Everett Pepperrell Wheeler

The Modern Law of Carriers

THE

MODERN LAW OF CARRIERS:

OR THE

LIMITATION OF THE COMMON-LAW LIABILITY OF COMMON CARRIERS

UNDER

THE LAW MERCHANT, STATUTE AND SPECIAL CONTRACTS.

By EVERETT P. WHEELER,
OF THE NEW YORK BAR.

NEW YORK:
BAKER, VOORHIS & CO., LAW PUBLISHERS,
66 NASSAU STREET.
1890.

Everett Pepperrell Wheeler

The Modern Law of Carriers

ISBN/EAN: 9783337397586

Printed in Europe, USA, Canada, Australia, Japan

Cover: Foto ©Suzi / pixelio.de

More available books at **www.hansebooks.com**

PREFACE.

The liability of common carriers at common law has been settled by a series of decisions, and is accurately stated in numerous text-books. But in my professional experience I have found no text-book which fully considered the limitations placed upon such liability by the law merchant, by statutes and by special contract. To supply this deficiency I have prepared the present volume. I have for thirteen years devoted to it such time as I could take from the labors of an engrossing profession, and I trust it will be useful to my brethren of the bar.

The first part of the book is devoted to the rights and obligations of maritime carriers; the second is more general, and applies to carriers both by land and sea.

I have been aided in the collation of cases by several gentlemen of the bar, and especially by Mr. Wyllys Hodges, Mr. Ferdinand Shack and Mr. Seth S. Terry. Mr. Hodges and Mr. Terry have assisted to prepare the index. I am glad to tender to them all my sincere thanks.

EVERETT P. WHEELER.

NEW YORK, *January* 24, 1890.

TABLE OF CONTENTS.

PART FIRST.

LIMITATIONS UPON THE LIABILITY OF COMMON CAR-
RIERS BY THE LAW MERCHANT, AS ADOPTED IN
THE UNITED STATES.

CHAPTER I.

CHAPTER II.

CHAPTER III.

PART SECOND.

LIMITATION OF LIABILITY BY CONTRACT.

CHAPTER IV.

TABLE OF CASES.

For the sake of brevity, the abbreviation R. R. is used herein for Railroad Company, and R. Co. for Railway Company.

B

C

THE

MODERN LAW OF CARRIERS.

THE

MODERN LAW OF CARRIERS.

PART I.

LIMITATIONS UPON THE LIABILITY OF COMMON CAR-
RIERS BY THE LAW MERCHANT AS ADOPTED
IN THE UNITED STATES.

CHAPTER I.

THE ADOPTION OF THE LAW MERCHANT IN THE
UNITED STATES.

The law of the United States is as composite as the
people. Its basis is the common law of England, but that
law has been modified to suit our circumstances and
character. The language of the Constitution which confers upon the Federal Courts "admiralty and maritime
jurisdiction," has been interpreted in no narrow sense,
and those courts have administered the maritime law of
Europe, as adopted in America, as well as the local jurisprudence of each State which forms part of the American
Commonwealth. In no country, therefore, is the responsibility of the judge and the lawyer more onerous.

The common law of England and the civil law of
Rome imposed upon him who undertook the task of carrying goods for the public the severe responsibility of an
insurer. His sole exemption was for losses caused by the
act of God or the public enemy.[1] In no other way it was

---

[1] See the statement of the rule in "The Maggie Hammond," 9
Wallace, 435, 444 (1869).

1

thought could fidelity be ensured. This rule originated in times when transportation, both by land and water, was insecure, and when the risk of collusion between the carrier and pirates or thieves was great.

As commerce increased, the necessity for protection and encouragement to it became more apparent. The security afforded by Government to peaceful traders on land was made adequate, and the rule itself to them became less oppressive. But from many perils by sea Government could afford no protection. Ship building developed into a science, and the size and cost of vessels increased. It was seldom practicable for a navigator to own the ship he commanded. It became important, therefore, to encourage capitalists to invest their money in the building and purchase of ships. But under the stringent rule already mentioned, the person who owned a ship which carried a valuable cargo, might be bound for many times the value of his investment in the ship, and thus put at risk his whole fortune.

To lighten his responsibility, the maritime countries of the continent of Europe provided at an early day that the liability of a shipowner to freighters and passengers should not exceed the value of his interest in the ship and her freight.

There were other reasons for this provision, in addition to those already mentioned, which deserve consideration. The carrier on land could supervise the agents employed by him to a much greater extent than the carrier by water. The captain and crew, when once they had sailed from the home port, were beyond the control of the owner, and the lives of the master and mariners being at stake there was supposed to be less likelihood of their negligence.

To what extent this provision has been adopted and become law in the United States will first be considered.

That it has been with reference to our own merchant marine is clear.   The Act of March 3, 1851 [chap. 43, 9 U. S. Stat. at Large, 635], which has been re-enacted in the Revised Statutes ["Title 48th, Regulation of Commerce and Navigation," chap. 6, sects. 4282–4289], contains the first statutory provisions on this subject of general application to be found in America, though local Statutes had previously been passed in Maine and Massachusetts.

In determining the force and effect of this Statute it is very material to consider its relation to the maritime law by which other countries are governed.   The distinction between municipal regulations and laws affecting the commerce between nations has long been recognized. The former vary with the needs and institutions of each particular country.   The latter are most useful when they are most harmonious and uniform.

The Mediterranean Sea was once the home of the commerce of what was then the civilized world.   In the states bordering upon it a body of customs and sea-laws sprung up.   They had their origin in the necessities of commerce.   They differed in many respects from the civil law which was, in effect, the common law of those states. When the Hanse towns along the Baltic became prosperous, and when France began to send ships from her Atlantic ports, most of these usages and customs were transported to the North.   They were administered by courts of special jurisdiction, which came in time to be called Courts of Admiralty, or Tribunals of Commerce. These usages and customs were codified and promulgated at different times and by different governments.   Of these Codes, the celebrated Ordonnance de la Marine is the most complete.   But it is true of all of them, that while in form they are decrees emanating from the highest power in the State, in reality they simply give form and expression to laws or customs previously known and recognized.

Take, for example, the Ordonnance already referred to. It begins:

"Louis, by the grace of God, King of France and Navarre, . . . We do speak, ordain, declare and make known our will as follows. . . ."

Yet all the writers on the subject agree that most of the provisions of the Ordonnance had been for centuries in force among the principal maritime nations of Europe.[1]

It is to be especially noticed that the authorities just cited uniformly speak of the Ordonnance not merely as a statute or a decree of Louis XIV, which on its face it purports to be, but as a code or digest of the existing maritime law.

When, therefore, we find it declared in the Ordonnance (Book 2, title 8, article 2) that the liability of the ship-

---

[1] In reference to this ordinance of Louis XIV, Chancellor Kent says (Comm., Vol. 3, pp. 16, 17):

"The whole law of navigation, shipping, insurance and bottomry was systematically collected and arranged. . . . Every commercial nation has rendered homage to the wisdom and integrity of the French Ordinance of the Marine, and they have regarded it as a digest of the maritime laws of civilized Europe."

As long ago as 1759, Lord Mansfield, in Luke v. Lyde, 2 Burrows, 882, cites it as an authority and says: "It was collected and compiled under authority of M. Colbert."

Emerigon says in his preface to his treatise on Insurance, p. ii: "The ancient maritime laws are the sources which were open to the compilers of the ordinance, and from which those must draw who would go to the fountain head." He then gives a sketch of the different compilations before the ordinance, and adds, p. xv: "The ordinance of 1681 is a compilation of all these ancient laws." (*Les anciennes lois maritimes sont les sources qui furent ouvertes aux redacteurs de l'Ordonnance, et dans lesquelles doivent puiser ceux qui veulent remonter aux principes." "L'ordonnance de 1681 est un composé de toutes ces anciennes lois.*"

Azuni on Maritime Law, Vol. 1, p. 393 (Am. ed. of 1806), says: "The ordonnance has become in some sort the common law of all the neighboring nations."

See also Bedarride, du Commerce Maritime, tome 1, sections 10, 18, pp. 14, 21.

owner for the negligence of the master is discharged by the abandonment of the ship and freight,[1] we can only conclude that this provision was, as long ago as the reign of Louis XIV, the established maritime law of continental Europe. A still older compilation, the Consolato del Mare, contains a provision to the same effect, as to the liability of the owner, although it did not undertake to provide a remedy by which this limitation of liability could be enforced.[2]

The courts of Holland recognize the same right on the part of the owner, and the same rule is acknowledged throughout the continent of Europe.[3]

In England, however, this rule never was fully adopted. The decisions of the courts of that country before the time of Lord Mansfield had little or no reference to the commercial law of Europe. For this there were many reasons.

The English, before the discovery of the mariner's compass in the twelfth century, were not and could not be a commercial people. The tenacity with which they clung to their local privileges, and especially to the right of trial by jury of the vicinage, led them to look with distrust and jealousy upon the Court of Admiralty, and its powers were greatly restricted so long ago as the reign of Richard II. The pride with which the English

---

[1] Valin Comm. Sur. l'Ord., Vol. 1, p. 490, ed. 1841, p. 568, ed. 1776;
[2] Peters' Adm, Dec. Appendix, p. xvi.
  Bedarride, du Commerce Maritime, Vol. 1, sections 273, 276, 279, 287. In section 279, Bedarride says : "In no case can the ship owner be made liable by any consequence of the voyage beyond his interest in the ship itself."
  In sect. 287 he says : "The right to abandon the ship and freight exists where the negligence or willful tort or quasi tort (quasi delit) is imputable to the crew or to the captain himself."
[3] The Rebecca, 1 Ware Rep. 195 (1831); The Phebe, Ware, 265 (1834). See, also, Pardessus Lois Maritimes, Vol. 2, p. 161.
[3] Valin. Comm., Vol. 1, p, 568 (ed. 1776); Liv. 2, tit. 8, art. ii; Ib. Vol. 1, p. 490 (ed. 1841); 3 Kent's Comm. 218; Force v. Providence Washington Ins. Co., 35 Fed. Rep. 769 (1888).

have always regarded the common law of that country made their courts look with suspicion upon any other system of jurisprudence.

The colonists in that part of America which now forms the United States were English, it is true. But the altered circumstances of the new country to which they came, and the fact that their very existence depended on commerce, led them to modify in many respects the rigid rules of the common law. It is to be remembered also that they came to America when the commercial spirit was acquiring that strength which has made England a great maritime country.

There is good reason to think that the Colonial Admiralty Courts claimed and exercised the full jurisdiction which was the prerogative of the English Admiralty before the time of Richard II. But, however this may be, the farseeing men who framed our Constitution, did not intend to limit the courts of this country by any such narrow bounds as those to which the English Admiralty Courts were subjected. This, after long discussion, is definitely settled. The opinion of Chief Justice Taney, in the Genesee Chief,[1] states very clearly the reasons for this decision. The limitations upon the powers of the English Admiralty were inapplicable to the condition of the colonies, and of the new country to which the framers of the Constitution gave a stable government, with powers adequate in all its branches, executive, legislative and judicial.

Still it does not necessarily follow, because our Admiralty Courts have the jurisdiction of similar courts in continental Europe, that they will, in all things, be guided by the decisions of these courts, or administer precisely the same law as they. But the history of the case of the

---

[1] 12 How. 443 (1851).

Norwich Trans. Co. *v.* Wright,[1] leads to the conclusion that the Statute of 185: adopted the rule of the maritime law already quoted from the ordonnance of Louis XIV, and that our Admiralty Courts will enforce it in all its fullness.

A libel *in personam* to recover damages for a collision between the steamer City of Norwich and a schooner, was filed in the District Court of Connecticut. While it was pending, the respondent set up as a defence the provisions of the Act of March 3, 1851.[2] The District Court held that these could not be administered by a Court of Admiralty, and that the remedy of a party seeking relief under them was in equity. The decree was affirmed by the Circuit Court. The Supreme Court reversed this decision, and held that a Court of Admiralty was the appropriate tribunal, because it administered the maritime law, of which this provision for limiting the liability of ship owners formed a part.[3]

The question then came up as to the extent of this limitation. Under the English statute of 7 George II (1734), and the subsequent acts of 26 George III (1786) and 56 George III (1813), it had been held that the words "The value of the vessel and her freight then pending," meant her value immediately before the injury complained of, and that this was the amount for which the owners were liable.[4] The consideration was pressed upon the

---

[1] 13 Wallace, 104 (1871); s. c. on Second Appeal, *sub nom.* Place *v.* Norwich Trans. Co., 118 U. S. 468 (1885). The decision in 13 Wall. reversed s. c. 1 Bened. 156 (1867); 8 Blatchf. 14 (1870).

[2] 9 U. S. Stat. at Large, 635.

[3] See second note, chap. 3, *post.*

[4] Gale *v.* Laurie, 5 B. & Cress. 156 (1826); Brown *v.* Wilkinson, 15 Mees. & Wels. 390 (1846); Lloyd *v.* Guibert, L. R. 1 Qu. B. 119 (1865).

At an earlier day a different decision has been suggested by Bayley, J., in Wilson *v.* Dickson, 2 B. & Ald. 2 (1818). At p. 15 he said: "Possibly (I only say possibly) the Legislature, from motives of policy, might think that persons who had embarked their property in shipping

court that the American statute was simply a re-enactment
of the English statute, and that on well settled rules of
construction the interpretation which had been put upon
its language by the English courts must be taken to be
the intent of the Legislature.

But the court held that the statute was the adoption,
not of an English municipal regulation, but of a well settled rule of the law merchant, and that this rule was the
law for our courts. According to this rule the abandonment of the interest of the owner in the ship and freight
discharged him from further liability. The doctrine was
based on the reasons before stated, and was the outgrowth
of the necessities of commerce, and not of any arbitrary
enactment.[1]

Another point made in the City of Norwich illustrates
the subject under consideration. It was argued that the
Act of 1851 was unconstitutional; that it was a mere municipal regulation, and so not within the power of Congress. But the court here, as in the Genesee Chief, already cited, avoid this question by planting their decision
on the maritime law, and the grant to the Federal courts
of Admiralty and maritime jurisdiction. In this respect,
also, the City of Norwich is parallel to the Genesee Chief,
and the two should be read together.[2]

should, on giving up all they had ventured in a particular voyage, be
relieved from any further responsibility."

[1] Butler v. Boston & Savannah S. S. Co., 130 U. S. 527 (1889); The
Epsilon, 6 Bened. 378 (1873). In Spring v. Haskell, 14 Gray (Mass.)
309 (1859), the court followed the English rule, being governed by the
Mass. statute. So did Grier, J., in Barnes v. Steamship Co., 25 Legal
Int. 196; s. c., 6 Phila. 479 (1868).

[2] In The Ventura (Lord v. Steamship Co.), 102 U. S. 541 (1881),
affi'g s. c. 4 Sawyer, 292 (1877), the act was held valid as a regulation
of commerce.

The opinion of the Supreme Court of the United States in The Atlas,
93 U. S. 302 (1876), implies that the law, thus stated, is applicable to
all vessels, whether foreign or domestic.

Clifford, J., states it as follows: " Owners of ships or vessels are not
liable, under existing laws, for any loss, damage or injury by collision,
if occasioned without their privity or knowledge, beyond the amount

The considerations thus far suggested lead inevitably to the conclusion that the Act of 1851[1] is the adoption of the rule of the maritime law of Europe already stated, as a regulation of commerce between this country and foreign nations, and of our domestic commerce. If it were a mere municipal regulation it would be limited in its scope to American vessels As a regulation of commerce it applies to all vessels which come to our ports.

It was so held by the United States Supreme Court in the Scotland,[2] as it had been previously by the Circuit

---

of their interest in such ship or vessel and her freight pending at the time the collision occurred.'

In a more recent case, Providence & N. Y. S. S. Co. v. Hill Mfg. Co., 109 U. S. 578 (1883), the court held the act to be constitutional, and say of it: "It is not only a maritime regulation in its character, but it is clearly within the scope of the power given to Congress to regulate commerce."

[1] Re-enacted in the Revised Statutes, sections 4281–4287. Section 4283 is printed erroneously in one particular in the first edition. The word "lost," as printed in the fourth line of that section, is "loss" in the original act.

[2] 105 U. S. 24 (1881); rev'g s. c. sub nom. Dyer v. National S. S. Co., 14 Blatchf. 483 (1878). In that case the Supreme Court say:

"Our law adopts the maritime rule of graduating the liability by the value of the ship after the injury as she comes back into port, and the freight actually earned, and enables the owners to avoid all responsibility by giving up ship and freight, if still in existence, in whatever condition the ship may be, and with such surrender subjects them only to a responsibility equivalent to the value of the ship and freight as rescued from the disaster.

"But whilst the rule adopted by Congress is the same as the rule of the general maritime law, its efficacy as a rule depends upon the statute, and not upon any inherent force of the maritime law. As explained in the Lottawanna (21 Wall. 558 [1874]), the maritime law is only so far operative as law in any country as it is adopted by the laws and usages of that country. This particular rule of the maritime law had never been adopted in this country until it was enacted by statute, and therefore whilst it is now a part of our maritime law it is nevertheless statute law, and must be interpreted and administered as such. Then does it govern the present case ? In administering justice between parties, it is essential to know by what law or Code, or system of laws, their mutual rights are to be determined. When they arise in a particular country or State, they are generally to be determined by the laws of that State. Those laws pervade and give them their color and legal effect. Hence, if a collision should occur in British waters, at least between British

Court for the Southern District of New York, in Levinson *v.* The Oceanic Steam Nav. Co., after very full argument and careful consideration.[1]

The American statute of April 29, 1864,[2] on the rule of the road at sea, is an instance of a similar adoption by this country of rules in reference to collisions which had previously been adopted by other maritime countries,

---

ships, and the injured party should seek relief in our courts, we would administer justice according to the British law, so far as the rights and liabilities of the parties were concerned, provided it were shown what that law was. If not shown, we would apply our own law to the case. In the French or Dutch tribunals, they would do the same. But, if a collision occurs on the high seas, where the law of no particular State has exclusive force, but all are equal, any forum called upon to settle the rights of the parties would *prima facie* determine them by its own law as presumptively expressing the rules of justice; but if the contesting vessels belonged to the same foreign nation, the court would assume that they were subject to the law of their nation, carried under their common flag, and would determine the controversy accordingly. If they belonged to different nations, having different laws, since it would be unjust to apply the laws of either to the exclusion of the other, the law of the forum, that is the maritime law, as received and practiced therein, would properly furnish the rule of decision. In all other cases each nation will also administer justice according to its own laws, and it will do this without respect of persons, to the stranger as well as to the citizen. If it be the legislative will that any particular privilege should be enjoyed by its own citizens alone, express provision will be made to that effect. Some laws, it is true, are necessarily special in their application to domestic ships, such as those relating to the forms of ownership, charter-party and nationality; others follow the vessel wherever she goes, as the law of the flag. such as those which regulate the mutual relations of master and crew and the power of the master to bind the ship or her owners. But the great mass of the laws are, or are intended to be, expressive of the rules of justice and right applicable alike to all.

But it is enough to say, that the rule of limited responsibility is now our maritime rule. It is the rule by which, through the act of Congress, we have announced that we propose to administer justice in maritime cases. We see no reason, in the absence of any different law governing the case, why it should not be applied to foreign ships as well as to our own, whenever the parties choose to resort to our courts for redress. Of course the rule must be applied, if applied at all, as well when it operates against foreign ships as when it operates in their favor.

[1] Albany Law Journal, Vol. 17, p. 285 (1878), and note.
[2] R. S. sect. 4233.

and which are applied by the courts of America to all collisions whether between foreign or American ships or both. Indeed the jurisprudence of this country is full of instances in which our courts in questions of maritime law have followed the rule prevailing in continental Europe rather than the English rule.

Take, for example, the decisions in reference to memorandum articles, so called, in a policy of insurance. The rule on the Continent of Europe is that when goods are warranted " free of particular average," or " free from average, except general," the insured cannot recover for a total loss of a part of any particular lot of goods. The English rule was for a long time different. But as long ago as 1800, the Supreme Court of New York adopted the Continental rule, and the decision was followed by the Supreme Court of the United States.[1]

It is a very significant fact, that the King's Bench, in Lord Mansfield's time, had adopted the Continental rule. It deserves notice that the English courts have finally returned to the rule originally laid down by him.[2]

So, in Thomas v. Osborn,[3] the Supreme Court, in opposition to the English, followed the Continental rule that the master has power, without a bottomry bond, to create a lien on his vessel for repairs and supplies furnished in a foreign port.[4]

It need, therefore, excite no surprise that the courts of this country should have refused to follow the English decisions under the statute of George II. It was held by Lord Stowell in the Carl Johan, cited by counsel in the

---

[1] 2 Arnould on Ins. 1038–1041.

[2] Ralli v. Janson, 6 Ellis & Bl. 422 (1856).

[3] 19 How. 22 (1856).

[4] For other instances, see the learned opinion of Chancellor Kent, in Palmer v. Lorillard, 16 Johns. 348, 361 (1819).

Dundee,[1] that this act was a municipal regulation only, and had no application to foreign vessels, and would not be administered by a Court of Admiralty. Those courts, he said, sat to administer the general maritime law, and not the local statutes of any particular country. Had that great man, who did so much to give clearness and precision to the practice and law of the English Admiralty, and whose native vigor has perhaps never been surpassed in any court, been as familiar with the civil law and the maritime law of Europe as Lord Mansfield, the decision in the Carl Johan would have been different. Taking his premises that his court sat to administer the general maritime law, finding the doctrine already adverted to a part of that law, he would have applied it in the case before him.

One objection that was taken to this view deserves consideration. Why, it was said, was not this alleged rule discovered and enforced in America before 1851? Why was it not pleaded as a defence in the suits growing out of the loss of the Lexington?[2] The answer to this last question is obvious. The loss of the Lexington was caused by negligence in her construction and equipment, and to losses such as this the rule does not apply. It does not exonerate ship owners from losses caused by their own negligence.[3]

The rule protects owners from ruin, which would otherwise overtake them from the fault of their agents,

---

[1] 1 Hagg. Adm. 113, 121 (1823); and see The Girolamo, 3 Hagg. Adm. 186 (1834).

[2] N. Y. Steamboat Co. v. Merchants' Bank, 6 How. U. S. 344 (1848).

[3] "The surrender by the owner of his interest in the ship and freight does not relieve him from liability for damages caused by the inherent defect (*vice propre*) of the ship. This is really an act of his own (*un fait personnel*) in respect to which the right to abandon does not exist." Court of Cassation, April 11, 1870; Journal du Palais, Table Complementaire, Vol. 1, Title Navire, sect. 75.

without any fault of their own. As was said by Hull, J., as long ago as the Year Books, 2 H. IV, fol. 18, p. 6:

"This were against all reason to put blame or fault upon a man when there is none in him, for the negligence of his servants cannot be said to be his own."

It must be remembered that disasters requiring the interposition of this rule are comparatively rare, and that so far as cargo is concerned, ship owners commonly protect themselves by exceptions in their bills of lading. Indeed, the fact that there is no reported case in this country prior to 1851, in which a passenger sued for injuries received by a marine disaster, is cogent evidence that the justice and reason of the rule already stated were so manifest that no one cared to challenge it.

It will be useful in this connection to consider to what extent the courts of this country have held that there is a law merchant, independent of our local and municipal jurisprudence, which has become such by the general—not necessarily the universal—consent of commercial nations.

That there is such a general law merchant, forming part of the jurisprudence of this country, is shown by a long series of decisions.[1]

---

[1] Watson v. Tarpley, 18 Howard, 517 (1855); Carpenter v. Ins. Co., 16 Peters, 495 (1842); Gloucester Ins. Co. v. Younger, 2 Curtis, 338 (1855).

In Swift v. Tyson, 16 Peters, 1 (1842), the court says, p. 19: "The true interpretation and effect of contracts and other instruments of a commercial nature are to be sought, not in the decisions of local tribunals, but in the general principles and doctrines of commercial jurisprudence. Undoubtedly the decisions of the local tribunals upon such subjects are entitled to, and will receive, the most deliberate attention and respect of the court, but they cannot furnish positive rules or conclusive authority by which our own judgments are to be bound up and governed. The law respecting negotiable instruments may be truly declared in the language of Cicero, adopted by Lord Mansfield in Luke v. Lyde (which it should be noticed was a case arising upon a bill of lading), 2 Burr. R. 882, 887 (1759), to be in a great measure, not the law of a single country only, but of the commercial world. *Non erit alia lex*

*How is this Law to be Proved? Whence does it
Arise?*—Not, certainly, from any purely municipal reg-

---

*Romae, alia Athenis, alia nunc, alia posthac, sed et apud omnes gentes, et
omni tempore, una eademque lex obtinebit."*
The decision has been repeatedly followed, and is well settled law.
Meade *v.* Beale, Taney Dec. 339 (1848); Austen *v.* Miller, 5 McLean,
153 (1849); The Ship George, Olcott, 89 (1845); Pine Grove *v.* Talcott,
19 Wallace, 666 (1873); Robinson *v.* Commonwealth Ins. Co., 3 Sumner,
220 (1838).

In the latter case Story, J., says (p. 225): "I am aware that a rule
somewhat different has been laid down by the Supreme Court of Massachusetts, for whose judgments I entertain the most unfeigned respect.
But questions of a commercial and general nature like this, are not
deemed by the courts of the United States to be matters of local
law in which the courts of the United States are positively bound by
the decisions of the State courts. They are deemed questions of
general commercial jurisprudence, in which every court is at liberty
to follow its own opinion, according to its own judgment of the weight
of authority and principle."

2 Parson's Marit. Ins. 207, and note, is to the same effect. It was,
however, held in an early case in Michigan—Rossiter *v.* Chester, 1
Doug. (Mich.) 154 (1843)—that the law merchant was no part of the
common law.   But this statement is not supported by the best English
authorities.

Blackstone says in his Commentaries, Vol. 1, p. 273: "No municipal laws can be sufficient to order and adjust the new, extensive and
complicated affairs of traffic and merchandise, *neither can they have a
proper authority for this purpose.* For, as these are transactions carried on between subjects of independent States, the municipal laws
of one will not be regarded by the other. For which reason the affairs
of commerce are regulated by a law of their own, called the law merchant, or *lex mercatoria,* which all nations agree in and take notice
of."

So in Vol. 4, p. 67: "In mercantile questions, such as bills of exchange, and the like; in all the marine cases relating to freight, average,
demurrage, insurance, bottomry, and others of a similar nature, the law
merchant. which is a branch of the law of nations, is regarded and constantly adhered to. So, too, in all disputes relating to prizes, ship-
wrecks, to hostages and ransom bills, there is no other rule of decision,
but this great universal law, collected from history and usage, and
such writers of all nations and languages as are generally approved and
allowed of."

That Courts of Admiralty have jurisdiction to administer this general maritime law is equally well settled. Sir James Marriott, Lord
Stowell's predecessor, said in the Columbus, Collectanea Juridica, p.
75:
"The Court of Admiralty is a court of mixed jurisdiction. It will
judge of the custom or law of the sea, the custom of civilized nations,
and the common sea law of the realm."

Lord Stowell declared the same rule in the Carl Johan, before cited,

ulation. Not necessarily from any international convention. But by the common consent of commercial nations. Its beginning may be hid in the mists of antiquity. But each nation, as it adopts any particular provision or rule, formulates its consent in some way. France did it by the Ordonnance of Louis XIV. The United States did the same by the Act of 1851. When the consent is thus formulated, the law becomes for that nation the law of the sea, to be administered by its courts, in reference to all vessels trading to its ports. When they come to us for our trade, and seek the custom of our merchants, they submit themselves to the whole body of our law, and are entitled to its benefits.

In thus adopting and giving full force and effect to the rule limiting the liability of ship-owners, the courts of this country have followed the course of the continental courts in reference to the civil law. That law is the common law of most continental countries. On the subject under consideration it agrees with the English common law. How was it modified? Not by a mere municipal regulation, but by ordinances or decrees, the precise analogue of our statute of 1851, recognizing or adopting a rule different from that of the civil law, and bringing the country by whose sovereign it was promulgated into line with other commercial countries, thus forming a maritime law.[1]

There is no novelty in thus applying a statute to per-

---

and it has become elementary. In the Eagle, 8 Wall. 15 (1868), it was held that there was a maritime lien upon the offending vessel for damages caused by a collision in Canadian waters, although the local law gave no such lien. See, also, the Milford, Swabey, 362 (1858).

[1] An illustration of this is to be found in General Order 253, of the U. S. Navy Department, July 16, 1880. It begins: "A revised code of 'Regulations for Preventing Collisions at Sea' having been approved by nearly all the maritime nations of the world, and adopted by them to go into effect on the 1st of September, 1880, thus becoming an integral part of the law of the sea, it is hereby adopted for the naval service of the United States."

sons other than the citizens of the country by whose legislature the statute is enacted.   For example many of the old and strict rules in regard to corporate powers and corporate action have ceased to be applicable to the conditions of modern society, and are no longer enforced by the courts.   In the Bank of Augusta v. Earle[1] it was held that a corporation could transact business beyond the limits of the jurisdiction which created it, and was by necessary consequence subject to the laws of the country where it located its offices and did its business.[2]

Now that corporations have practically become partnerships with limited liability, and do business all over the world, it seems hard to conceive that the point should ever have been seriously contested.

In like manner it is not easy to give any reason why a corporation which does business in a country other than that which incorporated it, and is subject to the laws of that State, should not be entitled to their benefit.

It is a general rule in the construction of statutes that "if the law makes no exception the court can make none."[3]

---

[1] 13 Peters, 519 (1839).

[2] To the same effect are Cowell v. Springs Co., 100 U. S. 55 (1879); Lafayette Ins. Co. v. French, 18 How. U. S. 404 (1855); Dryden v. Grand Trunk Railway, 60 Maine, 512 (1872).

[3] Collins v. Carman's Exr., 5 Md. 503, 533 (1854); Warfield v. Fox, 53 Penn. 382 (1866); Beckford v. Wade, 17 Vesey, 87 (1805). So in Demarest v. Wynkoop, 3 Johns. Ch. 142 (1817), Chancellor Kent said: "General words in the statute must receive a general construction, and if there be no express exception, the court can create none."   See, also, U. S. v. Coombs, 12 Peters, 72 (1838).

In construing this very statute, the N. Y. Commission of Appeals say: "Where general words are used the courts are not at liberty to insert limitations not called for by the sense or the objects, or the mischiefs of the enactment.   Chamberlain v. Western Transportation Co., 44 N. Y. 305, 309 (1870).   And they held that it was to be construed liberally.

There are many instances of the application of this rule.   In the Marianna Flora, 11 Wheat. 1 (1826), the Act of March 3, 1819, chapter 75, came under consideration.   Section 2 of that act authorized the President

It is worthy of notice that in the revision of the statutes of the United States the Act of 1851 is codified as part of title 48: "Regulations of commerce and navigation," sections 4282–4289. It will be observed, on a critical examination of the sections of this title, that they apply to foreign as well as to domestic vessels, unless it is otherwise expressed.[1]

·Section 4274 limits the provisions of the title "relating to the transportation of passengers" to United States vessels. Why the necessity of this section, unless, if it had not been inserted, they would have applied to all vessels? Could it be argued for a moment that sections 4278–4279, regulating the transportation of nitro-glycer-

---

to empower United States vessels to subdue "any armed vessel or boat . . . which shall have attempted or committed any piratical aggression . . . upon any vessel of the United States." A Portuguese vessel was seized by a United States cruiser, and sent into port for adjudication under the provision of this statute. She was libelled and condemned. On appeal, Judge Story, delivering the opinion of the court, said (p. 39):

"It has, indeed, been argued at the bar that even if this attack had been a piratical aggression it would not have justified the capture and sending in of the ship for adjudication, because foreign ships are not to be governed by our municipal regulations. But the Act of Congress is decisive on this subject. It not only authorizes a capture, but a condemnation in our courts for such aggressions, and whatever may be the responsibility incurred by the nation to foreign powers in executing such laws, there can be no doubt that the courts of justice are bound to obey and administer them."

So in the case of the Southern Life Ins. Co. v. Packer, 17 N. Y. 51 (1858), it was held by the N. Y. Court of Appeals that the Act of 1850, that "No corporation shall interpose the defense of usury," applied to foreign as well as domestic corporations. The court put the decision on two grounds: 1. There is nothing expressed in the act from which such a limitation could be presumed. Its language is general. 2. There is nothing in the purview of the act from which an intent to confine it to domestic corporations could be inferred.

The pilotage laws of New York were held to be operative beyond the territorial limits of that State so far as commerce to and from it was concerned. The Nevada, 7 Bened. 386 (1874); Cisco v. Roberts, 36 N. Y. 292 (1867).

The same rule is stated by Dr. Lushington in the Milford, Swabey, 362 (1858).

[1] Compare section 4197 with section 4212.

2

ine and prohibiting such transportation upon passenger vessels, would not apply to a British ship bringing this dangerous substance to our ports? Then why do not the seven following sections apply equally to foreign vessels engaged in commerce with this country? The language of the former is no more general than that of the latter.

Another argument has been presented in reference to this subject. It is said that the courts of this country ought not to allow this limitation of liability in favor of the owners of a foreign vessel, when the laws of the country to which that vessel belongs recognize and enforce a different rule.

So far as known, England is the only maritime country whose law differs on this subject from our own. But it must be remembered that under the present provisions of the English Merchant Shipping Act, 17 and 18 Vict. c. 104, section 403, it is applicable to foreign as well as English vessels, and that it limits the liability by an arbitrary sum, £8 per ton for injuries to cargo and £15 per ton for injuries to passengers. This may be and often is a sum less than the value of the interest of the owner in the ship and freight after the injury. A case of limitation was heard in New York in which it was considerably less.[1] So that the English law now differs from our own only in fixing, for convenience sake, an arbitrary limit. There is a comity, a recognition by England, of the rule referred to, which goes far enough to justify our courts in applying our own rule to English vessels, even if the only question were one of comity.[2]

---

[1] The Star of Scotia, U. S. District Court, Southern District of New York, Choate, J. (1876), not reported.

[2] There is nothing unprecedented in the application in one court of a rule of damages different from that which prevails in another. At common law, for example, a party whose negligence contributes to a collision can recover nothing. In Admiralty the damages are divided. The Atlas, 93 U. S. 302 (1876); Arctic Ins. Co. v. Austin, 69 N. Y. 470 (1877); Lord v. Hazeltine, 67 Maine, 399 (1877).
Before the passage of the act referred to in the text it was held that

But the question is not one of comity. America is just as much interested as England in the commerce between the two countries, and our right to regulate it is just as clear. If, in the judgment of our Legislature, commerce is promoted and attracted to our ports by the adoption of this liberal commercial regulation, our courts cannot refuse to carry out this beneficent policy.[1]

---

the owner of a British ship could limit his liability for damage done to a foreign ship by a collision on the high seas within three miles of the British coast. General Iron Screw Co. *v.* Schurmanns, 1 Johns. & Hem. 180 (1858). It was held otherwise if the collision happened at a distance more than three miles from the British coast. Cope *v.* Doherty, 4 K. & J. 367 (1858); s. c. on appeal, 2 De Gex & J. 614 (1858).

[1] The oral argument in the Scotland, 105 U. S. 24 (1881), was, probably, as forcible and thorough as any that has ever been had on an Admiralty appeal. The following extracts from it and from the colloquy between the court and counsel will not be without interest. Mr. Butler was for the English ship-owner, Mr. Carter for the libellant.

Mr. Butler. That these English owners should go scot-free seems to my friends, in the language of Bunyan, like grace abounding to the chief of sinners. They want to establish a doctrine of election by which this benefit of the Admiralty law shall be conferred alone upon American citizens.

Bradley, J., to Mr. Carter. You claim full damages? Mr. Carter. Yes.

Bradley, J. By what law? Mr. Carter. By our customary law always administered in our courts.

Bradley, J. That is municipal law? Mr. Carter. Yes.

Bradley, J. Then why may not our statutes apply to foreigners? Mr. Carter. The body of rules on which commercial nations unite may be called the general Admiralty law. When that concurrence exists that law exists. When it does not, the law does not exist.

Waite, C. J. Does that concurrence exist in this case? Mr. Carter. No.

Waite, C. J. Then what law would apply? Mr. Carter. Our own rule of justice. No maritime law exists. The statute does not apply and there is no general Admiralty law on the subject.

Waite, C. J. Are there two rules in the United States—one applicable to citizens of the United States, and another to foreigners? Mr. Carter. Yes.

Waite, C. J. Is there anything in the statute to indicate that? Mr. Carter. The rule of construction already stated indicates it.

Waite, C. J. Isn't it rather the inference that it was intended to apply to the citizens of all countries when they seek redress in the courts of this country?

Bradley, J. Has any difficulty been raised since the Act of Parliament was passed extending to foreign vessels? Mr. Carter. No.

Bradley, J. Then there is no intrinsic difficulty in the subject.

The cases in which it is sought to apply the rule of the maritime law which has thus been considered are, ordinarily, actions of tort, brought to obtain redress for injuries, caused on the high seas by the negligence of the master or other officer of the vessel committing the tort.

Indeed, it was for many years a mooted point whether the rule referred to had any application to actions brought to enforce contracts made by the master, as distinguished from actions to recover damages occasioned by his negligence. The commentators and the courts of France were at variance. It was finally settled that the rule applied to both classes of cases. But in practice its application is infrequent, except to protect the owner from unlimited liability for the negligence of his agent.[1]

---

[1] An account of the controversy on this subject will be found in Bedarride, du Commerce Maritime, Tome 1, sects. 270, 271. Valin was of opinion that the right to limit the owner's liability extended only to losses caused by the misconduct (*delits* or *quasi delits*) of the master or crew. Emerigon (Contrat a la Grosse, chap. IV, section 11, paragraphs 1 and 2) takes the ground that by the maritime law the right of limitation extends to breaches of a contract made by the master. The opinion of Emerigon finally prevailed, and the matter was set at rest in France by an amendment to the Code Napoleon, adopted in 1841.

The Report of M. Camille Perier to the Chambre de Paris (Moniteur Universel, 23 Mars. 1841) on this subject will well repay perusal. A copy is to be found in the Astor Library, New York.

CHAPTER II.

THE UNITED STATES STATUTE.

The Act of 1851, has been re-enacted without material change in the Revised Statutes, sections 4282 to 4289, inclusive.

These sections of the Revised Statutes are *in pari materiâ* with the Act of 1851, and to be construed as effecting no change in the law, unless the words of the subsequent act require it. It is settled after full deliberation and elaborate argument that no change has been made by the revision.[1]

And the Statute should be liberally construed to pro-

---

[1] " When the meaning is plain, the courts cannot look to the Statutes which have been revised, to see if Congress erred in that revision, but may do so when necessary to construe doubtful language used in expressing the meaning of Congress. If, then, in the case before us, the language of sect. 4820, was fairly susceptible of the construction claimed by the Government as well as of the opposite one, the argument from the provision of the Statute as it stood before the revision would be conclusive." United States *v.* Bowen, 100 U. S. 508, 513 (1879).

" On these differences of language," said Mr. Justice Blatchford, in Thomassen *v.* Whitwill, 21 Blatchf. 45 ; s. c. 12 Fed. Rep. 891 (1882); affd. 118 U. S. 520 (1886), " it is contended that the Revised Statutes exclude a limitation of the liability of a part owner to the value of his interest in the vessel and freight, and do not provide for any limitation short of the interest of the owner or owners, collectively, in the whole vessel. There is no force in this contention. By section 1 of the Revised Statutes, it is provided, that in determining the meaning of the Revised Statutes, words importing the singular number may extend and be applied to several persons or things, and words importing the plural number may include the singular. It was undoubtedly because of this general provision that the language of the Act of 1851 was condensed in the revision. Read by the light of such general provision, and in view of the principles on which the revision was made, it must be held that the new language in sections 4283 and 4285, is the result merely of revision, simplification, re-arrangement and consolidation, with a view to the re-enactment of the same substance and meaning."

mote the beneficial end for which it was enacted, *i. e.*, of advancing the commerce of the country.[1]

Section 4282 is as follows :

"No owner of any vessel shall be liable to answer for or make good to any person any loss or damage which may happen to any merchandise whatsoever, which shall be shipped, taken in, or put on board any such vessel, by reason or by means of any fire happening to or on board the vessel, unless such fire is caused by the design or neglect of such owner." [2]

The true interpretation of this section gave rise to a conflict of opinion between the courts of the States of New York and Massachusetts and the Federal Courts. A libel was filed by the owners of the Oceanus to limit their liability for the loss by fire of the cargo of that vessel. The court sustained the libel and granted an injunction against all proceedings at law. Some of the shippers had brought an action at law to recover for the loss to their goods. The Superior Court of the city of New York[3] stayed all proceedings in this suit, but the Court of Ap-

---

[1] Providence & N. Y. S. S. Co. *v.* Hill Mfg. Co., 109 U. S. 578, 589 (1883).

Chamberlain *v.* Western Trans. Co., 44 N. Y. 305 (1871). In this case the court say, p. 309 : "This is not in any sense a penal statute, nor is it in any way derogatory to natural right, and hence I know of no rule of law that requires that it should be strictly construed, It is true that it changes the common law, but there can be no reason for applying the rule of strict construction to the vast body of statute laws which change the common law. The prior law, whether it be statute or common law, is to prevail, unless the subsequent statute, by a fair and proper construction, repeals or modifies it. This statute is rather a remedial statute. It was enacted to remedy the rigor of the common law, which it was deemed unwise, on grounds of public policy, to continue. It should, therefore, be construed, if not liberally, at least fairly, to carry out the policy which it was enacted to promote." To the same effect is the Warkworth, 9 Prob. Div. 20 (1884).

[2] This section does not apply to express companies who ship goods on .steam vessels, but do not charter them. Hill Mfg. Co. *v.* Boston & Lowell R. R. Co., 104 Mass. 122 (1870).

[3] Knowlton *v.* Providence & N. Y. S. S. Co., 35 N. Y. Superior Ct. 572 (1873).

peals reversed the order and held,[1] that the effect of the
Statute was not merely to limit the liability of the ship-
owner in case of loss by fire, but to take it away altogether,
so far as the cargo was concerned, unless the owner himself was at fault.   It therefore held that this defense
could be pleaded in any suit brought by the shipper,
and that no proceedings in Admiralty were necessary or
proper.[2]

There can be no doubt on the language of the Statute,
that the defense, in case of fire, is complete.[3] The question therefore is merely in what forum this defense shall be
tried.   The advantage of the Admiralty proceeding is,
that all parties claiming to recover can be brought in and
the issue tried in one suit.   It is strictly analogous to a
bill in equity, in the nature of a bill of interpleader, in
which all parties claiming an interest in the subject-matter
of the controversy are brought in.   A multiplicity of suits
is thus avoided, and the whole matter determined in one
action.[4]   And on these grounds the Supreme Court of the
United States has overruled the New York and Massachusetts decisions, and sustained the Admiralty jurisdiction in such cases.   And it distinctly held that the pro-

---

[1] Knowlton v. Providence & N. Y. S. S. Co., 53 N. Y. 76 (1873).

[2] s. p., Hill Mfg. Co. v. Providence & N. Y. S. S. Co., 125 Mass. 292
(1878); s. c. 113 Mass. 495 (1873).
In Moore v. Am. Trans. Co., 24 Howard, U. S. 1 (1860), the
defense under this Section of the Statute was pleaded in an action at
law, and the defense was sustained in the Supreme Court. No affirmative proceedings were taken by the owner in admiralty or otherwise.
This is clearly an adjudication that the defense can be pleaded in an
action at law. In this respect it is analogous to the decision in the
Scotland, 105 U. S. 24 (1881); 118 U. S. 507 (1886).
On the other hand the owners may still be sued at law, and are
liable in the action to the extent of their interest in the vessel and her
freight, for any loss of or injury to the cargo. Spring v. Haskel, 14
Gray (Mass.), 309 (1859).

[3] Walker v. Transportation Company, 3 Wall. 150 (1865).

[4] Of this class of cases, N. Y. & N. H. R. R. Co. v. Schuyler, 17 N.
Y. 592 (1858), is the most notable example.

ceedings taken by the Providence and New York Steam Ship Co. were a bar to all suits to recover damages for losses caused by this fire.[1]

When the cargo is discharged and placed upon a wharf alongside the ship, the effect of the act to take away the liability of the owner, for the loss by fire of the goods discharged ceases, unless the goods are destroyed in consequence of the vessel taking fire.[2]

It will be observed that this section is limited to the case of "loss or damage to merchandise." It does not, as does section 4283, contain also the words "goods, property." Whether passenger's trunks, not in the custody of their owners, but placed in the baggage compartment of a steamer, can be called merchandise, is as yet undecided.[3]

It has been held that horses and trucks in custody of teamsters who, together with their teams, take passage on a ferry boat, are not merchandise, and that section 4282 does not apply to the loss of such horses and trucks.[4] On the other hand, under the Statute of 1851, it was held that the ordinary baggage of passengers on a steamboat was "goods," and that the ship-owner was not liable for its loss, caused by fire, without his design or neglect.[5]

---

[1] Providence & N. Y. S. S. Co. v. Hill Mfg. Co., 109 U. S. 578 (1883). At p. 589 the court say of the statute: "Its value and efficiency will also be greatly diminished, if not entirely destroyed, by allowing its administration to be hampered and interfered with by various and conflicting jurisdictions."

[2] The Egypt, 25 Fed. Rep. 320 (1885); The Tangier, 1 Cliff. 396; s. c. 21 Law Rep. 612 (1858). It was held in Morewood v. Pollock, 1 Ell. & Bl. 743 (1853), that the corresponding section of the English Statute did not apply to the destruction by fire of goods on board lighters, being transported to the ship. Under the United States Statute, as amended in 1886 (24 U. S. Stat. at Large, p. 80), the owner of the lighter certainly would not, in such case, be liable.

[3] Heye v. North German Lloyd, 33 Fed. Rep. 60 (1887).

[4] The Garden City, 26 Fed. Rep. 766 (1886).

[5] Chamberlain v. Western Trans. Co., 44 N. Y. 305 (1871); revg. s. c. 45 Barb. 218 (1866).

This word "goods" is omitted in Section 4282 of the Revised Statutes. Yet it is well settled, as shown in the previous part of this chapter (page 2), that the re-enactment of the law of 1851, in the Revised Statutes, was not intended to change the meaning of the former act. The words, "any merchandise whatsoever," should therefore be considered as synonymous with "any goods or merchandise whatsoever." This decision of the Commission of Appeals is not referred to in the opinion in The Garden City.[1] Moreover the decision of the point was not necessary in that case.

It may therefore be said that the meaning of the words "any merchandise whatsoever," is still unsettled. The expressions of the Commission of Appeals in the Chamberlain case as to the construction of the act of 1871, are so similar to those of the United States Supreme Court in the Providence S. S. case (*ante*, p. 22, note 1), that there is reason to believe that this court would give to the words an ampler significance than is given in the Garden City.

It is not within the scope of this treatise to examine in detail the meaning of the words "design or neglect," used in this section. The word neglect must be considered as synonymous with negligence, and that is so fully and accurately treated by Shearman and Redfield in their admirable work on Negligence that it is unnecessary to do anything here except refer to the decisions upon this very section.

It is neglect on the part of the ship-owner to omit to maintain in proper order apparatus required by law to be kept on board for the purpose of extinguishing fires.

This section does not limit the liability of a ship-owner for neglect to secure for the owner of baggage, indemnity for injury to it by fire and water used to extinguish the

---

[1] The Garden City, 26 Fed. Rep. 766 (1886).

fire, which ought to have been the subject of a general average contribution.[1]

Section 4283, is as follows :

" The liability of the owner of any vessel, for any embezzlement, loss, or destruction, by any person, of any property, goods or merchandise shipped or put on board of such vessel, or for any loss, damage or injury by collision, or for any act, matter or thing, loss,[2] damage, or forfeiture, done, occasioned, or incurred, without the privity or knowledge of such owner or owners, shall in no case exceed the amount or value of the interest of such owner in such vessel, and her freight then pending."

It has been questioned whether the language of this section is broad enough to cover the case of an injury to the person. No doubt the first part of the section is in terms confined to the case of injury to the cargo. But the language that follows is much broader. Judge Benedict held in the case of the Epsilon,[3] that this covered injuries to the person caused by the explosion of a boiler on board a vessel in the East River. This is clearly right on principle. The maritime law knows no distinction in jurisdiction, between maritime torts causing injury to persons and

---

[1] Heye v. North German Lloyd, 33 Fed. Rep. 60 (1887). In this case the baggage compartment took fire. It was held that this was a risk to the ship, that the injury to the baggage, caused by extinguishing the fire, was a sacrifice for the general good, and therefore the subject of a general average contribution, and that the ship-owner ought to have collected this for the benefit of the owners of the baggage, and was liable to them for this neglect, though not liable directly for the injury done by the fire. It was questioned also, whether damage by water, used in putting out the fire, came within this section.

[2] This is erroneously printed "lost" in the first edition of the Revised Statutes. The true text is "loss."

[3] 6 Bened. 378 (1873); s. p., The City of Columbus, 22 Fed. Rep. 460 (1884); affd. sub nom. Butler v. Boston & Savannah S. S. Co., 130 U. S. 526 (1889); The Seawanhaka, re Long Island, &c., Trans. Co., 5 Fed. Rep. 599 (1881); Rounds v. Providence & N. Y. S. S. Co., 14 R. I. 344 (1885); The Alpena, 8 Fed. Rep. 280 (1881). The French law is the same. D'Orbigney contre Guerin, Cour de Cassation; Sirey de Villeneuve, 1876, partie 2, p. 214. Couder, Dict. de Droit Comm., tome 1, p. 412, § 66.

those causing injury to cargo. But the act does not apply to injuries done on the land by a tort committed on the water.[1] It does apply to injuries done wherever the Admiralty jurisdiction extends.[2]

The liability of the owner of a ship, by the negligence of whose servants injury is done to another ship, is limited by the Statute, as well as his liability for injuries to the cargo, carried upon his own vessel.[3]

The meaning of the important words in the foregoing section, "without the privity or knowledge of such owner or owners," has not been definitely determined. It will be observed that the words used to express the condition upon which the owner is allowed to limit his liability are different from those in the preceding section. Under the terms of that section the owner is not liable in any amount whatever, for any loss or damage which may happen to any merchandise on board a vessel, by means of fire happening to or on board the vessel, "unless such fire is caused by the design or neglect of such owner."

The opinion was at one time expressed, by the New

---

[1] The Admiralty has no jurisdiction in such case: "The true meaning of the rule of locality in cases of marine torts was that the wrong must have been committed wholly on navigable waters, or at least the substance and consummation of the same must have taken place upon those waters to be within the admiralty jurisdiction." The Plymouth, 3 Wallace, 20 (1866), as stated in *Ex parte* Phenix Ins. Co., 118 U. S. 610, 618 (1886). In this latter case a writ of prohibition was granted to restrain the District Court for the Eastern District of Wisconsin from entertaining jurisdiction of the petition of a ship-owner to limit its liability for damage done by a fire on land caused by the negligent navigation of its vessel. The opinion of the District Court is reported, 26 Fed. Rep. 713 (1886), *sub nom. In re* Goodrich Trans. Co. This case is therefore overruled, and so is *In re* Vessel Owners' Towing Co., 26 Fed. Rep. 169 (1886). So is also the Epsilon, 6 Bened. 378, 381, 391 (1873); so far as it sustains the jurisdiction in a limited liability proceeding to enjoin the prosecution of such claim.

[2] Butler *v.* Boston & Savannah S. S. Co., 130 U. S. 527 (1889).

[3] Norwich Co. *v.* Wright, 13 Wall. 104 (1871); revg. s. c. 8 Blatchf. 14 (1870).

York Court of Appeals, that the words were nearly or quite synonymous.[1]

But the Supreme Court of the United States takes an entirely different view of the language of the two sections. In the case of the Providence and New York S. S. Co. *v.* Hill Mfg. Co.,[2] which has been stated in the previous part of this chapter, that court considered the contention, which had been approved by the Supreme Court of Massachusetts and by the Court of Appeals of the State of New York, that the third section of the Act of 1851, re-enacted in section 4283 of the Revised Statutes, had no application to a loss by fire, and that the first section of the original act, re-enacted in section 4282 of the Revised Statutes was the only provision in force relating to this subject. The Supreme Court distinctly overruled the decisions of both these courts on this subject, and held that both sections were applicable to the case of a loss by fire, and that the owner, in case of loss by fire not caused by his design or neglect, might still desire to limit his liability to his interest in the vessel and her freight then pending, and might therefore properly take proceedings under the subsequent section. The opinion of the court on this subject can best be expressed in their own language, which will be found in the note.[3]

---

[1] Peckham, J., Knowlton *v.* Pro. & N.Y. S. S. Co., 53 N.Y. 76 (1873), at page 84, says:

"It is claimed that this first section is subject to the third, and embraced within its provisions. If it were so intended it is singular that the difference in the conditions of liability should be so slight. They are, in fact, substantially alike—so near as to evince no difference of purpose."

[2] 109 U. S. 578 (1883).

[3] "The owners may not be able, under the first section, to show that it happened without any neglect on their part, or what a jury may hold to be neglect; whilst they may be very confident of showing, under the third section, that it happened without their 'privity or knowledge.' The conditions of proof, in order to avoid a total or a partial liability under the respective sections, are very different." Providence & N Y. S. S. Co. *v.* Hill Mfg. Co., 109 U. S. 578, 602 (1883).

It would therefore seem to be clear that the Supreme Court at least inclined to the opinion, that there might be a neglect, imputable to the owner under section 4282, which could not yet be said to have caused a loss with his "privity or knowledge" under section 4283. The question therefore recurs: what is meant by these latter words?

In the first place it would seem to be clear, in the case of a corporation, that there are some officers of such corporation whose privity or knowledge, within the meaning of this statute, must be said to be the privity and knowledge of the corporation itself. The Supreme Court of Massachusetts has held distinctly that the acts, intentions and neglects of the president and directors of a corporation are those of the corporation itself.[1]

It is true that the decision in this case was reversed by the U. S. Supreme Court. But the reversal was not at all for error in the proposition thus stated. This is entirely in accord with the reasoning of the U. S. Supreme Court in a prior case,[2] and is believed to express a correct proposition. It is entirely in harmony, also, with the decisions of courts in actions for negligence, and in the determination of the validity of clauses of exemption in bills of lading.

---

[1] Hill Mfg. Co. v. Prov. & N. Y. S. S. Co., 113 Mass. 495 (1873). At page 500, Gray, C. J., says:

"If the owners are a corporation, the president and directors are not merely the agents or servants, but the representatives of the corporation; and the acts, intentions and neglects of such officers are those of the corporation itself (21 How. 202, 210, 211 [1858]; 3 Allen, 433, 441 [1858]). To hold otherwise would be wholly to exempt all steamship companies from loss by fire of goods on board their ships, however carelessly or imperfectly they built their furnaces and engines. Such a construction is too novel and unreasonable to be entertained."

[2] Philadelphia, W. & B. R. R. v. Quigley, 21 How. U. S. 202 (1858), held that a corporation which is impersonal can only act through agents, and is liable for torts committed by the directors in the course of the business of the company, e. g., a libel published by them during an investigation into its affairs.

In the former class of cases it is well settled that
while a master is not liable to a servant for injuries
caused by the negligence of a fellow-servant, yet that
this rule does not extend so far as to exempt the master from liability for failure to perform a duty which the
law itself devolves upon him. Among these duties is that
of supplying the servant with apparatus or machinery
reasonably safe for his use in the work in which he is employed.[1]

But still the distinction between these actions for negligence, and cases arising under the Limited Liability
Act, is manifest. In the former the negligence of the
agent is imputed to the principal; in the latter it is not.[2]
The principal is not liable for loss incurred "without his
privity or knowledge." These words point to a fault, personal to the principal as distinguished from the negli-

---

[1] Hough v. Railway Co., 100 U. S. 215 (1879). At page 220, the court
say: "The true view is that, as corporations can act only through superintending officers, the negligences of those officers, in respect to other
servants, are the negligences of the corporation." To the same effect
are the New York cases. "The master is liable to his servant for any
injury happening to him from the misconduct or personal negligence of
the master, and this negligence may consist in the employment of unfit
and incompetent servants and agents, or in the furnishing for the work
to be done, or for the use of the servant, machinery or other implements
and facilities improper and unsafe for the purposes to which they are to
be applied." Wright v. N. Y. Cen. R. R., 25 N. Y. 565 (1862). Loughlin
v. State, 105 N. Y. 159 (1887). At page 162, the court say: "The master is sometimes responsible for the negligent act of one servant causing
injury to a co-servant. But this liability, when it exists, does not rest
upon the doctrine of *respondeat superior*, but solely upon the ground
that in the particular case the co-servant whose act or neglect caused
the injury was, by the appointment of the master, charged with the performance of duties which the master was bound to perform for the protection of his servants, a failure to perform which, or a negligent performance of which by a servant delegated to perform them, is regarded
in law the master's failure or negligence, and not merely the failure or
negligence of the co-servant."

[2] Walker v. Transportation Co., 3 Wall. 150 (1865); The Whistler,
2 Sawy. 348 (1873). These were cases of loss by fire. Wilson v. Dickson, 2 Barn. & Ald. 2, 13 (1818); The Warkworth, 9 Prob. Div. 20
(1883).

gence of the agent. The decisions in negligence cases are, therefore, not controlling in questions arising under the Limited Liability Statute.[1]

In cases arising under bills of lading containing exemptions from liability for certain specific risks, it has uniformly been held that if the real cause of the loss was the insufficient construction, equipment or stowage of the vessel, the owner would be liable, and that in such case the negligence causing the loss was his negligence, and imputable distinctly to him.[2]

---

[1] Craig v. Continental Ins. Co., 26 Fed. Rep. 798 (1886). In this case it was held that the negligence of the wrecking agent of an insurance company, who ordered a wreck to be towed into port without sufficient previous examination, could not be said to be with the privity or knowledge of the company itself.

[2] The Hadji, Circuit Court, S. D. New York, 20 Fed. Rep. 875, 878 (1884); affg. 16 Fed. Rep. 861 (1883).

Wallace, J. "It is the duty of a common carrier by water to provide a vessel tight, stanch and fit for the employment for which he holds it out to the public. Ang. Carr., sect. 173. The breach of this duty is the personal default of the vessel owner. Lyon v. Wells, 5 East, 428 (1804). The loss sustained by the libelants, therefore, arose from the carrier's own negligence."

In s c. in the District Court, 16 Fed. Rep. 861, 864, 865 (1883), the court say:

"The damage to the goods on board the Hadji did not arise from any peril of the sea or dangers of navigation, nor, properly considered, from anything external to the ship herself. It arose exclusively from the insecure and insufficient structure or repair of the vessel. The damage was not from sea-water taken in through stress of weather or perils of the voyage, but from the faulty construction of the tanks, whereby the water used as ballast escaped and injured the cargo. The character of the defects, as disclosed by the evidence, shows that they were such as should have been guarded against in the construction of the vessel, or ascertained in her repairs and equipment for the voyage. They were such defects as made her unseaworthy for the safe transportation of goods, and, as the immediate and proximate cause of the loss, they were not within the ordinary risks of marine insurance. Arn. Ins. 775; Copeland v. N. E. Marine Ins. Co., 2 Metc. 432 (1841); Gen. Mut. Ins. Co. v. Sherwood, 14 How. (U. S.) 361 (1852). It is impossible, as it seems to me, not to hold that this constitutes, in law, negligence as respects her seaworthiness and proper equipment for the voyage, for which her owners must be held answerable. Clifford, J., in Richards v. Hansen, 1 Fed. Rep. 54, 58, 62 (1879)." Lyon v. Wells, 5 East, 428 (1804).

In this case yarn was shipped on a lighter which turned out to be

Other cases on this subject are considered in the first section of the fourth chapter. It is believed that their reasoning is applicable to the true construction of the words under consideration. Such a construction would tend materially to increase the safety of vessels going to sea, and of the cargo and persons on board. It is possible for owners, by the use of proper precautions, to provide a seaworthy vessel. Where there are statutory requirements as to her equipment or construction, these can be observed, and the fact whether or not they have been observed can generally be discovered before she sails upon her voyage. Still there may be a secret defect, which could not be discovered by the exercise of reasonable care. For loss occasioned by such a cause the owner should still be able to limit his liability. Yet it cannot be said that there is any reported decision precisely in point upon this subject. The nearest approach to such a decision is to be found in the case of The Ventura, decided in the U. S. Circuit Court for the District of California, and affirmed by the Supreme Court of the United States.[1]

---

leaky, and the yarn was injured. Held that owner was liable for full amount of loss, even assuming the validity of a notice that he would not be liable for any loss except from negligence of master or crew, and then only to the extent of 10 per cent. The law implies a promise that the vessel shall be tight and capable of carrying the cargo. The court said that when she is leaky, "this we consider as personal neglect of the owner, or more properly as a non-performance on his part of what he had undertaken to do, viz., to provide a fit vessel for the purpose." To the same effect is Kopitoff v. Wilson, 34 Law Times (N. S.), 677 (1876).

[1] Lord v. Goodall Co., 4 Sawyer, 292 (1877); affd. sub nom. Lord v. S. S. Co., 102 U. S. 541 (1881). The report of the decision of the Supreme Court does not touch this question in any way, but passes simply on the constitutionality of the act, when applied to vessels on a voyage from one port to another port of the same State. Nor did the facts of that case require the expression of an opinion upon the point under consideration, for the injury there did not happen from any defect in the construction of the machinery. But, nevertheless, Mr. Justice Sawyer, in the Circuit Court, expresses his opinion as to the meaning of the statute in the following language, which seems to the author to be the best statement of its meaning that has yet appeared:

In the absence of any authoritative decision on the

"As used in the statute, the meaning of the words 'privity or knowledge' evidently is a personal participation of the owner in some fault, or act of negligence causing or contributing to the loss, or some personal knowledge or means of knowledge, of which he is bound to avail himself, of a contemplated loss, or of a condition of things likely to produce or contribute to the loss, without adopting appropriate means to prevent it. There must be some personal concurrence, or some fault or negligence on the part of the owner himself, or in which he personally participates, to constitute such privity, within the meaning of the act, as will exclude him from the benefit of its provisions. (3 Wall. 153 [1865]; 113 Mass 499 [1873].)   It is the duty of the owner, however, to provide the vessel with a competent master and a competent crew, and to see that the ship, when she sails, is in all respects seaworthy.   He is bound to exercise the utmost care in these particulars—such care as the most prudent and careful men exercise in their own matters under similar circumstances ; and if, by reason of any fault or neglect in these particulars, a loss occurs, it is with his privity, within the meaning of the act.   But the owner, under this act, is not an insurer.   If he exercises due care in the selection of the master and crew, and a loss afterwards occurs from their negligence, without any knowledge or other act or concurrence on his part, he is exonerated by the statute from any liability beyond the value of his interest in the ship and the freight then pending.   So, also, if the owner has exercised all proper care in making his ship seaworthy, and yet some secret defect exists which could not be discovered by the exercise of such due care, and the loss occurs in consequence thereof, without any further knowledge or participation on his part, he is in like manner exonerated, for it cannot be with his ' privity or knowledge,' within the meaning of the act, or in any just sense, and the provision is that ' The liability of the owner   .   .   .   for any act, matter or thing, loss, etc., .   .   .   occasioned without the privity or knowledge of such owner or owners shall, in no case, exceed the amount or value of the interest of such owner in such vessel and her freight then pending.'   This language is broad, and takes away the quality of warranty implied by the common law against all losses except by the act of God and the Public Enemy."

In a case in the Supreme Court of the State of New York, Chisholm v. Northern Transportation Co., 61 Barb. 363, 390 (1872), the court considered this question, and Mr. Justice Talcott, who delivered the opinion, expressed the following views:

"While it is, perhaps, true that any defect in the construction or fitting of the ship and its appurtenances, by means whereof loss or damage is occasioned, is to be attributed to the negligence of the owner, notwithstanding the construction which the Federal Court has put upon the exemption in the first section, yet even in that case the owner is only liable to the value of his interest in the ship and freight, unless he has knowledge of, or is privy to, the defect."   This case did not call for the expression of an opinion on this subject.   It was an action at law to recover damages caused by fire.   And the opinion thus expressed

3

subject, we naturally seek for light from the continental
and English authorities.

It was held by the French Court of Cassation, in 1870,
that the owner had no right to limit his liability for a loss
occasioned by the intrinsic weakness or insufficiency of
the ship itself, and that this was his personal fault, in respect of which the right to abandon the vessel did not exist.[1]

The English statutes on this subject originally used
the same expression—"privity or knowledge"—as that
in the American statute, but no case has been found
in which those words were considered. The words were
subsequently altered so as to read "without their actual
fault or privity."[2]

Under this amended statute, it has been held that the
owner may limit his liability for a defect in navigation

---

can not be considered as entitled to the same weight as that of Mr. Justice Sawyer.

In the Ella, 8 Am. Law Reg. 206 (1860), it was held by the District
Court of South Carolina that a loss caused by unseaworthiness of the
vessel was incurred "with the privity or knowledge of the owner." But
this case held that the Act of 1851 did not apply to the owner's contract liability. In this respect it is overruled, and on the other point
can hardly be considered as controlling.

[1] Couder Dict. de Droit Commercial, vol. 1, p. 413, title Armateur,
sect. 75. "Il faut également rattacher au même principe la solution qui
décide que le proprietaire respond indefiniment des conséquences du
vice propre du navire; il y a là, en fait personnel, au regard du-
quel la faculté d'abandon n'existe point."

Couder cites some conflicting decisions on this subject in the tribunals of first instance. But it would appear to be set at rest in France
by a decision of the Court of Cassation, rendered April 11, 1870, which
he cites. He does not give its title, and whether it is the same as the
following decision, reported in full in the Journal du Palais for 1870, I
am unable to ascertain.

Arnaudin v. Adm. de la Marine, Journal du Palais (1870), p. 633.
The Court of Rennes, referring to Article 216 of the Code du Commerce, says:

"Que le premier, concernant l'abandon, n'accorde cette faculté à
l'armateur que pour lui permettre de s'affranchir de la responsabilité
des faits de son capitaine et *nullement de ses obligations personnelles*."
This was affirmed in the Court of Cassation, *Ibid*, p. 634.

[2] 102 Stat. at Large, 435; 25 and 26 Vict., chap. 63, sect. 54.

caused by the negligence of some person on board the ship, which "consisted in putting a screw wrongly or carelessly into the steam steering-gear."[1] In other words, such negligence happened without the actual fault or privity of the owner.

There can be no doubt that "the owner is not liable beyond his interest in the vessel and her freight, for the misconduct of the officers and mariners of the vessel, in which he does not participate personally."[2]

Section 4286 is as follows :

"The charterer of any vessel, in case he shall man, victual and navigate such vessel at his own expense, or by his own procurement, shall be deemed the owner of such vessel within the meaning of the provisions of this Title relating to the limitation of the liability of the owners of vessels; and such vessel, when so chartered, shall be liable in the same manner as if navigated by the owner thereof."

A very singular question has arisen as to the meaning of the words "owner" in section 4282, and "charterer" in section 4286. A railroad company contracted to deliver goods at a point beyond the terminus of its line, and in performance of this contract delivered them to a connecting line of steamships. While in the possession of this line, and on board one of its ships, they were destroyed by fire, without the design or neglect of the first carrier. It was held that the first carrier was not the owner or charterer of the vessel on which the loss occurred, and therefore not entitled to the benefit of the act.[3]

---

[1] The Warkworth, 9 Prob. Div. 20 (1883); affd. *Ibid*, 145 (1884); s. c. 51 Law Times Rep. 558.

It is obvious, from the report of this case, that the defect was not in the original construction. Indeed, the Master of Rolls, at p. 146 of the Report, says that if the defect had been in the ship when she was constructed, but was latent, and not discoverable before the accident, the shipowner would not have been liable at all, irrespective of the statute.

[2] Walker *v.* Western Transp. Co., 3 Wall. 150 (1865).

[3] Rice *v.* Ontario S. Co., 56 Barb. (N. Y.) 384 (1869); Hill Mfg. Co. *v.* Boston, &c. R. R., 104 Mass. 122 (1870).

This decision seems to be warranted by a strict construction of the terms of the contract. Yet it presents the singular anomaly of making the carrier on whose line the loss did not occur liable, while the carrier on whose line it did occur is discharged. Contracts by one carrier to transport goods or passengers to a point beyond its own line, on what is known as a through bill of lading, are common. Their validity is now well settled. It has been held that unless there is some limitation to the contrary in the contract, the carrier making it is liable for a loss caused by the negligence of the connecting carrier.[1]

It would seem probable that if this question should again arise and be thoroughly discussed, it would be held that the carrier issuing a through bill of lading would be an owner of the vessels engaged in performing the through contract, within the meaning of section 4282. Certainly it would not be contended that the statute is applicable only to the registered owner of a vessel. The beneficial owner is liable for supplies furnished the ship. The registered owner, if he have no beneficial interest in the ship, is not. In other words, the beneficial owner is treated as the real owner to all intents and purposes, except so far as the requirements of the registration acts are concerned.[2] And by parity of reason it would seem just to hold that a carrier who participates in the earnings of a vessel forming part of a through line, and has the right to contract for transportation upon her, is owner *pro hac vice*, and within the equity of the Act of Congress.

It is very common to provide in these through bills of lading that each carrier shall be liable only for loss or damage occurring on his own line. Under such a contract the question under consideration could not arise.

Sections 4284 and 4285 relate to the legal proceedings

---

[1] *Ante*, p. 35, n. 3; *post*, ch. 13, sect. 3; Quimby *v.* Vanderbilt, 17 N. Y. 306 (1858); Insurance Co. *v.* Railroad Co., 104 U. S. 146 (1881).
[2] Macy *v.* Wheeler, 30 N. Y. 231 (1864).

to be taken by the owner in order to obtain the benefit of the statute, and will be considered in the third chapter.

Section 4287 is as follows:

"Nothing in the five preceding sections shall be construed to take away or affect the remedy to which any party may be entitled, against the master, officers, or seamen, for or on account of any embezzlement, injury, loss or destruction of merchandise, or property, put on board any vessel, or on account of any negligence, fraud, or other malversation of such master, officers, or seamen, respectively, nor to lessen or take away any responsibility to which any master or seaman of any vessel may by law be liable, notwithstanding such master or seaman may be an owner or part owner of the vessel."

Even if the master be a part owner, and the loss or damage be caused by his negligence, so that the right of action, preserved by this section, exists against him, the other part owners are not thereby rendered liable, if the loss or damage be occasioned without their privity or knowledge.[1] In such case it has been held that no right of action exists against the vessel on which a fire takes place, but that the remedy is solely *in personam* against the negligent part owner.[2]

If a part owner is on board, and has taken part in the navigation of the vessel, but is asleep at the time of the negligence which caused the injury, it not being his

---

[1] *Re* Leonard, 14 Fed. Rep. 53 (1882); Wilson *v.* Dickson, 2 Barn. & Ald. 2 (1818). This was an action at common law against the owners. Judgment was rendered in favor of all except the captain.
The Spirit of the Ocean, 1 Br. & Lush. 336 (1865); s. c. 34 Law Jour. Adm. 74; The Obey, L. R. 1 Adm. 102 (1866).

[2] The Bark Whistler, 2 Sawy. 348 (1873). This case was decided under the peculiar provisions of Section 1 of the Act of 1851. In a case where the damage was by collision, Dr. Lushington held that the interest of all the owners was properly libelled *in rem*, but that the Admiralty would not make a decree against the master, who was a part owner, and whose negligence caused the collision, for the difference between the amount of the loss and the value of the offending vessel and her freight. The Volant, 1 W. Rob. 383 (1842).

watch, and there being nothing which called for special vigilance, it cannot be said that the loss was incurred with his privity or knowledge.[1]

Section 4289, as originally enacted, was as follows:

"The provisions of this Title relating to the limitation of the liability of the owners of vessels, shall not apply to the owners of any canal-boat, barge or lighter, or to any vessel of any description whatsoever, used in rivers or inland navigation."[2]

There has been considerable diversity of opinion as to the true construction to be given to the words "inland navigation."

In Moore v. Am. Transportation Co.[3] it was held by the U. S. Supreme Court, affirming the decision of the Supreme Court of Michigan,[4] that the navigation of the great lakes was not "inland navigation" within the meaning of this act, and that it was as applicable to a vessel engaged in traffic between Buffalo and Detroit as to a vessel plying between New York and Liverpool.

It is applicable to vessels engaged in navigating Long Island Sound.[5]

It is not limited to vessels plying between ports of different States. If they are not confined to rivers or inland navigation, they can avail themselves of the provisions of the act, although plying between ports and exclusively upon waters of the same State. The Act of 1851 was a regulation of inter-State and foreign commerce. But it

---

[1] The Maria & Elizabeth, 12 Fed. Rep. 627 (1882); The Obey, L. R. 1 Adm. 102 (1866).

[2] The Maritime Law is the same. Couder, Dict. Droit Comm., title Armateur, sect. 109.

[3] 24 How. U. S. 1 (1860).

[4] 5 Mich. 368 (1858); s. P, Re Vessel Owners' Towing Co., 26 Fed. Rep. 169 (1886); Wallace v. Providence & S. S. S. Co., 14 Fed. Rep. 56 (1882).

[5] The Seawanhaka, re Long Island Transp. Co., 5 Fed. Rep. 599 (1881); Wallace v. P. & S. S. S. Co., 14 Fed. Rep. 56 (1882).

was more. It was a declaration and adoption of the Maritime Law in its application to the jurisdiction and decision of Courts of Admiralty,[1] and is therefore applicable, so far as its terms extend, to commerce upon all waters within the jurisdiction of our Admiralty Courts.

But a steamer plying exclusively on a river is excluded from the benefit of the act by the terms of section 4289.[2] The name of the stream, however, is not conclusive. If it be really an arm of the sea, like the East River, vessels plying on it are not engaged in river navigation, and the act applies to and protects their owners.[3]

Some of the questions as to the application of this section to inland waters are now removed by subsequent legislation amending the original statute.

In 1884 an additional statute was passed.[4]

Sec. 18. That the individual liability of a ship-owner shall be limited to the proportion of any or all debts and liabilities that his individual share of the vessel bears to the whole; and the aggregate liabilities of all the owners of a vessel on account of the same shall not exceed the value of such vessels and freight pending; *Provided*, That this provision shall not affect the liability of any owner incurred previous to the passage of this act, nor prevent any claimant from joining all the owners in one action; nor shall the same apply to wages due to persons employed by said ship-owners.

This section does not seem to have yet been construed by the courts. It was perhaps intended as a legislative interpretation of section 4283 of the Revised Statutes with

---

[1] Lord *v.* Steamship Co., 102 U. S. 541 (1880); The Seawanhaka *Re* Long Island Transp. Co., 5 Fed. Rep. 599 (1881); *Re* Norwich & N. Y. Trans. Co., 17 Blatchf. 221 (1879). The contrary was held in Spring *v.* Haskell, 80 Mass. (14 Gray) 309 (1859).

[2] Plant *v.* Stovall, 40 Ga. 85 (1869).

[3] The Garden City, 26 Fed. Rep. 766 (1886).

[4] 23 U. S. Stat. at Large, 57; Act June 26, 1884, sect. 18.

which it is coterminous.   Under the Revised Statutes the liability of the owner is limited to the value of his interest in ship or vessel, and it would seem obvious that the owner of the fourth part of a ship could not be made personally liable for more than one-fourth part of her value, that is, in the language of the statute of 1884 "the proportion his individual share of the vessel bears to the whole."

It will be noticed that *all* liabilities are mentioned in the statute of 1884, while in the Revised Statutes the limitation is confined to liability for "*any embezzlement*," &c. It is not believed that since the act of 1851 the owners were ever held liable in a separate suit to an amount exceeding the value of their vessel, for separate embezzlements, collisions, or otherwise, except in the cases hereinafter referred to, where such losses occured during different voyages.[1]   But as such questions might arise, the statute of 1884 seems intended to imply that the owner should not be liable for the aggregate amount of losses caused by the ship during a given voyage, to an amount greater than "the value of such vessels and freight pending."

Further question might have been made as to whether this statute of 1884 acting as an amendment of sect. 4283

---

[1] After the passage of this Act of 1884 it was held in the Great Western; Thommessen *v.* Whitwill, 118 U. S. 520; s. c. 30 Lawyers' Ed. 156 (1886), that where a vessel committed a maritime tort and was afterwards stranded and wrecked, her value, for the purpose of limited liability proceedings was to be taken as that of the wreck.   The reasons given for this decision would be equally applicable if the wreck had been caused by a second tort which inflicted injury upon another vessel.

See also The City of Norwich, 118 U. S. 500 (1886).   It is to be noticed that the liability to action for successive losses was (Brown *v.* Wilkinson, 15 Mees. & Wels. 397 [1846]) given as a reason in favor of the English rule which fixed the value of the offending vessel as that just *before* the commission of the tort.

The present English rule fixes the limit of liability for damage caused on any one occasion at £8 per ton.   But where the offending vessel ran into one vessel and then immediately after in consequence of the same act of improper navigation ran into and sank another, it was held that the loss to both vessels was caused "substantially at the same time, and on the same occasion."   The Rajah, L. R. 3 Adm. 539 (1872).

of the Revised Statutes, therefore repealed by implication section 4289 of the Revised Statutes, which limits it.

Repeals by implication are not favored, and statutes *in pari materiâ* should be construed together.   If construed in the light of these well settled rules of construction, it is believed that the statute of 1884 did not repeal section 4289 of the Revised Statutes, and that the limitation contained in the latter limited the statute of 1884, although not referred to in it.

That this view is correct would seem to be now determined by a still later statute which not only recognizes the continued existence of section 4289, but amends it. This later statute was passed in 1886,[1] and is as follows:

Sec. 4. That section forty-two hundred and eighty-nine of the Revised Statutes be amended so as to read as follows :

Sec. 4289. The provisions of the seven preceding sections, and of section eighteen of an act entitled "An act to remove certain burdens on the American merchant marine and encourage the American foreign carrying trade, and for other purposes," approved June twenty-sixth, eighteen hundred and eighty-four, relating to the limitations of the liability of the owners of vessels, shall apply to all sea-going vessels, and also to all vessels used on lakes or rivers or in inland navigation, including canalboats, barges, and lighters.

Whether this important extension to rivers and inland waters, of the limitation of shippers' liability, is intended to include waters lying entirely within any State, as it does in terms, and if so, whether this extension is valid, are questions which must be left for the courts to determine in the future.   They have not yet been considered in any important case which the author has been able to discover.[2]

---

[1] 24 U. S. Stats. at Large, 80; Act June 19, 1886, sect. 4.

[2] In Chappell *v.* Bradshaw (C. C. D. Md.), 35 Fed. Rep. 923 (1888), it was held that the statute of 1884 did not repeal section 4289 of the Revised Statutes and that the act of 1886 was not retroactive.

Having thus considered in detail these sections of the act of 1851, as re-enacted and amended, we proceed to consider some questions that have arisen in regard to the act, considered as a whole.

The language of the statute is general and applies to liability for the negligence of the master and mariners, as well as for their willful torts.[1]

The act applies to enrolled and licensed, as well as to registered vessels.[2]

It is immaterial that the contract of transportation was made on land and included land carriage. If the loss or injury was done or occasioned on the water, the owner is entitled to the benefit of the act.[3]

It has been held that the liability of the owner of a vessel can only be limited under the law to loss or damage occurring on the last voyage in which she engaged. The court put this on the language of the statute, and on the ground that it could not have been the intention of the law to allow owners to let claims accumulate against the vessel, on various voyages, until they amounted in the aggregate to more than her value and then abandon her.[4]

A railway company owning a ship can take advantage of the act.[5]

---

[1] Stinson v. Wyman, 2 Ware (Davies), 172 (1841). This decision was rendered under the language of the Maine statute, which was similar to that of the United States Act of 1851.

[2] Wallace v. Providence & S. S. S. Co., 14 Fed. Rep. 56 (1882). The law is apparently stated to be otherwise in Chisholm v. Trans. Co., 61 Barb. 363 (N. Y.) 1872. But the word "not" in Judge Talcott's opinion (p. 386) was obviously inserted by a mistake either of the copyist or reporter. The decision was that the act did apply to a vessel of that class.

[3] Wallace v. Providence & S. S. S. Co., 14 Fed. Rep. 56 (1882).

[4] The Alpena, 8 Fed. Rep. 280 (1881). The continental law is otherwise. It was held by the Court of Cassation, Dec. 31, 1856, that the owner of a vessel could limit his liabilty for a loss occurring on a previous voyage, in cases where no suit against the vessel or her owners was brought until after the termination of the intermediate voyage. Journal du Palais, Table complementaire, vol. 1, p. 118, section 34.

[5] London & S. W. Ry. Co. v. James, L. R. 8 Ch. App. 24 (1872).

ERRATA.—*Page 43. twelfth line from the top.*

For the word *least,* at the beginning of the line, read *most.*

The act applies to a vessel in a wrecked condition, though she cannot propel herself either by sail or steam, or carry cargo. She is still a vessel.[1]

The owner's personal liability is not extended by the execution of a bottomry bond by the master.[2]

Two questions have arisen under these sections of the statute with reference to the Admiralty rule of apportioning damages where both parties are at fault.

Where a collision occurs and both vessels are in fault, the practice in the American admiralty courts is to render a single judgment in favor of the owners of the one injured least, against the other, for half the amount of the difference between their respective losses. It follows that the owners of a vessel which is actually lost and sunk by a collision can not when both vessels are to blame, claim to limit their own liability for the collision to the value of the wreck, and at the same time recover against the other vessel the entire half of the damage sustained by them.[3]

---

[1] Craig *v.* Continental Ins. Co., 26 Fed. Rep. 798 (1886).

[2] Naylor *v.* Baltzell, Taney, 55, 60 (1841).

[3] The North Star, 106 U. S. 17, 22 (1882). In this case the Court say: "These authorities conclusively show that, according to the general maritime law, in cases of collision occurring by the fault of both parties, the entire damage to both ships is added together in one common mass, and equally divided between them, and thereupon arises a liability of one party to pay to the other such sum as is necessary to equalize the burden. This is the rule of mutual liability between the parties." This overrules the decision of the English Court of Appeals in Chapman *v.* Royal Netherlands Steam N. Co., L. R. 4 Prob. Div. 157 (1879). That decision was by a divided court reversing the decision of Sir George Jessel, which was in harmony with that of the Supreme Court. On the question of the weight of authority, the Supreme Court were well warranted in considering the judgment of the Master of the Rolls and Justice Brett as quite equal to that of the two Lord Justices who took the opposite view.

This decision in the Chapman case was overruled in the House of Lords, July 26, 1882. Stoomvaart Maatschappy Nederland *v.* Peninsular & Oriental S. N. Co., L. R. 7 App. Ca. 795 (1882). This case was not brought to the attention of the Supreme Court, but it is referred to by the reporter. The Judgment was that "the owners of the steam vessel Voorwaarts are entitled to prove against the fund paid into the court under that judgment, for a moiety of the loss and damage sustained by them, less

Where cargo is injured by a collision between two vessels, and it is held that both are to blame, the owner of the cargo recovers a moiety of his loss from each of the offending vessels. If one of them is not of value sufficient to pay this moiety, the other is liable for the amount of the deficiency.[1] If the owner of the cargo proceed against only one of the offending vessels, he recovers his whole damage.[2] Whether the owner of the libelled vessel could, in such case, have process to compel the other wrong-doer to appear and respond to the alleged wrongful act, the Supreme Court did not determine;[3] but on principle it would seem that in Admiralty this right should exist.[4]

If the owner of one of the injured vessels be also the owner of the cargo on board, and he desires to limit his liability for the injury done to the other vessel, he can do so without abandoning his interest in his cargo.[5]

The method, according to which the computation of

---

a moiety of the loss and damage sustained by the steam vessel Khedive, and to be paid in respect of the balance due to them after such deduction, *pari passu*, with the other claimants out of such fund." The Jose E. More, 37 Fed. Rep. 122 (1888).

[1] The Alabama and The Gamecock, 92 U. S. 695 (1875); The Washington and The Gregory, 9 Wall. 513 (1870). These cases overrule The City of Hartford and The Unit, 11 Blatchf. 290 (1873), and The Milan, 1 Lush. 388 (1861). The earlier English decisions on this rule of dividing the damages are fully stated in The Milan. See The Britannic, 39 Fed. Rep. 395 (1889).

[2] The Atlas, 93 U. S. 302 (1876); rev'g s. c. 10 Blatchf. 459 (1873); 4 Bened. 27 (1870).

[3] The Atlas, 93 U. S. 302, 317 (1876). This case had been decided in the Circuit Court on the ground that " a libellant could not, by proceeding against one of the offending vessels alone, deprive her owners of the right to such contribution from the other vessel, and of the means of enforcing it." This was so stated by Judge Woodruff in The City of Hartford and The Unit, 11 Blatchf. 290, 293 (1873).

[4] The Canima, 17 Fed. Rep. 271 (1883). The decree in this case accomplished the result indicated in the text, though by a different method, owing to the fact that on one libel the owners of both ships were before the Court.

[5] The Bristol, 29 Fed. Rep. 867 (1887). The French law is the same as shown in this case, p. 873.

damage and consequent recovery are to be determined in a case where both vessels are to blame, is fully stated in the Bristol. Briefly it may be said that in such case, the owner of the cargo on the abandoned vessel recovers half his loss from the other vessel, less the net salvage upon his own vessel, which, under the Statute, is the limit of his liability for the tort of his vessel.[1]

We have now considered the case of a collision where both vessels are at fault, and the cargo on board of one of them belongs to the owner of the injured vessel. But it more frequently happens that the cargo on the injured vessel belongs to some person other than the owner of the vessel herself. In such case, as has been shown, he is entitled to recover the whole of his damage. If the owners of the vessel on which his cargo was laden succeed in limiting their liability, he is entitled to recover the entire value of his cargo from the other vessel, and the weight of authority at present is, that in making up the statement of the account as between the respective owners, any right of action of the owners of the injured vessel against the other must be transferred to the trustee in the limited liability proceedings, if a trustee be appointed, or else included in the stipulation given for value. This question was considered and not decided in the Leonard case,[2] but the earlier and subsequent cases support the proportion just stated.[3] In effect, therefore, there would be brought

---

[1] The Bristol, 29 Fed. Rep. 867 (1887). If the injury had been to the person, instead of the property, of the owner of the offending vessel, he would in like manner have recovered only half of his damages. The Juniata, 93 U. S. 337 (1876).

[2] Re Leonard, 14 Fed. Rep. 53 (1882).

[3] The C. H. Foster, 1 Fed. Rep. 733 (1880); Atlantic Mut. Ins. Co. v. Alexandre, 16 Fed. Rep. 279 (1883); The Hercules, 20 Fed. Rep. 205 (1884); and see The Eleanora, 17 Blatchf. 104 (1879). This is stated as an inference from the decisions cited *ante*, p. 43, n. 3, and p. 44, n. 1 and 2.

In re Petition Norwich & N. Y. Trans. Co., 17 Blatchf. 221, 234 (1879), Strong, J., says:

"There is nothing in the act of Congress to indicate that the trans-

into court in the limited liability proceedings taken by
the owners of the sunken vessel, not simply the value of

---

fer of the interest of the owner to a trustee was intended to have any
different effect from that of an ordinary transfer of personal property,
which, neither in law or equity, carries with it insurance or any collateral contract."

It may be contended that this transfer should not carry with it any
right of action for the injury to the vessel transferred. The act certainly does not say that any such right shall be assigned, and in Denn
v. Reid, 10 Peters, 528 (1836), the Supreme Court said: "But it is not
for the court to say, when the language of the statute is clear, that it
shall be so construed as to embrace cases because no reason can be assigned why they were excluded from its provisions."

The phrase in the statute—"interest of the owner"—is often used
as expressive of the extent of the owner's aliquot share in the vessel.
The several part owners are tenants in common "with each other of
their respective shares, each having a distinct, although individual interest in the whole." Abb. on Shipping, 97 ; 1 Phill. Ins., sect. 380.

It may well be, therefore, that the Supreme Court will ultimately
determine that the transfer of the owner's interest transfers his share,
whatever that may be, but does not transfer his right of action for a
previous injury to such share. This would be in analogy to the well-
settled rule in Admiralty that it is the ship, and not the owner, which
is to be considered as the wrong-doer. For example, in The China, 7
Wallace, 53, 68 (1868), the Supreme Court say:

"The Maritime Law as to the position and powers of the master
and the responsibility of the vessel, is not derived from the civil law of
master and servant, nor from the common law. It had its source in the
commercial usages and jurisprudence of the middle ages. Originally
the primary liability was upon the vessel, and that of the owner was
not personal, but merely incidental to his ownership, from which he was
discharged either by the loss of his vessel, or by abandoning it to the
creditors. But while the law limited the creditor to this part of the
owner's property, it gave him a lien or privilege against it, in preference
to other creditors."

So in The Malek Adhel, 2 How. U. S. 210, 234 (1844), the court say:

"The ship is also by the general maritime law held responsible for
the torts and misconduct of the master and crew thereof, whether arising
from negligence or a willful disregard of duty; as for example in cases
of collision and other wrongs done upon the high seas or elsewhere,
within the admiralty and maritime jurisdiction, upon the general policy
of that law, which looks to the instrument itself, used as the means of
mischief, as the best and surest pledge for the compensation and indemnity to the injured party."

It would seem, therefore, that the proposition stated in the text can
hardly be said to be settled beyond controversy. The cases cited, however, show that the weight of authority in the District and Circuit Courts
at present supports it.

the wreck, but also the proportion of the damage which they would be entitled to recover against the other vessel. The value of the wreck and the value of the recovery would form a fund for distribution.

The insurer who pays a loss on cargo is subrogated to the rights of its owner, but he occupies no better position, and can recover only half the loss in a case in which that would have been the extent of the owner's recovery.[1]

It must be remembered that damage done to cargo in either vessel is a part of the loss or damage caused by a collision, "and it is wholly immaterial in which vessel the damaged cargo happens to be."[2]

Two other sections of the Revised Statutes remain to be considered :

Section 4281 is as follows :

"If any shipper of platina, gold, gold-dust, silver, bullion or other precious metals, coins, jewelry, bills of any bank or public body, diamonds or other precious stones, or any gold or silver in a manufactured or unmanufactured state, watches, clocks or time-pieces of any description, trinkets, orders, notes or securities for payment of money, stamps, maps, writings, title deeds, printings, engravings, pictures, gold or silver plate or plated articles, glass, china, silk in a manufactured or unmanufactured state, and whether wrought up or not wrought up with any other material, furs or lace, or any of them, contained in any parcel or package, or trunk, shall lade the . same as freight or baggage, on any vessel, without, at the time of such lading, giving to the master, clerk, agent or owner of such vessel receiving the same, a written notice of the true character and value thereof, and having the

[1] The Bristol, 29 Fed. Rep. 867 (1887). This was decided on the authority of Phœnix Ins. Co. v. Erie Trans. Co., 117 U. S. 312 (1886). Simpson v. Thomson, L. R. 3 App. Ca. 279 (1877).

[2] Leonard v. Whitwill, 10 Bened. 638, 658 (1879); The Bristol, 29 Fed. Rep. 867 (1887). See the decree in The Eleanora, 17 Blatchf. 88, 105 (1879).

same entered on the bill of lading therefor, the master and owner of such vessel shall not be liable as carriers thereof in any form or manner, nor shall any such master or owner be liable for any such goods beyond the value, and according to the character thereof, so notified and entered."

This statute was passed in its original form, March 3, 1851. It then read as follows :

"SEC. 2. And be it further enacted, That if any shipper or shippers of platina, gold, gold-dust, silver, bullion or other precious metals ; coins, jewelry, bills of any bank or public body ; diamonds or other precious stones, shall lade the same on board of any ship or vessel, without, at the time of such lading, giving to the master, agent, owner or owners of the ship or vessel receiving the same, a note in writing of the true character and value thereof, and have the same entered on the bills of lading therefor, the master and owner or owners of the said vessel shall not be liable, as carriers thereof, in any form or manner. Nor shall any such master or owners be liable for any such valuable goods beyond the value and according to the character thereof so notified and entered." [1]

The statute was afterwards amended so as to include many other articles than those enumerated in the statute of 1851 (among them pictures), and was also amended by the addition of the words, "contained in any parcel, or package, or trunk," and also by the insertion after the words "shall lade the same," of the words "as freight or baggage." [2]

In this amended shape it appears in the United States Revised Statutes to-day. It would be difficult to find a plainer indication of the legislative intent that the statute should cover every kind of case under which such enum-

---

[1] U. S. Statutes at Large, vol. 9, p. 635.

[2] U. S. Stat. at Large, vol. 16, p. 458, chap. 100, sect. 69 (Feb. 28 1871).

erated articles might be put on board, than is shown by
the insertion of the words "as freight or baggage," above
referred to.   It was held in Massachusetts that the original
statute did not apply to the baggage of passengers.[1]

But it would seem clear that baggage, as well as
freight, are within the terms of the law as amended.[2]   It
has, however, been held in New York that a passenger
who puts articles of jewelry, such as she is accustomed to
wear upon her person, in a trunk which she takes with
her on a steamer, is not a shipper of such jewelry, within
the meaning of the act, and that the carrier is liable for
their loss, although the passenger has given no notice of
the character and value thereof to the master or agent of
the ship.[3]

The statute is so comprehensive in terms that the carrier would not be liable, even for negligence, in a case
covered by it.[4]

It is enough if the "notice of the true character and
value" is contained in the bill of lading.   It need not be
a separate notice.[5]

The remaining section requiring consideration is section 4493, which is as follows:

SEC. 4493. Whenever damage is sustained by any

---

[1] Dunlap v. The International Steamboat Co., 98 Mass. 371 (1867).
Under the statute of 1851 the Commission of Appeals of New York
held that the words, "any goods or merchandise whatsoever," in the
first section of that act, applied to personal baggage.   Chamberlain v.
Western Transportation Co., 44 N. Y. 305 (1871).

[2] Wheeler v. Oceanic Steam N. Co., 52 Hun, 75; s. c. 5 N. Y. Supp.
101 (1889).

[3] Carlson v. Oceanic Steam Nav. Co., 109 N. Y. 359 (1888).

[4] The statute is founded upon the British statute, 1 Wm. IV, chap.
68. Under that statute it was held that a carrier would not be liable even
for gross negligence.   Hinton v. Dibbin, 2 Ad. & Ellis, N. S. (Qu. B.)
646 (1842).

[5] Watson v. Marks, 2 Am. Law Reg. 157 (1853).   Under the English statute it has been held that a description of the goods shipped, as
"one box containing about 248 oz. of gold-dust," was not a sufficient
statement of value.   Williams v. African S. S. Co., 1 Hurlst. & N. 300
(1856).   This seems a very technical construction.

4

passenger or his baggage, from explosion, fire, collision or other cause, the master and the owner of such vessel, or either of them, and the vessel, shall be liable to each and every person so injured, to the full amount of damage, if it happens through any neglect or failure to comply with the provisions of this Title, or through known defects or imperfections of the steaming apparatus, or of the hull; and any person sustaining loss or injury through the carelessness, negligence, or willful misconduct of any master, mate, engineer or pilot, or his neglect or refusal to obey the laws governing the navigation of such steamers, may sue such master, mate, engineer or pilot, and recover damages for any such injury caused by any such master, mate, engineer or pilot.

It was held, under the provisions of the section of which this is a re-enactment, that damages sustained by a passenger or his baggage from any of the causes therein mentioned, is not included within the loss, the liability for which can be limited under section 4283.[1] The decision in the Carroll case was placed on the ground that the object of the Act of 1851 was to limit the common-law liability of carriers of goods. It has, however, been shown that the Act of 1851 applies to the liability of carriers for injuries to persons as well as injuries to goods. But the case is sustainable on the express language of the section which, so far as passengers and their baggage are concerned, is clear enough. But when a loss of goods happens through failure to comply with the provisions of the title of which the section just quoted forms a part, or through known defects or imperfections of the steaming apparatus, or of the hull, the question will arise whether the loss was incurred with the privity or knowledge of the owner.

Under the familiar rule that statutes which are *in*

---

[1] Act of Feb. 28, 1871; U. S. Stat. at Large, vol. 16, p. 446; Carroll *v.* Staten Island R. R. Co., 58 N. Y. 126 (1874); Chisholm *v.* Northern Transp. Co., 61 Barb. 393 (1872).

pari materiâ are to be construed together, it would seem reasonable to maintain that a vessel which is not equipped in accordance with the sections of the same title, is defectively equipped with the privity or knowledge of the owner, because of the duty to provide such equipment imposed upon him by the statute.[1]   On the other hand it may fairly be argued that if the carrier cannot, under the Act of 1851, limit his liability for a loss caused by such defective equipment, there would have been no occasion for passing the Act of February 28, 1871, section 43, re-enacted as above stated.   No decisions are reported from which any inference can be drawn upon this subject.

The validity of the act of which this section formed a part was at one time disputed, but it seems clear that it is a regulation of commerce, and as such it was held valid by the Supreme Court.[2]

None of the sections of the statute which have been referred to have the effect to oust the jurisdiction of the State courts of all common law actions.   These may still be prosecuted, and if it should not become necessary to invoke the aid of the admiralty proceedings authorized by the act, and the rules of the Supreme Court adopted in conformity to it, the defence under the statute can still be asserted in these suits.   In other words there is nothing in the U. S. Statute, which ousts the jurisdiction of common law courts of actions to recover damages for marine torts.[3]

But where several actions have been brought, or several claims have been made against one defendant to recover damages for a marine tort, it seems clear that the only remedy available to the defendant is that provided

---

[1] It was so held in England *v.* Gripon, 15 La. Ann. 304 (1860).

[2] Sherlock *v.* Alling, 93 U. S. 99 (1876).

[3] Chappell *v.* Bradshaw, 128 U. S. 132 (1888); Dougan *v.* Champlain Trans. Co., 56 N. Y. 1 (1874); Carroll *v.* Staten Island R. R. Co., 58 N. Y. 126 (1874).

for by the admiralty rules. The effect of the commencement of proceedings in Admiralty for that purpose, is to
oust the jurisdiction of the State courts. Whether or not
the Admiralty Court has authority to grant an injunction
is a point not yet finally determined, but it is settled by
the Supreme Court of the United States that the pendency
of the Admiralty proceeding is a bar to the prosecution of
actions in common law courts, to recover damages for the
tort respecting which the petition in limited liability proceedings has been filed. If, notwithstanding the interposition of this defence, the State court should assert jurisdiction and render judgment adversely to the defendant, this
judgment can be reviewed by writ of error out of the Supreme Court.[1]

---

[1] Providence & N. Y. S. S. Co. *v.* Hill Mfg. Co., 109 U. S. 578, 600
(1883).

CHAPTER III.

An owner or charterer of a ship or vessel desiring to avail himself of the limitation of liability which has thus been considered, may, if there be only one claim against him, or the several claimants have brought but one suit, plead his defense in bar of the action or in mitigation of damages.[1] If he desires to take affirmative proceedings to limit his liability, he must file his libel in a district court of the United States. A bill in equity, for the purpose of limiting liability, is not maintainable in the United States.[2]

"The said libel or petition shall be filed, and said proceedings had, in any district court of the United States in which said ship or vessel may be libelled to answer for any such embezzlement, loss, destruction, damage or injury; or if the said ship or vessel be not libelled, then in the district court for any district in which said owner or owners may be sued in that behalf. When the said ship or vessel has not been libelled to answer the matters aforesaid, and suit has not been commenced against the said owner or owners, or has been commenced in a district other than that in which the said ship or vessel may be,

---

[1] The Scotland, 105 U. S. 24 (1881). So he, may if the loss be total, even if there be several suits. Craig v. Continental Ins. Co., 26 Fed. Rep. 798 (1886).

[2] Goodrich Trans. Co. v. Gagnon, 36 Fed. Rep. 123 (1888); s. c. Chicago Legal News, Aug. 25, 1888; Elwell v. Geibei, 33 Fed. Rep. 71 (1887). In both these cases the tort was done by a vessel on the water to persons or property on land. But this fact was held not to confer jurisdiction on the Circuit Court in equity. See The Mary Lord, 31 Fed. Rep. 416 (1887); Providence & N. Y. S. S. Co. v. Hill Mfg. Co., 109 U. S. 578, 593 (1883); Norwich Co. v. Wright, 13 Wall. 104, 123 (1871). It is a curious fact that in England the remedy by statute was original in equity.

the said proceedings may be had in the district court of the district in which the said ship or vessel may be, and where it may be subject to the control of such court for the purposes of the case as hereinbefore provided. If the ship have already been libelled and sold, the proceeds shall represent the same for the purposes of these rules."[1]

There remains the case of a ship-owner whose ship has become a total loss, and who has not yet been sued. He can obtain relief in the district into which the rem-

---

[1] Admiralty Rule 57, promulgated May 6, 1872, 13 Wall. xiii; as amended April 27, 1889, 130 U. S. 705; *In re* Leonard, (D. C., S. D. N. Y.) 14 Fed. Rep. 53 (1882). In this case the district court, in Leonard *v.* Whitwell, 10 Bened. 638 (1879), had held that both of two colliding vessels were at fault, and that each should pay half the damages. The owners of one of the vessels—an American schooner—thereafter filed their libel in the Southern District of New York, to limit their liability for the loss to the value of their interest in the vessel and her freight. The owners of the other vessel—a British steamer—excepted to the jurisdiction. The collision occurred on the high seas, fifteen miles south of Long Island. It was held that the libel was properly filed in the Southern District, because the litigation as to the liability for the collision took place there; the stipulation representing the value of the steamer was filed there, and the amount of the recovery by the schooner against the steamer would be paid into court there.

In Wallace *v.* Providence & Stonington S. S. Co. (C. C. Mass., Lowell and Nelson, JJ.), 14 Fed. Rep. 56 (1882), it was held that the libel could be filed in any district where the carrier was sued. But this must be taken with the limitation that no libel in Admiralty has been filed against the vessel. If such libel has been filed, the proceedings to limit liability must be taken in the district court in which such libel was filed. The Luckenback, 26 Fed. Rep. 870 (1886). This rule was applied in The Luckenback to a case in which a decree upon the original libel had been rendered in the District Court and affirmed in the Circuit Court, and an appeal had been taken to the Supreme Court of the United States before the commencement of the proceedings to limit liability. Judge Brown in that case expresses the opinion that Admiralty Rule 58 (13 Otto, xiii, Desty Fed. Proc. 761) applies only to cases where a decree in a proceeding to limit liability is reversed in the Supreme Court, and the cause remanded to the Circuit Court, or where such proceeding is pending in the Circuit Court on appeal. This opinion was not necessary to the decision of that case, but it has been followed by Colt, J., in the First Circuit, and expresses the practice. The Mary Lord, 31 Fed. Rep. 416 (1887).

The question as to the validity of these Admiralty Rules was raised in Providence & N. Y. S. S. Co. *v.* Hill Mfg. Co., 109 U. S. 578 (1883). The court held them to be valid.

nants of the vessel have been brought.   The filing of the stipulation for the value of his interest in the ship and her freight brings into court the *res* itself, and is, to all intents and purposes, substituted for it.[1]

The District Court of the district to which the vessel is bound, has jurisdiction of a proceeding to limit the liability of her owner, upon the filing in that court of the transfer of the interest of the owner in her wreckage and freight, though she was wrecked within another district. In this case the proceedings of the wreckage and freight were paid into court.[2]

The libel, in addition to the usual requirements, must contain five articles:

First. The pleader must state whether he elects to contest his client's liability altogether, or to admit this, and simply seek to limit it.   In the English practice the question of liability cannot be tried in the action brought to limit it.   This must be tried in an action at law, or upon a libel in Admiralty, and the suit for the limitation of liability is stayed to await the result of such action.   But in this country both questions can be determined in one suit.   If the pleader proposes to contest the owner's liability altogether, he should state, in detail, the grounds of

---

[1] Whenever a stipulation is taken in an Admiralty suit, for the property subjected to legal process and condemnation, the stipulation is deemed a mere substitute for the thing itself, and the stipulators liable to the exercise of all those authorities on the part of the court which it could properly exercise if the thing itself were still in its custody.   The Palmyra, 12 Wheat. 1, 10 (1827); The City of Norwich, 118 U. S. 468, 489 (1886).

Admiralty Rule 57: "If the ship have already been libelled and sold, the proceeds shall represent the same for the purposes of these rules."   But if a libel *in rem* is filed, and a stipulation for the value of the vessel at that time is given, this stipulation is not conclusive as to her value immediately after the committing of the tort, respecting which proceedings to limit the owner's liability are subsequently taken. The City of Norwich, 118 U. S. 468 (1886); The Doris Eckhoff, 30 Fed. Rep. 140 (1887).

[2] *Ex parte* Slayton, 105 U. S. 451 (1881); The Alpena, 8 Fed. Rep. 280 (1881).

his defense—much as he would in an answer or plea in an action brought to recover damages for the injury the shippers or passengers have suffered.

Second. The pleader must determine and allege in his libel whether the owner abandons his interest in the ship and her freight then pending, or elects to give a stipulation for their value. Ordinarily it is for the shipper's interest that the owner should himself take the steps necessary to save all that can be saved. He is more familiar with the facts necessary to be known to make this salvage of any value. It is, therefore, more in harmony with the spirit of the rule to give the stipulation. The doubts which have been expressed as to whether the giving such a stipulation is a compliance with the Maritime law, seem, therefore, unreasonable.

Third. The libel must state, as nearly as may be, the particulars of the loss by reason of which the owner seeks the protection of the court :

Fourth. Also that the loss took place without his privity or knowledge :

Fifth. And that the owner seeks the benefit of the limitation of liability given by the statute and by the Maritime law.

It is not necessary to aver that the claims against the vessel exceed her value.[1]

When the libel is filed, the next step is to give notice to all persons, claiming to recover damages for the loss in question, to come into court and assert their claims. And if the libel tenders a stipulation for value instead of making an abandonment the claimants are entitled to be heard on the question of value.

The court makes an order referring it to a commissioner to fix the amount of the stipulation, which must be for the value of the libellant's interest in the vessel and her freight

---

[1] The Garden City, 26 Fed. Rep. 766 (1886).

advertised in a manner to be fixed by the court, and notice must also be given to all persons who have commenced actions against the libellant to recover damages for the loss in question. This may be given either personally or by mail, and it may be given to them or their attorneys in the suits so begun.

It was claimed in the Levinson case, already referred to,[1] that the service of this notice on the attorneys was insufficient to give the court jurisdiction of the client. The Circuit Court, however, held otherwise.

That this decision was right is manifest from a consideration of the nature of the proceedings to limit the liability of a ship-owner. These are primarily *in rem*, inasmuch as their first object is to bring into court and surrender, in one form or another, the vessel and her freight then pending. The decree barring claims *in personam* against the owner is incidental to the proceeding *in rem*. Jurisdiction of this suit *in rem* is gained by the filing of the petition and the offer to surrender the vessel and her freight. The process issued upon the filing of this libel is "due process of law," being in strict conformity with the immemorial practice of courts of admiralty. The proceedings before the commissioner are simply to fix the amount of the stipulation. Courts, both of law and admiralty, have always assumed to fix the amounts of bonds and stipulations, and this is often, in the first instance, done *ex parte*. If the amount of the stipulation in these proceedings were to be fixed *ex parte*, it would be open to any person interested afterwards to contest the amount, and claim that it be increased. It is therefore more convenient that all known claimants should be notified, and this question of the amount of the stipulation settled at the outset. But there are frequently some claimants then unknown, who afterwards appear in answer to the monition. It seems certain

---

[1] Levinson *v.* Oceanic Steam Nav. Co., 17 Albany L. J. 285 (1876).

then pending.   Notice of the hearing before him must be that these would have the right to ask the court to increase the amount of the stipulation.   It is to be observed that the statute does not provide for the appraisement, and the rule leaves the manner of making it in the discretion of the court.   In the Levinson case, the question as to the proper manner of giving notice of appraisement was treated as the same as that of the jurisdiction obtained by the issue of the monition.   And no doubt it is well that the notice of the hearing upon the application to fix the amount of the stipulation should be served in the way in which monitions are served.   This method, also, is not provided for by statute, but it is in conformity with the ancient practice of courts of admiralty, and is therefore due process of law.[1]

In the Levinson case, attorneys had been entrusted by the claimants with the prosecution of their claims, and notice of the proceedings to limit the shipowner's liability was therefore properly served upon them.

The legislature may and often has authorized the courts to determine how notice of proceedings in court shall be given.   It is no doubt true that process in a pro-

---

[1] In the matter of the Empire City Bank, 18 N. Y. 199 (1858), the court say, p. 215:

"It may be admitted that a statute which should authorize any debt or damages to be adjudged against a person upon a purely *ex parte* proceeding, without a pretence of notice or any provision for defending, would be a violation of the constitution, and be void; but where the legislature has prescribed a kind of notice by which it is reasonably probable that the party proceeded against will be apprised of what is going on against him, and an opportunity is afforded him to defend, I am of opinion that the courts have not the power to pronounce the proceedings illegal. . . . If we hold, as we must in order to sustain this legislation, that the constitution does not positively require personal notice in order to constitute a legal proceeding due process of law, it then belongs to the legislature to determine in the particular instance whether the case calls for this kind of exceptional legislation, and what manner of constructive notice shall be sufficient to reasonably apprise the party proceeded against of the legal steps which are taken against him."

To the same effect is Levinson v. Oceanic Steam Navigation Co., 17 Albany L. J. 285 (1876).

See also cases cited in next note.

ceeding *in personam* must be served within the jurisdiction of the court from which it issues. If this be done, the service need not be personal. Indeed, both at common law and in equity, original process could regularly be served by leaving a copy at the defendant's residence.

But in a proceeding *in rem*, the rule as to service within the jurisdiction does not apply. Notice must be given, but when given it is notice to all the world. And this doctrine is constantly applied to proceedings not strictly *in rem*, but of a kindred character, as for example proceedings to wind up the affairs of a bank, of a partnership, of a deceased person, of a bankrupt.[1]

The next question to examine is as to the extent of the stipulation which the commissioner must require to be given. In general it must be, to use the language of the statute, for "the interest of such owner in the vessel or her freight then pending." But questions of great importance have arisen upon the construction of these terms.

---

[1] The Empire City Bank, 18 N. Y. 199 (1858); Campbell *v.* Evans, 45 N. Y. 356 (1871); *re* N. Y. Elevated R. R., 70 N. Y. 327, 357 (1877); *re* Village of Middletown, 82 N. Y. 201 (1880); Matter of the Harmony F. & M. Insurance Co., 45 N. Y. 310 (1871). The constitutional provision that no person shall be deprived of property, &c., without due process of law does not require proceedings according to the common law or personal notice. It is sufficient if a kind of notice is provided which is reasonable. Happy *v.* Mosher, 48 N. Y. 313 (1872). (This was a case of claims against vessels.) Rockwell *v.* Nearing, 35 N. Y. 302 (1866); Gray *v.* Schenck, 4 N. Y. 460 (1851); Jackson *v.* Babcock, 16 N. Y. 246 (1857); Swan *v.* Williams, 2 Mich. 427 (1852); Curry *v.* Mount Sterling, 15 Ill. 320 (1853); Redfield on Railways, sect. 72; Methodist Prot. Church *v.* Baltimore, 6 Gill (Md.) 391 (1848); State *v.* Mayor, &c., of Jersey City, 4 Zab. (N. J.) 662 (1855); Nicholls *v.* Bridgeport, 23 Conn. 212 (1854); Hildreth *v.* City of Lowell, 11 Gray (Mass.) 345 (1858).

In Stewart *v.* Board of Police, 25 Miss. 479 (1853), the court held that in laying out a new road no notice to the owners of land over which it passed was necessary. They refer to the practice in admiralty and exchequer courts. "The seizure of the thing on which the judgment is to operate is considered constructive notice to everybody in interest." But this proposition can hardly be considered as sound law in any State but Mississippi. The usual rule is that reasonable notice of some sort must be given even though the proceeding be *in rem*.

FIRST. *Insurance.*—On the hearing before the Commissioner, the claimants have no right to have the amount of any insurance on the vessel or freight included in the stipulation.[1]

SECOND. *Advance Freight and Passage Money.*—It has been contended that the amount of any advance freight or passage money received by the libellant should be included in the stipulation. If the voyage was broken up by the disaster causing the loss, so that the passengers or cargo were not transported to their destination, the passenger or shipper would, by the American rule, which is in conformity with the law merchant, have a right to the return of the money paid in advance for transportation.[2]

---

[1] The City of Norwich, 118 U. S. 493 (1886); s. c. *sub nom. In re* Petition Norwich & N. Y. Trans. Co., 17 Blatchf. 227 (1879); 8 Bened. 317 (1875); The Scotland, 118 U. S. 507 (1886); The Phestigo, 2 Flipp. C. C. 466 (1879); The City of Columbus (D. C. Mass.), 22 Fed. Rep. 461 (1884). See text to notes 1 and 2, page 70, *infra.*

By the Prussian law as it existed before 1862, the owner was obliged to surrender the amount of his insurance as well as his interest in the vessel. But this was changed in that year by the adoption of the Code of the Germanic Confederation. Pöhls: Darstelling des Handelsrechts, vol. 3, p. 234.

[2] The continental law allows prepaid freight and passage money to be recovered, if the goods or passengers are not transported to their destination by reason of disaster. Ord. de la Mar. tit. du Fret. art. 18 (Valin Comm., vol. 1, p. 661); Roccus de Nav. et Maulo, n. 80; Cleirac, Les Us et Contumes de la Mer, 42; Code du Commerce, art. 302.

In the U. S. the first reference to this subject appears to have been made by Chief Justice Kent in 1808, in Watson *v.* Duyckinck, 3 Johns. 335, 337. "The general rule undoubtedly, is that freight is lost unless the goods are carried to the port of destination. The rule seems to go farther and to oblige the master, in case of shipwreck, to restore to the shipper the freight previously advanced."

In The Kimball, 3 Wall. 37 (1865), the U. S. Supreme Court holds accordingly, and Justice Field says, p. 44 : "Freight being the compensation for the carriage of goods, if paid in advance, is in all cases, unless there is a special agreement to the contrary, to be refunded, if from any cause not attributable to the shipper the goods be not carried." The principle thus asserted represents the law in the U. S. Atwell *v.* Miller, 11 Md. 348 (1857); Lee *v.* Barreda, 16 Md. 190 (1860); Griggs *v.* Austin, 3 Pick. 20 (1825); Brown *v.* Harris, 2 Gray, 359 (1854), passage money;

It would seem to follow that in such a case the money which is thus held by the libellant should not be paid into court or included in the amount of the stipulation. It can hardly be contended that a claim for its return would be provable against the amount so paid into court. It is not a claim for loss, damage or injury incurred during the voyage, but rather a cause of action to recover the consideration for a contract which the other contracting party has failed to perform.[1]

Benner *v.* Equitable Safety Ins. Co., 6 Allen, 222 (1863), charter party case.

In The Scotland, 118 U. S. 507 (1886), it appeared that the advance passage money was refunded in part, and in part used to forward the passengers by another vessel, and it was held that the owner was not chargeable with any portion of it. A claim for return of advance freight is not barred by abandonment proceedings, and it will not be stayed. *Re Petition*, Liverpool & G. W. S. Co., 3 Fed. Rep. 168 (1880). In Wilson *v.* Dickson, 2 Barn. & Ald. 2, 15 (1818), it was held that "freight due or to grow due" meant the entire freight for the voyage, whether paid in advance or not. But this seems clear under the English act, the language of which, in this particular, differs from ours.

[1] Upon this, as upon so many other points of maritime law, the rule adopted by the English courts differs from that of the continental authorities, and from that adopted in this country. Freight once paid cannot, it is held in England, be recovered back, even though the voyage be broken up, and the cargo never delivered. Byrne *v.* Schiller, L. R. 6 Ex. 319 (1871); Hicks *v.* Shield, 7 E. & B. 633 (1857); Jackson *v.* Isaacs, 3 Hurl. & N. 405 (1858); De Cuadra *v.* Swan, 16 C. B. (N. S.) 772 (1864); Allison *v.* Bristol Marine Ins. Co., L. R. 1 App. Cas. 209 (1876).

It has, however, come to pass, owing to the fact that most of the commerce between Europe and America is conducted in British bottoms, that a great deal of the litigation in our Courts of Admiralty relates to British vessels. In no case, however, as yet, has the owner of a British vessel, who has taken proceedings in our court to limit his liability, been required to give a stipulation for an amount sufficient to cover the advance freight or passage money paid him. Freight is seldom, but passage money is almost always paid in advance.

It is believed that the courts of this country will apply the American rule in such cases, and not require the British owner, in case of loss, to stipulate for a larger amount than an American owner would be required to do. Freight or passage money received by him before the beginning of the voyage can hardly be described as freight then (that is at the time of the disaster) pending.

The words " freight then pending," include the earnings of the vessel in carrying the goods of the owners of
the vessel.[1]

The extended examination which has been given in
the first chapter to the case of the Norwich Transportation
Co. v. Wright, 13 Wall. 104 (1871), makes it unnecessary
to do more than repeat here that in estimating the value
of the owner's interest in the vessel, the period of time at
which the value of the interest is to be fixed is after the
tort respecting which the claim is made.[2]

It necessarily follows that if the ship sink, and be
afterwards raised, the value of the owner's interest is to be
determined by ascertaining the value of the wreck when
raised, and deducting therefrom the cost of raising her.
And in like manner any enhancement of the value by
reason of repairs put upon the vessel is not to be considered in estimating the value of the owner's interest in
her.[3]

The principles bearing on this subject are discussed in Chapter
Eighth, " The Conflict of Laws."

[1] Allen v. Mackay, 1 Sprague, 219 (1854).

[2] The time at which the value is to be determined has sometimes
been stated to be " immediately after the injury." But in a case where
the vessel is liable for an injury, was subsequently wrecked on the same
voyage, and was abandoned to the underwriters, it was held that the
limit of liability was the value of the wreck. The court points out that
this necessarily follows from the language of sect. 4284, which gives the
owner a right to limit his liability by a surrender, and that all claimants
for injuries happening on the same voyage share in the fund. Cases
where the time " immediately after the injury " has been fixed, were
either cases involving only the question of subsequent additions to the
value of the vessel, as by raising the wreck or repairs put upon it; or
cases involving the contention that the value immediately before the
injury was that by which the limit of liability must be determined.
" The termination of the voyage is the point of time at which the value
of the offending vessel is to be taken." When, therefore, after the
injury has been done, the offending vessel puts back and is by the
negligence of her navigators sunk, the voyage terminates with the
sinking, and the value of the wreck is the value of the owner's interest.
The Great Western, 118 U. S. 520 (1886); The City of Norwich, 118
U. S. 468 (1886). See, also, next note.

[3] The Norwich & N. Y. Transp. Co.. after obtaining the favorable

The rules of evidence in the Federal Courts of each
District are generally the same as those in the State

---

decision of the Supreme Court in the Wright Suit (13 Wall. 104 [1871]),
filed a petition in the District Court of the United States for the Eastern
District of New York to obtain the benefit of the Act of Congress as
construed by the Supreme Court. Accordingly, the court made an
order staying all proceedings in the other suits, and referring the matter
to the clerk to report the value of the owner's interest in the vessel and
her freight. Upon exceptions to his report as to value, the court say :
" Value was properly ascertained by taking what she was proved to be
worth after she had been raised and deducting therefrom the expenses
of raising her. Equally unfounded is the proposition that the expenses
of raising the boat and the expenses of her subsequent repairs shall be
added to the aforesaid value. The exceptions which claim that such
expenses should have been added to the amount reported, are also overruled."

Re Norwich & N. Y. Transp. Co., 8 Bened. 314 (1875). This case
was affirmed in the Circuit Court, 17 Blatchf. 221 (1879), and in the
Supreme Court, *sub nom.* The City of Norwich, 118 U. S. 468, 492
(1886). The court says:

" If, however, by reason of the loss or sinking of the ship the voyage is
never completed, but is broken up and ended by causes over which the
owners have no control, the value of the ship (if it has any value) at the
time of such breaking up and ending of the voyage must be taken as
the measure of the owner's liability. In most cases of this character no
freight will be earned ; but if any shall have been earned, it will be
added to the value of the ship in estimating the amount of the owner's
liability. . . If this view is correct it follows, as a matter of course,
that any salvage operations, undertaken for the purpose of recovering
from the bottom of the sea any portion of the wreck, after the disastrous
ending of the voyage as above supposed, can have no effect on the
question of the liability of the owners. Their liability is fixed when
the voyage is ended. The subsequent history of the wreck can only
furnish evidence of its value at that point of time. . . Having fixed
the point of time at which the value is to be taken the statute does the
rest. It declares that the liability of the owner shall in no case exceed
the amount or value of the interest of such owner in such vessel and
her freight then pending. If the vessel arrives in port in a damaged
condition, and earns some freight, the value at that time is the measure
of liability; if she goes to the bottom and earns no freight, the value
at that time is the criterion. . . . It follows from this, that the proper valuation of the steamer was taken in the court below, namely, the
value which she had when she had sunk and was lying on the bottom
of the sea. That was the termination of the voyage." The Scotland,
118 U. S. 507 (1886); The Great Western, 118 U. S. 520 (1886).

In the first reported American decision upon the Statute of 1851,
Watson *v.* Marks, 2 Am. Law Reg. 165, Judge Kane said : " It is impossible to give effect to the fourth section of the Act of Congress unless we suppose that in cases of affreightment, at least, the measure of his

Courts of the State of which the Federal District forms a part.[1]

It has, however, become the practice in the Federal Courts in the Southern District of New York, and probably in other districts, to admit evidence of the value of sister ships, upon the hearing before the commissioner as to the value of the vessel whose owner is seeking to limit his liability. The rule is otherwise in the courts of the State of New York.[2]

The amount of the stipulation for the value of the owner's interest in the freight then pending is limited to the net, and not the gross, freight. That is to say, the crew's wages, port charges, and other expenses necessary to enable the owner to realize his freight monies, and which are a lien upon them, must be deducted from the

---

(ship-owner's) liability is the value of the vessel and freight at the time of suit brought." The section referred to by Judge Kane is that incorporated in sect. 4285, of the Revised Statutes, and relates to a transfer of the owner's interest to a trustee. No doubt if such a transfer should be made it would convey the vessel as she was at the time of the transfer. But as has been stated, the usual and generally preferable practice is to give a stipulation for value, and to this Judge Kane's reasoning does not apply.

[1] The rules of evidence prescribed by the laws of a State are rules of decision for the U. S. Courts, while sitting within the limits of such State, under the 34th section of the Judiciary Act. Ryan v. Bindley, 1 Wall. 66 (1863); Owings v. Hall, 9 Pet. 607, 625 (1835); Fowler v. Hecker, 4 Blatchf. 425 (1860); Vance v. Campbell, 1 Black, 427 (1861); Wright v. Bales, 2 Black, 535 (1862).

But "the laws of the State are only to be regarded as rules of decision in the Courts of the United States, where the constitution, treaties or statutes of the United States have not otherwise provided. When the latter speak, they are controlling. That is to say, on all subjects on which it is competent for them to speak. There can be no doubt that it is competent for Congress to declare the rules of evidence which shall prevail in the courts of the U. S., not affecting rights of property, and where Congress has declared the rule, the State law is silent." Conn. Mut. Life Ins. Co. v. Schaefer, 94 U.S. 457 (1876); Potter v. Nat. Bank, 102 U. S. 163 (1880); King v. Worthington, 104 U. S. 44 (1881).

[2] Blanchard v. N. J. Steamboat Co., 59 N. Y. 292 (1874). In that case the court say (p. 300): "It was not competent for the defendant to prove the value of the Telegraph by showing the value of other vessels with which she might be compared."

gross freight. This would seem to follow logically from the decision that the time at which the value of the vessel is fixed is immediately after the disaster.[1] No freight, except what is actually earned, is to be "added to the value of the ship in estimating the amount of the owner's liability."[2] Conversely whatever freight is actually earned on the voyage is to be added to the value of the ship, and will not be apportioned *pro rata itineris* up to the time of the disaster.[3]

When the commissioner has fixed the amount which the libellant must pay into court, or for which he must give a stipulation, the report must be filed and notice thereof given in the usual manner. If exceptions to it are filed, they are brought to a hearing upon notice to the exceptant's proctors when the order of the court fixing the amount of the stipulation or payment into court has been made.

A monition issues requiring all persons who have

---

[1] This was so held by Judge Choate in the matter of the Petition of Corry & Co. (owners of the Star of Scotia), not reported (1883). It is analogous to the rule as to general average. In adjusting general average in New York, the common practice is to deduct from the gross freight one-half, as an equivalent for the crew's wages, port charges, &c. Marvin on Average, 71; Dixon on Average, 149.

In The Abbie C. Stubbs, 28 Fed. Rep, 719 (1886), Judge Nelson, in his Massachusetts district, held otherwise, and refused to allow a deduction for the wages expended after the collision, or for the expense of a tug in towing the vessel into port. In The Jose E. More, 37 Fed. Rep. 132 (1888), it was held that all expenses incurred after collision were to be deducted from gross freight.

[2] The City of Norwich, 118 U. S. 468, 492 (1885).

[3] The Abbie C. Stubbs, 28 Fed. Rep. 719 (1886). In this case it was, however, held that "sums paid salvors for services rendered in getting the vessel off the beach, and also a contribution in general average for the cargo jettisoned" were extraordinary expenses. incurred for the preservation of the vessel and freight, as well as of the cargo, and for the common benefit after the libellants' lien had attached. Deductions on account of them were therefore allowed. "The salvage expenses are to be apportioned upon the vessel, freight and cargo in proportion to their respective values, and the shares belonging to the vessel and freight are to be deducted from the proceeds in the registry. The general average contribution, apportioned upon the vessel and freight for cargo jettisoned, is to be deducted in full."

5

claims against the libellant by reason of the loss, damage or injury mentioned in the libel to appear and file exceptions or answer thereto. This monition is to be served in the same way as the ordinary monition in admiralty suits *in rem*.

On its return-day, if exceptions or any answer to the libel be filed, they are brought to a hearing in due course. If none be filed, an interlocutory decree is entered referring it to a commissioner to take proof of the facts and circumstances stated in the libel and to advertise for claims against the libellant respecting the loss, damage or injury in the libel mentioned.

In the first case of limitation of liability, which was seriously contested in the Southern District of New York, the claimants filed no answer to the libel, but contested on the hearing upon the interlocutory decree the right of the libellant to sustain the cause of action alleged in the libel. They contended that the loss of the steamer Atlantic was caused by a defective equipment, viz.: Want of a supply of coal sufficient for her voyage.

It is submitted, however, as the better practice, to interpose such a defence as this by way of answer to the libel. The interlocutory decree proceeds on the ground that the libellant has, by entering the default of all persons who have not answered or filed exceptions, established his standing in court.

In like manner in the same case, the libellant contested before the commissioner its liability altogether, alleging that the loss of the Atlantic was caused by a current of unusual force, the strength and direction of which could not be discovered from the ship.

But the more regular way of raising this issue is by an answer denying the averment of the libel. The reference to the commissioner should be simply a reference to compute.

It was no doubt equitable in the case referred to, in

view of the novelty of the proceeding, that the time of all persons to contest the allegations of the libellant should thus have been extended. But it is believed that the practice suggested is more in harmony with that usually adopted by courts of admiralty.

The report of the commissioner should fix the amount of the injury sustained by each person whose claim was in evidence before him, and should apportion the fund among the claimants in proportion to the amount of each claim.

In distributing the amount for which the owners of a vessel are held to be liable in a proceeding to limit their liability, the distribution must be made solely among those who are injured by the negligence complained of. Liens for seamens' wages, money borrowed, pilotage, &c., are not entitled to payment out of this fund.[1]

In the English practice the plaintiffs in any suits brought against the libellant to recover for the loss, damage or injury in question, have the right to costs in case the question of liability is determined against the libellant. And a similar rule seems to prevail in this country. No doubt the court in which such a suit was pending would not allow it to be discontinued except on payment of costs. It may be added that costs were recovered in the actions at law, brought by all the claimants for loss sustained by the wreck of the Atlantic, who proved their claims before the commissioner.[2]

---

[1] The Marit and Elizabeth, 12 Fed. Rep. 627 (1882); The Enterprise, 1 Lowell, 455 (1870); The Linda Flor, Swabey Adm. 309 (1857).

The law was so stated by Mr. Justice Bradley, delivering the opinion of the Supreme Court, in Norwich Co. v. Wright, 13 Wall. 122 (1871): "Liens for reparation for wrong done are superior to any prior liens for money borrowed, wages, pilotage, &c. But they stand on an equality with regard to each other, if they arise from the same cause."

It must, of course, be understood that this exclusion of these liens does not affect the individual liability of the owner for the wages or other similar claim. The Linda Flor, and The Enterprise, *supra*.

[2] Similar rulings were made in The Benefactor, 103 U. S. 245 (1880), and The Garden City. 27 Fed. Rep. 234 (1886).

In Place v. The Norwich Trasportation Co., the costs taxed to the

If exceptions are filed to this report, they are brought to a hearing in the usual way. When these are finally disposed of and an order made upon the report, the money called for by the stipulation, must be paid into court, and the final decree of distribution is then entered.

The 54th admiralty rule of the Supreme Court provides for granting an injunction against "the further prosecution of all or any suit or suits against said owner or owners in respect of any such claim or claims."

In Dial v. Reynolds,[1] that court says that no court of the United States, except under the bankrupt act, can grant an injunction against proceedings in a State court. This was prohibited by the act of March 2, 1793 (1 Stat. 33), U. S. R. S., sect. 720.

But the attention of the Supreme Court was not called to the power of the District Court, sitting in admiralty, in this class of cases, nor did the facts in Dial v. Reynolds call for so general statement. And it is believed that the

---

petitioner in the District Court were $20 docket fee, and $20 fee on reference for each claim proved against the amount of the stipulation. The appellant in that case argued in the Supreme Court that this was erroneous:

1st. Because the petitioner did not succeed on the controversy as to its being liable at all, and

2d. Because in any case only one docket fee and one fee on reference should have been allowed.

The opinion of the Supreme Court takes no notice of the point, and although the decree was affirmed, yet perhaps it may be considered that the question is open.

In the Matter of the Atlantic, not reported (Southern District of New York, 1872), only one docket fee and one fee on reference was allowed. It would seem on principle that this is more correct taxation than that of the clerk in the case of The City of Norwich. The various claims presented are all in one matter. In surplus and remnant proceedings, it has been the practice, so far as the writer can learn, to tax only one fee, although numerous claims are presented. Were the rule otherwise, it might often happen, as it did in the case of The City of Norwich, that the amount allowed the petitioner for costs, and paid out of the fund in court, would be much more than that distributed to the various claimants.

[1] 96 U. S. 340 (1877).

"appropriate proceedings" mentioned in section 4284 necessarily involve the granting the injunction provided for in rule 54.[1]

This rule is itself a more specific expression of opinion on this subject, and while it is true that the Court has in one instance[2] held that a rule previously adopted by it was unconstitutional and invalid, yet this was so exceptional a case that it can hardly be expected to occur again.

It is clear that if no such injunction could be granted the provisions of the act would, in many cases, be inoperative. Judgments might be recovered at law and collected before a decree in Admiralty could be obtained, which would be pleadable in bar in the action at law. The practice in Admiralty in this class of cases has uniformly been to grant such injunctions.

If a suit against the owner for damages caused by the collision or other injury in question is pending in a State court, or at law in the Circuit Court, it would be unsafe to allow the suit to proceed to judgment before commencing proceedings in Admiralty to limit the owner's liability. This would then be *res adjudicata*, and the judgment in the State court would be entitled, under art. IV, sect. 1, of the Constitution of the United States, and sect. 905 of the U. S. Revised Statutes, passed in pursuance therewith, to "have such faith and credit given to them in every court within the United States as they have by law or usage in the courts of the State from which they are taken." It is clear that in any State of this Union the

---

[1] Sect. 720 of R. S. prohibiting injunctions against State courts, if it would apply to admiralty proceedings, is limited by sect. 4285, which provides that "all suits for such damage shall cease." The Oceanus, 6 Benedict, 258 (1872); Prov. & N. Y. S. S. Co. *v.* Hill Mfg. Co., 109 U. S. 578 (1883).

[2] *Ex parte* Garland, 4 Wallace, 333 (1867). The admiralty rules in question were held to be valid in Providence & N. Y. S. S. Co. *v.* Hill Mfg. Co., *supra*.

judgment of a Court of Record would be conclusive as to the extent of the liability of the person against whom it was rendered.[1]

It is therefore expedient in all cases where suits at law have been commenced against the owner of a vessel, and he is entitled to avail himself of the provisions of law limiting his liability, and is desirous at some time of so doing, that he should obtain an injunction from a District Court of the United States against the prosecution of such action at law.

It is in the discretion of the court in which the proceeding is pending, to charge the owner with interest, by way of damages, upon the value of his interest in the ship and freight. This is true, even in a case where the owner actually received in cash the value of this interest, long before the period when he paid it into court.[2]

It is submitted, however, that the Circuit Court in this instance did not charge the owner with interest, owing to the novelty of the questions involved, and the uncertainty which had prevailed as to the practice, and that hereafter interest would probably be charged against the owner, from the time the proceeds of his interest in the ship and freight came into his hands.

When the abandonment may be made.—The owner

---

[1] The question of negligence, if determined in the first instance, upon a libel against the offending ve·sel, becomes *res adjudicata*. and cannot be reopened upon a proceeding to limit her owner's liability. The Maria and Elizabeth, 12 Fed. Rep. 627 (1882).

[2] The Scotland, 118 U. S. 507 (1886). The usual practice in the English courts is to allow interest in such cases. African Steamship Co. *v.* Swanzy, 25 L. J. N. S. Ch. 870 (1856); General Iron Screw Collier Co. *v.* Schurmanns, 29 L. J. N. S. Ch. 877 (1860); Nixon *v.* Roberts, 30 L. J. N. S. Ch. 844 (1861); Straker *v.* Hartland, 34 L. J. N. S. Ch. 122 (1865); Smith *v.* Kirby, L. R. 1 Qu. B. Div. 131 (1875); The Sisters, 2 Aspinall's Maritime L. C. N. S. 589 (1875); The Northumbria, L. R. 3 Ad. & Ec. 6 (1869).

In The Jose E. Moore, 37 Fed. Rep. 132 (1888), interest was allowed from the date of the District Court judgments. So it was in The Manitoba, 122 U. S. 97 (1887).

may offer to surrender his interest in the vessel and her freight, or give a stipulation for their value, and thus take the benefit of the law limiting his liability to such value, at any time before the entry of the final decree against him, in any District Court of the United States.   He may also do so during the pendency of an appeal to the Circuit Court from a final decree against him in the District Court.[1]

It is not necessary that the owner should take affirmative proceedings in Admiralty to limit his liability.   The rules on this subject enable him to bring all parties having claims against him before the court in one proceeding. But "where all the parties injured are represented as libellants or intervenors in the cause, an answer setting up the defense of limited responsibility is fully adequate to give the ship-owners all the protection which they need."[2]

---

[1] The French law is the same, but the French courts hold that such an abandonment comes too late after an appeal has been taken to the Court of Cassation, which is the French tribunal corresponding most nearly to the Supreme Court of the United States.

Journal du Palais, vol. 9, tit. Navire, sects. 301-304.

Ibid. Table Complementaire, vol. 1, p. 118, sect. 32.

[2] The Scotland, 105 U. S. 24 (1882); revg. s. c. *sub nom.* Dyer *v.* National Steam Nav. Co., 14 Blatchf. 483 (1878).

In this case that portion of the answer which it was held was sufficient to set up the defense was as follows: "Respondents, further answering, say that said steamer Scotland was by said collision sunk and destroyed, and that there is no liability *in personam* against these respondents for said loss of The Kate Dyer."

This overrules The Maria and Elizabeth, 11 Fed. Rep. 520 (1882), so far as it is inconsistent.   It does not appear in that report whether the defense under the Act of Congress was set up in the answer.   And it does appear in the report of the same case on a later hearing (12 Fed. Rep. 627 [1882]), that the libellant contended that the loss was incurred with the privity or knowledge of one of the owners.   It has been held that the answer in a suit at law setting up limited liability proceedings must allege the surrender of the ship or a stipulation for its value, or else its total loss.   Feldman *v.* De Nederlandsche, &c. Co., City Court of N. Y., Daily Register, Sept. 20, 1884.

Such a surrender or its equivalent is necessary where there are many claimants, and it is desired to restrain them from proceeding with their several suits.   But in The Great Western, 118 U. S. 520

In such case "it will be sufficient if the amount is paid after the trial of the cause and the ascertainment of the amount of liability in the decree. Payment and satisfaction of the decree will be a discharge of the owner as against all creditors represented in the decree.[1]

The surrender of the owner's interest may be made, and he may take the benefit of the limitation of liability provided by law, although he has previously abandoned the vessel and freight to the underwriters.[2]

This seems, at first, anomalous, but is justified by the French authorities for the reason that the lien in Admiralty of all persons having claims against the ship and freight continues to bind both, even after they are transferred to a *bona fide* vendee,[3] and the insurer, therefore, receives the transfer of the owner's interest, subject to the right of the owner to surrender them in discharge of his liability for any loss, damage or injury caused by the ship or her navigators without his privity.

In The Great Western[4] the Supreme Court arrived at

(1886); affg. s. c. *sub nom.* Thommessen *v.* Whitwill, 21 Blatchf. 45; 12 Fed. Rep. 891 (1882), the court say (p. 525):

"The answer, as originally framed, set up the defense that the liability of the respondent was limited to the amount or value of his interest in The Great Western and her freight upon the voyage, and averred that that interest was of no value. The issue being thus raised, the respondent was entitled to have the decree against him in that cause limited to the amount which should be shown, by the proofs on the trial, to be the value of said steamer and freight at the termination of the voyage. He did not need to make any surrender or attempt at a surrender. A surrender of the vessel, or payment of her proceeds, or value, into court would have been necessary in order to bring other creditors into concourse with the libellants; but for the mere defense of that cause it was not necessary."

[1] The City of Norwich, 118 U. S. 468, 503 (1886); The Great Western, 118 U. S. 520 (1886); affg. s. c. *sub nom.* Thommessen *v.* Whitwill, 21 Blatchf. 45 (1882).

[2] This is the French law. Journal du Palais, vol. 9, title Navire, sect. 210; Thommessen *v.* Whitwill, 12 Fed. Rep. 891 (1882).

[3] Sheppard *v.* Taylor, 5 Pet. 675, 712 (1831); The Rebecca, Ware 187, 212 (1831).

[4] 118 U. S. 520 (1886).

the same conclusion, but by a different process of reasoning. The limitation of liability under the United States Statute does not depend upon the surrender by the owner of his interest. He may, instead, pay its value into court, and in that case what he does or has done with his interest, itself, in the ship and freight, is immaterial.

If, at the conclusion of the proceedings, it should appear that the total amount of the claims proved and allowed is less than the value of the vessel, the jurisdiction of the court will not thereby be ousted, provided the amount of the claims was for more than her value.[1]

It has been more common, in proceedings to limit the liability of owners, to give a stipulation for the value of the interest of the owner in the abandoned vessel. But in some cases the alternative of the statute has been followed, and a conveyance has been made to a trustee appointed by the court. This, as has been shown, is strictly analogous to the practice in the Continental courts. The first point to be considered is the citizenship of the trustee. Most nations require that the title to their own ships should be held by citizens of the country to which the ship belongs. If the wreck abandoned is a British ship, the trustee must be a British subject; if it be an American ship, the trustee must be an American citizen. It is usual to require the trustee to give a bond for the faithful discharge of his duty, in a sum to be fixed by the court. He should, after his appointment and qualification, proceed, with reasonable diligence, to sell the vessel. The same may be at auction or at private sale, as the court may direct. The marshal is not entitled to a commission

---

[1] Briggs v. Day, The H. W. Hills, 21 Fed. Rep. 727 (1884). In this case Judge Brown says: "There may also be other claims hereafter presented." This could only happen if the court should reopen the case to allow additional claims to be proved. Ordinarily the claims not presented within the time fixed by the court are barred. See The Garden City, 26 Fed. Rep. 766 (1886).

on the proceeds of such sale, but if the proceeds are paid into court, the clerk is entitled to a commission on the proceeds, even though the liability of the owner be contested.[1]

---

[1] The Vernon, 36 Fed. Rep. 113 (1888).

PART II.

CHAPTER IV.

THE RIGHT OF THE CARRIER TO LIMIT HIS LIABILITY BY CONTRACT, AND BY RULES AND REGULATIONS OF HIS OWN, AS AFFECTED BY PUBLIC POLICY.

INTRODUCTION.

The same experience of the injustice, in many cases caused by the extreme liability imposed upon common carriers both by the common and the civil law, which gave rise to the limitations of the law merchant, so far as carriers by sea were concerned, was the origin of numerous attempts by carriers on land to limit their liability through the medium of notices and contracts. Lines of transportation for freight and passengers became more numerous, and it was claimed that the business could not be conducted at reasonable rates, unless some limitation could be placed upon this liability, which was, to almost all intents and purposes, that of an insurer. At first the courts were inclined to admit the right of the carrier to limit his liability by a mere notice.[1] But carriers speedily made an unreasonable use of the latitude thus afforded, and the language of their notices became so broad as practically to leave little responsibility of any sort. The natural result of this was,

---

[1] Covington v. Willan, Gow, 115 (1819); Peek v. North Staffordshire R. Co., 10 House of Lords Ca. 473 (1863).

that the right to restrict their liability at all came to be
disputed, and in several reported decisions it was held that
the liability of the carrier was created by law and could
not be modified or diminished by either notice or contract.
But these cases were finally upon more mature consideration modified, and the courts both in England and America,
both State and Federal, determined that the liability of the
carrier could be to a certain extent limited by contract between himself and the shipper or the passenger, but that
a mere notice from the carrier would not have this effect.[1]

In some cases it has been held that a notice assented to
by the shipper would constitute a contract.   These will be
considered in the tenth chapter.

A certain limited scope has also been allowed by the

---

[1] N. J. Steam Nav. Co. *v.* Merchants' Bank, 6 How. U. S. 344 (1848);
Dorr *v.* N. J. Steam Nav. Co., 11 N. Y. 485 (1854).   These two
cases were suits for goods destroyed by fire on the Steamer Lexington.
The latter case reversed s. c. 4 Sandf. S. C. R. 136 (1850), and over-
ruled Gould *v.* Hill, 2 Hill, 623 (1842); Hollister *v.* Nowlen, 19 Wend.
234; Cole *v.* Goodwin, *Ibid,* 251 (1838) ; Reno *v.* Hogan, 12 B. Monr.
(Ky.) 63 (1851); s. c. 54 Am. Dec. 513; Farmers & Mechanics' Bank *v.*
Champlain Transportation Co., 23 Vermont, 186 (1851); Farnham *v.*
Camden & Amboy R. R., 55 Penn. 53 (1867).
The following extract from the opinion in Derwort *v.* Loomer, 21
Conn. 244 (1851), will illustrate some of the causes that led to the decisions stated in the text.   " It is no apology that freight is put upon these
stages, as in this case, under public or any other notices.   The liability
continues the same.   Nor is it any apology that stage proprietors and
their drivers are accustomed to load stages with passengers and freight,
notwithstanding the state of the roads, until nothing more can be crowded
within or accumulated on the top.   It is high time that the law on
this subject should be better understood and regarded, and that such
unpardonable liberties should cease to be taken, by persons who stipulate to carry passengers safely, and without exposure.   Converting
coaches into freight wagons to transport iron and well nigh everything
else, is the last innovation upon the rights of the traveling community,
and it is one which we do not intend to sanction or countenance."
Transportation Co. *v.* Newhall, 24 Ill. 466 (1860); Lewis *v.* N. Y. Sleeping Car Co. & Wing *v.* Same, 143 Mass. 267 (1886).   In this case it was
held that a notice posted in a sleeping car that the company would not
be responsible to passengers for valuables, was of no avail as a defense,
and the company was held liable for a "reasonable amount of money
for traveling purposes stolen from the travelers' clothing while asleep."
The notice was not seen by the plaintiffs.

courts to rules and regulations made by the carrier respecting the conduct of his business.   The cases on this
subject will be considered in the seventh chapter.   With
these limitations, the rule that a carrier can limit his
liability by contract only is well established.

The next question of importance that arose for determination was, whether it was lawful to make a contract
exempting the carrier from liability for negligence, either
his own or that of his servants.   To an examination of
this question the remainder of this chapter will be devoted.

SECTION I.

PERSONAL NEGLIGENCE. DEFECTIVE EQUIPMENT.

A contract by which it is agreed that the carrier shall
not be liable for his personal negligence, is unreasonable
and invalid.[1]   The carrier may and generally does act by

---

[1] Keefe *v.* Boston & Albany R. R. Co., 142 Mass. 251 (1887);
Welsh *v.* Pittsburgh, Fort Wayne & Chicago R. R., 10 Ohio St. Rep. 65
(1859).   In this case the special contract which was for the transportation of live stock, expressly provided that the carrier should not be
liable for the unsafe condition of the doors of its cattle cars.   This
agreement was signed by the owner.   The doors of the cattle cars were
defective, they gave way while the train was in motion, the cattle fell
out and were injured.   It was held that the carrier was liable, and that
the clause to the contrary was void.   It is true that in this case the
owner observed the dangerous condition of the doors, and called the
attention of the carrier's agent to it.   The latter promised to have them
repaired.   This oral agreement, however, was before the written contract
was signed, and clearly was merged in the latter.   The evidence on this
subject was only admissible to rebut the presumption of concurrent
negligence, that might have arisen from the proof as to the shipper's
knowledge of the dangerous condition of the doors.

Hawkins *v.* Great Western R. R., 17 Mich. 57 (1868).   In this case
the contract provided for exemption from liability for the negligence,
"gross, or culpable or otherwise, on the part of the railway company's
agents or officers."   The court held that this did not exempt from
liability for damages caused by a defective car.   In Smith *v.* N. Y. Central R. R., 24 N. Y. 222 (1862), it was held that a contract exempting
the carrier from liability for personal injury, "from whatever cause,"
sustained by a drover accompanying cattle, did not relieve the carrier
from liability for the drover's death, which was caused by the use of an
unsafe and unsuitable car.   It is true that in this case, under the rule
laid down by later decisions, the language of the agreement was not

agents, and in the case of a corporation always must do so.
But nevertheless there is such a thing as negligence imputable to the carrier, whether a corporation or not, as
distinguished from the negligence of its agents. For
example, a railroad company is bound to provide a road-bed,
rails, ties, engines, cars, and appliances of all kinds, of the
best character and description that can reasonably be procured, and that are by other railroad companies recognized as desirable and proper to be used. It is not
bound to try experiments, but it is bound to keep up with
the process of invention, as tested by experience, and if
its agents fail to fulfill the duty thus devolved upon the
carrier, the breach of this duty is treated as the carrier's
personal negligence.[1]

---

broad enough to cover the negligence, even of an agent. Mynard *v.*
Syracuse, &c., R. R. Co., 71 N. Y. 180 (1877). But the court do not
put the decision in the Smith case upon this ground but on that already
stated.

In Indianoplis, Bloomington & Western R. R. *v.* Strain, 81 Ill. 504
(1876), it was held that the carrier was liable for injuries to live stock
caused by their escaping from a defective car, beyond the terminus of
the carrier's road. The special contract provided that the carrier
should not be liable for injuries beyond such a terminus, but the court
refused to construe this so as to exempt from liability for injuries caused
by its own defective car.

In England a stipulation exempting a carrier from injuries caused by
a defective car was held to be unreasonable and invalid. McManus *v.*
Lancashire & Y. R. Co., 4 H. & N. 327 (1854); Gregory *v.* West Midland Co., 2 H. & C. 944 (1864); *Contra,* Chippendale *v.* Lancashire and
Yorkshire R. Co., 15 Jur. 1106; s. c. 12 L. J. Q. B. 22 (1851).

In Ill. Cent. R. R. Co. *v.* Haynes, 63 Miss. 485 (1886), it was said
a shipper could only demand suitable, safe, and sufficient shipping, not
the best in use.

[1] Hall *v.* Conn. River Steamboat Co, 13 Conn. 326 (1839); Tuller
v. Talbot, 23 Ill. 357 (1860); Pittsburgh C. & St. L. R. R. *v.* Thompson,
56 Ill. 138 (1870); St. Louis & S. E. R'y Co. *v.* Dorman 72 Ill. 504
(1874); R'y Co. *v.* Hamilton, 76 Ill. 393 (1875); Same *v.* Durkin, 76 Ill.
395; Indianapolis, B. & W. R'y Co. *v.* Strain, 81 Ill. 504 (1876); Mc-
Donald & Wife *v.* Chicago & N. W. R'y Co., 26 Iowa, 124 (1868); Ingalls *v.* Bills, 9 Met. (Mass.) 1 (1845); McElroy *v.* Nashua & Lowell R.
R., 4 Cush. (Mass.) 400 (1849); Warren *v.* Fitchburg R. R., 8 Allen
(Mass.). 227 (1864); Smith *v.* New Haven & Northampton R. R., 12 *Ibid,*
531 (1866); Simmons *v.* New Bedford, etc., Steamboat Co., 97 Mass. 361
(1867); Dunn *v.* Grand Trunk R. R. Co., 58 Me. 187 (1875); Beard *v.*

The litigation on this topic has often arisen in that numerous class of cases in which employers, whether car-

---

Conn. & Pass. R. R. Co., 48 Vt. 101 (1875); Smith v. N. Y. Central R. R. Co., 24 N. Y. 222 (1862); Steinweg v. Erie R'y, 43 N. Y 123 (1870); Benzing v. Steinway, 101 N, Y. 547 (1886); Bevier v. Delaware & Hudson Canal Co., 13 Hun (N. Y.). 254 (1878); Potter v Sharp, 24 Hun (N. Y.), 179 (1881); Indianapolis, &c. R. R. v. Horst, 93 U. S. (3 Otto) 291 (1876); Steamboat " New World " v King, 16 How. (U. S.) 469 (1853); The Rover. 33 Fed. Rep. 515 (1887), S. D. of N. Y. In Smith v. British & N. A. R. M. S. P. Co., 86 N. Y. 408 (1881) ; affg. s. c. 46 N. Y. Superior Ct. 86 (1880), the plaintiff was a steerage passenger in one of defendant's steamships. She had a berth in a section built in two tiers. The tiers were defectively constructed and the upper tier fell in the night. The fall and screams of those occupying the berths so alarmed plaintiff that she became helpless. In this condi ion she was removed from her berth and placed upon her feet. Being unable to help herself she was thrown by the rolling of the ship against an open door and injured. It was held by a divided court that the defective construction of the berths was the real cause of the injury, and that the defendant was therefore liable.

In Indianapolis, &c., R. R. v. Horst, 93 U. S (3 Otto) 291 (1876), the plaintiff was injured while traveling on a freight train in charge of cattle. The court say: "Life and limb are as valuable. and there is the the same right to safety in the caboose as in the palace car. The rule is uniformly applied to passenger trains. The same considerations apply to freight trains; the same dangers are common to both. There is no reason in the nature of things why the passenger should not be as safe upon one as the other, with proper vig'lance on the part of the carrier. We do not mean all the care and diligence the human mind can conceive of, nor such as will render the transportation free from any possible peril, nor such as would drive the carrier from his business.

" It does not, for instance, require steel rails and iron or granite cross-ties, because such ties are less liable to decay, and hence safer than those of wood; nor, upon freight trains, air brakes, bell pulls, and a brakeman upon every car; but it does emphatically require everything necessary to the security of the passenger upon either. and reasonably consistent with the business of the carrier, and the means of convey nce employed."

s. p., Louisville & Nashville R. R. Co. v Oden, 80 Ala. 38 (1885). A shipper can only demand " suitable, safe, and sufficient " cars and equipment, not the "best and most improved in use." Illinois Cen. R. R. Co. v. Haynes, 63 Miss 485 (1886).

So where canvass and matting were ordinarily used indifferently as a packing, the canvass being the best, if the carrier use matting he does so at his peril, and is liable if injury is caused by its insufficiency. He is bound to use the best ordinary means. Hill v. Mackill, 36 Fed. Rep, 702 (1888).

The rule stated in Weston v. N. Y. Elevated R R. Co., 73 N. Y. 595 (1878), that " the defendant is not bound to keep its platform in such con di ion that it is impossible for passenger to slip, but in such a condi ion that person using ordinary care which people use when not apprised of

riers or not, have claimed a defense under the rule that an employer is not liable to one workman for injuries sustained by the negligence of a fellow workman.

It does not fall within the scope of this work to give a detailed analysis of these cases. But the principle which underlines them all is this—An employer owes a duty to his employé to furnish safe appliances for the work he is engaged to do. The omission of this duty is negligence. Whether the employer undertakes to discharge it in person or deputes it to some one else, is immaterial so far as his common law liability is concerned. In either case, the omission is the employer's personal negligence, and he is liable for all damages resulting from it.[1]

---

danger," was approved, but said to be too stringent for the case before the court where the carrier had not had reasonable opportunity to remove sleet which had formed on the steps of the car. Palmer v. Penn. R. R. Co., 111 N. Y. 488 (1888); reversing s. c. 4 N. Y. State Rep. 888 (1886).

So, it being conceded that there is an implied warranty of the carrier by water that his vessel is seaworthy, it was said in Bell v. Read, 4 Binn. (Penn.) 127 (1810), that a vessel need only be fit for the service she undertakes.

The rule stated in the text was extended to cars on a train provided by an independent car company, and for using which an extra fare was charged, and it was held that for a defect in such a car the carrier was liable. Penn. Co. v. Roy, 102 U. S. 451 (1880).

[1] Laning v. N. Y. C. R. R. Co., 49 N. Y. 521 (1872); Chapman v. Erie R. R., 1st Thomps. & Cook (N. Y.), 529 (1873); DeGraff v. N. Y. C. & H. R. R. R., 3 Thomps. & Cook (N.Y.), 255 (1874); Siger v. Syracuse, B. & N. Y. R. R. Co., 7 Lans. (N. Y.) 67 (1872); Baulec v. N. Y. & Harlem R. R., 59 N. Y. 356 (1874); Randolph v. Bost. & Albany R. R., 5 Weekly Digest, 150 (1877); Booth v. The Same, 73 N. Y. 38 (1878); Stevenson v. Jewett, 16 Hun (N. Y.), 210 (1878); Eagen v. Tucker, 18 Ibid, 347 (1879); Harvey v. N. Y. C. & H. R. R. R., 19 Ibid, 556 (1880); Jones v. The Same, 22 Ibid, 284 (1880); Painton v. Northern Central R. R. Co., 83 N. Y. 7 (1880); Fuller v. Jewett, 80 N. Y. 46 (1880); Kain v. Smith, 80 N. Y. 458 (1880); same case, 89 N. Y. 375 (1882). In Ellis v. N. Y., Lake Erie & W. R. R., 95 N. Y. 546 (1884), it was held that if the cause of the accident was partly the omission of the carrier to provide suitable appliances (in this case a buffer) and partly the negligence of the co-servant, the company is still liable. Huntingdon & Broad Top R. R. Co. v. Decker, 84 Penn. St. 419 (1877); Baker v. Alleghany Valley R. R. Co., 95 Ibid, 211 (1880); Cayzer v. Taylor, 10 Gray (Mass.), 274 (1857); Paulmier, Adm'r v. Erie R. R., 5 Vroom (N. J.), 151 (1870); Coombs v.

For this reason the rule stated in the beginning of this chapter must be considered as resting on a solid foundation of principle. And it is analogous to that of the law merchant, adopted by the United States, that the carrier's right to discharge himself from liability by abandoning his interest in ship and freight does not extend to cases where the loss is caused by his privity or personal negligence.

Cases have occurred in which the carrier provided suitable means of transportation, but his servants negligently omitted to use these and employed others which were unsuitable for the use of the particular kind of freight to be transported ; as, for example, using a grain and lumber car, the door of which was insecure, for the transportation of live stock. The contract provided that the carrier should not be liable for the negligence of his servants, and the validity of the exemption was sustained.[1]

Whether the distinction taken in this case will be approved in other States, does not yet appear. But the general rule stated at the beginning of this section is established not only in those States in which no contracts of exemption from negligence are held to be valid, but in other States, and it is sustained by the weight of authority

---

New Bedford Cordage Co., 102 Mass 572 (1869); Ford *v.* Fitchburg R. R. 110 *Ibid*, 240 (1872); Holden *v.* The Same, 129 *Ibid*, 268 (1880); O'Connor *v.* Adams, 120 *Ibid*, 427 (1876); Chicago & N. W. R. R. Co. *v.* Swett, 45 Ill. 197 (1867); Camp Point Mfg. Co. *v.* Ballou, 71 *Ibid*, 417 (1874); T. W. & W. R'y Co. *v.* Fredericks, *Ibid*, 294 (1874); Fairbank *v.* Haentzche, 73 *Ibid*, 236 (1874); Chicago & Great Eastern R. Co. *v.* Harney, 28 Ind. 28 (1867). The soundness of the distinction stated in text is denied in Illinois Central R. R. Co. *v.* Read, 37 Ill. 484 (1865), and Gulf, C. & S. F. R. Co. *v.* McGown, 65 Texas, 640 (1886), in both of which cases it was held that there was no distinction in the grade of corporate agents so far as the liability of the corporation was concerned, and that however subordinate the agent, his negligence was that of the corporation itself. Stipulations for exemption from liability therefore were held invalid.

[1] Wilson *v.* N. Y. C. & H. R. R. R., 97 N. Y. 87 (1884).

6

in England, where the validity of such contracts generally is upheld.[1]

SECTION II.

LAWFULNESS OF CONTRACT FOR EXEMPTION FROM LIABILITY FOR NEGLIGENCE OF THE CARRIER'S SERVANTS.

Let us now assume that the carrier has in all respects fulfilled the obligation thus devolved upon him. His ship, we will say, is constructed by skillful builders. She has every security against danger that experience has approved. Her officers and crew are men of skill, trusty and experienced. This certainly is all the carrier can do. Why, then, may he not lawfully stipulate by express contract that if these agents, in whose selection he has used diligence and prudence, betray their trust, and are careless or wicked, the carrier should not be liable?

Yet in a majority of the States of this Union such a contract of exemption is held to be against public policy, and therefore void. This is the rule in all the Federal Courts.[2]

---

[1] Tattersall v. The National S. S. Co., Limited, L. R. 12 Q. B. D. 297 (1884). This was a shipment of cattle under a bill of lading containing the following clause: "These animals being in sole charge of shippers' servants, it is hereby expressly agreed that the ship owners, or their agents or servants, are, as respects these animals, in no way responsible, either for their escape from the steamer or for accident, disease or mortality, and that under no circumstances shall they be held liable for more than £5 for each of the animals." The ship had previously carried diseased cattle and the loss arose from contagion communicated in consequence of her having been insufficiently cleaned. *Held* that the defendant was liable notwithstanding the exception in the bill of lading because the ship was not reasonably fit for the carriage of the cattle.

The question as the evidence from which a jury may properly infer defective construction of an engine is considered in Tanner v. N. Y. Cent. & H. R. R. R. Co., 108 N. Y. 623; s. c. 15 North East. Rep. 379 (1888).

[2] New Jersey Steam Navigation Co. v. Merchants' Bank, 6 How. (U. S.) 344 (1848); Phila. & Reading R. R. Co. v. Derby, 14 *Ibid*, 468 (1852); Steamboat "New World" *et al.* v. King, 16 *Ibid*, 469 (1853); York Company v. Central Railroad, 3 Wall. 107 (1865); Walker v. The

The rule is the same in many of the State Courts.[1]

Transportation Company, *Ibid*, 150 (1865); Express Co. *v.* Kountze Bros., 8 *Ibid*, 342 (1869); Railroad Company *v.* Lockwood, 17 *Ibid*, 357 (1873); Bank of Kentucky *v.* Adams Ex. Co., 93 U. S. 174 (1876). In the last case a stipulation that the express company was not to be liable for loss by fire, did not exempt the company from liability for damage by fire caused by the negligence of the servants of the railroad which had contracted with the express company to transport the goods. The court held the stipulation to be invalid on the ground that it was against public policy to sustain any exemptions from liability for negligence, under any circumstances. The Montana, 129 U. S. 397 (1889); affg. s. c. 22 Blatchf. 372 (1884); 17 Fed. Rep. 377 (1883); reported in Supreme Court, *sub nom.* Liverpool & G. W. Steam Co. *v.* Phenix Ins. Co.; Inman *v.* South Carolina R. Co., 129 U. S. 128 (1889); The City of Norwich, 4 Bened. 271 (1870); Rintoul *v.* N. Y. Central & H. R. R. R., 17 Fed. Rep. 905 (1883); Earnest *v.* Express Co., 1 Woods, 573 (1873).

But these courts permit a carrier to insure against the negligence of his servants, and also hold valid a contract with the shipper that the carrier shall have the benefit of the insurance. Phœnix Ins. Co. *v.* Erie Trans. Co., 117 U. S. 312, 324 (1885).

[1] Alabama.—Cent. R. R. & Banking Co. *v.* Smitha, 85 Ala. 47; s. c. 4 So. Rep. 708 (1888); Steele *v.* Townsend, 37 Ala. 247; s. c. 1 Ala. Sel. Ca. 201 (1861); Louisville & Nashville R. R. Co. *v.* Oden, 80 Ala. 38 (1885); Southern Express Co. *v.* Crook, 44 Ala. 468 (1870); South & N. Ala. R. R. Co. *v.* Henlein, 52 Ala. 606 (1875); Ala. G. S. R. R. Co. *v.* Little, 71 Ala. 611; s. c. 2 Ala. Law Journal, 141 (1882); Alabama G. S. R. R. Co. *v.* Thomas, 83 Ala. 343; s. c. 3 So. Rep. 802 (1888).

Arkansas.—Little Rock, M. R. & T. R. Co. *v.* Talbot, 39 Ark. 523 (1882).

California.—In this State it was held that an express company was liable for the negligence of the employes on a steamboat not belonging to nor managed by the express company, but which transported goods for it, although the contract with the shipper stipulated that the express company should not be liable " except as forwarder." Hooper *v.* Wells, 27 Cal. 11 (1864).

Delaware.—Flinn *v.* Phila., Wil. & Balt. R. R. Co., 1 Houst. 469 (1857).

Georgia.—Berry, *et al. v.* Cooper & Boykin Exrs., 28 Ga. 543 (1859); Georgia R. R. *v.* Gann, 68 Geo. 350 (1882).

Illinois.—Boscowitz *v.* Adams Ex. Co., 93 Ill. 523 (1879). But see Ill. Cent. R. R. Co. *v.* Jonte, 13 Bradwell, 424 (Ill. App. 1883), and cases cited; and see note 1, p. 86, *post.*

Indiana.—Evansville & C. R. R. Co. *v.* Young, 28 Ind. 516 (1867); Michigan S. & Northern Indiana R. R. Co. *v.* Heaton, 37 *Ibid*, 448 (1871); Adams Express Co. *v.* Fendrick, 38 *Ibid*, 150 (1871); Indianapolis, P. & C. R. R. *v.* Allen, 31 *Ibid*, 394 (1869); Mich. S. & N. I. R. R. *v.* Heaton, *Ibid*, 397, note (1869); Ohio & Miss. R. R. *v.* Selby, 47 *Ibid*, 471 (1874). These cases overrule the earlier decisions in that State. Wright *v.* Gaff, *et al.,* 6 Ind. 416 (1855); Indiana Central R. R. *v.* Mundy, 21 *Ibid*, 48 (1863). The last was a case of a passenger traveling on a free pass,

In analogy to the rule thus stated, it is held in some
States that a carrier cannot lawfully stipulate with its

who had contracted that the carrier should not be liable for injuries
caused by the negligence of its servants.   Held, that such agreement
did not cast upon such passenger any risks arising from the gross, or
from any, negligence of the servants of the company.   Thayer v. St.
Louis, Alton & Terre Haute R. R., 22 *Ibid*, 26 (1864).

Kansas.—St. Louis, K. C. & N. R. Co. v. Piper, 13 Kans. 505 (1874);
Kallman v. U. S. Ex. Co., 3 *Ibid*, 205 (1865).

Kentucky.—Louisville & Nashville R. R. Co. v. Brownlee, 14 Bush,
590 (1879); Orndorff v. Adams Express Co., 3 Bush, 194 (1867); Reno
v. Hogan, 12 B. Monr. 63 (1851).

Louisiana.—N. O. Mut. Ins. Co. v. N. O., Jackson & G. N. R. R.
Co., 20 La. Ann. 304 (1868).   But see note 1, *post*, p. 86.

Maine.—Sager v. Portsmouth, S. & P. & E. R. R. Co., 31 Me. 228
(1850).

Massachusetts.—School Dist. v. Boston, Hartford & Erie R. R. Co.,
102 Mass. 552 (1869); Lewis v. N. Y. S. C. Co., 143 Mass. 267 (1887).
In this case there was a sign that sleeping-car company would not be
liable, but the court said, as plaintiff did not see it, defendant could not
take advantage of it.   But see Hill v. Boston, Hoosac Tunnel & W. R.
R. Co., 144 Mass. 284 (1887), where a stipulation as to value was held
good in spite of negligence of the carrier.

Minnesota.—Shriver v. Sioux City & S. P. R. R. Co., 24 Minn. 506
(1878); Christenson v. Am. Ex. Co., 15 Minn. 270 (1870).

Mississippi.—Whitesides v. Thurlkill, 20 Miss. 599 (1849); Southern
Express Co. v. Moon, 39 Miss. 822 (1863).

Missouri.—Levering *et al.* v. Union Transp. & Ins. Co., 42 Mo. 88
(1867); Snider v. Adams Ex. Co., 63 Mo. 376 (1876); Lupe v. Atlantic
& P. R. R., 3 Mo. App. 77 (1876); Kirby v. Adams Ex. Co., 2 Mo. App.
369 (1876); Dawson v. Chicago & A. R. R., 79 Mo. 296 (1883); Carroll
v. Mo. Pacific Ry. Co., 88 Mo. 239 (1885).

Nebraska.—The Constitution of Nebraska (1875) provides that
"The liability of railroad corporations as common carriers shall never
be limited."   A railroad company which operates a line of railroad in
that State, although not incorporated under its laws, is subject to this
restriction, and cannot make a valid agreement to limit its liability.
Missouri Pac. R. R. v. Vandeventer, 3 Law. Rep. Ann. 129; s. c. 41
N. W. Rep. 998 (1889).

North Carolina.—A clause in a receipt permitting carrier to transport at his own convenience does not exempt him from liability for unreasonable detention of the goods; it is against public policy and the
statute.   Branch v. Wilmington & W. R. R. Co., 88 N. C. 573 (1883).

Ohio.—Jones v. Voorhees, 10 Ohio, 145 (1840); Davidson v. Gra-
ham, 2 Ohio St. 131 (1853); Graham & Co. v. Davis & Co., 4 *Ibid*,
362 (1854); Wilson v. Hamilton, *Ibid*, 722 (1855); Welsh v. P., Ft. W.
& C. R. R. Co., 10 *Ibid*, 65 (1859); Cleveland, P. & A. R. R. Co. v.
Curran, 19 *Ibid*, 1 (1869); C., H. & D. & D. & M. R. R. Co. v. Pontius,
Ibid, 221 (1869); Knowlton v. Erie R. Co., *Ibid*, 260 (1869).

employees, at the time and as part of their contract of
employment, that the carrier shall not be liable for injuries caused to them by the carelessness of other employees.[1]

Oregon.—Seller *v*. The Pacific, 1 Oreg. 409 (1861).

Pennsylvania.—Laing *v*. Colder, 8 Penn. 479 (1848); Camden *v*.
Amboy R. R. Co. *v*. Baldauf, 16 *Ibid*, 67 (1851); Penn. R. Co. *v*. Mc-
Closkey, 23 *Ibid*, 526 (1854); Goldey *v*. Penn. R. R. Co., 30 *Ibid*, 242
(1858); Powell *v*. Penn. R. R. Co., 32 *Ibid*, 414 (1859); Penn. R. R. Co.
v. Henderson. 51 *Ibid*, 315 (1865); Farnham *v*. Camden & Amboy R.
R. Co., 55 *Ibid*, 53 (1867); American Express Co. *v*. Sands, *Ibid*, 140
(1867); Penn. R. R. Co. *v*. Butler, 57 *Ib*. 335 (1868); Empire Transp.
Co. *v*. Wamsutta Oil Refining and Mining Co., 63 *Ibid*, 14 (1869); Grogan *v*. Adams Ex. Co., 114 *Ibid*, 523 (1886).

Texas.—Mo. P. Ry. Co. *v*. Cornwall, 8 S. W. Rep. 312 (1888); Missouri Pac. R. Co. *v*. Harris, 67 Texas, 166 (1886). In this case the tort
was not willful. Houston & T. C. R. R. *v*. Burke, 55 Texas, 323
(1881); Gulf, C. & S. F. R. R. Co. *v*. McGown, 65 Texas, 640 (1886);
Missouri Pac. Ry. *v*. Ivey, 71 Texas, 409; s. c. 9 S. W. Rep. 346 (1888).
In this case it was held that the carrier could not lawfully demand a
waiver of any of the common-law rights of the shipper, as a condition
precedent to receiving goods for transportation. Missouri Pac. R. Co.
v. Fagan, 9 S. W.Rep. 749 (1888).

Tennessee.—Merchants' Dispatch T. Co. *v*. Bloch, 86 Tenn. 392
(1888).

Virginia.—Va. & Tenn. R. R. *v*. Sayers, 26 Gratt. 328 (1875).

Wisconsin.—Carrier may exempt himself for liability where the carriage is absolutely gratuitous, but not if there is a partial consideration,
or gross negligence. Annas *v*. Milwaukee & Northern R. Co., 67 Wisconsin, 46 (1886).

[1] Lake Shore & M. S. Ry. Co. *v*. Spangler, 44 Ohio St. 471; s. c.
34 Alb. L. J. 423 (1886); Roesner *v*. Hermann, 8 Fed. Rep. 782 (1881).
The ground of the Ohio decision was that public policy demanded
that a common carrier should not exempt itself from liability for injuries to its servants caused by carelessness of those who are superior
in authority over them.

Western & A. R. R. Co. *v*. Bishop, 50 Ga. 465 (1873), was cited in
the Ohio case in support of the validity of the contract. It was there
held that such a contract, so far as it does not waive any neglect of the
company or its principal officers, is a legal contract, and binding upon
the employee. But the court add: "We do not say that the employer
and employee may make any contract—we simply insist that they stand
on the same footing as other people. No man may contract contrary to
law, or contrary to public policy or good morals, and that is just as true
of merchants, lawyers and doctors, of buyers and sellers, and bailors and
bailees, as of employers and employees."

In State *v*. Baltimore & O. R. Co., 36 Fed. Rep. 655 (1888), a clause
in the constitution of a relief association, which required a person ac-

On the other hand the English courts, and those of many States in the Union, recognize the validity of stipulations limiting the liability of carriers for the negligence of their servants, and enforce the contracts containing them.[1]

---

cepting the benefit of its funds to release a railroad company from any claim for damages caused by its negligence, was valid. To the same effect are Fuller *v.* Balt. & Ohio Employes' Relief Association, 67 Md. 433 (1887); Owens *v.* Balt. & O. R. R. Co., 35 Fed. Rep. 715 (1888).

In Mo. P. Ry. Co. *v.* Mackey, 127 U. S. 205 (1888), it was held that a statute rendering a railroad company liable to its employees, for the negligence of any of its agents, engineers, etc., was constitutional. s. p., Minneapolis & St. L. Ry. Co. *v.* Herrick, 127 U. S. 210 (1888).

An attempt, by contract, to make a cattle-guard employed by owner an employee of the carrier, so as to exempt the latter from liability to him, was held invalid in Missouri P. Ry. Co. *v.* Ivey, 71 Texas, 409; s. c. 9 S. W. Rep. 346 (1888).

[1] The Duero, L. R. 2 Adm. & Ec. 393 (1869); Taubman *v.* Pacific S. N. Co., 26 Law Times (N. S.), 704 (1872); Steele *v.* State Line S. S. Co., 3 App. Ca. 72 (1877); Manchester, S. & L. Railway *v.* Brown, 8 App. Ca. 703 (1883); *In re* Missouri S. S. Co, 58 Law Times (N. S.), 377 (1888); affd. Ct. Appeals, Weekly Notes, Notes of Cases, May 11, 1889, p. 90; Peek *v.* North Staffordshire Railway Co., 10 House of Lords Cases, 473 (1863). The English cases are fully stated in the opinion of Blackburn, p. 491, *et seq.* Carr *v.* Lancashire & York. R. Co., 7 Excheq. 707 (1852); Dodson *v.* Grand Trunk R. Co., 2 Nova Scotia Dec. 405 (1871).

Among the earlier English cases, see especially Hinton *v.* Dibbin, 2 Q. B. 646 (1842), and Wyld *v.* Pickford, 8 Mees. & Welsb. 443 (1841).

Connecticut.—Hale *v.* N. J. Steam Navig. Co., 15 Conn. 539 (1843); Lawrence *v.* N. Y., Providence & Boston R. R. Co., 36 Conn. 63 (1869).

Illinois.—Illinois Central R. R. Co. *v.* Morrison, 19 Ill. 136 (1857). In this case it was held that a carrier could limit his liability for the negligence of his agents, but not for their gross negligence. This is cited, with approval, in Illinois Central R. R. Co. *v.* Adams, 42 Ill. 474 (1867). Note 1, p. 83, *ante.*

Louisiana.—Higgins *v.* N. O., M. & C. R. R. Co., 28 La. Ann. 133 (1876). In this case, also, it is said that if the injury was occasioned "by the fraudulent, willful or reckless conduct of the agent," an agreement for exemption would be unlawful. See note 1, p. 82, *ante.*

Maryland.—Balt. & Ohio R. R. Co. *v.* Brady, 32 Md. 333 (1869).

Michigan.—Hawkins *v.* Great Western R. R., 17 Mich. 57 (1868); same case affirmed, 18 *Ibid*, 427 (1869).

New York.—Wells *v.* N. Y. Central R. R. Co., 24 N. Y. 181 (1862); affg. s. c. 26 Barb. 641 (1858); Perkins *v.* The Same, *Ibid*, 196 (1862); Smith *v.* The Same, *Ibid*, 222 (1862); Bissell *v.* N. Y. Central R. R. Co., 25 *Ibid*, 442 (1862). In this case the passenger who was injured (a

The question as to the carrier's right to contract for exemption from liability for the negligence of his servants, is complicated in the earlier cases by a discussion as to the consideration paid by the passenger for his carriage. There is a class of cases where a passenger traveling on a free ticket, having paid no fare whatever, has received injury, and where the ticket contained a printed form called an agreement, to the effect that the company should

---

cattle drover) was transported at a reduced rate of fare. This was the consideration for the agreement that the carrier should not be liable for negligence. This was held sufficient. See *post*, ch. IV, sect. 4.

Poucher *v.* N. Y. Central R. R. Co., 49 N. Y. 263 (1872). This also was a case of personal injuries to a drover accompanying cattle transported by the carrier. Cragin *v.* N. Y Central R. R. Co., 51 N. Y. 61 (1872); Spinetti *v.* Atlas S. S. Co., 80 N. Y. 71 (1880); revg. s. c. 14 Hun, 100 (1878); Parsons *v.* Monteath, 13 Barb. 353 (1851); Moore *v.* Evans, 14 *Ibid*, 524 (1852); Heinman *v.* Grand Trunk R. R. Co., 1 Buffalo Superior Ct. Rep. 95 (1866).

The Supreme Court of New York has gone so far, in sustaining the validity of such stipulations, as to enjoin one citizen of New York from suing another upon a contract made with a carrier, to recover damages for injuries caused by the negligence of the carrier's servants, in the courts of a State where clauses of exemption from liability for injuries so caused are held to be unlawful. Dinsmore *v.* Neresheimer, 32 Hun, 204 (1884).

These cases overrule the earlier decisions in New York. Cole *v.* Goodwin, 19 Wend. 251 (1838); Gould *v.* Hill, 2 Hill, 623 (1842); Dorr *v.* N. J. Steam Nav. Co., 4 Sandford Superior Ct. Rep. 136 (1850); Stoddard *v.* The Long Island R. R. Co., 5 *Ibid*, 180 (1851); Bissell *v.* N. Y. Central R. R., 29 Barb. 602 (1859); see Stedman *v.* Western Trans. Co., 48 Barb. 97 (1866).

But the contract against negligence must be express; mere general expressions will not answer. Canfield *v.* B. & O. R. R. Co., 93 N. Y. 532 (1883). See *post*, ch. X, sect. 3.

New Jersey.—Ashmore *v.* Penn. Steam Towing & Transportation Co., 4 Dutcher, 180 (1860); Kinney *v.* Central R. R., 32 N. J. Law (3 Vroom.), 407 (1868); affd. 34 N. J. Law, 514 (1870). This was a case of a passenger traveling on a free pass, who had contracted that the carrier should not be liable for injuries caused by the negligence of its servants.

Vermont.—Kimball *v.* Rut. & Burl. R. R. Co., 26 Vt. 247 (1854); Mann, *et al. v.* Birchard, *et al.*, 40 *Ibid*, 326 (1867).

Western Virginia.—Baltimore & Ohio R. R. *v.* Rathbone, 1 W. Va. 87 (1865). In this case it is said that the exemption will not be extended to a loss occasioned by the malfeasance or fraud of the carrier's servants.

not be liable for any injury or loss to the passenger, whether arising from negligence of its servants or otherwise. In these cases the courts in some of the States have held that the contract was a legal one, and that no degree of negligence on the part of the carrier's agents could make the carrier liable for injury to the person traveling on such a free ticket.[1]

---

[1] Wells *v.* N. Y. C. R. R. Co., 24 N. Y. 181 (1862); affirming s. c. 26 Barb. 641 (1858); Perkins *v.* N. Y. C. R. R. Co., 24 N. Y. 196 (1862); Boswell *v.* H. R. R. R. Co., 5 Bosw. (N. Y.) 699 (1860). In the latter case, the passenger injured had charge of cattle, which were being transported on the railroad, and received a pass from the carrier, which contained a stipulation that by accepting or using it he expressly released the company in consideration of this pass, and the reduction of the freight below tariff rates, from all liability for injury to said stock or for injury to his person or stock from any cause whatever. The court held that under such contract the carrier was not liable for an injury to the drover. In this case, however, the injury occurred without willful fault or gross negligence on the part of the carrier's agents. On the other hand, it can hardly be said that a person who travels upon such a ticket as that pays no consideration whatever for his carriage. None, it is true, is specifically paid, but the carriage of himself as well as of the live-stock which he accompanies is paid for by the price which is paid in gross. If there be anything in the distinction which some courts have attempted, between cases where no consideration whatever is paid for transportation, and cases where some consideration is paid, the Boswell case should be included in the latter class. See, also, Ohio & Miss. R. R. Co. *v.* Selby, 47 Ind. 471 (1874); Pennsylvania R. R. Co. *v.* Henderson, 51 Pa. 315 (1865). In Myers *v.* Wabash & St. Louis R. Co., 90 Mo. 98 (1886), a reduced rate of freight was held to be a valid consideration for the owner's assuming part of the risk. Carroll *v.* Missouri Pacific R. Co., 88 Mo. 239 (1885) was a case of injury to a drover traveling on a pass, with stock, held that a stipulation for exemption from liability was invalid. The same rule was applied to the case of a person traveling on a free pass in Gulf, C. & S. F. R. R. *v.* McGown, 65 Texas, 640 (1886). See *post*, ch. IV, sect. 4.

In another of the free ticket cases, the court held that a person accepting such a ticket might contract that the company should not be liable for ordinary negligence, but that a contract exempting from negligence would not be so construed as to exempt the carrier from liability for willful default or tort of his servant. Mobile & Ohio R. R. Co. *v.* Hopkins, 41 Ala. 486 (1868).

In R. R. Co. *v.* Stevens, 95 U. S. 655 (1877), the United States Supreme Court had under consideration a question of the carrier's liability for damages to a passenger who was traveling on a free pass which contained a stipulation exempting the company from liability for the negli-

Many of the courts which hold such a stipulation invalid extend their ruling so far as to maintain that the carrier shall not be permitted to stipulate for exemption from liability for the negligence of another carrier employed by it to perform the work of transportation. It is not customary in the United States for railroad companies to undertake the transportation of small and valuable parcels by their own servants. This is commonly done by what are called||express companies. These sometimes furnish their own cars, and sometimes engage space on the cars of the railroad companies. In either case it is the railroad company that hauls the freight, and thus performs the work of transportation. The parcels are commonly received and delivered by the servants of the express company, and are in their custody during the transit. When these express companies first were charged as common carriers, they sought to exempt themselves from liability for the negligence of the servants of the railroad companies with which they contracted, by the provision that the express company should be liable as forwarders only. This, however, did not accomplish the purpose for which it was

---

gence of its servants. It, however, appeared in this case that though the passenger paid no pecuniary consideration for his transportation, he was in fact traveling at the request and for the benefit of the company, and the court held that under such circumstances the carrier was liable for injuries to him, but declined to say that had he been traveling without paying any consideration to the railroad company, such a stipulation might not be valid.

Ill. Central R. R. Co. *v.* Read, 37 Ill. 484 (1865) was another free ticket case. There was no pretence that any consideration of any kind was paid for the ticket, but the carrier was held liable for the gross negligence of its servants, notwithstanding the clause on the ticket purporting to exempt the carrier from liability for negligence.

Where an express messenger is allowed to ride on a baggage car and carry his goods, the privilege is a good consideration for the exemption of the carrier from liability for injuries to the messenger arising from his being in that car, and the carrier is not liable to him for the negligence of its own baggage men. Bates *v.* Old Colony R. R. Co., 147 Mass. 255; s. c. 38 Albany L. J. 297 (1888).

intended. Notwithstanding such agreement, the express company is held to be liable as carrier, although both it and its servants are free from blame. This is contrary to the rule of *respondeat superior*, and throws liability on a carrier which would not be imposed upon the owner of real estate for the negligence of his contractor's servants. But the views of public policy entertained by the courts referred to have induced them to extend the rule as far as has just been stated.[1]

In some of the States and in Great Britain, statutes have been passed limiting the right of the carrier to make special contracts with a shipper or passenger, which exempt

---

[1] Bank of Kentucky v. Adams Ex. Co., 93 U. S. 174 (1876); Hooper v. Wells, 27 Cal. 11 (1864); Galt v. Adams Ex. Co., McArthur & Mackey (D. C.) 124 (1879); Langworthy v. N. Y. & Harlem R. R., 2 E. D. Smith (N. Y.), 195 (1853); Boscowitz v. Adams Ex. Co., 93 Ill. 523 (1879); Merchants' Dispatch T. Co. v. Bloch, 86 Tenn. 392 (1888). See, for an apparent exception, American Ex. Co. v. Second National Bank, 69 Penn. 394 (1871).

The rule stated in the text has been applied conversely. In Thorpe v. N. Y. C. & H. R. R. R. Co., 13 Hun, 70 (1878), the railroad company was held liable for the misconduct of the servants of a drawing-room car company, in using unnecessary violence in evicting a passenger who had taken a seat in the drawing-room car without paying extra fare, he having been unable to procure a seat in the ordinary cars. This decision was, however, clearly right, irrespective of any question of public policy. It is well settled that a carrier owes a duty to passengers contracting with it, to protect them from unlawful violence or ill treatment while on its vehicles. Putnam v. Broadway & Seventh Av. R. R., 55 N. Y. 108 (1873); Williams v. Pullman Car Co., 40 La. Ann. 417; s. c. 4 So. Rep. 85 (1888). In the same case (40 La. Ann. 87; 3 So. Rep. 631 [1888]), it was held that the Pullman Car Co. was not responsible, there being no contract between them and the plaintiff. See, also, as to holder of free railway pass having paid for seat in a Pullman Car, Ulrich v. N. Y. C. & H. R. R. R. Co., 108 N. Y. 80 (1888).

In an Alabama case the court put the carrier's liability on the ground of contract, and therefore held that some of the joint owners of a steamboat were not liable for the loss of goods transported under a special contract with the other joint owners by which the freight payable for the transportation was to be taken in extinguishment of a debt due from the shipper to the parties with whom he contracted. Jones v. Sims, 9 Porter (Ala.) 236 (1839).

the carrier from liability for the negligence of its agents or servants, or prohibiting such contracts altogether.[1]

There is a class of cases in which courts appear to intimate that under no circumstances will a stipulation to exempt a carrier from liability for the gross negligence of his servants be supported, although a contract of exemption from liability for ordinary negligence might be. It

---

[1] Iowa Code, sect. 1307. In Rose v. Des Moines Valley R. R. Co., 39 Iowa, 246 (1874), it was held that this statute was applicable to contracts with passengers as well as with shippers of freight. In another case in the same State, the court held that the provisions of the Code on this subject were applicable, although the contract for the transportation of the goods in question was made at a reduced rate, and the shipper in consideration of such reduction contracted that the company should not be liable for loss caused by the negligence of its agents. Brush v. S., A. & D. R. R. Co., 43 Iowa, 554 (1876).

An act was passed in Kentucky in 1870 authorizing the Louisville & Nashville R. R. Co. to make special contracts for transportation of live-stock. It was, however, held that this statute should not be construed so as to authorize the company to contract for exemption from liability for negligence of its servants. Louisville, Cin. & Lex. R. R. Co. v. Hedger, 9 Bush (Ky.), 645 (1873).

In Great Britain, section 7 of the Railway and Canal Traffic Act (17 and 18 Vict. c. 3) (1854), enacted that stipulations limiting the liability of a common carrier within the United Kingdom should be invalid, unless, in the opinion of the court before which a case arising under them came to be tried, such stipulations were "just and reasonable." See Brown v. Manchester, Sheffield and L. R. Co., L. R. 9 Qu. B. Div. 230 (1882).

A similar provision exists in Texas; Rev. Stat., art. 278. Houston & T. C. R. R. v. Burke, 55 Texas, 323 (1881). It was held, however, that this was not infringed by a provision in a bill of lading that the carrier, if he paid a loss, should have the benefit of any insurance effected by the shipper upon the cargo injured or lost. British F. M. Ins. Co. v. Gulf, C. & S. F. R. Co., 63 Texas, 475 (1885); see, also, The Titania, 19 Fed. Rep. 101 (1883).

The general railroad act of Michigan, Session Laws, 1855, p. 173, prohibited railroad companies formed under it from restricting their common law liability. It was held in McMillan v. Mich. S. & N. Ind. R. R., 16 Mich. 79 (1867), that this statute did not render invalid an agreement between the carrier and the shipper, expressly releasing the carrier from part of his common law liability.

The constitution of Nebraska, adopted in 1875, provides that "the liability of railroad corporations as common carriers shall never be limited." Missouri Pac. R. Co. v. Vandeventer, 3 Law. Rep. Ann. 129; s. c. 41 N. W. Rep. 998 (1889).

is believed, however, that the tendency of the decisions at the present time, is to treat this distinction claimed to exist between the different degrees of negligence, as impracticable, and that there are probably few States in the Union in which a court would now support the validity of a stipulation exempting a carrier from liability for ordinary negligence, and at the same time charge the carrier under such a contract with liability for gross negligence.[1]

One modification of the rule, which the courts have adopted, as to the validity of contracts for exemption from liability for specified causes, must be borne in mind. Any departure by the carrier from the stipulated mode of transportation will deprive him of the benefit of any clauses in the contract limiting his liability, and during the period of such departure his full liability at common law is reinstated. If, for example, the contract with the shipper provides that the transportation shall be entirely by rail, and the carrier at some intermediate point transfers the goods to a steamboat, the entire provisions of the contract which

---

[1] Austin v. Manchester S. & L. R. Co., 10 Comm. B. 454, 474 (1850); Hinton v. Dibbin, 2 Qu. B. 646 (1842), per Denman, C. J.; Railroad Co. v. Lockwood, 17 Wall. 357 (1873); see Ohio & Miss. R. R. v. Selby, 47 Ind. 471, 484 (1874).

This distinction as to gross negligence is taken in the following, among other cases: Ill. Central R. R. Co. v. Morrison, 19 Ill. 136 (1857); Ill. Central R. R. v. Read, 37 Ill. 484 (1865); Thayer v. St. Louis A. & T. H. R. R. Co., 22 Ind. 26 (1864); Mich. S. & N. Ind. R. R. v. Heaton, 37 Ind. 448 (1871); Southern Ex. Co. v. Armstead, 50 Ala. 350 (1874); Arnold v. Illinois Central R. R., 83 Ill. 273 (1876). In the latter case it was held to be gross negligence in an express company to deposit goods on the platform of a railroad station at the end of its route, and give no notice to the consignee, although when the goods were received for transportation it notified the consignor that it had no agent at the place of destination. But it is now settled law in Alabama and Indiana, that no stipulation exempting the carrier from liability for negligence is valid; see cases cited under note 1, p. 83, ante.

In Wisconsin it is held that a carrier may relieve himself from liability for the ordinary or slight negligence of his servants, but not for their gross negligence. Annas v. Milwaukee & N. R. Co., 67 Wis. 46 (1886).

limit the carrier's liability, are displaced, and become in-operative.[1]

One of the leading cases on this subject rests the de-cision upon the ground that the injury is really caused, not by negligence on the part of the carrier, but by an entire and willful abandonment of all effort to perform the

---

[1] Collins *v.* Bristol and Exeter R. Co., 11 Excheq. 790 (1856); Blos-som *v.* Griffin, 13 N. Y. 569 (1856); Magnin *v.* Dinsmore, 70 N. Y. 410 (1877); Graham *v.* Davis, 4 Ohio St. 362 (1854); Fatman *v.* Cincinnati, H. & D. R. R. Co., 2 Disney (Ohio), 248 (1858); Galveston H. & H. R. Co. *v.* Allison, 59 Texas, 193 (1883); Robinson *v.* Merchants' Despatch T. Co., 45 Iowa, 470 (1877).

In this latter case, the stipulation of the contract was that the goods should be transported "through, without transfer, in cars owned and controlled by the company." The goods, however, were transferred to other cars, and while in these cars were burned. It was held that the carrier was liable for the loss notwithstanding the contract contained an express stipulation exempting him from loss by fire.

In Hand *v.* Baynes, 4 Whart. (Pa.) 204 (1839), the contract stated that the transportation was to be by canal. On reaching the canal, the master of the vessel was informed that the locks were out of order, and that his vessel could not go through. He consequently undertook to go by Chesapeake Bay, and while engaged in the voyage the vessel and cargo were lost in a storm. The court held that the stipulation as to the method of transit, was absolute, and that the carrier was liable, although the loss was occasioned by a peril of the sea.

The disability in this latter case was strictly analogous to that caused by a blockade. In such case, the rule is well settled, that if the blockade is likely to be continued, it is the duty of the carrier to return to the port of departure.

In Hunnewell *v.* Taber, 2 Sprague 1 (1854), the bill of lading con-tained a clause, "not accountable for leakage." The carrier failed to comply with an agreement as to the method of caring for the casks, and it was held that he was liable for the injury caused by leakage, notwith-standing the clause of exemption.

So a failure by a carrier to deliver to the stipulated connecting line makes him liable as insurer for injury on the line to which the goods are delivered. Isaacson *v.* N. Y. Central & H. R. R., 94 N. Y. 278 (1884). But a carrier may stop at an intermediate port not mentioned in his bill of lading if it is his custom to do. Lowry *v.* Russell, 8 Pick. (Mass.) 360 (1829).

In Johnson *v.* the N. Y. Cent. R. R. Co., 31 Barb. (N. Y.) 196 (1857), it was held that a deviation rendered necessary by unforeseen circum-stances was justifiable. Where a bill of lading authorizes a vessel "to call at any port or ports," this means in course of her voyage, and does not justify her in going 40 miles out of her course to pick up a disabled vessel. Ardan S. S. Co. *v.* Theband, 35 Fed. R. 620 (1888).

contract, which of itself constitutes a breach of the carrier's duty, and takes the case entirely out of the scope of the clauses of limitation.[1]   But if there be good cause for the deviation, it has been sustained and approved.[2]

The diversity in the decisions that have been cited is to be regretted.   It is difficult for a lawyer to undertake to hold the scales when tribunals of learning, ability and experience have differed.   Nevertheless, a few observa-

---

[1] Keeney v. G. T. R. Co., 47 N. Y. 525 (1872); affirming same case 59 Barb. 104 (1870).   This was the case of a live-stock contract, which provided that the owner should undertake "all risk of loss, injury, damage and other contingencies, in loading, unloading, conveyance, and otherwise," and that the carriers "do not undertake to forward the animals by any particular train or at any specified hour, neither are they responsible for the delivery of the animals within any certain time, or for any particular market."   The carrier, in order to forward more rapidly other freight which had been entrusted to it, switched the cars containing the cattle to a side track, and allowed them to remain there for two or three days in a position where they could not be unloaded, fed, or watered.   In this case, manifestly, there was a breach of the carrier's obligation to forward freight without discriminating in favor of one shipper against another.   See also Clark v. St. Louis, K. C. & N. R. Co., 64 Mo. 440 (1877).   On a somewhat similar principle it has been held, that where a carrier receives goods to be transported with directions to forward them at once, and the goods are allowed to remain in the carrier's warehouse for his own convenience, the carrier is liable for the destruction of the goods by fire before the commencement of the transit.   Moses v. B. & M. R. R. Co., 24 N. H. 71 (1851); Heyl v. Inman S. S. Co., 14 Hun (N. Y.), 564 (1878).

In Magnin v. Dinsmore, 70 N. Y. 410 (1877), the court held that a carrier is liable for conversion of the goods transported or for the willful misfeasance of his servants in transporting the same, notwithstanding a special contract exempting the carrier for liability for loss from negligence of his servants.   In other words, it is held that willful conversion or misfeasance is not negligence.   The court, however, say that to prove conversion of the goods under such a bill of lading, it is not enough to prove a technical conversion, such as demand and refusal, but that an actual wrongful withholding or disposal of the goods must be established to show misfeasance.   An affirmative act of wrong doing must be proved.

[2] In Regan v. Grand Trunk R. Co., 61 N. H. 579 (1881), "the defendant's undertaking was to carry the plaintiff's goods from Groveton to Portland, and deliver them to the boat for transportation to the consignee at Boston."   Transportation by the boat became impossible, owing to a storm.   The goods were perishable, and it was held that the carrier did right to forward them by rail, but was bound to notify the consignee of the change of route.

tions on the merits of the rule adopted by the English, French, and many American courts may not seem out of place.

First, then, it is one of the maxims of the common law, that *modus et conventio vincunt legem*. That is to say, in the absence of positive prohibition or well settled public policy having the force of positive prohibition, the agreement of the parties is the law of the case. In the next place, it is to be observed that it is always dangerous for a court to undertake to determine public policy. That would seem to be properly the province of the Legislature. It is true that some rules are so firmly established by common consent, that there needs no legislative declaration to establish them, yet it must also be admitted that these rules are few. It is also true, that what may be at one time a wise public policy, under different circumstances and at different times may cease to be unwise, yet no one knows better than a lawyer how difficult it is to induce a court which has once laid down a rule on the subject to recede from it. What was originally public policy becomes adjudication and has the force of an adjudication, and sometimes under different circumstances becomes a public detriment instead of a public benefit.[1]

Again it would seem that the very fact that so many courts of learning and ability had determined that a particular agreement was not against public policy, was sufficient at any rate to show that there was doubt enough

---

[1] Some very judicious observations on this subject will be found in the Girard Will Case, 2 How. (U. S.) 197 (1844); Hollis *v.* Drew Theol. Sem., 95 N. Y. 166 (1884); Kellogg *v.* Larkin, 3 Chandler (Wis.), 133, 142 (1851).

In Hadden *v.* The Collector, 5 Wallace, 107, 111 (1866), the court say: "What is termed the policy of the Government with reference to any particular legislation is generally a very uncertain thing, upon which all sorts of opinions, each variant from the other, may be formed by different persons. It is a ground much too unstable upon which to rest the judgment of the court in the interpretation of statutes."

on the subject to induce another court to refrain from saying that the case was so clear that it did not admit of doubt.

Another consideration, which does not appear to have been adverted to by the United States Supreme Court, until very recently, would seem to be entitled to even more weight than those which have been suggested.

It was, as already shown, enacted by the Federal Legislature in 1851, that the owner or charterer of a ship might limit his liability for the neglect of his agents by abandoning his interest in the vessel and her freight then pending, and that he is not liable at all for loss from fire caused by the neglect of his agents. How, then, in the face of such a legislative declaration, can it be said that an agreement limiting his liability for the negligence of his agents is against public policy?

Again, in the first section of the act of March 3d, 1851, it was provided "that nothing in this act contained shall prevent the parties from making such contract as they please, extending or limiting the liability of such owner."[1]

Whatever reasons may originally have existed for the requirement that a carrier should answer for all loss arising from the negligence of his agents, there would seem to be no good reason why a carrier who takes all reasonable precautions to secure competent and faithful agents, should be liable for a fault on their part, of which he has no knowledge and which he could not in any way prevent. The business of carriers has assumed such vast proportions that it is impossible for them to exercise personal

---

[1] It was held in Walker v. The Transportation Company, 3 Wallace, 150 (1865), that this provision did not apply to an implied, but only to an express agreement. But it does apply to an express agreement, and would seem a recognition of the validity of such an agreement.

It is true that this portion of the original act has not been re-enacted in the Revised Statutes, but as a legislative declaration on the subject of public policy it would seem entitled to as much weight as if it had been.

supervision over all their employees.   And it would seem unjust to impose upon them an absolute responsibility, for which no contract is allowed to provide and against which no amount of care can furnish an entire safeguard.

The question is really one of the amount of consideration that the shipper or passenger is willing to pay.   He is not bound to accept the qualified engagement from the carrier, but may insist that his goods shall be carried under the common law liability of such carrier.   On the other hand, it would seem unjust to say that if he were willing for a less remuneration to contract for the carriage of his goods, and thus act as his own insurer, or procure insurance elsewhere, he should not be allowed to do so.

For these reasons it is believed that the doctrine of the English and New York Courts is just, and that in the future it should prevail as the law of the whole country.[1]

It is admitted by all courts, however, and this should be borne distinctly in mind, that no language, however general, will be construed as relieving the carrier from liability for the negligence of his agents unless this is distinctly and specifically expressed in the contract.[2]

SECTION III.

LIVE STOCK CONTRACTS.—INTRINSIC DEFECTS.

The common law liability of a carrier may also be limited by the intrinsic character of, or defects in the sub-

---

[1] The French law on this subject is in conformity with the decision of the English and some of the State courts of the United States.   The French authorities on this subject are stated in the very able brief of appellant's counsel in 129 U. S., pp. 417, 418.   The German, Italian and Dutch authorities, cited on the same and following pages, show that the law of those countries is the same as the French law.   This law had been differently stated in Bedarride's Droit Commercial, Titre VI, des Commissionaires, sect. 252, p. 268.   Sect. 251, p. 267, applies to loss from defect in ship or vehicle.

[2] See cases cited, Chap. X, sect. 3.

ject-matter of the contract. When slavery existed in the United States this limitation was applied to contracts for the carriage of slaves, and it was held that the carrier, in such cases, was not an insurer but a carrier of passengers, and was liable only for want of care and skill.[1]

This rule has found its most frequent illustration in the case of contracts for the transportation of live stock. The carrier who undertakes the carriage of living animals is not answerable for damages caused by the conduct or propensities of the animals themselves. "In other respects the common law responsibilities of the carrier will attach."[2]

There are cases which hold that in the absence of a special contract the extent of the carrier's liability for in-

---

[1] Boyce *v.* Anderson, 2 Peters, 150 (1829); Clark *v.* McDonald, 4 McCord (S. C.), 223 (1827) ; Williams *v.* Taylor, 4 Porter (Ala.), 234 (1836).

[2] South & North Ala. R. R. *v.* Henlein, 52 Ala. 606 (1875); Agnew *v.* Steamer Contra Costa, 27 Cal. 425 (1865); Indianapolis & St. Louis R. Co. *v.* Jurey, 8 Bradwell (Ill. App.), 160 (1880); Chicago, R. I. & P. R. R. *v.* Harmon, 12 *Ibid*, 54 (1882); McCoy *v.* The K. & D. M. R. Co., 44 Iowa, 424 (1876); Evans *v.* Fitchburg R. R., 111 Mass. 142 (1872); Smith *v.* New Haven & N. R. R., 94 Mass. 531 (1866); Chicago, St. L. & N. O. R. R. *v.* Abels, 60 Miss. 1017 (1883); Clarke *v.* Rochester & S. R. R., 14 N. Y. 570 (1856); Mynard *v.* Syracuse, B. & N. Y. R. R., 71 N. Y. 180 (1877); Cragin *v.* New York Central R. R., 51 N. Y. 61 (1872); Bamberg *v.* South Carolina R. R., 9 South Car. 61 (1877); Palmer *v.* Grand Junction R. Co., 4 Mees. & Wels. 749 (1839); Kimball *v.* Rutland & Burlington R. R., 26 Vt. 247 (1854). *Cf.* Missouri Pacific Ry. Co. *v.* Harris, 67 Texas, 166 (1886); Missouri Pacific R. Co. *v.* Fagan (Texas), 9 S. W. Rep. 749 (1888); Rixford *v.* Smith, 52 N. H. 355 (1872); Maslin *v.* Baltimore & O. R. R., 14 W. Va. 180 (1878).

In Myrick *v.* Michigan Central R. R. Co., 107 U. S. 102, 107 (1882), the court say: " Although a railroad company is not a common carrier of live animals in the same sense that it is a carrier of goods, its responsibilities being in many respects different, yet when it undertakes generally to carry such freight it assumes, under similar conditions, the same obligations, so far as the route is concerned over which the freight is to be carried."

In some States, however, the rule appears to be different. It is there held that railroads are not bound to receive live stock as common carriers, and if they carry them at all, may do so under a different liability from that of other freight. See *post*, p. 105, note 1.

juries to live stock is as great as it would be under a contract for the carriage of inanimate objects.[1]

---

[1] Wilson *v.* Hamilton, 4 Ohio St. Rep. 722 (1855); Kansas Pacific R. Co. *v.* Nichols, 9 Kansas, 235 (1872). In this case the court laid down the rule, that whenever a railroad company receives cattle or live stock to be transported over its road, such company assumes all the responsibilities of a common carrier of freight, except so far as such responsibility may be modified by special contract.

In Nebraska it is held that a special contract for the carriage of live stock which provides that the carrier shall not be liable as such for injury to the stock is invalid, and that the carrier cannot thus divest itself of its common law liability. Atchison & Nebraska R. R. *v.* Washburn, 5 Neb. 117 (1876); see Hooper *v.* Wells, 27 Cal. 11 (1864). In Illinois a somewhat more liberal rule has been laid down. In Illinois Central R. R. *v.* Morrison, 19 Ill. 136 (1857), the carrier agreed to carry cattle at less than the usual rates, and the shipper, in consideration of this, agreed that the transportation should be at his risk, and that they should be in custody of his agent. Held that the carrier under such circumstances was liable only for the gross negligence or willful misfeasance of his servants.

But in Saint Louis & S. E. R. Co. *v.* Dorman, 72 Ill. 504, 506 (1874), the court say: "The common law liability of a carrier to deliver live animals is not different from that where the delivery of merchandise or other dead matter is concerned. Cars of sufficient strength for such purpose should always be provided, and the want of them is negligence."

In Alabama it is held that a contract exempting the carrier from liability for negligent injuries to cattle, not arising from gross negligence, is invalid. E. Tenn., Va. & G. R. R. *v.* Johnston, 57 Ala. 596 (1884).

In Georgia it is held that a carrier and shipper may lawfully agree that the former shall not be liable for any damage to live stock from any cause (*e. g.* overloading or heat), except that resulting from the conduct or running of its trains. Mitchell *v.* Georgia R. R., 68 Ga. 644 (1882).

In the same State a stipulation exempting the carrier from liability for injury to live stock caused by collision or derailment is held unlawful. Georgia R. R. *v.* Spears, 66 Ga. 485 (1881); s. c. 42 Am. Rep. 81.

In this case the court say : "At common law the only exceptions to the liability of the common carrier for losses were, where they occurred by the act of God or the public enemy. But to these have since been added cases where the goods were lost by their own decay, from an inherent infirmity, or by the fault of the owner himself. And still later and from the necessity and justice of the case, another exception has been introduced in favor of the carrier of live stock, of accountability for its loss or injury resulting from its own uncontrollable vicious propensities, and the damages incident to its carriage from its inherent natural character. So that it now seems to be settled that a carrier of living animals as freight is a common carrier as to such

It certainly is the carrier's duty to guard against injuries which would naturally, in the absence of appropri-

---

freight, and liable as such, with the foregoing exception. That is to say, he is liable as in other cases, except from the act of God, the public enemy, or of the animals themselves, unless he has further protected himself by contract."

In Ritz v. Penn. R. R., 3 Phila. 82 (1858), Woodward, J., said: "The common law duties and liabilities of common carriers attach to the carriers of live stock. If they hold themselves out to the world as carriers of this species of property, they are bound to receive and transport all that is offered to them on the tender of reasonable compensation for the service. An actual tender is not necessary if the party avers and proves his readiness to pay the money for the carriage. They are bound to provide suitable vehicles for the transportation, with all reasonable equipments, and servants to take care of them, and in general, to use all the diligence which prudent and cautious men usually employ for the preservation of property entrusted to their care. . . . I hold all stipulations and agreements void that have for their object the licensing of negligence on the part of a common carrier. No matter how distinct the terms of a release or valuable the consideration in which it is founded, the carrier is still bound, on principles of social duty, to carry with ordinary diligence and care. The want of these is negligence, and for that he is responsible in damages. Stipulations for exemption are against the policy of the law, and therefore the law will not enforce them."

In England stipulations that horses shall be carried at the owner's risk are held to be reasonable and valid. McCance v. London & N. W. R. Co., 7 H. & N. 477 (1861); Gannell v. Ford (Q. B.), 5 Law Times, N. S. 604 (1862); Harrison v. London, B. & S. R., 2 B. & Sm. 122 (1860); s. c. 8 Jurist, N. S. 740; 31 Law Journal (Q. B.), 113; Great Northern Railway Company v. Morville, 16 Jur. 528; s. c. 21 L. J., Q. B. 319 (1852).

They are not, however, valid, so far as they purport to relieve the carrier from liability for defective equipment. Ante, Ch. IV, sect. 1, pp. 77, et seq.

In Squire v. N. Y. Cent. R. R. Co., 98 Mass. 239 (1867), it was held that an express stipulation that a carrier should not be liable for injuries to live stock in consequence of their own intrinsic defects differs very little, if at all, from the rule of law when there is no contract.

In Texas and Missouri a railroad receiving cattle receives them as a common carrier and cannot exempt itself from liability for negligence. Missouri Pac. R. Co. v. Harris, 67 Texas, 166 (1886); Clark v. St. Louis, R. C. & N. R. Co., 64 Missouri, 440 (1877).

Under the Texas statute providing that carriers shall not limit "the liability as it exists at common law," it is held that they are made common carriers of live stock, and are liable for injuries to cattle to the same extent as for injuries to other property. Gulf, C. & S. F. Ry. v. Trawick, 68 Texas, 314 (1887). Yet the court admits that at common law carriers are not liable for injuries arising from the "uncontrollable vicious propensities of live stock." And in Penn. it is held, even in contracts

ate care, be caused by the natural propensities of the animals carried.[1]

In one case the duties and liability of a carrier of live stock are assimilated to those of an inn-keeper.[2]   But the cases generally do not go to this extent, nor can it be considered as settled law that there is any obligation on the part of the carrier to feed and water the stock.   It has

---

for the carriage of live stock, that the carrier cannot exempt himself from the consequences of gross negligence.   Penn. R. R. v. Raiordan, 119 Penn. 577; s. c. 13 Atl. Rep. 324 (1888).

[1] Clarke v. Rochester & Syracuse R. R., 14 N. Y. 570 (1856).   In this case a horse was tied by a halter to the side of the car; he fell during the journey and was choked.   The evidence tended to show that if a servant of the carrier had inspected the car from time to time, the horse could have been saved.

The court said: "The plaintiffs contend for the rule that the carrier is bound to transport in safety and deliver at all events, save only the known cases in which a carrier of ordinary chattels is excused, while the defendants maintain that they are not insurers at all against the class of accidents which arise from the vitality of the freight.   We are of opinion that neither of these positions is well taken.   The carrier of animals, by a mode of conveyance opposed to their habits and instincts, has no such means of securing absolute safety.   They may die of fright, or by refusing to eat; or they may, notwithstanding every precaution, destroy themselves by attempting to break away from the fastenings by which they are secured in the vehicle used to transport them, or they may kill each other.   In such cases, supposing all proper care and foresight to have been exercised by the carrier, it would be unreasonable in a high degree to charge him with the loss.   But the rule which would exempt the carrier altogether from accidents arising out of the peculiar character of the freight, irrespective of the question of negligence, would be equally unreasonable.   It would relieve the carrier altogether from those necessary precautions which any person becoming the bailee, for hire, of animals is bound to exercise, and the owner, where he did not himself assume the duty of seeing to them, would be wholly at the mercy of the carrier.   It was for the jury to say whether prudence did not require that a servant of the defendants should have been stationed in or about the horse car, so as to observe the conduct and condition of the animals constantly or at intervals."

Gulf, C. & S. F. R. Co. v. Ellison, 70 Texas, 491; s. c. 7 S. W. Rep. 785 (1888).   He must at least use ordinary care.   German v. Chicago & N. W. R. R., 38 Iowa, 127 (1874).

[2] Porterfield v. Humphreys, 8 Humph. (Tenn.) 497 (1847).   And accordingly it was held in this case that the owner of a steamboat was liable for the value of a horse which he was transporting, and which, being insecurely fastened, got loose in the night and jumped overboard.

been held that such obligation will not be implied from a stipulation, in the contract for their carriage, that in case of accident or delay, the owners are "to feed, water, and take proper care of the stock."[1]

Special contracts for the carriage of such stock are very common, and have received from the courts a liberal construction. Thus, for example, when the shipper contracted that the carrier should not be answerable for delays, and that the owner's agent was to take care and charge of the stock, and the cars were detained by a snowstorm, it was held that the carrier was not bound to afford facilities for unloading the cattle at the place where the delay occurred. and thus enable the owner's agent to take proper care of them.[2]

Such contracts will be construed with reference to their subject-matter and to its intrinsic qualities. Thus, a contract provided that the shipper should assume all risk which the animals might receive in consequence of any of them being wild, unruly, etc., or from delays. It was held that this referred only to injuries caused to the ani-

---

[1] Louisville & Nashville R. R. v. Trent, 11 Lea (Tenn.), 82 (1883). In Dunn v. Hannibal & St. Jo. R. R., 68 Mo. 268 (1878), it was held that a carrier which was prevented at the junction of a connecting line from forwarding mules immediately, was bound to feed and water them, although they were accompanied by the owner, who had contracted to take care of them while in transit. But this was put on the ground that the delay at the connecting point was due to the carrier's negligence. In New York, on the other hand, it is settled that the carrier, if delay in transportation occur, is not bound to unload the cattle, but is bound, upon request, to afford reasonable facilities to enable the owner so to do, even if this should require the carrier to send forty miles for an engine. Bills v. N. Y. Central R. R., 84 N. Y. 5 (1881); s. c. 53 N. Y. 608 (1873). In England it is held that when a horse is shipped "at owner's risk" the carrier is not bound to water and feed them while he is at the terminal station, awaiting delivery. Wise v. Great Western R. Co., 1 Hurlst. & N. 63 (1856); Central R. R. & Banking Co. v. Smitha, 4 So. Rep. 708; s. c. 85 Ala. 47 (1888). In Mo. Pacific Ry. Co. v. Fagan, 9 S. W. Rep. (Texas), 749 (1888), a carrier of live stock was held bound to feed and water them.

[2] Penn v. Buffalo & Erie R. R., 49 N. Y. 204 (1872); Bankard v. B. & O. R. R. Co., 34 Md. 197 (1870).

mals themselves by delay, and not to other losses, such as depreciation in market price.[1]

Such contracts cannot relieve the carrier from his obligation to provide suitable vehicles for the transportation of the cattle.[2]

But if the shipper, from choice, selects cars not belonging to the carrier for the transportation of his stock, the carrier is not liable for defects in such cars.[3]

The carrier may make reasonable rules and regulations in regard to the transportation of live stock, which will be binding upon the drover accompanying such stock.[4]

---

[1] Sisson *v.* Cleveland & Toledo R. R. Co. *et al.*, 14 Mich. 489 (1866). In this case Cooley, J., said: "The defendants claim in this Court that the action cannot be sustained in any event, because, by the express terms of the contract, they are not to be liable for delays. We do not so read the contract. As we read this agreement, it refers to loss or damage to the party by reason of injuries to the stock, caused by delay, etc., upon the cars, and to loss or damage by reason of delay in loading or unloading, and has no reference to other losses which the delays of the carriers may cause to the shipper. There are good reasons for an agreement of this description, growing out of the manner in which cattle are usually transported; the owner or his agent accompanying and taking charge of them, and being on hand to prevent injuries of the kinds specified, while no care of the owner could prevent other delays, or protect against losses which might follow incidentally from other delays. The stipulation appears to us carefully worded to cover such injuries and losses as the owner might guard against, while it studiously avoids including losses like the one complained of here." To the same effect are Ball *v.* Wabash, St. L. & P. R. Co., 83 Mo. 574 (1884); Holsapple *v.* Rome, W. & O. R. R., 86 N. Y. 275 (1881); Mynard *v.* Syracuse, B. & N. Y. R. R., 71 N. Y. 180 (1877); revg. s. c. 7 Hun, 399 (1876).

[2] Rhodes *v.* Louisville & Nashville R. R., 9 Bush (Ky.), 688 (1873). In this case the special agreement provided that the owner of the cattle should assume all injury which might be occasioned by their escaping, or by fright or their own viciousness, as well as any other injury which might happen to them incidental to railroad transportation, not caused by the fraud or gross negligence of the railroad company. Held, that while this special contract devolved on the owner the personal care of the cattle, with the duties and risks connected with it, it did not exonerate the company from responsibility for damages resulting from a failure to provide a suitable and safe car for the carriage of the cattle.

[3] See cases fully stated in Chapter IX.

[4] The cases as to reasonable regulations are stated in Chapter VII. Dietrich *v.* Penn. R. R., 71 Penn. 432 (1872), was the case of a

The principles just stated apply with equal force to contracts for the carriage of perishable property.

The carrier is not liable for injuries caused by its intrinsic defects.[1]   But he is bound to take reasonable means to guard against such injuries, to use special diligence to avoid delay in its transportation,[2] and to give it a preference in transportation over non-perishable goods, if he is not able to forward both at once.[3]

And he is to take notice of any marks upon the package containing the goods, which indicate the character of its contents.[4]

---

stock dealer traveling on a drover's ticket, but not at the time in charge of stock.

[1] Evans *v.* Fitchburg R. R., 111 Mass. 142 (1872).

[2] Michigan Central R. R. *v.* Curtis, 80 Ill. 324 (1875).   In this case the first carrier was held liable for injuries done to plants by frost upon a connecting line, it being shown that the injury would have been avoided had the goods been promptly delivered.

In the transportation of meat it has been held that a provision in a bill of lading that a carrier should not be liable for decay did not protect him from anything more than the decay due to the intrinsic tendency of the meat, and not from bad judgment of the captain in persisting in his voyage after breaking his shaft, when by turning back he might have saved the meat.   The jury had found that it was negligent in the captain to persist in continuing his voyage under the circumstances.   Sherman *v.* Inman Steamship Co., 26 Hun, 107 (1881).

Missouri Pac. Ry. *v.* Cornwall, 70 Texas, 611; s. c. 8 S. W. Rep. 312 (1888).

[3] Marshall *v.* N. Y. Central R. R., 45 Barb. (N. Y.) 502 (1866).   In this case the judge at Circuit charged that "where two kinds of property are delivered at the same time by different owners, one of which kind is perishable and the other not, preference is to be given to that which is perishable in transportation, and if either must wait, it must be that which is not perishable."   This charge was sustained on appeal.   The court say: "The question how the carrier was employed, and how he used and employed his means of transportation during any given period when property was delayed, would always be a proper subject of inquiry, and that on this inquiry proof that his means of transportation were employed in transporting perishable property, in preference to other property received at the same time, would always be held a sufficient excuse for delay."

[4] Hastings *v.* Pepper, 11 Pick. (Mass.) 41 (1831).   In this case the box contained oil of cloves, and the mark held sufficient to notify the carrier was: "Glass—with care—this side up."   Held, the carrier was bound to so carry it.   See American Ex. Co. *v.* Perkins, 42 Ill. 458 (1867).

It has even been intimated by one learned judge that the carrier is not bound to receive fragile goods except under a contract limiting his common-law liability. And in Michigan, Kentucky and Tennessee it seems to be the rule that a railroad company is not, at common law, a carrier of live stock, and may lawfully refuse to receive it for transportation, and that it makes itself liable as common carrier for that species of property only by assuming to carry it as such.[1]

---

[1] Mich. S. & N. Ind. R. R. Co. v. McDonough, 21 Mich. 165 (1870); Lake Shore & Mich. S. R. R. Co. v. Perkins, 25 Mich. 329 (1872); Baker v. Louisville & N. R. R. Co., 10 Lea (Tenn.), 304 (1882); Louisville, C. & L. R. R. Co. v. Hedger, 9 Bush (Ky.), 645 (1873). In People v. Babcock, 16 Hun (N. Y.), 313 (1878), a mandamus asked to compel a carrier to receive live stock for transportation under the common-law liability of common carriers, was refused by the Supreme Court of New York.

In the Perkins case the court say (p. 335): "It must be admitted as settled law that where one has already assumed the character of common carrier he may, in special cases, by express agreement, exclude particularly common-law duties and liabilities, and that when this is done his common-law character as common carrier will be cut short, at least to the extent of the variation made by the agreement; and if such is the consequence of an agreement limiting his liability, by one already a common carrier, it seems reasonable to conclude that one who has never assumed or offered to carry chattels of a certain class except upon special terms exempting him from all the important duties and liabilities of the common carrier, cannot be classed among common carriers of property of that kind, or be made answerable in the character of a common carrier as to such property."

Where a railroad company has been accustomed to receive and carry live stock subject to conditions, it is, subject to those conditions, a carrier of live stock, and bound to furnish cars; and if on any emergency it cannot do so, it is bound to be diligent in notifying a proposed shipper. Ayres v. Chicago & N. W. Ry., 71 Wis. 372; s. c. 37 N. W. Rep. 432 (1888).

In East Tenn. & Ga. R. R. v. Whittle, 27 Geo. 535 (1859), it was held that if a railroad company chartered cars to the owner of live stock for its transportation, he could not claim that the company was a common carrier, but that he could sue on an implied agreement that the cars were "in good condition and substantial," and would be carried safely and in the usual time to their destination, and that opportunity for attending to the stock would be given.

In a similar case it was held that the railroad company "stood in the relation of the common carrier" to the owner of the live stock, and this is believed to be the better rule. Peters v. New Orleans, J. & G. N. R. R., 16 La. Ann. 222 (1861).

It is not easy to reconcile the cases which have been referred to. But there is a distinction between them which may be noted. In those stated at the beginning of the chapter it either appeared, or it was assumed by the court, that the corporation sued had held itself out as a carrier of live stock for all who should choose to employ it for that purpose.[1] In the cases in Michigan, Kentucky and Tennessee the attention of the court appears rather to be directed to the proposition, that no person is bound to be a common carrier of everything that offers, but may lawfully hold itself out as a common carrier of one kind of freight and not of another. Many railroads, in cities, are carriers only of passengers and mails. And in the future it is likely that some ocean steamers may in like manner limit their employment.

SECTION IV.

THE CARRIER'S LIABILITY AS AFFECTED BY THE QUESTION OF CONSIDERATION.

It was at one time contended with much earnestness on behalf of the carrier that he was liable only upon his contract, and consequently that the law imposed no liability upon him in the case of a gratuitous undertaking to carry a passenger. But the courts finally held otherwise, and it is now well settled that the carrier owes a duty to all upon his vehicle, independent of contract, and that the breach of this duty is negligence for which he is liable.[2]

---

[1] In Moulton *v.* St. Paul, Minn. & Man. R. Co., 31 Minn. 85, 87 (1883), the court say: "A railroad company which undertakes to transport live stock for hire, for such persons as choose to employ it, assumes the relation of a common carrier, and becomes chargeable with the duties and obligations which are incident to that relation." See Maslin *v.* Baltimore & Ohio R. R., 14 W. Va. 180 (1878); Coup *v.* Wabash, St. L. & P. R. Co., 56 Mich. 111 (1885). This was a contract for a menagerie train. It was held that the railroad company, in respect to this train, was not a common carrier.

[2] Philadelphia & Reading R. R. *v.* Derby, 14 How. U. S. 467, 485 (1852); Waterbury *v.* N. Y. Central & H. R. R. R. Co., 17 Fed. Rep.

In the case of drovers accompanying live-stock and receiving passes for this purpose, and of mail agents who

---

671 (1883). The note to this contains an admirable collection of authorities. Keep *v*. Indianapolis & St. I. R. R., 3 McCrary, 208, 302 (1881 and 1882); Lemon *v*. Chanslor, 68 Mo. 340 (1878); Evans *v*. St. Louis, I. M. & S. R. Co., 11 Mo. App. 463 (1882); New Orleans, J. & G. N. R. R. *v*. Hurst, 36 Miss. 660 (1859); Hurt *v*. Southern R. R. Co., 40 Miss. 391 (1866); Nolton *v*. Western R. R., 15 N. Y. 444 (1857); see Saltonstall *v*. Stockton, Taney Dec. 11 (1838); Buffalo, &c. R. R. *v*. O'Hara, 11 Am. Law Record, 554, Supreme Court Penn. (1882); Camden & A. R. R. *v*. Bausch, 6 Central Rep. 121, Supreme Court Penn. (1887); Heirn *v*. M'-Caughan, 32 Miss. 17 (1856). In Cleveland *v*. N. J. Steamboat Co., 68 N. Y. 306 (1877), the court put the liability of the carrier on the ground that the person injured in that case was liable for the payment of his passage-money, though he had not actually paid it. See Jones *v*. Sims, 9 Porter (Ala.), 236 (1839). In Gillenwater *v*. Madison & Indianapolis R. R., 5 Ind. 339 (1854), the defendants employed plaintiff to frame and build a bridge on their road, across a creek, and while he was engaged in the work directed him to proceed in their cars to Greenwood, and assist in loading timbers for the bridge. While on their cars, as directed, through the negligence of defendant's servants the train was derailed, and plaintiff was injured. Held that he was a passenger, and that the defendant was liable for the injury. In Doran *v*. East River Ferry Company, 3 Lansing (N. Y.), 105 (1870), the plaintiff paid ferriage for one trip, on which she was safely carried. She remained on board during several other trips. No additional ferriage was paid by or asked from her. Held that she could recover for injuries caused by defendant's negligence while the boat was entering the ferry-slip on the last of these trips.

In these cases it may be said that there was either a consideration, or a liability, to pay fare, which made the contract more than gratuitous. But in Mobile & Ohio R. R. *v*. Hopkins, 41 Ala. 486 (1868), the court held that a carrier was liable for the loss of baggage caused by the negligence of its servants, although the owner was riding on a free pass, which contained a stipulation that the carrier should not be liable under any circumstances, whether of the negligence of his agents or otherwise, for any injury to the person or property. Griswold *v*. N. Y. & N. Eng. R. R. Co., 53 Conn. 371 (1885), s. c., 55 Am. Rep. 115, held that under such circumstances the carrier was not liable for the negligence of its servants which caused the death of the person using the pass. s. p.; Kinney *v*. Central R. R., 34 N. J. (Law). 513 (1869). In many of the negligence cases cited in Chapter IV this question of consideration is discussed. The courts that have held contracts exempting a carrier from liability for the negligence of his servants to be void, have generally treated the element of consideration as immaterial. See U. S. Express Co. *v*. Bachman, 2 Cin. Super. Ct. Rep. (Ohio), 251 (1872); Bissell *v*. N. Y. Central R. R., 25 N. Y. 442 (1862); revg. s. c. 29 Barb. 602 (1859). On the other hand, in Orange Co. Bank *v*. Brown, 9 Wend. 85 (1832), some of the old cases are cited with apparent approval in which it is said that

accompany the mails, but pay no money for their transportation, it is believed that the consideration paid for transporting, in the one case the stock and in the other case the mails, would be sufficient even if the liability rested on this ground only.[1] An express agreement that the drover

---

the carrier's liability depends upon the consideration paid him. But in Carroll *v.* Staten I. R. R. Co., 58 N. Y. 126 (1874), the court say that the duty imposed by law upon the carrier of passengers to carry them safely, as far as human skill and foresight can go, exists independently of contract. For a negligent injury to a passenger an action lies against the carrier, although there be no contract, and the service he is rendering is gratuitous; and, whether the action is brought upon contract or for failure to perform it, the liability is the same. s. p., Littlejohn *v.* Fitchburg R. R., 2 Lawyers' Rep. Ann. (Mass.) 502 (1889).

But a reduction in the rate of fare is a valid consideration for certain limitations in the contract to carry, as the limit to the length of time in which a passenger ticket is good. Pennington *v.* Phila., W. & B. R. R. Co., 62 Md. 95 (1883); Johnson *v.* Same, 63 Md. 106 (1884). In Higgins *v.* N. O., M. & C. R. R. Co., 28 La. Ann. 133 (1876), a railroad was held not liable, to a newsman traveling under a free pass, for injuries arising from causes not amounting to fraudulent, willful or reckless conduct of the defendant.

And in Annas *v.* The Milwaukee & N. R. R., 67 Wisc. 46 (1886), the court says, referring to the rule of the Federal and other Courts, that the carrier cannot lawfully limit his liability for negligence:

"It will be found, by an examination of the large number of cases in which this rule is held, that they are cases arising out of the carriage of goods for hire, or where the carriage of the passenger was for a consideration, received either directly or indirectly." And the court found only four cases—and those in State courts, where the rule was applied to a gratuitous passenger.

In McCall *v.* Brock, 5 Strob. (S. C.) 119 (1850), the Court says that the carrier may except, by notice or stipulation, every risk incident to his undertaking. If he make no stipulation, he gets a higher rate of freight as insurance. In such a case the shipper is not bound to show negligence.

In Way *v.* Chicago, R. I. & P. R. Co., 73 Iowa, 463; s. c. 35 N. W. Rep. 525 (1887), it was held that although plaintiff was wrongfully upon the car under another person's pass, the carrier was liable for so recklessly and negligently moving its cars that an injury might have been expected.

In East Line & R. R. R. R. *v.* Lee, 71 Texas, 538; s. c. 9 S. W. Rep. 605 (1888), the owners of a leased line, which was operated by a lessee, were held liable for injuries to a passenger on a ticket issued by the lessee, which were caused by the officers of the latter. As to Pullman Car Companies, see Chap. IV, sect. 2, p. 90, note 1, *ante.*

[1] Railroad Co. *v.* Lockwood, 17 Wall. 357 (1873); Ohio & Miss. R. Co. *v.* Selby, 47 Ind. 471, 492 (1874); Ohio & Miss. R. Co. *v.* Nickless

employed by the shipper shall be considered as an employé of the railroad company is an evasion of the rule

71 Ind. 271 (1880); Missouri Pac. R. Co. v. Ivey, 71 Texas, 409; s. c. 9 S. W. Rep. 346 (1888); Hammond v. North Eastern R. R. Co., 6 So. Car. 130 (1874); Cleveland, P. & A. R. R. v. Curran, 19 Ohio St. 1 (1869).

In the latter case the carrier, in making a contract for the shipment of live stock at a specified rate, delivered to the shipper, without any additional consideration, a "drover's pass," entitling him to go with his stock, and to return on a passenger train.   In the written agreement for transporting the stock, the holder of the ticket was referred to as "riding free to take charge of the stock."   On the pass was an indorsement that it was a "free ticket," and that the holder assumed all risk of accident, and agreed that the company should not be liable under any circumstances, whether of negligence by the company's servants or otherwise, for any injury to his person or property, and that he would not consider the company as common carriers, or liable as such. Held, that the pass and the agreement for transporting the stock constituted, together, a single contract, and that the holder, both while going with his stock and returning, was not a gratuitous, but a paying passenger.   The stipulation exempting the company from liability for negligence was held to constitute no defense to an action brought by the shipper for personal injury, caused by the negligence of servants of the company in the management of its trains.   Penn. R. R. Co. v. Henderson, 51 Penn. 315 (1865); Buffalo, &c. R. R. Co. v. O'Hara, 11 Am. L. Record (Penn.), 554 (1882).

In Bissell v. N. Y. Central R. R., 25 N. Y. 442 (1862), it was held that the provisions of the general Railroad Act of New York, Laws 1850, chap. 140, sect. 36, did not increase the carrier's liability, nor diminish his right to contract for exemption.   In this case the proposition stated in the text was discussed, but not decided.   The court held that a reduced rate of freight on cattle, and the carriage of a drover without charge additional to the freight, was a sufficient consideration for an agreement by the drover to ride at his "own risk of personal injury from whatever cause."

Bankard v. Baltimore & O. R. R. Co., 34 Md. 197 (1870), held that a reduction in freight was a good consideration for an agreement that the carrier should only be liable for injury to cattle caused by gross negligence.

Where the contract secured exemption from certain risks in consideration of a reduced rate of freight, the shipper was allowed to introduce evidence that the rate was not, in fact, reduced, and it was held that the representation, if false, constituted a fraud.   McFadden v. Mo. Pacific Ry. Co., 92 Mo. 343 (1887).

When an express agent is allowed to ride free, a contract of exemption against the negligence of the carrier's employees is valid in Massachusetts; Bates v. Old Colony R. Co., 147 Mass. 255; s. c. 17 North Ea. Rep. 633 (1888); distinguishing Railway Co. v. Lockwood, on the ground that the injury might not have happened to a passenger.

In California it is held, that in the case of an express agent on the

forbidding exemption from negligence, and is therefore void.[1]

In like manner the price that a passenger pays for his ticket is the consideration for the carriage of his baggage as well as his person.[2]

It will be found that the same courts which hold a contract with a drover or passenger, limiting the carrier's liability for negligence, to be valid, adopt substantially the same rule whether there be express consideration for the contract of carriage or not. On the other hand most of the courts which hold such contract void in the one case, hold it to be equally void in the other. To this, however, there are some exceptions.[3]

---

train paying no fare, the consideration paid for carrying the express packages would be sufficient. Yeomans v. Contra Costa S. N. Co., 44 Cal. 71 (1872).

[1] Missouri Pac. R. Co. v. Ivey, 71 Texas, 409; s. c. 9 S. W. Rep. 346 (1888).

[2] Wilson v. Grand Trunk R., 56 Me. 60 (1868). In this case it was held that baggage, forwarded by the passenger's direction, subsequently to his journey, in the absence of any special agreement with or negligence on the part of the carrier in not forwarding it before, must pay freight like any article of merchandise. In Pierce v. Milwaukee & St. Paul R. Co., 23 Wis. 387 (1868), the goods transported were empty bags. The contract provided that they should be transported free. Freight had been paid for their transportation when full, and it was held that this was really a consideration for the agreement to return the empty bags without additional charge.

[3] In Montana it is held that although a common carrier is held to the highest degree of care towards a passenger who pays his fare, the law only requires ordinary care towards a "dead-head" or trespasser. Higley v. Gilmer, 3 Montana, 90 (1878); s. c. 35 Am. Rep. 450.

In Gray v. Missouri River Packet Co., 64 Mo. 47 (1876), it is held that a carrier who transports property gratuitously is liable for injury thereto only in cases of gross negligence; but that, in the absence of an express agreement to the contrary, a promise to pay a reasonable sum for freight arises by implication.

In New Jersey it is held the carrier may exempt itself from all liability where the passenger is carried as a mere gratuity. Kinney v. Central R. R. Co. of New J., 34 N. J. Law, 513 (1869).

In Camden & A. R. R. Co. v. Bausch, 6 Cent. Rep. 121 (1887), the Pennsylvania Supreme Court, by an equally divided court, affirmed a decision of the Common Pleas that the New Jersey rule was otherwise if, in fact, there was a consideration for the carriage of the passenger. In

The rule just stated as to the carrier's liability has been so applied as to charge a carrier for the loss of goods carried over its railroad by an express company,[1] and for the loss of goods received by it for transportation when its line was in part under the direction and control of the military authorities, provided the carrier accepted and agreed to carry the goods,[2] and for the loss of goods received by it for transportation and destroyed by fire at a station on a part of its line leased to another company.[3]

The doctrine of the cases just cited should not, however, be extended. The decisions were probably right, but the facts in each case were peculiar. The proposition is not tenable that a carrier by land is liable for the loss of all goods carried over his line, even though they be in his own vehicle. No one would claim that the owner of a ship, who charters her for a voyage, is liable for injuries caused by the negligence of a master employed, paid and directed exclusively by the charterer. And the same

---

the Federal Courts it is settled that a person who rides on a free pass at the request and for the benefit of the carrier, can recover damages for the carrier's negligence, notwithstanding a stipulation to the contrary. Grand Trunk Ry. *v.* Stevens, 95 U. S. 655 (1877).

[1] Bank of Kentucky *v.* Adams Express Co., 93 U. S. 174 (1876); Hooper *v.* Wells, 27 Cal. 11 (1864); Langworthy *v.* N. Y. & Harlem R. R., 2 E. D. Smith (N. Y.), 195 (1853). In this case there was a private arrangement between the railroad and express companies for the transportation of light freight, of which the public had no notice, and the goods in question were delivered at the cars; whether to the express agent or to the railroad baggage-master, was not clearly stated in the testimony. Held immaterial.

[2] Illinois Central R. R. Co. *v.* Ashmead, 58 Ill. 487 (1871); distinguished from Ill. Central R. R. Co. *v.* McClellan, 54 Ill. 58 (1870); and see Chap. XIV, sect. 4, *post.*

[3] Langley *v.* Boston & Maine R. R., 10 Gray (Mass.), 103 (1857). And in this case and the Ashmead case, cited in the previous note, it may fairly be claimed that the carrier was liable upon his contract, and that, had it not been for this, there would have been no liability. The lessee of a railroad is liable in case of injury to a person at a crossing, even though the ultimate cause of the injury was a defect in the original construction of the road. It knowingly maintains a nuisance. Wasmer *v.* Delaware, L. & W. R. R., 80 N. Y. 212 (1880).

principle must apply on land.   Thus it was held[1] that the owner of goods transported on cars chartered by the owner of them, a railroad company, to an individual cannot recover from the company for injuries to the goods caused by the negligent stowage of the charterer.   And a receiver of a railroad in one State, who with others takes a lease of a connecting railroad in another State, and operates it, is liable for negligence of persons employed by him to operate the road.[2]   On the other hand where a railroad is operated by a receiver or assignee in bankruptcy the corporation to which it belongs is not liable for the negligence of the servants of the assignee or the receiver.[3]

In the long controversy as to the validity of contracts for the exemption of the carrier from liability for the negligence of his servants, to which reference has so often been had, the question of the consideration for such exemption has been frequently considered.   If it can be shown that there was no consideration for such a contract, it will not be valid.   For example, in a case where a railroad was bound by previous contract with the government to carry a mail agent free of charge, it was held that a contract between him and the carrier that the latter should not be held liable for damage caused by the negligence of its servants, was void for want of consideration.[4]

On the other hand it has been held that the carrier is not liable for the non-delivery of goods which he has agreed to carry gratuitously,[5] but that if the agreement for carriage is silent as to compensation, an agreement to pay a reasonable sum for the same will be implied.[6]

---

[1] East Tenn., Va. & G. R. R. v. Whittle, 27 Ga. 535 (1859).

[2] Kain v. Smith, 80 N. Y. 458 (1880); Rogers v. Wheeler, 43 N. Y. 598 (1871); Metz v. Buffalo, C. & P. R. R., 58 N. Y. 61 (1874).

[3] In Ohio & Miss. R. Co. v. Nickless, 71 Ind. 271 (1880), the injury complained of occurred before the appointment of the receiver. The action was brought afterwards. Held that the action was sustainable.

[4] Seyboldt v. N. Y., L. E. & W. R. R. Co., 95 N. Y. 562 (1884).

[5] Chouteau v. Steamboat St. Anthony, 16 Mo. 216 (1852).

[6] Kirtland v. Montgomery, 1 Swan (Tenn.), 452 (1852).

The further consideration of the question as to the extent of the carrier's liability when he undertakes to transport passengers or goods free of charge does not fall within the scope of this work.   The reader is referred to the cases on the subject, which are cited in the note.[1]

---

[1] Passengers.—Rose v. Des Moines Valley R. R., 39 Iowa, 246 (1874); Jacobus v. St. Paul & Chicago R. Co., 20 Minn. 125 (1873); Blair v. Erie R. Co., 66 N. Y. 313 (1876); Hammond v. N. E. R. R., 6 Rich. (S. C.) 130 (1874); The New World v. King, 16 How. U. S. Rep. 469 (1853).

Goods.—Boyd v. Estis, 11 La. Ann. 704 (1856); Knox v. Rives, 14 Ala. 249 (1848); Flint & Marquette R. Co. v. Weir, 37 Mich. 111 (1877).

Cases of Implied Compensation.—Russ v. The War Eagle, 14 Iowa, 363 (1862); Gray v. Missouri R. Packet Co., 64 Mo. 47 (1876).

Where the liability is statutory, as in cases where death results, the liability is limited by statute.   Under the Massachusetts statute, there must be culpability on the part of the carrier in order to give right of action when death ensues.   Littlejohn v. Fitchburg R. R., 2 Lawyers' Rep. Ann. 502 (Mass., 1889).

CHAPTER V.

The courts have shown more liberality towards carriers, in their attempts to limit the amount for which they can be made liable, than in dealing with any other limitations which they have sought to place upon their common-law liability. The earlier cases maintained the carrier's right to limit the amount of his liability by a simple notice.[1] Judge Cowen recognized this right in his opinion delivered in the leading case in New York,[2] in which it was held that a carrier could not, even by express contract, restrict in other respects his common-law liability.

Subsequent cases have not generally admitted that the amount of the carrier's liability could be limited by notice to the shipper.[3] But almost all agree that such a limita-

---

[1] Harris v. Packwood, 3 Taunt. 264 (1810); Batson v. Donovan, 4 B. & Ald. 21 (1820).

Lord Ellenborough said, in Maving v. Todd, 1 Starkie, 72 (1815): "Since they can limit it to a particular sum, I think they may exclude it altogether."

[2] Cole v. Goodwin, 19 Wendell, 251 (1838). In Hollister v. Nowlen, 19 Wend. 234 (1838), Judge Bronson recognized this distinction. He quotes all the old cases as to notice. It was held, however, that notice that the carrier would not be liable at all, was ineffective to limit his liability as to amount. Judge Nelson's opinion in Orange Co. Bank v. Brown, 9 Wend. 85 (1832), contains a *dictum* to the same effect as that of Judge Cowen's, stated in the text.

[3] Southern Express Co. v. Armstead, 50 Ala. 350 (1873). In Illinois and New Hampshire the distinction is adhered to. Moses v. Boston & Me. R. R., 4 Foster (24 N. H.), 71 (1851); Western Trans. Co. v. Newhall, 24 Ill. 466 (1860). In Oppenheimer v. U. S. Ex. Co., 69 Ill. 62 (1873), the court say: "In respect to those duties designed simply to enjoin good faith and fair dealing, a notice alone, if brought home to the knowledge of the owner of the property delivered for carriage, will be sufficient." In that case the appearance of the box did not indicate

tion is valid if agreed to by him,[1] even though injury

---

that its contents were valuable, and the receipt delivered by the carrier to the shipper contained a clause limiting the liability as to amount if the value was not disclosed, and the court held that it was not necessary to introduce affirmative evidence of the shipper's assent.   In other words, they treated the receipt as a notice.   In Illinois affirmative evidence of assent by the shipper, to the terms of a carrier's contract, is necessary.   See Ch. X, sect. 2.

The statement in the text is based upon the numerous decisions cited in the introduction to Chapter IV, to the effect that the carrier's liability can only be limited by contract, and not by notice.   Yet, even so late as 1878, there seems to be a recognition by the New York Court of Appeals of the earlier rule, allowing a notice brought home to the shipper to limit the amount of the carrier's liability.   Baldwin *v.* Liverpool & G. W. S. Co., 74 N. Y. 125 (1878).   See, also, the Fraloff case, *post*, p. 119, note 1.   It is true that the observations on this subject in each of these cases are *dicta*, but they appear to have met the concurrence of the court, and it may be that, if the question should hereafter arise, these *dicta* will be the rule of decision.

And the carrier's liability certainly cannot be limited by a rule or custom without notice to the shipper.   McCune *v.* Burlington, C. R. & N. R. Co., 52 Iowa, 600; s. c. 3 N. W. Rep. 615 (1879).

[1] Boorman *v.* American Ex. Co., 21 Wis. 152 (1866); Fay *v.* The New World, 1 Cal. 348 (1850).   In this latter case the agreement was that no compensation should be paid and no responsibility incurred. There was no negligence.   The agreement was held valid.   Newstadt *v.* Adams, 5 Duer. 43 (1855); Moriarty *v.* Harnden's Ex., 1 Daly, 227 (1862); Baxendale *v.* Great E R. Co., L. R. 4 Q. B. 244 (1869); Brehme *v.* Adams Ex. Co., 25 Md. 328 (1866); Lawrence *v.* N. Y., P. & B. R. R., 36 Conn. 63 (1869); Belger *v.* Dinsmore, 51 N. Y. 166 (1872); Elkins *v.* Empire Trans. Co., 81 Penn. (32 P. F. Smith), 315 (1876); Chicago, R. I. & P. R. R. *v.* Harmon, 17 Ill. App. 640 (1885); Brown *v.* Wabash, St. L. & P. R. Co., 18 Mo. App. 568 (1885).   In M'Cance *v.* London & N. W. R. Co., 3 H. & C. 343 (1864); s. c. Exchq. Cham., 34 L. J. (Exchq.) 39, the decision was put on the ground that both parties had assumed to act on an agreed state of facts, to wit: an admission as to the value of the horses being transported, and that this was therefore binding on both.

In St. Louis, I. M. & S. R. Co. *v.* Lesser, 46 Ark. 236 (1885), it was held that if a partial injury should occur, amounting to less than the amount specified as the value of the animal transported, the damages should abate *pro rata.*

In Brehme *v.* Adams Ex. Co., *supra*, plaintiff delivered to defendant a package of merchandise to be transported from New York to Baltimore.   The contract was evidenced by a printed receipt, signed by the agent of the express company, containing a stipulation that in no event "shall the holder hereof demand beyond the sum of $50, at which the article forwarded is hereby valued, unless otherwise herein expressed, or unless specially insured, and so specified in this receipt."   The contents of the package were light and costly goods, worth $675.   This was not known to the express company; no statement of its value was made by

should be done or loss occur through the negligence of the carrier's servants.[1]

---

the plaintiffs, and no special insurance effected. Held, that the receipt constituted a contract between the parties for the carriage of the package, binding upon both, and that the plaintiff could only recover the sum at which the package was valued in the receipt, with interest thereon.

[1] The leading case is Hart v. Pennsylvania R. R., 112 U. S. 331 (1884); affg. s. c. 2 McCrary, 333 (1881). In this case the stock to be transported was valued in the bill of lading at a fixed sum, and the clause was held valid, though the loss arose from negligence. The court say, "As a general rule, and in the absence of fraud or imposition, a common carrier is answerable for the loss of a package of goods, though he is ignorant of its contents, and though its contents are ever so valuable, if he does not make a special acceptance. This is reasonable, because he can always guard himself by a special acceptance, or by insisting on being informed of the nature and value of the articles before receiving them.

"If the shipper is guilty of fraud or imposition, by misrepresenting the nature or value of the articles, he destroys his claim to indemnity, because he has attempted to deprive the carrier of the right to be compensated in proportion to the value of the articles and the consequent risk assumed, and what he has done has tended to lessen the vigilance the carrier would otherwise have bestowed. 2 Kent. Com. 603, and cases cited; Relf v. Rapp. 3 Watts. & S. 21 (1841); Dunlap v. International Steamboat Co., 98 Mass. 371 (1867); N. Y. C. Railroad Co. v. Fraloff, 100 U. S. 24 (1879).

"This qualification of the liability of the carrier is reasonable, and is as important as the rule which it qualifies.

"There is no justice in allowing the shipper to be paid a large value · for an article which he has induced the carrier to take at a low rate of freight on the assertion and agreement that its value is a less sum than that claimed after a loss. It is just to hold the shipper to his agreement, fairly made, as to value, even where the loss or injury has occurred through the negligence of the carrier. The effect of the agreement is to cheapen the freight and secure the carriage, if there is no loss; and the effect of disregarding the agreement, after a loss, is to expose the carrier to a greater risk than the parties intended he should assume. The agreement as to value in this case stands as if the carrier had asked the value of the horses, and had been told by the plaintiff the sum inserted in the contract.

"The limitation as to value has no tendency to exempt from liability for negligence. It does not induce want of care. It exacts from the carrier the measure of care due to the value agreed on. The carrier is bound to respond in that value for negligence. The compensation for carriage is based on that value. The shipper is estopped from saying that the value is greater. The articles have no greater value for the purposes of the contract of transportation between the parties to that contract. The carrier must respond for negligence up to that value.

The rigor of the rule declared by the Federal and many of the State Courts, which rejected stipulations exonerat-

---

It is just and reasonable that such a contract fairly entered into, and where there is no deceit practiced on the shipper, should be upheld. There is no violation of public policy. On the contrary, it would be unjust and unreasonable, and would be repugnant to the soundest principles of fair dealing and of the freedom of contracting, and thus in conflict with public policy, if a shipper should be allowed to reap the benefit of the contract if there is no loss, and to repudiate it in case of loss. . . .

" The subject matter of a contract may be valued, or the damages in case of a breach may be liquidated in advance. In the present case, the plaintiff accepted the valuation as 'just and reasonable.' The bill of lading did not contain a valuation of all animals at a fixed sum for each, but a graduated valuation according to the nature of the animal. It does not appear that an unreasonable price would have been charged for a higher valuation."

In accord with the Hart case are the following decisions in

Federal Courts.—Muser v. Holland, 17 Blatchf. 412 (1880); s. c. 1 Fed. Rep. 382 (1880); Earnest v. Express Co., 1 Woods, 573 (1873); Hopkins v. Westcott, 6 Blatchf. 64 (1868).

Alabama.—Louisville & N. R. Co. v. Sherrod, 4 So. Rep. 29 (1888); s. c. 84 Ala. 178.

Illinois.—Oppenheimer v. U. S. Ex. Co., 69 Ill. 62 (1873).

Massachusetts.—Hill v. Boston, H. T. & W. R. R., 144 Mass. 284 (1887); Graves v. Lake Shore & M. S. R. R. 137 Mass. 33 (1884); Squire v. N. Y. Central R. R., 98 Mass. 239 (1867); Judson v. Western R. R., 6 Allen, 486 (1863).

Missouri.—Harvey v. Terre Haute & I. R. R., 74 Mo. 538 (1881).

New York.—Magnin v. Dinsmore, 70 N. Y. 410 (1877); 62 N. Y. 35 (1875); 56 N. Y. 168 (1874); Steers v. Liverpool, N. Y. & P. S. S. Co., 57 N. Y. 1 (1874); Belger v. Dinsmore, 51 N. Y. 166 (1872).

Pennsylvania.—Farnham v. Camden & A. R. R., 55 Penn. St. 53 (1867); Elkins v. Empire Trans. Co., 81 Penn. (32 P. F. Smith), 315 (1876); Newburger v. Howard, 6 Phila. 174 (1866).

These appear to be overruled by Grogan v. Adams Ex. Co., 114 Penn. St. 528 (1886). This considers and disapproves the Hart case.

To the contrary are the following cases:

Federal Courts.—The Hindoo, 1 Fed. Rep. 627 (1880); The City of Norwich, 4 Bened. 271 (1870). In this case, however, it is to be observed that the bill of lading did not in terms exempt the carrier from liability for negligence; The language was: "No package, if lost, damaged, or stolen should be deemed of greater value than $100, unless specially receipted for." These cases are no longer authority in the Federal Courts as they are clearly overruled by the Hart case.

Alabama.—Mobile & Ohio R. R. v. Hopkins, 41 Ala. 486 (1868); Ala. G. S. R. R. v. Little, 71 Ala. 611 (1882); L. & N. R. R. v. Oden, 80 Ala. 38 (1885); S. & N. Ala. R. R. v. Henlein, 52 Ala. 606 (1875); s. c. 56 Ala. 368 (1876).

Indiana.—Adams Express Co. v. Harris, 21 N. East. Rep. 340

ing the carrier from liability for loss or injury caused by
the negligence of his servants, led to the insertion of
these clauses limiting the amount of the carrier's liability.   Other forms of contract were resorted to in order to
restrict the application of the decisions referred to.   One
of the most common of these is a clause that "in case of
loss, damage or non-delivery, the ship-owner shall not be
liable for more than the invoice value of the goods."
Clauses in this and similar language are valid.   They do
no more than liquidate the damages for a breach of the
contract of affreightment.[1]

The Supreme Court of the United States has held that

(1889).   In this case the court drew attention to the fact that it did
not appear that the limitation was in consideration of a lower rate of
freight.

Kansas.—Kansas City, St. J. & C. B. R. R. v. Simpson, 30 Kans.
645 (1883); s. c. 2 Pac. Rep. 821.

Minnesota.—Moulton v. St. Paul, M. & M. R. Co., 31 Minn. 85
(1883); s. c. 16 N. W. Rep. 497; 47 Am. Rep. 781.

Mississippi.—Chicago, St. L. & N. O. R. R. v. Abels, 60 Miss. 1017
(1883); Southern Ex. Co. v. Moon, 39 Miss. 822 (1863).

Ohio.—U. S. Ex. Co. v. Backman, 28 Ohio St. 144 (1875); s. c. 2
Cinc. 255.

Pennsylvania.—Grogan v. Adams Ex. Co., 114 Penn. 523; s. c. 5
Central Rep. 298 (1886); expressly declining to follow Hart v. Penn. R.
Co., supra.

Tennessee.—Cunard v. E. T. V. & G. R. R., 16 Lea (Tenn.), 225
(1886); s. c. 57 Am. Rep. 226.

Wisconsin.—Black v. Goodrich Trans. Co., 55 Wis. 319 (1882); s. c.
13 N. W. Rep. 244; 42 Am. Rep. 713; distinguishing Hart v. Ry.;
Magnin v. Dinsmore, &c.

[1] Brown v. Cunard S. S. Co., 16 N. East. 717 (1888) (Mass.); criticis-
ing The Lydian Monarch, infra ; The Aline, 25 Fed. Rep. 562 (1885);
The Lydian Monarch, 23 Fed. Rep. 298 (1885); The Hadji, 18 Fed.
Rep. 459 (1883); Rosenfeld v. Peoria, D. & E. Ry. Co. (Ind.) 2 North
Eastern Rep. 344 (1885); So. & N. Ala. R. R. Co. v. Henlein, 52 Ala. 606
(1875); s. c. 56 Ala. 368 (1876).   And a stipulation that the value of the
goods shall be estimated at the place of shipment is valid.   Phœnix Ins.
Co. v. Erie & W. Trans. Co., 117 U. S. 314, 322 (1886).

Under such a stipulation, if a part only of the goods should be
damaged, and those not damaged sell for more than the invoice value,
this does not lessen the carrier's liability for the goods which are
damaged, and which, in consequence, sell for less than their invoice
value.   Pearse v. Quebec S. S. Co., 24 Fed. Rep. 285 (1885.)

a carrier may make reasonable regulations on the subject of valuation, and that they are binding if knowledge of them is brought home to the passenger. In the same case it was held that in the absence of such knowledge the regulations were not binding, and that the carrier was liable for the full value of costly laces belonging to the passenger, and contained in trunks having no external indication of their value.[1]

---

[1] N. Y. Central R. R. *v.* Fraloff, 100 U. S. 24 (1879). In Magnin *v.* Dinsmore, 62 N. Y. 35 (1875), the court say: " Where there is no special contract limiting the common law liability of the carrier, nor any notice so specially brought home to the knowledge of the shipper as to have that effect, the shipper is not bound to disclose the value of the goods unless he is asked thereof by the carrier." *Cf.* Hart *v.* Penn. R. R., 112 U. S. 331 (1884).

In the Fraloff case the plaintiff, who was a woman of large wealth and high social position, visited America. She brought with her six trunks of ordinary travel worn appearance, containing wearing apparel, including valuable dresses and laces which she had been accustomed to wear on different occasions. She delivered to the carrier at Albany for transportation as her baggage, to Niagara Falls, two of these trunks, which contained the larger portion of her laces. During the transit, the locks of one of the trunks was broken, and more than 200 yards of lace abstracted. The main contention of the carrier was that good faith required the passenger when delivering her trunks for transportation, to inform its agents of the peculiar character and extraordinary value of the laces in question, and that her failure in that respect, whether intentional or not, was in itself a fraud upon the carrier which would prevent any recovery.

The Supreme Court held that in the absence of legislation limiting the responsibility of the carriers for the baggage of passengers, as well as of reasonable regulations upon the subject by the carrier himself, of which the passenger has knowledge, and also in the absence of inquiry of the passenger as to the value of the articles carried, the mere failure of the passenger to disclose the value of his baggage is not a fraud upon the carrier which defeats all right of recovery.

On the question whether in a given case the quantity and value of the passenger's baggage is reasonable or not, due consideration must be given to the circumstances of the individual, his wealth, social position and the peculiar objects of his journey, and while the carrier is not to be made responsible for such unusual articles as the exceptional fancies, habits or idiosyncrasies of some particular individual may prompt him to carry, still he is liable for what persons in his station or pursuit in life usually carry for their comfort, convenience and gratification upon such journeys.

This case distinctly concedes that the carrier may make reasonable regulations on this subject, which will be binding if brought home to

The same rule of construction applies to contracts or notices by which it is sought to limit the amount of the carrier's liability, as to those by which he attempts to limit the liability altogether.   In either case he is liable to the full amount of the damages for injury or loss caused by the negligence of his servants, unless the intention that he shall not be liable for negligence is distinctly expressed.   No general words will suffice for this purpose.[1]

Where the direction, C. O. D. $292, was written on the face of the bill of lading, it was held that this was sufficient notice to the carrier of the value of the goods shipped.   The bill of lading contained the usual clause that the article was valued at $50, unlesss otherwise stated therein.[2]

_____

the knowledge of the shipper; and so the Supreme Court of North Carolina said, Smith *v.* North Carolina R. R., 64 N. C. 235 (1870), "They may reasonably qualify their liability for the loss of brittle, perishable, or unusually valuable articles."

[1] Wescott *v.* Fargo, 61 N. Y. 542 (1875); affg. s. c. 6 Lansing 319 (1872).   The fact that there are other clauses in the contract exempting the carrier from liability for loss from certain specified perils, occasioned by the negligence of his servants is immaterial.   The clause limiting the liability as to amount must be construed by itself.   At p. 554, the court say : " ' Nor shall this company be liable for any loss or damage of any box, package, or thing for over fifty dollars, unless the just and true value thereof is herein stated.'   There is in this phraseology no such clear and distinct expression of exemption from loss by negligence as the case of Magnin *v.* Dinsmore requires, and it has been already shown that there was, as in that case, sufficient evidence of negligence to justify a finding to that effect."   s. p., Black *v.* Goodrich Trans. Co., 55 Wis. 319 (1882); Magnin *v.* Dinsmore, 56 N. Y. 168 (1874).   See the fuller statement of this case Chapter IX; Vroman *v.* American Ex. Co., 5 Thomps. & Cook (N. Y.), 22; s. c. 2 Hun, 512 (1874); Prentice *v.* Decker, 49 Barb. (N. Y.) 21 (1867); Smith *v.* N. Y. Central R. R., 29 Barb. (N. Y.) 132 (1859); Indianapolis & C. R. R. Co. *v.* Cox, 29 Ind. 360 (1868).   This was a case of passenger's baggage.   The limitation sought to be effected was stamped on the baggage check.

[2] Van Winkle *v.* Adams Express Co., 3 Robt. N. Y. 59 (1864).   In Wilson *v.* Freeman, 3 Campb. 527 (1814), it was held that verbal notice to the carrier's agent of the value of the goods accompanied with an offer to pay whatever sum should be required as freight was sufficient

The carrier may, by agreement, limit his liability for articles of a fragile nature, the character of which is not marked upon them, or which are not securely packed;[1] and for articles of especial value, such as jewelry[2] or musk.[3]

After considerable discussion it is settled that the word article, in a bill of lading containing such a limitation, means a package, and not each piece or thing contained in such package.[4]

---

to charge the carrier with liability for the full value of the goods notwithstanding a notice by him to the contrary. So in Down v. Fromont, 4 Campb. 40 (1814), it was held that if the goods delivered were obviously worth over the amount limited in the notice no express statement of their value was necessary.

[1] Boorman v. Am. Ex. Co., 21 Wis. 152 (1866). In this case the question as to the effect of negligence was not decided.

[2] The Bermuda, 23 Blatchf. 554; s. c. 27 Fed. Rep. 476 (1885); affd. 29 Fed. Rep. 399 (1886).

[3] The Denmark, 27 Fed. Rep. 141 (1886). In this case the question as to the effect of negligence did not arise.

[4] Wetzell v. Dinsmore, 54 N. Y. 496 (1873); Wyld v. Pickford, 8 Mees. & Wels. 443 (1844); Berntein v. Baxendale, 6 Comm. B. (N. S.) 251 (1859); Henderson v. London & N.W. R. L. R. Co., 5 Exch. 90 (1870); Baxendale v. Great E. R. L. R. Co., 4 Qu. B. 244 (1869).

In Boscowitz v. Adams Ex. Co., 93 Ill. 523 (1879), it was held that a stipulation in an express receipt for 3 bales that the company is not to be liable "for any loss or damage of any box, package, or thing for over $50," means $50 for each bale or package.

In Wetzell v. Dinsmore, defendant received a package containing three cases of pills worth $113.50 per case. The receipt contained a clause that the holder should not demand more than $50 for any loss or damage at which "the article forwarded" is valued, and which shall constitute the limit of the liability of the company. The three cases were separately addressed to plaintiffs and were wrapped up with a proper cover in a single package similarly addressed. But one of the cases reached plaintiffs. Held, that "the article forwarded" was the single package, and that plaintiff's were not entitled to recover $50 upon each of the missing cases. Had each case to defendant's knowledge contained a different kind of drug, whether the same rule would have been applied, quere.

In Wyld v. Pickford, the carrier gave notice to the shipper that he would not be responsible for the loss or damage to the goods unless a higher than the ordinary rate of insurance be paid for the carriage. The shipper delivered the goods after receiving this notice. It was held that this amounted to a special contract to carry the goods on the terms

A different rule had been laid down by the New York Common Pleas, and by the U. S. Circuit Court for the Southern District of New York,[1] but these cases can no longer be considered as authority.

Where the bill of lading provided that the carrier should not be liable for more than the invoice value of the goods, it was held that this did not mean liable to pay more damage than the invoice value of the goods shipped, but that the carrier would not be liable for more than the invoice value of the particular goods damaged.[2]

---

stated, but that the carrier was not exempted thereby from all responsibility; but was bound to take ordinary care in the carriage of the goods, and liable not only for any act which would amount to a total abandonment of his character of a carrier, or for willful negligence, but also for a conversion by a mis-delivery arising from the failure to exercise ordinary care.

[1] Earle *v.* Cadmus, 2 Daly, 237 (1867); Hopkins *v.* Westcott, 6 Blatchf. 64 (1868). The latter decision was by Judge Smalley at Nisi Prius.

[2] Pearse *v.* The Quebec Steamship Co., 24 Fed. Rep. 285 (1885); see Brown *v.* Cunard S. S. Co., 16 North E. Rep. 717 (1888) Mass.

In the latter case it was held that although, after damage, the goods are still worth the invoice value, the actual damage up to the amount of the invoice value must be paid.

CHAPTER VI.

TIME AND MANNER OF PRESENTING CLAIMS.

The carrier may lawfully, by contract with the shipper, regulate the time within which claims against himself must be presented, and limit his liability to cases in which the claim shall be presented within the time stipulated by the contract.[1] But the contract will not be enforced unless its terms afford to the shipper a reasonable opportunity to present his claim.[2]

---

[1] Express Co. v. Caldwell, 21 Wall. 264 (1874); Southern Ex. Co. v. Hunnicutt, 54 Miss. 566 (1877); U. S. Ex. Co. v. Harris, 51 Ind. 127 (1875); Weir v. Express Co., 5 Phila. 355 (1864); Southern Express Co. v Glenn, 16 Lea (Tenn.), 472 (1886); Lewis v. Great Western R. Co., 5 H. & N. 867; s. c. 29 L. J. Exch. 425 (1860). Similar clauses (30 days) in policies of insurance are held valid. Steen v. Niagara Fire Ins. Co., 89 N. Y. 315 (1882); Wilkinson v. First Nat. Fire Ins. Co., 72 N. Y. 499 (1878). So they are in telegraph contracts. Cole v. Western Union Tel. Co., 33 Minn. 227; s. c. 22 N. W. Rep. 385 (1885); Wolf v. Western Union Telegraph Co., 62 Penn. 83 (1869); Young v. Western Union Tel. Co., 34 N. Y. Super. Ct. 390 (1872).

[2] Missouri Pacific R. Co. v. Harris, 67 Texas, 166 (1886). There is some conflict in the authorities as to what will be a reasonable time. This depends primarily upon the circumstances of each case. In Express Co. v. Caldwell, 21 Wall. 264 (1874), the time limit of ninety days from delivery to the carrier was held a reasonable one. But the court put this on the ground that the time for the transit was short—only one day. Such a clause was held invalid in Porter v. Southern Express Co., 4 So. Car. 135 (1872). A clause limiting the time to 30 days was held invalid in Southern Express Co. v. Caperton, 44 Ala. 101 (1870). A similar clause was held to be reasonable and valid in Hirshberg v. Dinsmore, 12 Daly (N. Y.), 429 (1884); Smith v. Dinsmore, 9 Daly (N. Y.), 188 (1880); Kaiser v. Hoey, 1 N. Y. Supp. 429 (1888). A clause limiting the time to five days from the loss was held valid in Chicago & Alton R. R. v. Simms, 18 Ill. App. 68 (1885); Dawson v. St. Louis, K. C. & N. R. Co., 76 Mo. 514 (1882). Forty days after occurrence of damage were held to be a reasonable time in Gulf, C. & S. F. Ry. Co. v. Trawick, 68 Texas, 314 (1887). On the other hand in the same State, a limitation of sixty days from shipment was held unreasonable. Pacific Ex. Co. v. Darnell, 6 S. W. Rep. 765 (1887). The reason-

So also the carrier and shipper may lawfully contract to limit the liability of the carrier to cases in which a

---

ableness of such a condition was admitted in Glenn *v.* So. Exp. Co., 86 Tenn. 594; s. c. 8 S. W. Rep. 152 (1888), but it was held that if the omission to present the claim within the stipulated time was not caused by any fault or negligence of the owner of the goods he could recover. A mere custom as to presenting claims will not limit the shipper's right, unless he had a reasonable opportunity to present his claim. Missouri Pac. R. Co. *v.* Fagan (Texas), 9 S. W. Rep. 749 (1888). Seven days from delivery to the consignee were held to be a reasonable time in Lewis *v.* Great Western R. Co., 5 H. & N. 867; s. c. 29 L. J. Exch. 425 (1860). In Weir *v.* Express Co., 5 Phila. 355 (1864), the limitation for presentation of claims was "within thirty days after the time when said property has or ought to have been delivered." The court say: "This is a very reasonable and proper provision to enable the defendants, while the matter is still fresh, to institute proper inquiries and furnish themselves with evidence on the subject. The defendants do a large business, and to allow suits to be brought against them, without such notice, at any length of time, would be to surrender them bound hand and foot to almost every claim which might be made. It would be next to impossible when a thousand packages, large and small, are forwarded by them daily, to ascertain anything about the loss of one of them at a distance of six months or a year."

In Porter *v.* Southern Ex. Co., the court said : " The view of this clause, taken by the defendants, is, that it operates as a limitation on that part of the contract that requires the delivery at the designated point of the same articles delivered to the defendant for conveyance. The effect of this would be that by the terms of the contract the defendants would be bound in general terms to deliver to the plaintiffs at a certain point, and yet the plaintiffs would not be entitled to enforce such obligation unless demand therefor was made within ninety days. It is not to be presumed that language employed in a contract was intended to impose obligations on one of the contracting parties, and yet not to create rights of a corresponding character in the other party. Certainly language that will reasonably bear any other construction should not be allowed to have such effect. If the construction contended for by the defendants is sound, then the ninety days clause was intended to operate with force and effect like that of the Statute of Limitations upon the plaintiff's right of action arising on a breach of the express contract to convey and deliver. We must exclude all other reasonable constructions before ascribing to the parties such an intent."

In a case where the goods were to be transported from Indiana to Georgia and the country was in an unsettled condition, it was held that a condition that the claim must be presented within thirty days after date of receipt by the carrier was unreasonable and invalid. Adams Express Co. *v.* Reagan, 29 Ind. 21 (1867).

A condition printed on a telegraph blank "that no claim for damages shall be valid unless presented in writing within twenty days from

claim for damages shall be presented in the manner prescribed by the contract.   A stipulation is valid which requires that claims for damages shall be presented at the
time the goods or cattle are received by the consignee or
before they are mingled with other goods or cattle.[1]

---

sending the message," was held reasonable and valid, in Heimann *v.*
Western Union Tel. Co., 57 Wis. 562 (1883). In the same case it was
held that delay in delivering the message, though occasioned by a mistake of the company, would not extend the time for presenting a claim
for damages, if a reasonable time was left after knowledge of the mistake, to present the claim. It was also held that the reasonableness of
the time fixed by the contract was a question of law to be determined
by the courts.

[1] A clause requiring goods to be examined before leaving the station,
as applied to a car load of cotton is not reasonable.   Capehart *v.* Seabord
& R. R. R., 81 No. Car. 438 (1879); overruling s. c. 77 No. Car. 355
(1877); Owen *v.* Louisville & N. R. R. (Ky.) 9 S. W. Rep. 698 (1888);
Rice *v.* Kansas Pacific R. Co., 63 Mo. 314 (1876); Sprague *v.* Missouri
Pacific R. Co., 34 Kans. 347 (1885); Goggin *v.* The Kansas Pac. Ry.
Co., 12 Kansas, 416 (1874). In this latter case there were special circumstances which somewhat restrain the full effect otherwise to be
given to the decision.   The stipulation was that "no claim for loss or
damage on live stock will be allowed unless the same is made in writing,
before or at the time the stock is unloaded."   The owner was well aware
of their condition when delivered to him, yet did not then, nor for
more than a year thereafter, make any demand in writing, for damage
sustained.   He signed the contract under protest after the cattle were
in the car, and verbally notified the servants of the company of the
damage before the cattle were unloaded ; and immediately after sought
for writing materials to make out a written notice to serve on the agents
of the company, but before he was able to find the materials and write
the notice, the cattle were unloaded, so that no notice was given.   The
court say: " It is no excuse for not performing a contract, that it was
signed under protest.   The plaintiff had his option to have his cattle
transported at the usual rates, and hold the company responsible as a
common carrier, or at special rates on lower terms, and with less responsibility on the part of the carrier. . . . Neither is the reason for not
giving the written notice sufficient. If the contract stipulation as to
written notice is valid, then the inability to procure writing materials at
the instant of unloading of the cattle, is no excuse for not giving notice
for more than a year afterward. . . .   The stipulation as to notice
contravenes no statute. The parties were competent to make the contract, and did make it, and it must be held good unless it is contrary to
public policy. . . .   The defendant was engaged in transporting
great numbers of cattle over its road, which were shipped further to
market, or so commingled with other stock that it would be impossible
to distinguish one carload from another, unless attention was called to

Such a restriction would not, however, apply to a claim for latent injuries, provided the claim were presented within a reasonable time after the discovery of the injury.[1] So a stipulation is valid that claims for loss or damage shall not be allowed or sued for unless written notice of the loss is given to the carrier.[2] But in such case it has

them immediately, and the object of the notice was to relieve the company from false and fictitious claims, by having an inspection of the cattle before they were removed or mingled with other cattle, and proper damages ascertained and allowed, of which reasons the plaintiff had full knowledge, and still chose to ship at reduced special rates. The reasons are cogent, and we are unable to see how it contravenes public policy that a special contract at reduced rates should stipulate that reasonable notice of injury should be given. . . . But such a contract should be reasonable, and not such as to be a snare or fraud upon the public. What is a reasonable time must depend upon many circumstances. In this case the plaintiff accompanied the cattle, feeding and superintending them, and by his reply admits that he knew of the injury at the time of the unloading, and could have given the notice immediately had he chosen to do so. Unless the notice was given immediately it would be of no value to the defendant. Under these circumstances, we cannot hold that the time when the notice was to be given was unreasonable. Of course it is not understood by the phrase 'before or at the time the stock is unloaded,' that it must be the identical moment, but so immediately that the object sought by the notice can be attained. Nor would such a notice be reasonable in the case of an ordinary shipper who did not accompany and superintend his stock, nor would it probably prevent a recovery for injuries sustained which could not readily be seen, and actually should not be discovered till the time for giving the notice had expired. Yet, in such a case, good faith would require notice so soon as the injury was known."

A stipulation that no recovery for injuries to live stock shall be had unless notice of the claim be " given to some officer of the carrier or its nearest station agent before said stock is delivered from its place of destination or place of delivery to the shipper, and before said stock is mingled with other stock," was held unreasonable and ambiguous in Smitha v. Louisville & N. R. R., 86 Tenn. 198; s. c. 6 S. W. Rep. 209 (1887).

[1] Memphis & Charleston R. R. v. Holloway, 9 Baxter (Tenn.), 188 (1877). In this case the loss occurred from the abstraction of goods from a box, and could not be ascertained at the time of delivery. Ormsby v. Union Pacific R. Co., 4 Fed. Rep. 170, 706 (1880). This was a case of illness of live stock.

[2] Hirshberg v. Dinsmore, 12 Daly (N. Y.), 429 (1884); Chicago & Alton R. R. v. Simms, 18 Ill. App. 68 (1885); and see Smitha v. Louisville & N. R. R., note 1, *ante*, pp. 125, 126.

been held that the carrier must show that he had an officer
to whom the notice could be given, and at the place at
which the contract required it to be given.[1] The contract
of the first carrier may lawfully provide that all claims
for damages shall be presented at the office of shipment
with the carrier's receipt or bill of lading attached within
a specified time. In case the claim is against one of the
connecting lines, the clause as to presentation at the place
of shipment is not to be understood literally. In such
case the claim may be presented to some agent or officer
of the company against which the claim is made.[2] This
limitation as to the time within which claims must be
presented cannot be effected by a mere notice.[3] Such a
clause will not be extended so as to apply to cases where
the injury is shown to have been caused by the carrier's
negligence, unless so expressed in terms.[4] A contract is
frequently made that the carrier will transport goods from
the vendor to the vendee, collect the price and remit the
same to the vendor. A stipulation that a claim for loss
of the goods must be presented within a specified time
has no application to the agreement contained in the same
contract to collect and remit the price, and a failure to
present, within the time so specified, the claim for a breach

---

[1] Good v. Galveston, H. & S. A. R. Co. (Texas), 11 S. W. Rep. 854
(1889); Missouri Pacific R. Co. v. Harris, 67 Texas, 166 (1886). These
cases overrule Missouri Pac. R. Co. v. Harris, 1 Texas Ct. App.
§ 1257 (1882); Texas Central R. R. v. Morris, 1 *Ibid*, § 374 (1883).

[2] U. S. Ex. Co. v. Harris, 51 Ind. 127 (1875).

[3] Browning v. Long Island R. R., 2 Daly (N. Y.), 117 (1867). In
this case the time specified (10 days) was held unreasonable.

[4] Vroman v. American M. U. Ex. Co., 5 Thomp. & Cook (N. Y.),
22; s. c. 2 Hun, 512 (1874); Westcott v. Fargo, 6 Lansing (N. Y.), 319;
s. c. 63 Barb. 349 (1872). This latter case was affirmed in the Commission of Appeals, 61 N. Y. 542 (1875), on the ground that a defense
under this clause must be specially pleaded. A different rule of pleading prevails in Indiana. There it is held that the defense is available
on demurrer. U. S. Exp. Co. v. Harris, 51 Ind. 127 (1875). It is,
however, to be observed that in the latter cases the special contract was
set out in the complaint.

of the latter agreement is no bar to a recovery.[1] In such contracts a clause is frequently added that the liability of the carrier while the goods are in its possession for the purpose of making such collection, shall be that " of warehouseman."   The two clauses should be construed together, and the time within which a claim must be presented for a failure to return the goods after the vendee has refused or neglected to pay for them, does not begin to run until such neglect or refusal.[2]

If the contract provide that an action upon it must be brought within sixty days after the loss, the time will not be extended by negotiations for a settlement, even though only twelve days remain after these are terminated.   In such case a failure to sue within the sixty days from the loss is a bar to a recovery.[3]   Still there seems no good reason to doubt that the same liberal rules which have been applied to suits upon policies of insurance will be applied to suits against carriers, and that the same conduct which has been held to amount to a waiver in the one case, will be given the like effect in the other.   Thus

---

[1] McNichol v. Pacific Ex. Co., 12 Mo. App. 401 (1882).   In such cases there are really two separate and distinct undertakings by the carrier, one to transport and deliver the goods, the other to collect and remit the price.

[2] Smith v. Dinsmore, 9 Daly (N. Y.), 188 (1880).   In this case the clauses under consideration were as follows: "In no event shall the Adams Express Company be liable for any loss or damage unless the claim therefor shall be presented to them in writing at their office within thirty days after the date of the bill of lading in a statement to which the receipt given to the shipper shall be annexed."   "If any sum of money, besides the charge for transportation, is to be collected from the consignee on delivery of the above described property, and the same is not paid within thirty days from the date of the bill of lading, the shipper agrees that this company may return said property to him at the expiration of that time, subject to the conditions of this receipt, and that he will pay the charges for transportation both ways; and that the liability of this company for such property while in its possession, for the purpose of making such collection, shall be that of warehouseman only."

[3] Thompson v. Chicago & Alton R. R., 22 Mo. App. 321 (1886).

it is held that if the contract requires that the claim be presented in writing, and it is presented orally, and no objection on that account is made by the carrier, the requirement as to writing is waived.[1]   And it has been held that the time is to be reckoned, not from the day when the loss occurs, but from the day when it is ascertained.[2] This last is a most reasonable decision.   It interprets the contract, not literally, but according to what may fairly be supposed to have been the intention of the parties when they made it.   This is the true rule of construction.[3]

Such stipulations, like all those which seek to limit a right of action, must be definite in order to be effective.   A clause which provides not that no claim shall be valid unless presented within a specified time, but merely that it must be presented within that time in order to receive attention, is ineffective.[4]

---

[1] Bennet *v.* Northern Pacific Ex. Co., 12 Oreg. 49 (1885); Rice *v.* Kansas Pacific R. Co. 63 Mo. 314 (1876).

[2] Ghormley *v.* Dinsmore, 51 N. Y. Super. Ct. 196 (1885).

[3] See Owen *v.* Louisville & N. R. R. (Ky.), 9 S. W. Rep. 698 (1888). An excuse for not presenting the claim within the time stipulated may be a question for the jury.   Glenn *v.* Southern Exp. Co., 86 Tenn. 594; s. c. 8 S. W. Reporter, 152 (1888).

[4] Dunn *v.* Hannibal & St. Jo. R. R., 68 Mo. 268 (1878).   In Sanford *v.* Housatonic R. R., 11 Cushing (Mass.), 155 (1853), the contract contained the clause : "Consignees of goods by this line are requested to notice any errors in regard to this line within twenty-four hours, or the company will consider their liability as ended."   This was held not to limit the liability of the carrier.   But the decision was placed partly on the ground that the consignee could not possibly, within the time specified, ascertain upon what line the loss occurred.

CHAPTER VII.

THE CARRIER'S RIGHT TO MAKE REASONABLE RULES AND REGULATIONS.

A common carrier may make reasonable rules and regulations for the convenient transaction of business between himself and those dealing with him, either as passengers or shippers, and thus to some extent limit his common law liability. The cases in which the carrier's liability may be limited by contract have already been considered. But there are certain rules which a carrier may make, and of which the passenger or shipper is bound to take notice, either absolutely or when proper measures have been taken to call attention to them. Of these the one absolute qualification seems to be that they should be reasonable.[1]

---

[1] Marriott v. London & S. W. R. Co., 1 C. B. (N. S.) 499 (1857); Garton v. Bristol & N. W. R. Co., 6 C. B. (N. S.) 639; s. c. 95 Eng. Comm. L. 639 (1859); Crouch v. London & N. W. R. Co., 14 C. B. 255; s. c. 78 Eng. Comm. L. 255 (1854); McRae v. Wilmington & W. R. R., 88 N. Car. 526; s. c. 43 Am. Rep. 745 (1883); South Fla. R. Co. v. Rhoads (Fla.), 3 Lawyer's Rep. Ann. 374 (1889); Sandford v. R. R. Co., 24 Penn. 378 (1855). In this case it was held that the power given by the charter of a railway company to regulate the transportation upon its road, did not give the right to grant exclusive privileges to a particular Express Company. The court said, page 383: "If it [the company] possessed this power it might build up one set of men and destroy others; advance one kind of business and break down another, and might make even religion and politics the tests in the distribution of its favors. . . . The rights of the people are not subject to any such corporate control."

Rogers Locomotive Works v. Erie R. Co., 5 C. E. Green (N. J.), 379 (1869); State v. Hartford & N. H. R. R., 29 Conn. 538 (1861). In this latter case the court held that a regulation made by the carrier in favor of a connecting railroad, excluding it from making its usual connections with a steamboat line was void, and that the carrier could be compelled by mandamus to deliver freight and transport passengers

The reasonableness of the rule generally depends upon the facts of the particular case. Where its reasonableness is in doubt, the burden of showing that the rule is reasonable is on the carrier.[1] Any general language in the carrier's charter giving him the power to establish rules and regulations will, however, be limited by the remaining portions of the charter so as to exclude the power to make rules inconsistent with his duties as a common

---

to the steamboat wharf to which its tracks extended. See the language of the court in National Docks R. Co. *v.* Central R. R., 32 N. J. Eq. 755 (1880).

On the other hand it was well said by the court in State *v.* Chovin, 7 Iowa, 204, 208 (1858): "All regulations will be deemed reasonable which are suitable to enable the company to perform the duties it undertakes, and to secure its own just rights in such employment; and also such as are necessary and proper to insure the safety and promote the comfort of passengers."

To the same effect is Commonwealth *v.* Power, 7 Metc. 596 (1844).

The law on the general subject under consideration was thus stated in Vedder *v.* Fellows, 20 N. Y. 126, 131 (1859): "I do not agree that the passengers upon our railroads deprive themselves of the right to complain of an unreasonable practice by voluntarily taking seats in the cars. The railroads are public institutions established by law for public accommodation. They have, except where they adjoin or are near navigable rivers, superseded all other extensive ways of conveyance, and have thus rendered travelers and owners of freight in a great measure dependent upon their means of locomotion. The companies have thus public duties to perform, and they ought not to, and in my opinion they cannot legally, subject either passengers or freight owners to regulations that are palpably unreasonable."

In England a contract which entirely discharges the carrier from all liability is unreasonable and void. McManus *v.* Lancashire & Y. R. Co., 4 H. & N. 327 (1859); Gregory *v.* West Midland R. Co., 2 H. & C. 944 (1864).

But where a carrier undertakes the whole carriage the shipper is not bound by the rules of a second carrier over whose route the goods are forwarded. Railroad Co. *v.* Pratt, 22 Wall. 123 (1874).

A rule which requires a passenger who has put too much fare in a lock-box to go to the end of the route to correct his mistake is unreasonable, if it can be corrected on the spot as by the fare of another passenger. Corbett *v.* Twenty-third St. R. Co., 42 Hun (N. Y.), 587 (1886).

In Hicks *v.* Hannibal & St. J. R. R., 68 Mo. 329 (1878), it was held, the rule or regulation, if relied on as a defense, must be pleaded.

[1] Peek *v.* N. Staffordshire R. Co., 10 H. of L. Ca. 473 (1862); Marriott *v.* London & S. W. R. Co., 1 C. B. (N. S.) 499 (1857).

carrier.[1] The reasonableness of a rule adopted by a carrier is a question of law to be decided by the court.[2] If, however, the facts were in dispute the question would become a mixed question of law and fact to be decided by the jury under proper instructions from the court.

SECTION I.

PROCURING TICKETS BEFORE ENTERING THE CARS

A railroad company has the right to require a passenger to procure and pay for a ticket before entering the car.[3]

---

[1] Chicago & N. W. R. R. *v*. People, 56 Ill. 365 (1870). This was an appeal from a judgment of mandamus, requiring a railroad company to deliver to the consignee, grain consigned to a particular elevator upon its line. Held that a contract or regulation made by the carrier to deliver grain only to certain elevators was inconsistent with its duty as a carrier, and therefore void; but that the carrier could not be compelled to deliver to elevators not upon its line, though upon a line of road with which it commonly connected. The court said, p, 383:

"It is claimed by counsel that the charter of respondent authorizes it to make such contracts and regulations as might be necessary in the transactions of its business. But, certainly, we cannot suppose the legislature intended to authorize the making of such rules or contracts as would defeat the very object it had in view in granting the charter. The company can make such rules and contracts as it pleases, not inconsistent with its duties as a common carrier, but it can go no further, and any general language which its charter may contain must necessarily be construed with that limitation. . . . The principle that a railroad company can make no injurious or arbitrary discrimination between individuals in its dealings with the public, not only commends itself to our reason and sense of justice, but is sustained by adjudged cases."

[2] South Florida R. Co. *v*. Rhoads (Fla.), 3 Lawy. Rep. Ann. 734 (1889); Illinois Cent. R. Co. *v*. Whittemore, 43 Ill. 420 (1867); Vedder *v*. Fellows; 20 N. Y. 126 (1859); Louisville, N. & G. S. R. Co. *v*. Fleming, 14 Lea, 128; s. c. 18 Am. & Eng. R. Cas. 347 (1884); Pierce *v*. Randolph, 12 Texas, 290 (1854). See *post*, Ch. VII, sect. 6.

[3] Burlington & M. R. R. *v*. Rose, 11 Neb. 177 (1881); State *v*. Goold, 53 Me. 279 (1865). In this case the court said (p. 281): " Railroad corporations have an undoubted right to fix and determine the rates of fare on their roads within the limits specified in their charters or by existing laws. They have also an undoubted right to make reasonable regulations as to the time, place and mode of collecting the same from passengers. They may reasonably require payment before the arrival of the train at the station where the passenger is to leave the

The existence of such a regulation will not be presumed. It must be proved by the carrier.[1] It is reasonable to enforce this regulation by requiring passengers who have not purchased tickets to pay in the car a sum additional to that usually required.[2] This regulation is sometimes put in the form of a charge made to those paying in the car which is in addition to the usual fare fixed by the company. Sometimes it is put in the form of a

---

cars. We see no reason to question their right to require payment in advance, to be made at a convenient office, and at convenient times; certainly, where there is no positive interdict to entering the cars without a ticket, as in this case. There is neither hardship nor unfairness toward the passenger who, ordinarily, can pay his fare and procure his ticket without trouble or delay, at the office. But to the company it is something more important than mere convenience that such regulations should be enforced. It is important in simplifying accounts. It is important to promote and secure safety, by allowing time to the conductor to attend to his proper duties on the train, and which would be often seriously interfered with if his time was taken up in collecting fares and exchanging money and answering questions. It is highly important as a check against mistakes or fraud on the part of the conductors, and as a guard against imposition by those seeking a passage from one station to another without payment." St. Louis, Alton & T. H. R. R., 43 Ill. 176 (1867); Hilliard v. Goold, 34 N. H. 230 (1856); Crocker v. New London, W. & P. R. R., 24 Conn. 249 (1855).

In Stephen v. Smith, 29 Vermont, 160 (1857), the court said (p. 163): "The discrimination in fare which is made by this company when tickets are purchased at the several stations, or when paid the conductor in the cars, is reasonable, as affording proper checks upon its accounting officers, and which they have a right to enforce. While the law requires of the company the adoption of such regulations as are necessary for the safety and convenience of passengers in their trains, they have also the right to adopt such reasonable regulations as are necessary for their own security; and these regulations are to be mutually observed. If they are not complied with by passengers, the company may not only refuse them admission within the cars, but if they are within they may remove them." Southern Kansas R. Co. v. Hinsdale, 38 Kans. 507; s. c. 16 Pac. Rep. 937 (1888).

[1] Avery v. Atchison, Topeka & S. F. R. R., 11 Kans. 448 (1873).

[2] R. R. Co. v. Skillman, 39 Ohio St. 444 (1883); Toledo W. & W. R. Co. v. Wright, 68 Ind. 586 (1879); State v. Chovin, 7 Iowa, 204 (1858); Chicago, B. & Q. R. R. v. Parks, 18 Ill. 460 (1857). In the last case it was held that a passenger who had paid one such additional charge to be carried to one station and decided there to go on, could be lawfully charged another.

deduction from the nominal fare made to those buying tickets at the station.[1]

In both cases the substance of the regulation is identical, and would undoubtedly be so considered by the courts unless the form were made material by some Statute, fixing the highest rate of fare per mile which the carrier can charge. Such Statutes generally contain a provision that a sum in addition to this legal rate may be charged to those who do not buy tickets before entering the cars, provided that a reasonable opportunity to purchase a ticket has been afforded before the departure of the train.[2]

In the absence of such a proviso, the rate charged in the cars must not exceed the statutory rate.[3]

It has been held that in the absence of such a statute the company is under no obligation to keep ticket offices open or afford any opportunity to passengers to purchase tickets at such offices. The same cases hold that in the absence of legislative restriction upon the rate of fare, a carrier may require passengers who are unable to purchase tickets, owing to the office not being open, to pay more in the cars than they would have been obliged to pay at the station.[4]

---

[1] State v. Goold, 53 Me. 279 (1865); Swan v. Manchester & L. R. R., 132 Mass. 116 (1882).

[2] Porter v. N. Y. Central R. R., 34 Barb. (N. Y.) 353 (1861); Nellis v. The Same, 30 N. Y. 505 (1864); Chase v. The Same, 26 N. Y. 523 (1863); Missouri Pacific R. Co. v. McClanahan, 66 Texas, 530 (1886); Everett v. Chicago, R. I. & P. R. Co., 69 Iowa, 15 (1886); Contra, De Lucas v. New Orleans & C. R. R. Co., 38 La. An. 930 (1886).

[3] Smith v. Pittsburg, F. W. & C. R. R., 23 Ohio St. 10 (1872).

[4] Crocker v. New London & W. & P. R. R., 24 Conn. 249 (1855). Bordeaux v. Erie R. Co., 8 Hun (N. Y.), 579 (1876). In this latter case the court, after citing some decisions in actions against the New York Central R. R. Co., said: "These cases were all actions for a penalty given by statute for taking illegal fares. The legal fare fixed by statute allowed said company to require the payment of five cents in addition to such fare, of any passenger who entered the cars without first having purchased a ticket for that purpose, at any station where a ticket office

It is a curious illustration of the American disposition to override individual rights, and subject them to real or imagined public convenience, that the unfortunate passenger who tried to vindicate his rights in Bordeaux *v.* Erie Railway Co., should have been subjected to an unmerciful snubbing by the court.

But other cases and with better reason lay down a different rule, and hold that the company has no right to exact a rate of fare in its cars higher than that charged for tickets at the office, when it deprives a passenger of the power to buy a ticket by keeping the office closed up to the time fixed for the departure of the train;[1] or by

---

is established and open; and said statute required the said company should keep the said office open at least one hour prior to the departure of each passenger train from such station.   But there is no such statute relating to the Erie Railway; and the charge of five cents required when the fare is paid to the conductor, is not an enhancement of the legal fare, but is within the limit of such fare.   On the contrary, the price of tickets sold at the offices is an abatement of the legal fare as fixed where the payment is made on the cars. . . .   How can the plaintiff base a claim to dictate the fare he should pay, upon his failure to find the defendant's ticket office open when he wished to purchase a ticket ? . . .   The courts cannot say when or for how long a time they should open such offices each day or otherwise.   If the plaintiff failed for any cause to procure a ticket, he had no right to get into the defendant's cars, except upon the implied engagement on his part to pay the fare fixed for and required of passengers without tickets."

In the Crocker case, the court held that the establishment of a ticket office, and fixing the rate of fare for persons buying tickets there, was a mere proposal which the company could withdraw at any time, and that it was withdrawn when the ticket office was closed.   This opinion was criticised in Jeffersonville R. R. *v.* Rogers, 28 Ind. 1 (1867); and in St. Louis, A. & C. R. R. *v.* Dalby, 19 Ill. 353 (1857); De Lucas *v.* New Orleans & Carrolton R. R., 38 La. Ann. 930 (1886); Curl *v.* Chicago, R. I. & P. R. Co., 63 Iowa, 417 (1884).

[1] Chicago, B. & Q. R. R. *v.* Parks, 18 Ill. 460 (1857); Chicago & Alton R. R. *v.* Flagg, 43 Ill. 364 (1867); DuLaurans *v.* St. Paul & Pacific R. R., 15 Minn. 49 (1870); Jeffersonville R. R. Co. *v.* Rogers. 38 Ind. 116 (1871); s. c. 28 Ind. 1 (1867); Paine *v.* C., R. I. & P. R. Co., 45 Iowa, 569 (1877).   In Pullman Palace Car Co. *v.* Reed, 75 Ill. 125 (1874), the court say (p. 130): " It is well recognized law, that carriers of passengers may lawfully require those seeking to be carried to purchase tickets, when convenient facilities to that end are afforded by the carrier, to exhibit them to persons designated by the carrier for that purpose, and to surrender them after securing their seats in the car or

not maintaining an office at the station.[1]   Unless the passenger have a reasonable opportunity to buy a ticket the carrier cannot lawfully exact an additional compensation on the ground that he has no ticket.[2]

It would seem that the latter rule is right on principle. The fallacy involved in the opinions of the court in the cases first stated consists in the assumption that there is no limit but the statutory one, to the rate of fares that a carrier may lawfully charge. It is, however, well settled that a carrier cannot lawfully charge more than a reasonable sum for the carriage of goods or passengers.

---

other vehicle used for transportation, when required by the person in immediate charge of the transportation. Such requirements cause but little, if any, inconvenience to the public, and may be indispensable to enable the carrier to protect itself against loss through the knavery of dishonest employees."

In the Jeffersonville case the court say: "If the plaintiff properly applied for a ticket and was unable, from any cause attributable to the company or its agents, to purchase one, he had a right, whatever that cause might have been, to be carried at the ticket rates."

In the Du Laurans case the court held distinctly that the shutting the ticket office did not constitute a withdrawal of the previous offer to carry passengers who should purchase tickets there at a certain fare, and that the company could not take advantage of its own wrong in closing the ticket office, but was bound to keep it open for a reasonable time. What would be a reasonable time to allow passengers an opportunity to procure tickets was held to be a question for the jury under proper instructions from the court.

In Nellis v. N. Y. Central R. R., 30 N. Y. 505 (1864), the court said: "To compel a passenger to pay a penalty because the company had deprived him of the power to travel for the regular fare, would be so oppressive and unjust that it would require a positive provision of a legislative act to induce any tribunal to sanction it. The statute is open to no such construction. The extra fare can only be demanded when the passenger fails to purchase his ticket at an established ticket office that is open. If it is not open, no ticket can be procured, and no right exists to demand the extra fare." In this case the train left at an hour in the night at which the railroad company was not required to open its ticket office. Hall v. South Carolina R. Co., 28 S. Car. 261; s. c. 5 S. Ea. Rep. 623 (1887); Brown v. Kansas City, F. S. & G. R. R., 38 Kans. 634; s. c. 16 Pac. Rep. 942 (1888).

[1] Poole v. Northern Pacific R. R., 16 Oregon, 261 (1888).

[2] Hall v. South Car. R. Co., 28 S. Car. 261; s. c. 5 South East. Rep. 623 (1887).

What in a given case will be a reasonable charge is not always easy to determine. But this much would seem to be clear that, as against the company, the rate it fixes for the price of a ticket from one place to another, is the reasonable compensation for carrying a passenger between the two. Hence it follows that the company cannot lawfully charge more. The cases referred to superadd one qualification to this rule—namely, that the carrier may also charge a reasonable sum for the trouble and risk to which it is put by the payment of fares in the cars, provided it gives a reasonable opportunity to pay them elsewhere. This proviso on principle is just as peremptory in the case of a rate of fare fixed by the company as one fixed by statute. The passenger who refuses to pay this additional sum, when its payment is lawfully required, is in the same plight as if he had refused altogether.

The question whether the carrier is bound to keep the ticket office open after the time fixed for the departure of the train, and until its actual departure, has been much discussed, and the decisions upon it are conflicting.[1] But

---

[1] In Chicago, B. & Q. R. R. v. Parks, 18 Ill. 460 (1857), the court say: "To justify the company in making this discrimination in the fare against the passenger who neglects to purchase a ticket at the company's office, the company must see to it that the fault was not that of its own agent, instead of the passenger. To justify this discrimination every reasonable and proper facility must be afforded the passenger to procure his ticket. They must furnish a convenient and accessible place for the sale of the tickets, with a competent person in attendance ready to sell them, which should be open and accessible to all passengers for a reasonable time before the departure of each train, and up to the time of its actual departure, so that it shall really be a case of neglect, and not of necessity, on the part of the passenger, and not the fault of the company." s. p., St. Louis, A. & C. R. R. v. Dalby, 19 Ill. 353 (1857).

But in St. Louis, Alton & Terre Haute R. R. v. South, 43 Ill. 176 (1867), the court laid down the rule that railroad companies are required to keep open their offices for the sale of tickets to passengers for a reasonable time before the departure of each train, and up to the time fixed by its published rules for its departure, and not up to the time of actual departure. And Breese, J., commenting upon the opinion in Chicago, B. & Q. R. R. v. Parks, 18 Ill. 460 (1857), said:

"In speaking, then, of the time of the actual departure of a train,

if the statute require it "to keep the office open at least one hour prior to the departure of each train," it must keep the office open until the train departs, even though it arrive late.[1]

Some Railroad Companies in America allow passengers to ride on freight trains, but require them in such cases to purchase tickets at a station before entering the train. Such a regulation is reasonable.[2] Even in such a

---

up to which the ticket office must be kept open, the court, unquestionably, meant to be understood as referring to the published fixed time which everybody knew. The presumption being that trains will arrive and depart on the schedule time, which time is notorious, no rule should be established that should apply, without much hardship and great inconvenience, to the departure of trains not on time. We do not recognize any right in any person to apply at a railroad ticket office after the time fixed and published for the departure of a train, and demand the same rights and privileges accorded to those who come at the proper time for their tickets. It is well known that trains are sometimes delayed for hours, and that it is unavoidable. Would it not be going too far to require the companies controlling them, to keep an agent at his post during all this delayed time?" s. p., Swan v. Manchester & L. R. R., 132 Mass. 116 (1882).

In the South case it was also held, that when a passenger willfully neglects to purchase a ticket as required, before entering the train, he cannot be expelled at a place other than a regular station. This ruling was, however, under a special statute of Illinois.

In other cases it has been held that the ticket office should be kept open until the departure of the train. Croker v. New London R. R., 24 Conn. 249 (1855); Hilliard v. Goold, 34 N. H. 230 (1856). The statute of Texas requires the company to keep the office open for half an hour prior to the departure of the train. Missouri Pacific Ry. Co. v. McClanahan, 66 Texas, 530 (1886).

[1] Porter v. N. Y. Central R. R., 34 Barb. (N. Y.) 353 (1861).

[2] Cleveland, Columbus & Cin. R. R. v. Bartram, 11 Ohio St. 457 (1860); Indianapolis, P. & C. R. Co. v. Rinard, 46 Ind. 293 (1874). In the latter case the court said: "Railroad companies may, doubtless, discriminate between the amount of fare where a ticket is purchased and where it is paid upon the train. Perhaps they could make regulations by which no one could be carried at all on trains carrying passengers without having previously procured a ticket. But if they could make such regulations still they would have no right to discriminate between persons, and sell tickets to some and refuse others, without some just cause. A person having duly applied for a ticket and having been refused, without just cause, would have the same right to be carried upon paying, or offering to pay, the ticket rate of fare, as if he had previously purchased a ticket."

case it is held that an opportunity to purchase a ticket must be afforded.[1]

SECTION II.

REQUIRING TICKETS TO BE SHOWN AND SURRENDERED.

A carrier may lawfully require passengers to exhibit their tickets whenever called upon to do so by the conductor of the train, or proper officer of the boat. A refusal to comply with this regulation will justify the carrier in removing the passenger from the train, even though he has paid his fare.[2]

It has been held that the officers of a steamboat were justified in detaining, for a reasonable time, a passenger who refused to produce his ticket, in order to enquire into the facts of the case, and that his having lost his ticket

---

[1] Illinois Central R. R. *v.* Johnson, 67 Ill. 312 (1873); Illinois Central R. R. *v.* Sutton, 53 Ill. 399 (1870); St. Louis & S. E. R. R. *v.* Myrtle, 51 Ind. 566 (1875). In the latter case the court laid down the rule, that a railroad company has a right to adopt a regulation that all persons who travel on a freight train shall procure a ticket before entering the cars; but such a regulation imposes upon the company the duty of having the ticket office open a sufficient length of time before the departure of the train to enable passengers to procure tickets. Notwithstanding such regulation on the part of the company, if a person desiring to take passage upon a freight train, endeavored to procure a ticket but could not do so in consequence of the absence of the agent, he had a right to travel on such train by paying, or offering to pay, the usual fare. See, also, Indianapolis & St. L. R. R. *v.* Kennedy, 77 Ind. 507 (1881).

[2] Louisville, N. & G. S. R. R. *v.* Fleming, 14 Lea (Tenn.), 128 (1884); Willetts *v.* Buffalo & Rochester R. R., 14 Barb. (N. Y.) 585 (1853); Havens *v.* Hartford & N. Haven R. R., 28 Conn. 69 (1859); Hibbard *v.* N. Y. & Erie R. R., 15 N. Y. 455 (1857); De Lucas *v.* New Orleans & Carrolton R. R., 38 La. Ann. 930 (1886); Bennett *v.* Railroad Co., 7 Phil. 11 (1868); Pullman Palace Car Co. *v.* Reed, 75 Ill. 125 (1874). In this latter case, however, the court held that if the conductor knew that the passenger had purchased a ticket and lost it, and that owing to its character (a sleeping car ticket good only for a particular berth and night) there was no danger of its being used by any one else, a removal from the car was unlawful. In the Willets case the refusal to show the ticket was due to the negligence of the father of an insane passenger who left his son in the train unguarded.

furnished no excuse for his not paying his fare again, and that the fact that he was not asked for his ticket on the boat warranted a finding that he knew he was to give it up when he left the boat.[1]

But a carrier cannot imprison or detain a passenger who, after the transit is completed, is unable to produce his ticket. The price of transportation is a debt, and the carrier has no lien on the person of the passenger for this sum.[2]

So the fact that the conductor knows that the passenger has had a ticket,[3] or is in the habit of using a commutation ticket regularly, which has not expired, will not prevent the enforcement of such a regulation.[4]

In such case, however, the commuter is entitled to a reasonable time to search for his ticket, and his expulsion without allowing him such time is unlawful.[5]

In the cases that have arisen in reference to commutation tickets this rule was expressed on their face. But the other authorities already referred to do not rest upon the validity of such a contract, but upon the reasonable-

---

[1] Standish v. Narragansett S. S. Co., 111 Mass. 512 (1873). The weight of authority is that the loss of a ticket does not excuse the passenger from compliance with the rule. In such case he must pay fare or leave the train. Louisville, N. & G. S. R. R. v. Fleming, 14 Lea (Tenn.), 128 (1884). See post, Ch. VII, sect. 9. It was, however, held otherwise in Butler v. Manchester, S. & L. R. Co. (Eng. Court of Appeals), 28 Am. Law Reg. 81 (1888); Jerome v. Smith, 48 Vt. 230 (1876); Cresson v. Philadelphia & R. R. R., 11 Phil. 597 (1875).

[2] Lynch v. Metropolitan Elevated R. Co., 90 N. Y. 77 (1882). In this latter case the regulation of the company was that the ticket should be surrendered as the passenger left its station at the end of his journey. He lost his ticket and refused to pay his fare a second time. It was held that it was unlawful for the company to detain him.

[3] Hibbard v. N. Y. & Erie R. R., 15 N. Y. 455 (1857).

[4] Ripley v. New Jersey R. R. & T. Co., 31 N. J. L. 388 (1866); Downs v. N. Y. & N. Haven R. R., 36 Conn. 287 (1869); Crawford v. Cincinnati, H. & D. R. R., 26 Ohio St. 580 (1875); Cresson v. Philadelphia & R. R. R., 11 Phila. 597 (1875).

[5] Maples v. N. Y. & N. H. R. R., 38 Conn. 557 (1871); Louisville, N. & G. S. R. R. v. Fleming, 14 Lea (Tenn.), 128 (1884). In this latter case the passenger was not a commuter.

ness of the regulation considered as a rule made by the carrier. So a custom which prevails on a railroad, that the conductor should take up the ticket soon after the beginning of the journey, and give the passenger a check instead, is reasonable.[1]

It is also reasonable to require that the passenger should surrender his ticket immediately after leaving the principal stopping place next before his point of destination, though there may be intermediate stations.[2] The reasoning of the opinion in this case is clear and cogent, and should be compared with that of the opinion in State v. Thompson, *infra* (n. 3).

It was held, however, in New Hampshire, that under such circumstances the passenger has a right to refuse to give up his ticket unless he is given a check, and that his expulsion because of such refusal is unlawful.[3] It is believed that this case would have been decided otherwise in those parts of the country where the giving of checks to passengers upon the surrender of their tickets is unusual. The right to such check can hardly depend upon anything but the usage of business.

The right of expulsion for refusing to show a ticket is not limited by statutory requirements in reference to expulsion for non-payment of fare.[4]

So also a rule that a coupon is not receivable for fare, when detached from the principal ticket or book to which it is attached when sold, is valid.[5] It has, however, been

---

[1] Northern R. R. v. Page, 22 Barb. (N. Y.) 130 (1856); Loring v. Aborn, 4 Cush. (Mass.) 608 (1849).

[2] The rule is thus stated in the only opinion reported in Vedder v. Fellows, 20 N. Y. 126 (1859). Some of the Judges concurred, but the point was not decided by the Court. See Pullman Palace Car Co. v. Reed, 75 Ill. 125 (1874).

[3] State v. Thompson, 20 N. H. 250 (1850).

[4] Illinois Central R. R. v. Whittemore, 43 Ill. 420 (1867).

[5] Marshall v. Boston & A. R. R., 145 Mass. 164; s. c. 5 New Eng. Rep. 172 (1887); Louisville, N. & G. S. R. R. v. Harris, 9 Lea (Tenn.),

held that if the two parts have been detached by inadvertence and both are presented at the same time to the conductor, they are valid.[1]

SECTION III.

LIMITING THE TIME OF VALIDITY OF TICKET.

A railroad company has the right to limit the time during which a ticket sold by it shall be valid.[2]

Especially may it do so in the case of a ticket sold at a reduced rate, as, for example, a commutation ticket, even though the number of trips allowed or the distance provided for by it (in case of a mileage ticket) shall not have been traveled.[3]

---

180 (1882); Walker *v.* Dry Dock, E. B. & B. R. R., 33 How. Pr. (N. Y.) 327 (1867); Houston & T. C. R. R. *v.* Ford, 53 Texas, 364 (1880).

[1] Wightman *v.* Chicago & N. W. R. Co., 73 Wis. 169; s. c. 40 N. W. Rep. 689 (1888).

[2] Hill *v.* Syracuse & Binghamton R. R., 63 N. Y. 101 (1875); Elmore *v.* Sands, 54 N. Y. 512 (1874); Wentz *v.* Erie Railway Co., 3 Hun (N. Y.), 241; s. c. 5 Thomps. & Cook, 556 (1874); State *v.* Campbell, 32 N. J. L. 309 (1867); Rawitzky *v.* Louisville & N. R. R. Co., 40 La. Ann. 47; s. c. 3 South Rep. 387 (1888); Barker *v.* Coflin, 31 Barb. (N. Y.) 556 (1860).

The reason given for the decision in the latter case was that it was only in this way that a carrier could protect itself from overloading. The court also say that the ticket with its indorsement was evidence of the contract between the carrier and the passenger, and that the carrier had a "right to make any special contract, not unreasonable or illegal." A mere notice on a ticket, not made known to the passenger, certainly does not constitute a contract with him. Quimby *v.* Vanderbilt, 17 N. Y. 306 (1858); Van Buskirk *v.* Roberts, 31 N. Y. 661 (1864); Rawson *v.* Penn. R. R. Co., 48 N. Y. 212 (1872); Elmore *v.* Sands, 54 N. Y. 512 (1874); Pennington *v.* Phil., W. & B. R. R. Co., 62 Md. 95 (1883).

No doubt the ticket is admissible in evidence with other facts and circumstances to show what the contract really was. Milnor *v.* N. Y. & N. H. R. R. Co., 53 N. Y. 363 (1873). But the rule laid down in the cases cited at the beginning of this note find their true foundation in the right of the carrier to make reasonable rules and regulations for the conduct of its business.

[3] Sherman *v.* Chicago & N. W. R. Co., 40 Iowa, 45 (1874); Powell *v.* Pittsburg, C. & St. L. R. R. Co., 25 Ohio St. 70 (1874); Lillis *v.* St. Louis, K. C. & N. R. Co., 64 Missouri, 464 (1877); Hall *v.* Memphis & C. R. Co. (U. S. C. Ct. W. D. Tenn.), 9 Fed. Rep. 585 (1881).

This time may be limited by a notice printed on the ticket, as for example: " Good for this day only," or " only good for twenty days from this date," if the date on which the ticket is sold be stamped upon the ticket.[1]

A State Legislature may, however, enact that such restrictions as to the time shall be invalid, and that a ticket shall be valid for six years notwithstanding the restriction. Such enactment is binding upon a foreign corporation doing business within the State.[2]

When the question of the validity of the limitation as to time was presented, there was some hesitation on the part of the courts in sustaining its validity unless actual notice of it were brought home to the passenger. In one case the fact is relied upon that the passenger knew that the through rate was less than the aggregate local rates.[3]

But the rule is sustainable—not on the ground of an assent on the part of the passenger constituting a contract—but on the ground that the regulation is a reasonable one which the company has a right to make, and of which it gives the passenger adequate notice by printing it on his ticket.

---

[1] Hill *v.* Syracuse, Bing. & N. Y. R. R. Co., 63 N. Y. 101 (1875); Elmore *v.* Sands, 54 N. Y. 512 (1874). In this case the court say of the carrier: " It had the right to make a rule that every passenger, when he entered the train, should pay his fare or produce a ticket showing his right to ride upon that train. Such a regulation is neither unreasonable nor illegal. It is not an uncommon one, and it is not important that we should perceive all the purposes which it subserves. It is sufficient that it is apparently useful for some purpose. If the ticket be required to be used on the day it is issued, the passenger cannot well use it for more than one trip, and the railroad company will have some information of the number of passengers to provide for on any day." Boice *v.* Hudson R. R. R. Co., 61 Barb. (N. Y.) 611 (1872); Boston & Lowell R. R. Co. *v.* Proctor, 1 Allen (Mass.), 267 (1861); Dietrich *v.* Penn. R. R. Co., 71 Penn. 432 (1872); McClure *v.* Phila., W. & B. R. R. Co., 34 Md. 532 (1871); Rawitzky *v.* Louisville N. Ry. Co., 3 So. Reporter, 387; s. c. 40 La. Ann. 47 (1888).

[2] Dryden *v.* Grand Trunk R. of Canada, 60 Me. 512 (1872).

[3] Shedd *v.* Troy & Boston R. R. Co., 40 Vt. 88 (1868).

This subject will be more fully considered in the eleventh section of this chapter.

Proof of a verbal statement by the ticket seller, after the ticket was sold that it would be good on any day, is not sufficient to extend its validity, in the absence of proof of authority on his part.[1]

A rule that the holder of an excursion ticket must present himself for identification at the office of the company at the terminal station, and that the ticket shall be valid only for a certain time after such identification, is reasonable.[2]

If the passenger begins his transit on the last day on which by its terms the ticket is valid, he has a right to complete it, although the transit is not complete until the following day, and he cannot lawfully be expelled from the train after midnight of the last day on which by its terms the ticket is valid.[3]

If the last day upon which by its terms the ticket can be used is Sunday, and the railroad company whose line completes the transit runs no train on that day the pas-

---

[1] Boice v. Hudson R. R. R. Co., 61 Barb. 611 (1872). See *post*, Ch. VII, sect. 9.

[2] Rawitzky v. Louisville & N. R. Co., 40 La. Ann. 47; s. c. 3 Southern Rep. 387 (1888).

[3] Evans v. St. Louis, Iron Mt. & S. R. Co., 11 Mo App. 463 (1882); Auerbach v. N. Y. Central R. R. Co., 89 N. Y. 281; s. c. 42 Am. Rep. 290; 21 Am. Law Reg. 790 (1882); revg. s. c. 60 How. Pr. 382 (1881); Georgia S. R. R. Co v. Bigelow, 68 Geo. 219 (1881).

It is not enough, however, that the passenger present himself at the station on the last day on which his ticket is valid, if the last train for that day has already left.   Arnold v. Penn. R. R. Co., 115 Penn. 135 (1887).

In Pennsylvania Co. v. Hine, 41 Ohio St. 276 (1884), it was held that the passenger was not entitled to use a ticket after the time limited by the terms printed on its face, although he was unable, owing to the delay of the carrier to use it before   The question as to whether the carrier "was liable for breach of contract because the train East of Pittsburg was so delayed that H. could not enter the train upon which his ticket gave him a right to ride, was not considered."   See *post*, Ch. VII, sect. 9.

senger is entitled to use his ticket on the Monday following.[1]

Indeed it may fairly be questioned whether this should
not be the rule whenever the last day of the term during
which the ticket can be used is a Sunday. It would seem
that the courts should apply to limited tickets the same
rule that has been applied in so many other cases; *e. g.*,
the date on which commercial paper, without days of
grace, is payable; on which a tenant must quit the demised
premises; within which legal papers must be served, and
the like.

SECTION IV.

REGULATING OR LIMITING THE TRIP UPON WHICH A TICKET CAN BE USED.

A carrier has the right to require that a passenger
who breaks his journey should have his ticket indorsed
by the conductor, and can lawfully refuse to accept the
ticket for the remainder of the journey if this regulation
be not complied with.[2]

Not only may the limitations already mentioned be
placed upon the passenger's manner of making his journey, but the carrier may establish a rule that the journey

---

[1] Little Rock & F. S. R. R. *v.* Dean, 43 Ark. 529 (1884).

[2] Beebe *v.* Ayres, 28 Barb. (N. Y.) 275 (1858); Dunphy *v.* Erie R.
Co., 42 N. Y. Superior Ct. Rep. 128 (1877). In this case the rule was
applied by the company to different divisions of its line, and this was
held to be reasonable and valid.

Denny *v.* N. Y. C. & H. R. R., 5 Daly (N. Y.), 50 (1874). In this
case, as also in Beebe *v.* Ayres, the rule hereinafter considered was applied, that a partial waiver would not be extended beyond its precise
terms. Yorton *v.* Milwaukee, L. S. & W. R. Co., 54 Wis. 234 (1882);
s. c. 11 N. W. Rep. 482. In this case the regulation of the company
permitted a passenger who had broken his journey to resume it without
further payment, if he procured from the first conductor a stop-over
check. This the passenger requested, but instead received a trip check.
The conductor of the train on which the passenger resumed his journey
refused to receive this, and ejected him. It was held that this was lawful.

10

shall be continuous, and that a passenger stopping over during its progress shall have no right to proceed further on the same ticket, but must pay fare for the remainder of the route.[1] The passenger may select the train, but when once the transit is commenced he has no right to change to another.[2] In the case of a passenger on a

---

[1] State v. Overton, 24 N. J. Law, 435 (1854); Dietrich v. Penn. R. R., 71 Penn. 432 (1872); Cheney v. Boston & Me. R. R., 11 Metc. (Mass.) 121 (1846); Gale v. Del., L. & W. R. R., 7 Hun (N. Y.), 670 (1876); Churchill v. Chicago & Alton R. R., 3 Am. Railway Rep. 430 (1873); Hatten v. R. R., 39 Ohio St. 375 (1883). In the Dietrich case the court quote with approval the case of State v. Overton. "The question is obviously a question of contract between the passenger and the company. By paying for passage, and procuring a ticket from Newark to Morristown, the passenger acquired the right to be carried from one point to the other without interruption. He acquired no right to be transported from one point to another upon the route, at different times and by different lines of conveyance, until the entire journey was accomplished. The company engaged to carry the passenger over an entire route for a stipulated price. But it was not part of the contract that they would suffer him to leave the train, and resume his seat in another train at any intervening point on the road. If the passenger chose voluntarily to leave the train before reaching his destination, he forfeited all rights under his contract. The company did not engage and were not bound to carry him in any other train, or at any other time, over the residue of the route."

[2] Gale v. Del., L. & W. R. R., 7 Hun, 670 (1876). In this case the court say: "After the plaintiff had commenced his journey on the train which he elected to take, he had the legal right to be carried to New York by that train, and the company was under legal obligations to carry him by that train. This right was reciprocal; that is, the defendant had a legal right to insist that the plaintiff's journey should be continued until it was completed, and that it should not be required to perform it in fragments."

Terry v. Flushing, N. S. & C. R. R., 13 Hun (N. Y.), 359 (1878); Stone v. Chicago & N. W. R. Co., 47 Iowa, 82 (1877). This was held in a case where the passenger was, by accident, left behind at a station, and sought to resume his journey on the next train, and tendered to the conductor a passage check that had been given him by the conductor of the previous train. This had, however, been intended simply for the conductor's convenience in collecting and assorting tickets. Breen v. Texas & Pacific R. R., 50 Texas, 43 (1878). A train or passage check which had printed upon it the words, "good for continuous passage only," came under consideration in Walker v. Wabash, St. L. & P. R. Co., 15 Mo. App. 333 (1884). It was held that the purchaser of such a check from the original holder had no right to use it for that portion of the transit which the original holder had not completed, although within the

steamboat, it is held that he may go ashore at places where the steamboat stops, and resume his journey on the same boat and trip without forfeiting his right to use his ticket.[1]

If the rule or the indorsement upon the ticket be, "Good for this trip only," the ticket may be used on a day subsequent to that on which it is issued, provided that the trip be continuous.[2]

The validity of a regulation requiring that the trip be continuous was sustained in a case where the passenger had surrendered his ticket.[3] But it is believed that this is an immaterial circumstance.

If the conductor refuse to receive the ticket, and requires the passenger to pay his fare, the conductor has no right to retain the ticket.[4]

This rule does not apply to the case of a ticket divided into coupons, each coupon covering the route of one of several connecting roads. In such case the traveler has the right to break his journey at the terminus of each road, unless some restrictions are printed on the ticket, or made known to the passenger when he buys it.[5] In such

---

time limited by the ticket which he purchased and had surrendered in exchange for this train check.

[1] Dice v. Willamette Trans. Co., 8 Oreg. 60 (1879).

[2] Pier v. Finch, 24 Barb. (N. Y.) 514 (1857). The court say: "A construction which would work a forfeiture of a right, which the plaintiff clearly had, for a valuable consideration paid, and which would enable the corporation to retain the consideration without performing the service, ought not, it seems to me, to be given to this language, if it is fairly and reasonably susceptible of any other. If it is susceptible of two interpretations, that should be preferred which will secure and preserve the rights of both parties, according to all canons for the interpretation of contracts."

[3] Cleveland, C. & C. R. R. v. Bartram, 11 Ohio St. 457 (1860). In this case the court said: "The plaintiff, after making his election of a train, and after giving in his ticket, had no right to make a re-election of trains while that train is in a reasonable manner performing the duties of the carrier."

[4] Van Kirk v. Penn. R. R., 76 Penn. 66 (1874).

[5] Brooke v. Grand Trunk R. Co., 15 Mich. 332 (1867); Palmer v.

case he may take his baggage from the custody of the carrier, and re-deliver it when he resumes his journey.[1] But a passenger holding such a ticket has no right to stop over at a way station.[2]

The rule just stated as to the effect of the limitation endorsed on the ticket or printed on its face applies equally to "lay-over" or "stop-over" tickets given by conductors to a passenger desiring to break his journey at an intermediate station, and resume it at a later day. The reason stated for this decision is the rule more fully considered hereafter, that the carrier has the right to treat the journey as an entirety, and is not bound to issue such tickets; and, if it does, may annex a condition as to the time within which they may be used.[3]

In one case the court has gone so far as to hold that a ticket for a trip between two stations is not valid for a trip to an intermediate station.[4] The ticket was an excursion ticket, and sold at a reduced rate, and by its terms was good "for a continuous trip only." But still, it would seem that in the absence of an express agreement to the contrary, the purchaser of a ticket to one place should have the right to ride upon that ticket part of the way only. The carrier may, perhaps, in the absence of legislation, charge more for a short haul than a long haul, but

---

Charlotte, C. & A. R. R., 3 S. Car. (N. S.) 580 (1871). In Hamilton v. N. Y. Central R. R., 51 N. Y. 100 (1872), Lott, Ch. Com., considers the question whether the holder of such a ticket has the right to stop at a station intermediate the termini specified on each coupon, and resume his journey, without paying fare, to the next terminus. He concludes that the passenger has no such right. The court did not pass on the question.

[1] Wilson v. Chesapeake & Ohio R. R., 21 Grattan (Va.), 654 (1872).

[2] McClure v. Phil., W. & B. R. R., 34 Md. 532 (1871); Little Rock & F. S. R. R. v. Dean, 43 Ark. 529 (1884).

[3] Churchill v. Chicago & Alton R. R., 67 Ill. 390 (1873); Wentz v. Erie R. Co., 5 Thomps. & Cook (N. Y.), 556; s. c. 3 Hun, 241 (1874); post, Ch. VII, sect. 9.

[4] Johnson v. Phil., W. & B. R. R., 63 Md. 106 (1884).

his right so to do, if it exist, is on the verge that separates the lawful from the unlawful, and ought to be strictly construed, and limited to the exact terms of the contract.

By statute in Maine, a regulation of the carrier or contract with him is invalid which purports to make a ticket invalid when the passenger has broken his journey. This statute has no extra-territorial operation, although the contract for the transportation is made in Maine. The courts of that State presume the law of other jurisdictions to be the same as the common law of Maine.[1]

SECTION V.

TICKETS NOT TRANSFERABLE.

A carrier may lawfully limit the use of a ticket to the person buying it, if the words "not transferable" or other equivalent expressions are printed on the ticket. In such case the buyer has not the right to sell it after having traveled part of the route, although his vendee takes passage on the same train.[2] But in such case the carrier has

---

[1] Carpenter *v.* Grand Trunk R. Co., 72 Me. 388 (1881).

[2] Post *v.* Chicago & N. W. R. R., 14 Neb. 110; s. c. 45 Am. Rep. 100 (1883); Cody *v.* Central Pacific R. R., 4 Sawyer, 114 (1876). In this case the court say: "A contract for one continuous emigrant passage from Omaha to San Francisco is not a contract to carry one man from Omaha to the next station, another to the next station, and so on through the entire line, but an entirely different contract, and one upon different terms and for a different rate of compensation. If this experiment should succeed, parties could readily arrange privately for local travel at through rates without the consent of the companies. A party might as well contract to carry a ton of freight from Omaha to San Francisco, and then insist that he could have a ton carried to the first station, and transfer a right to another party to carry another and different ton of freight to the next station, and so on through the entire line. The inconvenience and loss to the company would doubtless be greater than in the case of a passenger, but the difference is only in degree, not in principle."

no right to take the ticket from the vendee and expel him from the train.[1]

A person who gets possession of a free pass marked "not transferable," and personates the rightful owner, cannot recover damages for injuries caused by the negligence of the company's servants, not amounting to a willful tort.[2]

In the case of non-transferable tickets, as in the other classes of cases considered in this chapter, the conductor of a train may lawfully insist upon strict compliance with the carrier's rule, without regard to the question of the passenger's intent. Thus it was held that if a ticket, on its face not assignable, was made out in the name of the wrong person, the conductor could refuse to receive it when presented by the person for whom it was really purchased.[3]

And the carrier may lawfully forfeit a commutation ticket which, by its terms, is not assignable, if the holder, either intentionally or by negligence, has allowed some other person to use it.[4]

---

[1] Post v. Chicago & N. W. R. R., 14 Neb. 110 (1883).

[2] Way v. Chicago, R. I. & P. R. Co., 64 Iowa, 48 (1884); Toledo, Wabash & W. R. Co. v. Beggs, 85 Ill. 80 (1877). In the latter case the court say: "Was defendant in error a passenger on this train in the true sense of that term? He was traveling on a free pass issued to one James Short, and not transferable, and passed himself as the person named in the pass. By his fraud he was riding on the car. Under such circumstances the company could only be held liable for gross negligence which would amount to willful injury. But, on the assumption he was a passenger on the car, riding on a free ticket containing the usual conditions, as this did, then the case is like that of Illinois Central Railroad Co. v. Read, 37 Ill. 484 (1865), where it was held such a pass or ticket is a perfect immunity to the company for such unavoidable accidents as will happen to the best-managed railroad trains; not, however, shielding them from liability for gross negligence, or any degree of negligence having the character of recklessness."

[3] Chicago & N. W. R. R. v. Bannerman, 15 Ill. App. 100 (1884). In this case the error in the name upon the ticket was known to the person who purchased it. But this seems to be an immaterial circumstance. The real question is whether the conductor in any case is bound to look beyond the face of the ticket presented to him. See post, Ch. VII, sect. 9.

[4] Friedenrich v. Baltimore & O. R. R., 53 Md. 201 (1879).

But the ticket is assignable if no restriction be placed by the carrier upon its use before or at the time of the original purchase.[1]

SECTION VI.

THE RIGHT TO DESIGNATE THE CHARACTER OF THE CARS OR OTHER ACCOMMODATIONS PROVIDED, AND THE PERSONS WHO SHALL TRAVEL UPON OR USE THE SAME. THE PASSENGER'S RIGHT TO A SEAT.

A carrier may set aside a car for the accommodation of women, and may exclude all men, unaccompanied by women, from such car.[2] If, however, a man enters such car without objection, he cannot lawfully be removed from the same, except after reasonable notice, and with due regard to his safety.[3] And when the seats in the other cars are full, passengers not having seats may lawfully enter a car set apart especially for women and their escorts. In such case the carrier may select the persons who shall be allowed to enter the "ladies' car."

If a carrier provide special accommodation, as, for example, a chair car, he may charge an extra fare therefor, and exclude all persons who refuse to pay the extra fare.[4]

A carrier may exclude persons of color from a particu-

---

[1] Hudson v. Kansas Pacific R. Co., 3 McCrary, 249 (1882).

[2] Brown v. Memphis & C. R. Co., 7 Fed. Rep. 51 (1881); Chicago & N. W. R. Co. v. Williams, 55 Ill. 185 (1870); Memphis & C. R. R. Co. v. Benson, 85 Tenn. 627 (1887).

[3] Marquette v. Chicago & N. W. R. R., 33 Iowa, 562 (1871); Bass v. Chicago & N. W. R. R., 36 Wis. 450 (1874). And so if a man enter a limited express without objection he cannot be removed without reasonable notice and regard for his safety. Lake Shore & M. S. R. Co. v. Rosenzweig, 113 Penn. 519 (1886).

[4] Wright v. California Central R. Co., 20 Pac. Rep. (Cal.) 740 (1889). So he may exclude from an express train persons holding excursion tickets which are stated on their face not to be valid on express trains. Nolan v. New York, N. H. & H. R. R., 41 N. Y. Super. Ct. 541 (1876).

lar car when order and harmony are likely to be promoted thereby.[1]

---

[1] West Chester & Phila. R. R. *v.* Miles, 55 Penn. 209 (1867). But the Pennsylvania Act of 1867, Pamph. L. 38, which prohibits a carrier from making distinctions between passengers on account of race or color, prevents the carrier from excluding persons of color from the cars on which white persons holding similar tickets are allowed to ride. Central R. R. of N. J. *v.* Green, 86 Penn. 421 (1878); see Britton *v.* Atlanta & C. A. L. R. Co., 88 N. Car. 536; s. c. 43 Am. Rep. 749 (1883), in which it was held that if a carrier did not enforce its regulation on this subject, which the court held to be lawful, it was liable to make good any injury to a colored person riding in the car set aside for the whites.

In the Miles case the court say: " The right of the carrier to separate his passengers is founded upon two grounds—his right of private property in the means of conveyance, and the public interest. The private means he uses belongs wholly to himself, and imply the right of control for the protection of his own interest, as well as the performance of his public duty. He may use his property, therefore, in a reasonable manner. It is not an unreasonable regulation to seat passengers so as to preserve order and decorum, and to prevent contacts and collisions arising from natural or well known customary repugnancies, which are likely to breed disturbances by a promiscuous sitting. This is a proper use of the right of private property, because it tends to protect the interests of the carrier as well as the interests of those he carries. If the ground of regulation be reasonable, courts of justice cannot interfere with his right of property. The right of the passenger is only that of being carried safely, and with a due regard to his personal comfort and convenience, which are promoted by a sound and well regulated separation of passengers. An analogy and an illustration are found in the case of an inn-keeper, who, if he have room, is bound to entertain proper guests, and so a carrier is bound to receive passengers. But a guest in an inn cannot select his room or his bed at pleasure; nor can a voyager take possession of a cabin or a berth at will, or refuse to obey the reasonable orders of the captain of a vessel. But, on the other hand, who would maintain that it is a reasonable regulation, either of an inn or a vessel, to *compel* the passengers, black and white, to room and bed together ? If a right of private property confers no right of control, who shall decide a contest between passengers for seats or berths? Courts of justice may interpose to compel those who perform a business concerning the public, by the use of private means to fulfill their duty to the public, but not a whit beyond."

On the other hand it was held in Chicago & N. W. R. Co. *v.* Williams, 55 Ill. 185 (1870), that a colored woman could not lawfully be excluded from the "ladies' car" solely on account of her color, though the court express the opinion that separate seats in this car could lawfully be set apart for colored women. The reverse was held in Chesapeake, O. & S. W. R. R. Co. *v.* Wells, 85 Tenn. 613 (1887); and see Day *v.* Owen, 5 Mich. 520 (1858). If a carrier may classify passengers according to sex or color, he must give them equal accommodation and

But equally good accommodation must be provided in other parts of the car or boat.[1]   And in Iowa it was held that it was unreasonable to require persons of color to take their meals on the guard or in the pantry, and that it was unlawful to enforce such a regulation by forcibly removing a quadroon from the dining room.[2]   The change in public sentiment that has taken place in the United States, respecting the relations between the white and colored races, is visible in the decisions of the courts, and illustrates what Mr. Webster was perhaps the first to point out, that the reports contain important material for history.[3]

The carrier may set apart a table for the special use of the officers of the boat and exclude other persons therefrom.[4]

The carrier may require all persons wishing to ride on freight trains to procure a peculiar ticket;[5] and may re-

---

cannot put a colored woman, holding a first class ticket, into a smoking car against her will.   Gray v. Cincinnati S. R. Co. (C. Ct. S. D. Ohio), 11 Fed. Rep. 687 (1882); Houck v. Southern Pac. R. Co. (C. Ct. W. D. Texas), 38 Fed. Rep. 226 (1888); see, also, Green v. City of Bridgeton (U. S. D. Ct., Ga.), 9 Cent. L. J. 206 (1879).

[1] The Sue, 22 Fed. Rep. 843 (1885); Logwood v. Memphis & C. R. Co., 23 Fed. Rep. 318 (1885); Murphy v. Western & A. R. R., 23 Fed. Rep. 637 (1885).   The Civil Rights Bill, 1 Hughes 541, 547 (1875).   In the Logwood case Hammond, J., said: "Equal accommodations do not mean identical accommodations. . . . But in all cases the carrier must furnish substantially the same accommodations to all, by providing equal comforts, privileges and pleasures to every class."   In Hall v. De Cuir, 95 U. S. 485 (1877), the Supreme Court held that a statute of Louisiana, which was construed so as to forbid a carrier to exclude colored women from the cabin set apart for white women, was unconstitutional and void, so far as it related to interstate commerce.

[2] Coger v. Northwest Union Packet Co., 37 Iowa, 145 (1873).

[3] Address, Historical Soc., Feb. 23, 1852; Curtis' Life of Webster, vol. 2, p. 590.

[4] Ellis v. Narragansett S. S. Co., 111 Mass. 146 (1872).

[5] Law v. Illinois Cent. R. R., 32 Iowa, 534 (1871); Cleveland C. & C. R. R. v. Bartram, 11 Ohio, St. 457 (1860); Burlington & M. R. R. v. Rose, 11 Neb. 177 (1881); Falkner v. Ohio & Miss. R. Co., 55 Ind. 369 (1876); Lake Shore & M. S. R. Co. v. Greenwood, 79 Penn. 373 (1875); Lane v. E. T., Va. & Ga. R. R., 5 Lea, 124; s. c. 2 Am. & Eng. R. R. Cas. 278 (1880); Southern Kansas R. Co. v. Hinsdale, 38 Kans. 507;

fuse altogether to carry passengers upon freight trains
with or without a ticket, and either generally or to and
from particular stations,[1] and may exclude them from mail
and baggage cars.[2]

So the carrier may and should refuse to receive on its
cars or, if received by mistake, should expel therefrom all
persons who are disorderly or endanger the safety or interfere with the reasonable comfort and convenience of the
other passengers.[3]

But an intoxicated person who keeps quiet, and does not
interfere with others cannot lawfully be excluded,[4] unless

---

s. c. 16 Pac. Rep. 937 (1888); Thomas v. Chicago & G. T. R. Co., 40 N.
W. Rep. (Mich.) 463 (1888); Toledo, P. & W. R. R. v. Patterson, 63
Ill. 304 (1872); Illinois Central R. R. v. Nelson, 59 Ill. 110 (1871). In
this case the passenger had a first-class ticket. But it was held that a
regulation was reasonable which required a different ticket for freight
trains, and also that persons who took passage on freight trains could
only require that the train stop for them at a freight station. In Evans
v. Memphis & C. R. R., 56 Ala. 246 (1876), it was held that in such
case a reasonable opportunity to purchase the ticket must be afforded
or the exclusion will be unlawful. Dunlap v. Northern Pac. R. R., 35
Minn. 203 (1886); Indianapolis & St. L. R. R. v. Kennedy, 77 Ind. 507
(1881). If the carrier permit a passenger to ride on a freight train at
regular rates without any qualification, it must exercise the same care
as on passenger trains. New York, Chicago & St. L. R. Co. v. Doane,
115 Ind. 435; s. c. 15 West Rep. 465 (1888).

[1] Holmes v. Wakefield, 12 Allen (Mass.), 580 (1866); Arnold v. Ill.
Cent. R. R., 83 Ill. 273 (1876); Chicago & Alton R. R. v. Randolph, 53
Ill. 510 (1870); South & N. Ala. R. R. v. Huffman, 76 Ala. 492 (1884).

[2] Kentucky Central R. R. v. Thomas, 79 Ky. 160; s. c. 42 Am. Rep.
208 (1880); O'Donnell v. Alleghany V. R. R., 59 Penn. 239 (1868);
Houston & T. C. R. R. v. Clemmons, 55 Texas 88 (1881).

[3] Putnam v. Broadway & Seventh Ave. R. R., 55 N. Y. 108 (1873);
Atchison, T. & S. F. R. R. v. Weber, 33 Kansas 543 (1885); Louisville
& N. R. R. v. Logan (Ky.), 3 Lawy. Rep. Ann. 80 (1889); Sullivan v.
Old Colony R. R., 148 Mass. 119; s. c. 1 Lawy. Rep. Ann. 513 (1888);
Higgins v. Watervliet T. & R. R., 46 N. Y. 23 (1871). The last four
cases involved the ejection of intoxicated persons. The right to eject a
person using grossly profane or obscene language was sustained in Chicago, B. & Q. R. R. v. Griffin, 68 Ill. 499 (1873). And see St. Louis, A. &.
T. R. Co. v. Mackie, 71 Texas, 491 (1888). So the carrier may remove a
person who apparently has the smallpox, though it afterward turns out
that he had not. Paddock v. Atchison, T. & S. F. R. Co., 37 Fed. Rep.
841; s. c. 4 Lawy. Rep. Ann. 231 (1889).

[4] Milliman v. N. Y. Central & H. R. R. R., 66 N. Y. 642 (1876).

there is reason to believe that he will become offensive or annoying to the other passengers.[1] Some care for his safety must be taken, and it would be negligent to eject him in a place where he would be in danger of being run over by another train.[2]

The carrier may prohibit all persons from riding on the platform of its cars. This right in some States, as in New York,[3] is declared by statute, but there seems to be no reason to doubt that it exists independently of statutory regulation.[4] But this right implies an obligation on the part of the carrier to provide suitable accommodation elsewhere. If a car is crowded it is not negligent for a passenger to ride on the platform, and he is not bound to request other passengers to remove their parcels from the seats or to make room so as to enable him to sit down. It is the duty of the carrier to see that he has a seat.[5]

Standing on the platform has been held not to be of itself negligence, if notice of a regulation forbidding it has not been posted in the cars, especially when it appeared that the plaintiff found the car he entered crowded and had not time before the accident to find a seat in another.[6]

---

[1] Vinton v. Middlesex R. R., 11 Allen (Mass.), 304 (1865); Murphy v. Union R. Co., 118 Mass. 228 (1875).

[2] Haley v. Chicago & N. W. R. R. 21 Iowa, 15 (1866); Atchison, T. & S. F. R. Co. v. Weber, 33 Kansas, 543 (1885); Louisville & N. R. R. v. Logan (Ky.), 3 Lawy. Rep. Ann. 80 (1889).

[3] Railroad Act; Laws of 1850, Chap. 140, section 46.

[4] Moss v. Johnson, 22 Ill. 633 (1859); Virginia M. R. R. v. Roach, 83 Va. 375 (1887). It is the duty of a passenger to go inside if told to do so by the brakeman, even though there are no seats inside. Graville v. Manhattan R. R., 105 N. Y. 525 (1887); Alabama G. S. R. R. Co. v. Hawk, 72 Ala. 112; s. c. 18 Am. & Eng. R. R. Cas. 194 (1882).

[5] Willis v. Long Island R. R., 34 N. Y. 670 (1866).

[6] Colegrove v. N. Y. & N. H. R. R., 6 Duer (N. Y.), 382 (1857); affd. 20 N. Y. 492 (1859); Transfer Co. v. Kelly, 36 Ohio St. 86 (1880). It would probably be held otherwise in a case where sufficient accommodation was provided elsewhere and the passenger knew the place he selected to be more dangerous than inside the passenger car. Houston &

It has been held that while the carrier has the right to exclude from its cars persons who propose to enter them for immoral purposes, as, for example, gambling, yet if a ticket has been sold to such a person his fare must be returned before he can be lawfully ejected.[1]

This decision is opposed to the current of authority unless it be confined to the case of a person excluded simply because of his profession, and not for any actual misconduct.[2]

T. C. R. R. *v.* Clemmons, 55 Texas, 88 (1881). But see Graville *v.* Manhattan R. R., p. 155, note 4, *ante.*

[1] Thurston *v.* Union Pacific R. R. 4 Dill. 321 (1877.) In this case the court charged the jury: "The railway company is bound, as a common carrier, when not overcrowded, to take all proper persons who may apply for transportation over its line, on their complying with all reasonable rules of the company. But it is not bound to carry all persons at all times, or it might be utterly unable to protect itself from ruin. It would not be obliged to carry one whose ostensible business might be to injure the line; one fleeing from justice; one going upon the train to assault a passenger, commit larceny or robbery, or for interfering with the proper regulations of the company, or for gambling in any form, or committing any crime; nor is it bound to carry persons infected with contagious diseases, to the danger of other passengers. The person must be upon lawful and legitimate business. Hence defendant is not bound to carry persons who travel for the purpose of gambling. As gambling is a crime under the State laws, it is not even necessary for the company to have a rule against it. It is not bound to furnish facilities for carrying out an unlawful purpose. Necessary force may be used to prevent gamblers from entering trains, and if found on them engaged in gambling, and refusing to desist, they may be forcibly expelled. . . . After ticket is purchased and paid for, the railroad company can only avoid compliance with its part of the contract by the existence of some legal cause or condition which will excuse it. The company should, in the first case, refuse to sell tickets to persons whom it desires and has the right to exclude from the cars, and should exclude them if they attempt to enter the car without tickets. If the ticket has been inadvertently sold to such person and the company desires to rescind the contract for transportation, it should tender the return of the money paid for the ticket. If it does not do this, plaintiff may, under any circumstances, recover the amount of his actual damage, viz.: what he paid for the ticket, and, perhaps, necessary expenses of his detention."

[2] In Wright *v.* California Central R. Co., 20 Pac. Rep. (Cal.) 740 (1889), it was held that a person who was lawfully excluded from one car, and invited to sit in another, but who refused and left the train, could not recover damages because his ticket was not returned to him nor his fare refunded. It was held in Lemont *v.* Washington & G. R.

It is lawful to eject from a car or steamboat a person who attempted to ply thereon a calling, the object of which was to injure the business of the carrier.[1] The carrier may prohibit the sale of refreshments on the boat or train.[2]

The conductor or other person in charge of a train may dispense with the general regulations of the carrier, as to the place where passengers should ride. A passenger is justified in relying on the conductor's directions.[3]

R., 1 Mackey (D. C.), 180 (1881), that a carrier could lawfully remove from its car a person who it had reason to believe would be guilty of misconduct or indecency. On the other hand it was held in Brown v. Memphis & C. R. Co., 7 Fed. Rep. 51 (1881), that a woman of bad character, if she conducted herself properly, could not lawfully be excluded from the ladies' car.

[1] Jencks v. Coleman, 2 Sumner, 221 (1835). In this case the person excluded from the carrier's boat sought passage for the purpose of soliciting passengers to take a line of coaches in opposition to that with which the boat regularly connected. Judge Story charged that if the contract with the connecting line was reasonable and *bona fide* and not entered into for the purpose of an oppressive monopoly, and the exclusion of the plaintiff was a reasonable regulation in order to carry this contract into effect, it was lawful. No point was made in his case that the fare should have been returned. See p. 156, note 1, *ante*. Old Col. R. R. v. Tripp, 147 Mass. 35; s. c. 17 N. East. Rep. 89 (1888); Commonwealth v. Carey, 147 Mass. 40, note; s. c. 17 N. E. Rep. 97 (1888); Barney v. Oyster Bay & H. Steamboat Co., 67 N. Y. 301 (1876); The D. R. Martin, 11 Blatch. 233 (1873); see, also, Commonwealth v. Power, 7 Metc. (Mass.) 596 (1844); Markham v. Brown, 8 N. H. 523 (1837). But the mere wearing the uniform of an opposition company is not good cause for removal of the person wearing it. South Fla. R. Co., v. Rhoads, 3 Lawy. Rep. Ann. 133; 5 So. Rep. 633 (1889).

[2] Smallman v. Whilter, 87 Ill. 545; s. c. 29 Am. Rep. 76 (1877).

[3] Edgerton v. New York & H. R. R., 39 N. Y. 227 (1868); Carroll v. N. Y. & N. H. R. R., 1 Duer (N. Y.), 571 (1853); Phila. & Reading R. R. v. Derby, 14 How. (U. S.) 468 (1852); Lawrenceburg & Upper Miss. R. R. v. Montgomery, 7 Ind. 474 (1856); Penn. R. R. v. Henderson, 51 Penn. 315 (1865); Penn. R. R. v. McCloskey, 23 Penn. 526 (1854). In the McCloskey case, the plaintiff was a stockman, and was required by the regulations of the company to ride on the car containing his stock. By the conductor's directions he took a seat in another car, and while there was injured by an accident caused by the negligence of the company's servants. Had he remained in the stock car he would not have been injured. The court held that it was lawful for

It is to be observed that a passenger's non-compliance with the carrier's regulations is no bar to an action for injuries not caused by such disobedience but by negligence of the carrier, unconnected therewith.[1]

This is analogous to the well settled rule in collision cases that a violation of a regulation which has not contributed to produce the collision, is not a bar to a recovery at law, and does not in admiralty occasion a division of the damage.[2]

The decisions are not uniform as to whether the reasonableness of this class of rules is a question of law or fact.[3] On principle, if the facts are undisputed, the ques-

---

him to obey the conductor's directions, and that his doing so in violation of the general rules of the company constituted no defence. As to waiver of the carrier's rules, see Ch. VII, sect. 9, *post.*

The conductor's authority seems to be restrained to the trains. The company is not bound by his direction to the passenger what to do after leaving them. The reason the company is bound by the conductor's directions while the passenger is on the cars is that the passenger is bound to obey them. Cincinnati, H. & I. R. R. *v.* Carper, 112 Ind. 26 (1887).

[1] Lafayette & Indianapolis R. R. *v.* Sims, 27 Ind. 59 (1866); Lackawanna & Bloomsburg R. R. *v.* Chenewith, 52 Penn. 382 (1866); Britton *v.* Atlanta & C. A. L. R. R., 88 N. Car. 536 (1883).

In the Chenewith case the plaintiff, after being informed that it would be against the rules of the company to attach his freight car to a passenger train, persuaded the company's agents to attach it. He was injured by an accident caused by the negligence of the company in not providing a proper fence. The court held that as his violation of the rules of the company did not contribute to the accident, he was entitled to recover.

In Carroll *v.* N. Y. & N. H. R. R., 1 Duer (N. Y.), 571 (1853), the plaintiff was injured while sitting in the baggage car. This was in violation of a rule of the company, but no objection to his taking his seat there was made by the conductor, and it was shown that passengers did frequently sit there. The court held that the plaintiff could recover, as his being there did not tend, directly or remotely, to produce the act which caused the injury.

[2] The Farragut, 10 Wall. 334 (1870); Hoffman *v.* Union Ferry Co., 47 N. Y. 176 (1872).

[3] That it is a mixed question of law and fact. Day *v.* Owen, 5 Mich. 520 (1858); Bass *v.* Chicago & N. W. R. Co., 36 Wis. 450 (1874); Commonwealth *v.* Power, 7 Metc. (Mass.) 596 (1844); Jencks *v.* Coleman, 2 Sumner, 221 (1835); Brown *v.* Memphis & C. R. Co., 4 Fed. Rep. 37

tion of the reasonableness of a rule is for the court. If there is a conflict of evidence as to the facts, the question should be submitted to the jury, under appropriate instructions.

A passenger who has paid his fare has a right to a seat. But he cannot insist upon being transported free of charge unless a seat be given him. If a seat is not pro-vided his remedy is to leave the train and sue the carrier for the damage caused by its refusal or neglect to pro-vide a seat for him.[1]

SECTION VII.

RULES AND REGULATIONS AS TO THE STATIONS AT WHICH TRAINS SHALL STOP.

The carrier has also the right so to arrange his trains that some of them shall stop only at the principal sta-tions.[2]

It is the duty of the passenger to ascertain if the train he is about to take will stop at the station for which he has bought a ticket. If he fails to enquire, he has no right to insist that the train shall stop there.[3]

(1880). That it is a pure question of fact: State *v.* Overton, 24 N. J. Law, 435 (1854); Morris & Essex R. R. *v.* Ayers, 29 N. J. Law, 393 (1862). That it is a pure question of law: Chicago & N. W. R. Co. *v.* Williams, 55 Ill. 185, 188 (1870). See *ante,* p. 132, n. 2.

[1] Memphis & Charleston R. R. *v.* Benson, 85 Tenn. 627 (1887); Hardenbergh *v.* St. Paul, M. & M. R. Co., (Minn.) 38 N. W. Rep. 625 (1888). In Werle *v.* Long Island R. R., 98 N. Y. 650 (1885), the court say: "The sale of tickets by the defendant at that station for passage on that train bound it to furnish a safe and secure place for passengers to ride, and comfortable accommodations for their convenience."

[2] Dietrich *v.* Penn. R. R., 71 Penn. 432 (1872); Trotlinger *v.* East Tenn., V. & G. R. R., 11 Lea (Tenn.), 533 (1883); Logan *v.* Hannibal & St. Jo. R. R., 77 Mo. 663 (1883).

[3] Chicago & Alton R. R. *v.* Randolph, 53 Ill. 510 (1870); Ohio & Miss. R. Co. *v.* Applewhite, 52 Ind. 540 (1876); Pittsburg & St. L. R. Co. *v.* Nuzum, 50 Ind. 141 (1875); Duling *v.* Philadelphia, W. & B. R. R., 66 Md. 120; 5 Central Rep. 570 (1886); Chicago, St. L. & P. R.

The original direction given to the passenger as to the train he should take must be subject to subsequent modification to conform to the character of the route.[1]   And it is held that he may take a train which does not stop at the station to which his ticket entitles him to ride, break his journey at an intermediate station, and then proceed in a train which does stop at his point of destination.[2] This decision may at first seem inconsistent with some of those cited in Section IV of this chapter.   But the right thus maintained is generally conceded by railroads in this country.   It enables the traveler to make the larger part of his journey more rapidly and conveniently on an express train, and keeps local trains for local travel, and does not appear to have caused any of those supposed inconveniences to the carrier, the apprehension of which has

---

Co. v. Bills, 104 Ind. 13; s. c. 3 N. East. Reporter, 611 (1885); Fink v. Albany & S. R. R., 4 Lansing (N. Y.), 147 (1871); Atchison, T. & S. F. R. R. v. Gants, 38 Kans. 608 (1888); Dietrich v. Penn. R. R., 71 Penn. 432 (1872); Beauchamp v. International & G. N. R. Co., 56 Texas, 239 (1882); 9 Am. & Eng. R. R. Ca. 307.

The words, printed on a ticket, "good on passenger trains only," do not import an agreement that a particular train shall stop at every station.   Ohio & M. R. Co. v. Swarthout, 67 Ind. 567 (1879).   Nor do the words, on a ticket, "for this day and train only," amount to a representation that a particular train will stop at the station named in the ticket. Duling v. Philadelphia, W. & B. R. R., 66 Md. 120; 5 Central Rep. 570 (1886).

In both these cases it was held that the sale of a ticket for a particular station, just before the departure of a train, did not constitute a representation that the train would stop at that station.   Under circumstances somewhat special, the contrary was held in Mississippi, Mobile & O. R. R. v. McArthur, 43 Miss. 180 (1870).

Nor does the punching and taking up of a ticket for a particular station, after the conductor has informed the passenger that the train does not stop there, constitute an agreement that it shall.   Trotlinger v. E. Tenn., V. & G. R. R., 11 Lea (Tenn.), 533 (1883).

If a passenger gets on a train without inquiry as to the stations at which it stops, and it makes no stop until a station beyond that for which he has a ticket, he must pay the additional fare to the first usual stopping-place.   Atchison, T. & S. F. R. Co., v. Gants, 38 Kans. 608 (1888).

[1] Barker v. N. Y. Central R. R., 24 N. Y. 599 (1862).
[2] Richmond, F. & P. R. R. v. Ashby, 79 Va. 130; s. c. 52 Am. Rep. 620 (1884).

led some courts to hold that the traveler, irrespective of an agreement to the contrary, had no right to break his journey. The practice on some of the great routes, of running limited trains, for which seats must be specially engaged at an extra charge, is not inconsistent with the rule thus stated. The service on such trains is exceptional, and a matter of special agreement.

If a statute of the State where the station is situated require the train to stop there, a corporation incorporated under the laws of another State is bound to observe this requirement, and is liable in damages to a passenger whom it refuses to leave at that station.[1]

Stopping a train at a regular station is an invitation to the public to take passage thereon.[2]

SECTION VIII.

REGULATIONS AS TO BAGGAGE AND FREIGHT.

The carrier may make reasonable rules and regulations as to the place where the baggage of passengers shall be deposited. If the passenger is informed of such rules, and does not observe them, he cannot recover for the loss of his baggage.[3] And in general the carrier is

---

[1] Penn. R. R. v. Wentz, 37 Ohio St. 333 (1881). This was so held although the ticket contained a stipulation that the purchaser "agrees to use it only on such trains as regularly stop at both stations named." It would seem that the court might have held that this constituted a waiver by the passenger of the right given by the statute.

[2] Werle v. Long Is. R. R., 98 N. Y. 650 (1885).

[3] Gleason v. Goodrich Trans. Co., 32 Wis. 85 (1873). In this case the plaintiff was a passenger on defendant's steamboat, and knew that a room was provided in which baggage could be placed in charge of a porter and checked. He had a valise, which he placed in an unlocked stateroom, from which it was stolen. The carrier was held not to be liable. The plaintiff asked the clerk for a key to the stateroom, but none was provided. He told the clerk he wanted to put his valise in a safe place. He asked the cabin boys if it would be safe in the stateroom, and they replied in the affirmative. But all these inquiries were held not to absolve him from the consequence of his failure to get the valise

11

not liable for baggage not placed in his custody, nor entrusted to some person duly authorized to receive it, though there may be an exception to this rule so far as personal baggage, required for the passenger's use during the journey, is concerned.[1]

A regulation that passengers' baggage shall be delivered only at one of several stations at which a train regularly stops is unreasonable. The right of a passenger to stop at a particular station involves the right to have his baggage delivered to him there.[2]

The regulations considered in this chapter were chiefly made in reference to the carriage of passengers. But the carrier may lawfully make similar regulations in reference to freight. For example, it may provide a safer and more expensive conveyance for valuable live stock, and contract that it shall not be liable for damage to live stock carried at a cheaper rate in ordinary cars.[3]   The rules

---

checked at the parcel room, and it was also held that there was no delivery of the valise to the carrier's custody. The court, however, intimates that a rule requiring a passenger to surrender his hand-baggage would be unreasonable.

[1] McKee v. Owen, 15 Mich. 115 (1866); Forbes v. Davis, 18 Texas, 268 (1857); Cohen v. Frost, 2 Duer (N. Y.), 335 (1853); Steamboat Crystal Palace v. Vanderpool, 16 B. Monr. (Ky.) 302 (1855). See, however, the Steamboat H. M. Wright, Newberry Adm. 494 (1854), in which case the court holds that personal or hand-baggage need not be delivered to the carrier's actual custody in order to make him liable for its loss.   In McKee v. Owen, Christiancy, J., says that the liability of the carriers for the loss of baggage is that of an inn-keeper. But in Steamboat Crystal Palace v. Vanderpool the court says it knows of no case where this has been held.   In Louisiana the code assimilates the liability of common carriers to that of inn-keepers. Dunn v. Branner, 13 La. Ann. 452 (1858).   In Cohen v. Frost the plaintiff was a steerage passenger in defendant's ship. During the voyage his trunk was stolen. It had been in his exclusive possession and custody. Held, that he trusted to his own care and vigilance to protect him against its loss, and that the defendants were not liable. See, also, Ill Cen. R. R. v. Tronstine, 64 Miss. 834 (1887); I. & G. N. R. Co. v Folliard, 66 Texas, 603 (1886); Louisville, N. & G. S. R. R. v. Katzenberger, 16 Lea (Tenn.), 380 (1886).

[2] Pittsburg, C. & St. L. R. Co. v. Lyon, 123 Penn. 140 (1889).

[3] Robinson v. Great Western R. Co., 1 H. & R. 97 (1865).

stated in Chapter IV, as to the validity of contracts exempting from liability for negligence, would undoubtedly be applied in such a case.

SECTION IX.

WAIVER BY THE CARRIER.—THE PASSENGER'S REMEDY FOR THE VIOLATION OF A SPECIAL AGREEMENT MODIFYING OR WAIVING THE CARRIER'S RULES.

The carrier may waive strict compliance with its rules. But a partial waiver, as, for example, allowing a passenger to use a ticket for a portion of the journey beyond the time limited by it, will not be construed as a complete waiver. The carrier may afterwards enforce the rule, and refuse to allow the holder of the ticket to travel the remainder of the route unless he pays his fare.[1] It is held that the company's gate-keeper and train-despatcher has no authority to waive compliance with the conditions printed on a ticket, by assigning the passenger to a train on which he is not entitled to travel.[2] The rule already stated, as to the effect of a partial waiver, applies to a ticket good for a given number of miles, but limited as to time.[3]

---

[1] Stone v. Chicago & N. W. R. Co., 47 Iowa, 82 (1877); Dietrich v. Penn. R. R., 71 Penn. 432 (1872); Hill v. Syracuse & N. Y. R. R., 63 N. Y. 101 (1875).

[2] Johnson v. Phil., W. & B. R. R., 63 Md. 106 (1884).

[3] Sherman v. Chicago & N. W. R. Co., 40 Iowa, 45 (1874). So it was held in Wentz v. Erie R. Co., 5 Thomps. & Cook (N. Y.), 556; s. c. 3 Hun, 241 (1874), that such a limitation was not waived by the fact of checking baggage for a passenger who tendered such a ticket to the baggage master, although the latter punched it as if it had been a valid ticket. In Cloud v. St. Louis, I. M. & S. R. Co., 14 Mo. App. 136 (1883), this same rule was applied to a waiver by the conductor of one of the carriers forming part of a line of connecting carriers. It was held that this waiver did not bind the carriers forming the rest of the line, for the whole of which the ticket in question was sold. Oppenheimer v. Denver & R. G. R. Co., 9 Col. 320 (1886). In this case a mileage ticket, by its terms, was not good on a part of the route. Evi-

Where a railroad company is exempt from liability to a passenger by reason of his traveling on a free pass, it does not waive this exemption by accepting payment for drawing-room car ticket.[1]

The decisions are not harmonious as to the effect of the omission of the carrier's agent to enforce at the outset some rule which it has prescribed for the purpose of giving validity to the ticket. Some railroad companies require persons purchasing excursion tickets to sign the ticket when purchased, and procure it to be stamped by the company's agent before beginning the return trip, and make a rule that an unstamped ticket is invalid. In some States it is held that if the failure to stamp the ticket is due to the mistake or fault of the carrier's agent, and the passenger has done what he reasonably can to secure a proper ticket, the ticket is valid, and the carrier has no right to refuse to receive it, although it is not stamped in conformity with his rules.[2] On the other hand it was held, by the United States Supreme Court,[3] that even if the holder of the ticket applied at the proper office, and endeavored to procure his ticket to be stamped, but was unable to do so owing to the absence of the proper agent, the return ticket would nevertheless be invalid. But this was put on the ground that the agent whose default was the cause of the passenger's failure to procure his ticket to be stamped was not the agent of the defendant, but of

---

dence that similar tickets had been used upon that part of the route without objection was held to be inadmissible.

[1] Ulrick v. N. Y. Central & H. R. R. R., 108 N. Y. 80 (1888); revg. 13 Daly, 129 (1885).

[2] Head v. Georgia Pac. R. Co., 79 Geo. 358; 7 S. E. Rep. 217 (1887); Gregory v. Burlington & M. R. R. R., 10 Neb. 250 (1880); Kent v. Baltimore & O. R. R., 45 Ohio St. 284 (1887). See *ante*, p. 144, n. 2.

[3] Mosher v. St. Louis, I. M. & S. R. Co., 127 U. S. 390 (1888); affg. 23 Fed. Rep. 326 (1885). The same case held that a clause in a ticket, signed by the plaintiff, providing that no agent should have power to modify or waive the conditions of the ticket, was valid, and that it deprived the conductor of power to waive the condition in question.

a connecting line, for whose default, under the agreement, the defendant was not liable. In Massachusetts it is held that a conductor who delivers to a passenger who pays his fare a wrong ticket, does not bind the carrier so far as to make the ticket valid, and entitled the passenger to complete the trip for which he has paid.[1]

No doubt it would be inconvenient to compel a subsequent conductor to determine whether the passenger's statement that he has paid his fare is true or not. On the other hand the general rule that a principal is bound by the acts and declarations of an agent in and about the business which he is authorized to transact, no matter what his secret instructions may be, should not be departed from except for cogent reasons.

The question is really: What is the passenger's remedy for a violation by the carrier's agents of a special agreement made by him with other agents of the carrier, which modifies or waives in his case the carrier's general rules?

There is an irreconcilable conflict between the cases upon the question whether the conductor of a train is bound to accept the statement of the passenger respecting the contract alleged by him to have been made for his transportation. The tendency of the earlier cases was to hold that if the conductor did not do this, but acted in accordance with the rules of the carrier in reference to the facts, as they appeared to him, irrespective of the passenger's statement, and the jury should find that the passenger's statement was, in point of fact, true, and that he had made a contract with some officer of the carrier, the effect of which was to vary its rules, the carrier would be liable for any damages sustained by the passenger in conse-

---

[1] Bradshaw v. South Boston R. R., 135 Mass. 407; s. c. 46 Am. Rep. 481 (1883). In this case, however, it was held that the action should not be in tort, but for the breach of contract.

quence of his eviction from that train. All the cases agree that the carrier is liable in damages for the failure to perform a contract made by its authorized agent with the passenger.[1] But the question as to which they have

---

[1] The company is liable for the breach of a contract made by a ticket agent, that a particular train shall stop at a particular station for which a ticket is purchased. Marshall v. St. Louis, K. C. & N. R. Co., 78 Mo. 610; s. c. 18 Am. & Eng. R. R. Cas. 248 (1883). See ante, p. 144, n. 3.

In Lake Shore & M. S. R. Co. v. Pierce, 47 Mich. 277 (1882), the court held that the ticket agent was authorized to make such a contract and that the carrier was liable in damages for its breach, but that the passenger had no right to require that the train should stop at the particular station as represented by the ticket agent. In other words, his remedy is in damages, and he cannot insist upon the specific performance of the agreement. In view of the practice of forwarding passengers to the nearest largest station by express trains, and then on local trains to their destination, this appears to be a reasonable solution of the question stated in the text. In Alabama, however, it was held in a similar case that the passenger could recover damages for eviction from the train. Ala. G. S. R. R. v. Heddleston, 82 Ala. 218 (1886).

It is held that an agreement is valid between the passenger and conductor of a train, that it should stop at a particular station, at which it was not usual to stop. McGinnis v. Mo. Pac. R. Co., 21 Mo. App. 399; s. c. 4 West Rep. 797 (1886); Georgia R. R. & B. Co. v. McCurdy, 45 Geo. 288; s. c. 12 Am. Rep. 577 (1872).

In Hull v. East Line Red River R. R., 66 Texas, 619 (1886), a conductor had been in the habit of stopping at a place, not a station, and it was held that he must be considered as authorized to promise to let a passenger off there. In another case, however, it was held that the conductor had no authority to make an agreement that the train should stop at a station at which, according to the published time-table, the train was not to stop. Ohio & M. R. Co. v. Hatton, 60 Ind. 12 (1877). So it was held, in Pittsburg, C. & St. L. R. Co. v. Nuzum, 60 Ind. 533 (1878), that the ticket agent had no authority to bind the company by his statements as to the station at which a train would stop.

In St. Louis, A. & T. R. Co. v. Mackie, 71 Texas, 491; 1 Lawyers' Rep. Ann. 667; 9 S. W. Rep. 451 (1888), it was held that a passenger who had paid for first-class tickets, and, without negligence on his part, received second-class tickets, was entitled to ride first-class, and that the offer of the conductor, to allow him to ride first-class on paying the difference between first and second-class tickets, was no defense. In this case the passenger was not evicted, but made his journey in the second-class car.

In two cases in Maryland reliance was placed on the fact that the statement on the face of the ticket expressed the rights of the passenger, and that he was bound to know what these were, and had no right to rely on the statement of a ticket agent (Pennington v. Phil., W. & B. R. R., 62 Md. 95 [1883]); or of a gate agent (Johnson v. Phil., W. &

differed is as to the passenger's remedy. Can he stand
upon his rights as he understands them, resist an eviction
from the train by all the force at his command, and, if
the carrier is able—as it generally is—to bring superior
force to bear, claim damages for the injuries caused to
him by the forcible eviction? In the reported opinions on
this subject, this distinction between the right and the
remedy has not always been observed. When the court
has arrived at the conclusion that the contract of a company, in reference to the passenger's transportation, had
been violated, it has in some cases concluded that the passenger's remedy was to resist any eviction in violation of
this contract.[1] But this does not necessarily follow, and

B. R. R., 63 Md. 106 [1884]), in contradiction of the language of the
ticket.

[1] The passenger may stand upon his rights based upon the assur-
ances of the conductor (Tarbell v. No. Central R. R., 24 Hun [N. Y],
51 [1881]), or of the ticket agent, and if he is evicted in violation of the
agreement so alleged to have been made by him, he can maintain an action of tort against the company. Jeffersonville R. R. v. Rogers, 38
Ind. 116 (1871); Murdock v. Boston & Albany R. R., 137 Mass. 293
(1884); Head v. Georgia Pac. R. Co., 79 Geo. 358; 7 S. E. Rep. 217
(1887); Ala. G. S. R. R. v. Heddleston, 82 Ala. 218 (1886); Kansas
Pac. R. Co. v. Kessler, 18 Kans. 523 (1877). In Burnham v. Grand
T. R. Co., 63 Me. 298; s. c. 18 Am. Rep. 220 (1873), the court held
that the conductor should, before evicting the plaintiff, have offered to
return the excessive fare already paid, or to deduct it from the additional fare which he demanded. The case was one of a stop-over ticket,
and the question arose as to the alleged agreement with the ticket
agent, that the passenger might break his journey at an intermediate
station.

In the following case it was held that it was the conductor's duty to
accept the statement of a passenger as to his contract with the ticket
agent, irrespective of any statement upon the face of the ticket; and
that if the conductor should, in violation of this contract, attempt forcibly to expel the passenger, this would be an assault for which the carrier would be liable.

Hufford v. Grand Rapids & I. R. R., 64 Mich. 631; s. c. 7 West.
Rep. 859 (1887). In this case the court say: "The ticket given by the
agent to the plaintiff was the evidence agreed upon by the parties by
which the defendant should thereafter recognize the rights of plaintiff
in his contract, and neither the company nor any of its agents could
thereafter be permitted to say the ticket was not such evidence, and
conclusive upon the subject. Passengers are not interested in the in-

it is believed that the better opinion, and one which on the whole will tend to subserve the objects for which carriers are incorporated, is that the passenger should submit peaceably to the decision of the conductor, and not compel a stopping of the train, much less a forcible eviction, but seek his remedy—if his rights have been violated—by suit against the carrier for its breach of the contract.[1]

This seems to follow from the fundamental proposition that the carrier discharges not a private, but a public function, and in the discharge of this function it is necessary, for the safety of passengers, that the train should be run with punctuality, stopping only at the appointed places. The more complicated the railway system becomes, the more essential is it that the rules made by the carrier for the management of its train-service should be strictly observed.

The cases are especially conflicting where the attempt has been made to eject a passenger for failure to produce any ticket whatever, or one in accordance with the carrier's general rules. If the passenger originally had a ticket, which he has surrendered to a conductor, and no check or voucher has been returned to the passenger, it has been held that it was unlawful to eject him afterwards for failure to exhibit his ticket or pay his fare.[2]

---

ternal affairs of the companies whose coaches they ride in, nor are they required to know the rules and regulations made by the directors of a company for the control of the action of its agents and management of its affairs.''

If the agent of the carrier acts in good faith, the passenger should not offer exasperating resistance; and, if he does, can recover only the actual damage he sustains. Toledo, Wabash & W. R. Co. v. Wright, 68 Ind. 586 (1879).

[1] Hall v. Memphis & Charleston R. Co. (U. S. C. Ct., W. D. Tenn.), 15 Fed. Rep. 57 (1882); Chicago, B. & Q. R. R. v. Griffin, 68 Ill. 499 (1873); Penn. R. R. v. Connell, 112 Ill. 295 (1884); Southern Kan. R. Co. v. Rice, 38 Kan. 398; s. c. 16 Pacific Reporter, 817 (1888).

[2] Hamilton v. Third Ave. R. R., 53 N. Y. 25 (1873); Townsend v. N. Y. Central & H. R. R. R., 6 Thomps. & Cook (N. Y.), 495; s. c. 4

The same rule has been laid down in cases where the holder of an excursion ticket received from the first conductor a check, instead of his return ticket; or where, from any error of the first conductor, the passenger failed to receive a return ticket in due form.[1] Other cases maintain the reverse. These conflicting decisions are stated in the notes.

Hun, 217 (1875). In this case the Supreme Court said: "To require a passenger to show a ticket may be reasonable, but a company cannot require a passenger to comply with a regulation, compliance with which they have themselves prevented. Nor can it be said that the act of the conductor, in taking up the ticket, was wrongful toward the passenger. The company might take up their tickets whenever they chose, but they could not, by so doing, acquire the right to refuse to transport the passenger." Pittsburg, Cin. & St. L. R. Co. *v.* Hennigh, 39 Ind. 509 (1872); Palmer *v.* Charlotte, C. & A. R. R., 3 S. Car. (N. S.) 580 (1872); City & Suburban R. of Savannah *v.* Brauss, 70 Ga. 368 (1883).

The authority of the statement just quoted from the Townsend case is not unquestioned. Indeed, the law in New York is by no means free from doubt. On the first appeal in the Townsend case, 56 N. Y. 295 (1874), the opinion of Grover, J., which is the only one reported, maintains that the expulsion under the circumstances stated was lawful, but that the passenger had a remedy for the unlawful act of the first conductor in not giving him a proper check. It does not appear that this was concurred in by a majority of the court. And the General Term, in the same case, did not follow the rule thus stated, but held, as has been shown, that the expulsion was unlawful. And it was so held in the Hamilton case, in which the opinion was delivered by Grover, J., and in which the court was unanimous. The Townsend case in the Court of Appeals is cited without disapproval in Lynch *v.* Metropolitan El. R. Co., 90 N. Y. 77 (1882). In English *v.* Delaware & Hudson Canal Co., 66 N. Y. 454 (1876), the court do not overrule it, but distinguish it from the case of a passenger who has already paid his fare to the conductor who ejects him. In the latter case it was held that the passenger's resistance was lawful, and that he could recover for the injury caused him by the force used to overcome his resistance. The rule stated in Judge Grover's opinion in the Townsend case is in accord with Sheltin *v.* Lake Shore & M. S. R. Co., 29 Ohio St. 214 (1876).

[1] Lake Erie & Western R. Co. *v.* Fix, 88 Ind. 381 (1882); Philadelphia, W. & B. R. R. *v.* Rice, 64 Md. 63 (1885); Baltimore & O. R. R. *v.* Bambrey, 16 Atl. Reporter (Penn.), 67 (1888). It has, however, been held that in such cases the passenger's only remedy is an action against the company for the breach of the contract made by its agent. Frederick *v.* Marquette, H. & O. R. R., 37 Mich. 342 (1877). See St. Louis, A. & T. R. Co. *v.* Mackie, 71 Texas, 491; 1 Lawyers' Rep. Ann. 667; 9 S. W. Rep. 451 (1888). The Rice case should be compared with the other Maryland cases, *ante,* p. 166, n. 1.

The distinction is taken in some of the decisions thus cited, between the case of a passenger who has failed to receive from one conductor the evidence of his right to passage in a connecting train, and that of a passenger who is. evicted by the same conductor to whom he has paid his fare or surrendered his ticket.[1] There certainly is an important difference between the two cases. But it can hardly be said to be sufficient, clearly to outweigh the argument drawn from the inconvenience and danger to the public, involved in the stoppage of a train at an unusual place, and for an indefinite time.

SECTION X.

POWER OF CARRIER TO ENFORCE REASONABLE RULES.

The power to enforce reasonable rules and regulations made by the carrier must, of necessity, to a large extent be vested in the carrier's servants. Their rights in this particular find many illustrations in reported cases. The carrier may authorize his servants to remove from the cars, or other property belonging to him, a person who has, after reasonable notice of the established regulations and opportunity for compliance, neglected or refused to comply with them, or to pay his fare.[2]

---

[1] English v. Delaware & H. Canal Co., 66 N. Y. 454 (1876), and other cases cited, ante, p. 168, n. 2.

[2] Carpenter v. Washington & G. R. R., 121 U. S. 474 (1887); Havens v. Hartford & New Haven R. R., 28 Conn. 69 (1859); Landrigan v. The State, 31 Ark. 50 (1876); Barker v. Coflin, 31 Barb. (N. Y.) 556 (1860); Hibbard v. N. Y. & Erie R. R., 15 N. Y. 455 (1857); Cin. S. & C. R. R. v. Skillman, 39 Ohio St. 444 (1883); Louisville & N. R. R. v. Maybin, 5 So. Rep. (Miss.) 401 (1889).

The Landrigan case was an appeal from a conviction for assault and battery. Appellant was the watchman at the depot of a railroad company, which had adopted a regulation forbidding the entry of inn-keepers, or their agents, upon the platform of the depot for the purpose of soliciting patronage. The party assaulted, knowing the regulation, entered on the platform for the prohibited purpose. Appellant warned

The authorities are not uniform as to whether, when the removal is made from a train, it may be made anywhere, or only at a regular station.   In Minnesota, Maryland and Missouri it is held that he may be ejected anywhere.[1]   The same rule has been laid down in Michigan, Iowa, Indiana and Kansas, subject to the just qualification that reasonable care and prudence be exercised in the selection of the place for ejection.[2]   In other States, however, it is held that the ejection must be at a usual place for stopping the trains.[3]

---

him that he was violating the regulation, and notified him to desist; he refused, and thereupon appellant ejected him from the platform. Held, that the regulation was a reasonable one, and that the appellant committed no offense in enforcing it. Atchison, T. & S. F. R. R. v. Gants, 38 Kans. 608; s. c. 17 Pacific R. 54 (1888).

Memphis & C. R. R. v. Chastine, 54 Miss. 503 (1877). In this case the passenger had a ticket, for which he had paid in counterfeit notes. He was ignorant of the character of the notes. *Held*, that the apparent payment was really no payment at all.

[1] Wyman v. Northern Pacific R. R., 34 Minn. 210; s. c. 25 N. W. Reporter, 349 (1885).   In this case, however, the person ejected was a trespasser.   McClure v. Phil., W. & B. R. R., 34 Md. 532 (1871).   The court say (p. 538): "We cannot concur in the doctrine contended for by the counsel for the appellant, that a passenger having no ticket, and refusing to pay his fare, can only be put off at some station on the road. The establishment of such a principle would result in compelling railroad companies to carry a passenger to the station next to the one at which he entered the train, which might, and doubtless would often turn out to be, the very point to which he desired to be taken, and if the passenger were unknown to the conductor, the company would be without remedy."   To the same effect is Lillis v. St. L., K. C. & N. R. Co., 64 Mo. 464 (1877), in which the court say that a person who goes on board a train with a ticket which, by the terms on its face, has expired, and refuses to pay his fare, is a trespasser, although he has been advised that the ticket was valid.   Everett v. Chicago, R. I. & P. R. Co., 69 Iowa, 15 (1886).

[2] Great Western R. Co. v. Miller, 19 Mich. 305 (1869); Brown v. Chicago, R. I. & P. R. Co., 51 Iowa, 235 (1879); Toledo, W. & W. R. Co. v. Wright, 68 Ind. 586 (1879).   It was so held in this latter case, notwithstanding the existence of a statute similar to that of Illinois, quoted in note 3.   The court held this to be permissive only, and not mandatory.   Atchison, T. & S. F. R. Co. v. Gants, 38 Kans. 608 (1888).

[3] Chicago & Alton R. R. v. Flagg, 43 Ill. 364 (1867); Chicago, Burlington & Quincy R. R. v. Parks, 18 *Ib.* 460 (1857); Toledo, P. & W. R. R. v. Patterson, 63 Ill. 304 (1872).   In Illinois Central R. R. v. Sut-

No unnecessary violence should be used.[1] A passenger who has paid his own fare may be ejected for refusing

ton, 42 *Ib*. 438 (1867), the court recognize the proposition stated in the text. In that case, however, the passenger had endeavored to procure a ticket before entering the car—the regulation of the company requiring it—but had been unable to do so because the ticket office was closed. The court held that, as the company was itself at fault, it could not impose such a hardship upon the passenger as putting him off its train in any place except a regular station. In some States this matter is regulated by statute. The general railroad act of Illinois (Ill. R. S. [ed. 1883], ch. 114, sect. 94) provides that the conductor may, if the passenger refuse to pay the required fare, eject him " at any usual stopping-place." This means the place where passenger trains usually stop for passengers to get on and off. Illinois Central R. R. *v*. Latimer, 21 N. East Rep. (Ill.) 7 (1889). See, also, Ill. R. S., ch. 114, sect. 80, p. 1159. This was held to exclude the right of ejection at any other place, even though the passenger said that he would get off if the conductor would stop the train. Chicago & N. W. R. Co. *v*. Peacock, 48 Ill. 253 (1868). Under the New Hampshire statute (N. H. Gen. Laws, ch. 163, sect. 22) a "passenger station" was held to mean a place at which passenger tickets are usually sold. Baldwin *v*. Grand Trunk R. Co., 64 N. H. 596; 7 New Eng. Rep. 111; 15 Atl. Rep. 411 (1888). In New York the general railroad act, ch. 140, of 1850, sect. 35 (3 Rev. Stat. Banks Bros., 8 ed. 1760), requires that the ejection should be at a station or near a dwelling house. A similar provision is contained in the Rapid Transit Act, Laws 1875, ch. 606, sect. 29 (3 R. S. Banks Bros., 8 ed. 1831); and in the statutes of Vermont, Stephen *v*. Smith, 29 Vt. 160 (1857); and California, Wright *v*. California Central R. Co., 20 Pac. Rep. 740 (1889). Passengers on railroad trains have a right to seats, and if one refuses to pay his fare because no seat is furnished him, he cannot be ejected except at a regular station. Hardenburgh *against* St. Paul, M. & M. R. Co., 38 N. W. Rep. (Minn.) 625 (1888). In this case it is said that a trespasser can be ejected anywhere. This was so held in Illinois Central R. R. *v*. Whittemore, 43 Ill. 420 (1867); South Fla. R. Co. *v*. Rhoads, 3 Lawy. Rep. (Fla.) 733; 5 So. Rep. 633 (1889). In Florida there is a statute on the subject, but, like that of Illinois, it provides only for the case of a refusal to pay fare. A passenger who tenders sufficient fare to the station to which he wishes to go, which is wrongfully refused by the conductor, may lawfully insist that he be put off at once, and not be carried to the next station. Hall *v*. South Carolina R. Co., 28 S. Car. 261 (1887).

[1] Gallena *v*. Hot Springs R. R., 13 Fed. Rep. 116; s. c. 4 McCrary, 371 (1882); New Jersey Steamboat Co. *v*. Brockett, 121 U. S. 637 (1887); Law *v*. Illinois Cent. R. R., 32 Iowa, 534 (1871); Coleman *v*. New York & N. H. R. R., 106 Mass. 160 (1870); Great Western R. Co. *v*. Miller, 19 Mich. 305 (1869); Hanson *v*. European & N. A. R. Co., 62 Me. 84 (1873); State *v*. Ross, 26 N. J. Law, 224 (1857); Jardine *v*. Cornell, 50 *Ibid*, 485 (1888). Whether it has been or not, is a question for the jury. Arnold *v*. Penn. R. R., 115 Penn. 135; s. c. 6 Central Rep. 630 (1887).

to pay the fare of a child who is accompanying him, and under his charge.[1] It has been held that if the ejection be made in good faith, but not at a regular station, the aggrieved party can only recover the damages caused by the unsuitableness of the place.[2] The carrier's servants would not, in any case, be justified in ejecting a person from the cars while the train was in motion.[3] Some reasonable regard must be had for the safety of even a trespasser or intoxicated person, and especially for the safety of a sick person who is removed because his continuance in the car, in the condition in which he is, is inconsistent with the health or comfort of the other passengers.[4] In Connecticut it was held that the holder of a commutation ticket, who could not find it when its production was re-

---

But in Stone *v.* Chicago & N. W. R. Co., 47 Iowa, 82 (1877), it was held that a person ejected had no right of action because the company had not employed for his ejection gentlemanly, polite, or even sober, servants. Chicago, St. L. & P. R. R. *v.* Bills, 104 Ind. 13; s. c. 3 North Eastern Reporter, 611 (1885).

[1] Philadelphia, W. & B. R. R. *v.* Hoeflich, 62 Md. 300 (1884); Gibson and Wife *v.* E. Tenn., V. & G. R. Co., 30 Fed. Rep. 904 (1887).

[2] Toledo, Peoria & W. R. R. *v.* Patterson, 63 Ill. 304 (1872); Philadelphia, W. & B. R. R. *v.* Hoeflich, 62 Md. 300 (1884).

[3] Holmes *v.* Wakefield, 12 Allen (Mass.), 580 (1866); State *v.* Kinney, 34 Minn. 311; s. c. 25 N. W. Reporter, 705 (1885); Sanford *v.* Eighth Ave. R. R., 23 N. Y. 343 (1861).

[4] Arnold *v.* Penn. R. R., 115 Penn. 135; s. c. 6 Cent. Rep. 630 (1887); Railway Co. *v.* Valleley, 32 Ohio St. 345 (1877); Louisville, C. & L. R. R. *v.* Sullivan, 81 Ky. 624 (1884); Louisville & N. R. R. *v.* Logan, 3 Lawy. Rep. Ann. (Ky.) 80 (1889); Atchison, T. & S. F. R. R. *v.* Weber, 33 Kans. 543 (1885); Connolly *v.* Crescent City R. Co., 3 Lawy. Rep. 133 (1888). In McClelland *v.* Louisville, N. A. & C. R. Co., 94 Ind. 276 (1883), it was, however, held that if the conductor had once put the drunkard in a safe place, he was not bound to watch him, and keep him out of danger.

It was held, in Missouri, that a person who entered a car, under advice that a ticket which he had previously bought was still valid, although by its terms it had expired, and had resolved not to pay any fare, never became a passenger, but was a trespasser from the beginning, and could be ejected anywhere, and was not entitled to the benefit of the statute that passengers can only be ejected from the cars near a station or freight house. Lillis *v.* St. Louis, Kansas City & Northern R. Co., 64 Missouri, 464 (1877).

quired by the conductor, could only be ejected at a usual station, and regulation to the contrary was held unreasonable and void.[1] The passenger is entitled to a reasonable time to find and produce his ticket, or pay his fare.[2]

And if the passenger innocently violate a regulation, even if he is somewhat offensive in language or conduct, he is entitled to an explanation from the conductor.[3]

It has been held, after considerable discussion and some rulings to the contrary at *nisi prius*, that if a passenger has once been lawfully ejected from a train, or even if the train has been stopped for the purpose of ejecting him, he has no right to re-enter the same except at a regular station,[4] and not even then, unless he

[1] Maples v. N.Y. & N. H. R. R., 38 Conn. 557 (1871). In Downs v. N. Y. & N. H. R. R., 36 Conn. 287 (1869), the passenger had, by mistake, left his commutation ticket at home, and was unable to show it when called for; and it was held that, in conformity with an express stipulation in his contract with the company, the latter had the right to demand the ordinary fare for the passage, and that, upon his refusal to pay, the conductor lawfully ejected him from the cars at the next regular station. Maples v. N. Y. & N. H. R. R., 38 Conn. 557 (1871), differs from the case of Downs v. The Same, in that the plaintiff Maples had his commutation ticket about his person, and only requested a reasonable time to find it, which was denied; that there was no express stipulation in his contract with the company that he should pay his fare for the trip if his ticket was not shown to the conductor, to whom he was well known as a commuter; and finally, that he was ejected from the train at a place other than a regular station. In this case it was held that the ejection was unlawful.

[2] Maples v. N. Y. & N. H. R. R., 38 Conn. 557 (1871); Curl v. Chicago, R. I. & P. R. Co., 63 Iowa, 417 (1884); Robson v. N. Y. Central & H. R. R. R., 21 Hun, 387 (1880); Hayes v. New York Central & H. R. R., 18 Am. & Eng. R. R. Ca. (N. Y.) 363 (1884); Clark v. Wilmington & W. R. R., 18 Am. & Eng. R. R. Ca. (So. Car.) 366 (1885); International & G. N. R. R. v. Wilkes, 68 Tex. 617 (1887).

[3] Compton v. Von Volkenburgh, 34 N. J. Law, 134 (1870).

[4] O'Brien v. Boston & W. R. R., 15 Gray, 20 (1860); Nelson v. L. I. R. R., 7 Hun (N. Y.), 140 (1876); Hibbard v. N. Y. & Erie R. R., 15 N. Y. 455 (1857); Pease v. D., L. & W. R. R., 11 Daly (N. Y.), 350 (1883); s. c. 101 N. Y. 367 (1886); People v. Jillson, 3 Parker, C. C. 234 (1856); Hoffbauer v. D. & N. W. R. Co., 52 Iowa, 342 (1879); R. R. Co. v. Skillman, 39 Ohio St. 444 (1883); State v. Campbell, 32 N. J. Law, 309 (1867). In the Campbell case the passenger had purchased an "excursion ticket," on the face of which it was declared that it was "good for

one passage on the day sold only." The passenger, returning upon a subsequent day, purchased an ordinary ticket and entered a train. Being called on by the conductor for his ticket, he produced the return coupon of the spent excursion ticket, keeping the one he had just bought out of view. The coupon was refused and his fare demanded, and, not complying with the demand nor intimating that he had a valid ticket, he was ejected at a regular station, after considerable resistance, which caused delay and inconvenience to the train and other passengers. After his expulsion, and before the train started, he exhibited his valid ticket to the conductor and attempted to re-enter the train, but was prevented by force. Held, that the conductor had the right to exclude him.

O'Brien *v.* N. Y. C. & H. R. R. R., 80 N. Y. 236 (1880), holds: That where the train is stopped for the sole purpose of ejecting a passenger who has refused to pay his fare, he cannot regain his right to be carried by a tender; but where the train stops at a regular stopping-place, and the passenger, before being ejected—or others, in his behalf—offer to pay the full fare, it is the duty of the conductor to accept it; and if he refuses, and ejects the passenger, the company is liable. In Texas it is held that if the passenger's refusal to pay the fare demanded is not willful, but based on an honest mistake, the conductor is bound to allow him to remain on the train if he tender the right amount immediately after the bell to stop is pulled. Texas & P. R. R. Co. *v.* Bond, 62 Texas, 442 (1884). In Bland *v.* Southern Pacific R. R., 55 Cal. 570 (1880), it was held that where a passenger, who had no ticket, paid the conductor the price for a ticket, but not the additional charge exacted when fare was paid in the cars, the conductor could not lawfully eject him until after he returned the money, and that returning it after the ejection was insufficient to render the ejection lawful. Hoffbauer *v.* D. & N. W. R. Co., *supra*, tends to the contrary. In Chicago, B. & Q. R. R. *v.* Bryan, 90 Ill. 126 (1878), it was held that if the passenger had paid fare to the station at which he was evicted, he had the right there to re-enter the train upon paying fare from there to his destination.

In Louisville & Nash. R. R. *v.* Garrett, 8 Lea (Tenn.), 438 (1881), the court say: "His Honor (below) was correct when he told the jury, substantially, that if another person offered to pay the fare before ejection from the car, the carrier was bound to receive it and transport the passenger. It is unimportant to the carrier from whom the money comes. If it is the proper amount, he gets what he is entitled to, and must perform the duty imposed. To require that the passenger shall pay his own money would be absurd. If another party offers to pay for him, it is precisely as if the party, finding himself without money to pay, had borrowed the amount from one near him and tendered it. The conductor would have the same right to refuse to accept the money thus borrowed as to refuse the offer made in this case." In that case the offer was not made till after the bell-rope had been pulled for the train to stop, but court held it should have then been accepted and the passenger allowed to ride. s. p., Guy *v.* N. Y., O. & W. R. R., 30 Hun, 399 (1883).

In South Carolina R. R. *v.* Nix, 68 Georgia, 572 (1882), the court

pays his fare from the station at which he originally entered the train.[1]

The carrier's servants are bound to regard the age, condition of health, and other circumstances of the passenger before determining whether to eject him.[2]

The carrier has no right to detain a passenger at the station, at which he alights, until he produces a ticket or

---

held that the passenger would have the right to re-enter the train if he tendered the proper fare before the train started, but not afterwards.

In Gould v. Chicago, M. & St. P. R. Co., 18 Fed. Rep. 155 (1883), it was held that if the passenger had been abusive, and compelled the conductor to resort to violence, he could not require the carrier to receive him, even at a regular station; but that if no such misconduct were shown the rule would be otherwise.

[1] Stone v. Chicago & N. W. R Co.. 47 Iowa, 82 (1877); s. c. 29 Am. Rep. 458; Swan v. Manchester & L. R., 132 Mass. 116 (1882). In Louisville, N. & G. S. R. R. v. Harris, 9 Lea (Tenn.), 180; s. c. 16 Am. & Eng. R. R. Cas. 374 (1882), the right to re-enter the train at a station, even on tender of the full fare, was denied. In this case the passenger was a commuter, the violation of the rule which forbade him to detach coupons was technical only, and the rule seems to have been applied with needless severity.

[2] Sheridan v. Brooklyn City R. R., 36 N. Y. 39 (1867). In Louisville, Nashville & G. S. R. R. v. Fleming, 14 Lea (Tenn.), 128 (1884), it was held that if an infirm person told the conductor that his ticket was in his pocket, and the conductor undertook to search for it, "he should do so properly, and in good faith." But the obligation to search is denied. It was held, in Curl v. Chicago, R. I. & P. R. Co., 63 Iowa, 417 (1884), that if the passenger, through no fault of his own, had failed to get a ticket, and had only enough money to pay for one, but not the extra charge required from those who had no ticket, he was entitled to a reasonable time to obtain it from other passengers. In the Fleming case the court treat this as a question of contributory negligence, and state that the rule in Tennessee is different from that of other States, in that there contributory negligence may be shown in mitigation of damages, even in cases where, by reason of the willfulness of the tort committed by defendant's agents, it is not a defense. East Tenn., V. & G. R. R. v. Fain, 12 Lea, 35 (1883); Nashville & C. R. R. v. Carroll, 6 Heiskel, 347 (1871); Louisville & N. R. R. v. Burke, 6 Cold. (Tenn) 45 (1868); Nashville & C. R. R. v. Nowlin, 1 Lea, 523 (1878). It has been held that persons unable to take care of themselves must provide proper assistance, and cannot require the carrier to do so. New Orleans, J. & G. N. R. R. v. Statham, 42 Miss. 607 (1869); Hemingway v. Chicago, M. & St. P. R. Co., 72 Wis. 42; 37 N. W. 804 (1888); Willetts v. Buffalo R. R., 14 Barb. 585 (1853). Compare Owens v. Kansas City, St. J. & C. B. R. Co., 8 S. W. (Mo.) 350 (1888).

pays his fare.[1] But though there is no lien on the person, the carrier has a lien on the passenger's baggage for his unpaid fare.[2]

Where a commuter refused to show his ticket or pay his fare, it was held that the company might eject him or forfeit his ticket, but could not, on a subsequent occasion, refuse to sell him another commutation ticket.[3]

Where a passenger has been in the habit of improperly carrying merchandise in his trunk, the carrier may lawfully require him to sign a statement as to the contents of his trunk.[4]

In this class of cases we have no English authorities. In England no facilities are afforded for paying fare on the cars, and a ticket can only be procured before entering them.

SECTION XI.

WHETHER NOTICE OF THE RULES IS NECESSARY; AND IF SO, WHAT?

In many cases it is held that persons who deal with carriers, and especially passengers seeking to take pas-

---

[1] Lynch *v.* Metropolitan El. R. Co., 90 N. Y. 77 (1882); *ante*, pp. 139, 140, nn. 1, 2. In Sullivan *agst.* Old Colony R. Co., 18 N. East. (Mass.) 678; 1 Lawy. Rep. Ann. 513 (1888), a drunken and disorderly person was put into the baggage car, and carried to his destination. Held, that the company had a right to do this, and were not bound to put him into the hands of an officer at the next station.

[2] Roberts *v.* Koehler (U. S. C. Ct. Oregon), 30 Fed. Rep. 94 (1887).

[3] Atwater *v.* Delaware, L. & W. R. Co., 48 N. J. Law, 55 (1886).

[4] Norfolk & W. R. Co. *v.* Irvine, 5 S. E. Rep. (Va.) 533 (1888). Whether it can require an affidavit *quære*. But the court will not be critical as to the requirements of the carrier towards a passenger who is engaged in a deliberate attempt to make occasion for a suit against the carrier. Same *v.* Same, 7 S. E. Rep. (Va.) 233 (1888).

Where plaintiff was riding on a car with his assistant, under a drover's pass good only for one, and told the conductor if it was not right he might eject his assistant, the conductor would not be thereby justified in expelling the plaintiff. Missouri Pac. R. Co. *v.* Aiken, 9 S. W. Rep. (Texas), 437 (1888).

12

sage on railway trains, are bound to make enquiry as to the rules established by the carrier with reference to the proposed transit, and conform thereto, and that if no enquiry be made, the passenger is subject to the reasonable rules of the carrier even though unknown to him.[1]

On the other hand it is held that a regulation as to the time within which the ticket must be used is not valid unless some notice is given to the purchaser at the time he buys his ticket.[2] The same rule was applied, in Illinois, to a case where a man bought a ticket for himself and family, and the carrier's rule was that a son over twenty-one years of age, even though residing with his father, was not entitled to be transported under such a ticket.[3]

The decision of the court in any given case would

---

[1] Cheney *v.* Boston & Me. R. R., 11 Metc. (Mass.) 121 (1846); Elmore *v.* Sands, 54 N. Y. 512 (1874); Beebe *v.* Ayres, 28 Barb. (N. Y.) 275 (1858). In this latter case the court say of the passenger: "He is presumed to have purchased the ticket in reference to the regulations of the road." Northern R. R. *v.* Page, 22 Barb. (N. Y.) 130 (1856); Dunphy *v.* Erie R. Co., 42 N. Y. Super. Ct. 128 (1877). The same rule was laid down, as to the duty of the passenger to ascertain by enquiry what trains would stop at his place of destination, in Duling *v.* Philadelphia, W. & B. R. R., 66 Md. 120; 5 Cent. Rep. 570 (1886).

In McRae *v.* Wilmington & W. R. R., 88 N. C. 526; s. c. 43 Am. Rep. 745 (1883), the court say: "One who buys a ticket is bound to inform himself of the rules and regulations of the company governing the transit and conduct of its trains." It was held, therefore, that a passenger who bought an excursion ticket at less than usual rates, was bound to ascertain on what train his ticket would be good; that a rule of the carrier limiting its validity to a special excursion train was reasonable.

So it is held that a condition as to the continuity of the trip need not be printed on the ticket. Drew *v.* Central Pac. R. R., 51 Cal. 425 (1876); Oil Creek & Allegheny River R. Co. *v.* Clark, 72 Penn. 231 (1872). The regulations need not be communicated to the passenger, but he is bound by them, irrespective of notice. State *v.* Overton, 24 N. J. L. 435 (1854); Terry *v.* Flushing, N. S. & C. R. R., 13 Hun, 359 (1878); Dietrich *v.* Penn. R. R., 71 Penn. 432 (1872). In the Overton case, however, notice had been published. Atchison, T. & S. F. R. *v.* Gants, 38 Kans. 608; 17 Pac. Rep. 54 (1888). See cases, *ante*, p. 159, note 3, *post*, Ch. XI, sect. 1.

[2] Penn. R. R. *v.* Spicker, 105 Penn. 142 (1884).

[3] Chicago & N. W. R. Co. *v.* Chesholm, 79 Ill. 584 (1875).

doubtless depend upon the usages of the business of transporting passengers, and the extent to which the traveling public had conformed to them.   The giving of checks for baggage, the issuing of through tickets with a coupon for each railroad forming a part of the route, are now universal in the United States.   But there was a time in the history of railway transportation when these facilities were not customary.   Other usages spring up from time to time, and passengers and carriers will natu-rally conform to them, and special notice of them will neither be expected nor required.   It has become, for ex-ample, the universal custom of railway companies to print, and post in their offices, their time-tables, and of passen-gers to ascertain at what stations particular trains are to stop.   A passenger could not justly complain that the train he took did not stop at the station to which he was bound, if, with this usage in force, he should omit to in-quire whether a particular train was to stop at such sta-tion.

If the rules and regulations of the carrier are printed on the ticket delivered to the passenger, this is sufficient notice to him of the rules so printed.[1]   And in some cases it is held that posting the rules in a conspicuous place in the carrier's public office is sufficient notice to the public who do business there, if they have been posted long enough to enable persons in the exercise of due diligence to ascertain what the rules are.[2]

---

[1] Kelsey v. Michigan Central R. R., 28 Hun (N. Y), 460 (1882); Cresson v. Phil. & Reading R. R., 11 Phila. 597; S. C. 32 Leg. Int. 363 (1875).

[2] Burlington & M. R. R. v. Rose, 11 Neb. 177 (1881); Falkner v. Ohio & Miss. R. Co., 55 Ind. 369 (1876).   In Hart v. Baxendale, 6 Excheq. 769 (1851), it was held that posting a notice in the carrier's public office, that an increased charge would be made for the convey-ance of certain goods, was sufficient, though it was proved that the ship-per of the goods in question never saw the notice, and they were re-ceived by the carrier at the shipper's place of business.   Proof that regulations, purporting to be those of the carrier, were posted in its rail-

Notice that a coupon is not good if detached from its book, printed on the coupon and on the book, is sufficient.[1]

A former employee of the carrier is chargeable with knowledge of its rules.[2]

If the carrier desires to change its regulations in any particular in which they affect the traveling public, it should give reasonable notice of the change. Proof of personal notice is unnecessary, but the change should be so published as to give passengers reasonable opportunity to be informed of the change.[3]

---

road car is sufficient to show that they were, in fact, its regulations. Wright *v.* Cal. Cent. R. Co., 20 Pac. Rep. 740 (1889).

[1] Boston & Maine R. R. *v.* Chipman, 146 Mass. 107 (1888).

[2] Virginia Midland R. Co. *v.* Roach, 83 Va. 375 (1887).

[3] Kansas Pac. R. Co. *v.* Kessler, 18 Kans. 523 (1877); Lane *v.* E. Tenn., V. & Geo. R. R., 5 Lea (Tenn.), 124 (1880).

CHAPTER VIII.

CONFLICT OF LAWS.

There is probably no branch of the law more intricate, or more confused with conflicting decisions, than that which forms the subject of this chapter. The text writers have not succeeded any better than the judges in dealing with it. As judge-made law it has many defects and inconsistencies, but no codifier has yet shaped it into symmetry.

I shall not attempt to consider the subject at large. To do so would require a volume. But the questions upon carrier's contracts, in the decision of which the conflicting laws of different jurisdictions have been invoked, cannot be passed by without consideration. Lines of steamers link the continents. Lines of railroads span them. The laws of the country where the contract of affreightment is made differ from those of the country where its performance is to be completed. England has one policy as to stipulations limiting the liability of common carriers. The Federal courts declare another for the United States. Our different States disagree between themselves. Statutes have been passed which complicate the subject. Its difficulty has been enhanced by the changes in the method of doing business that have taken place during the past twenty-five years.

One of the most remarkable features in the history of this country during that time, has been the growth of great corporations, and the extension of their operations into many different States. American courts found in the British law the curious fiction, that for some purposes Scotland was a kingdom foreign to that of England. This was probably due to the prejudice entertained by the English of King James' time for their northern neighbors. Our courts adopted a similar rule, and held that the States of this Union were, for many purposes, foreign to each other. And this rule embarrassed them in dealing with corporations. Technically these are artificial beings, owing their existence only to the law of the State which created them, which law has no extra-territorial force. It was gravely questioned at one time whether a corporation had power to contract beyond the boundaries of the State under whose laws it was incorporated. It required the eloquence and the farseeing wisdom of Mr. Webster to convince the Supreme Court of the United States that this contention was too narrow and technical. In the celebrated "Alabama Appeal Cases," one of which only—The Bank of Augusta v. Earle—is reported,[1] it was held that a corporation incorporated under the laws of one State could make a valid contract in another, unless prohibited by the laws of that State. Since that time many States have adopted general laws for the creation of corporations, and they have practically become limited partnerships, capable of suing and being sued by the firm name, and having perpetual succession.

For a long time, too, it was questioned whether a common carrier incorporated under the laws of one State had any power to make a contract to transport persons or property beyond the limits of that State. In Bissell v. The Michigan Southern & N. Ind. R. R.[2] this defense of *ultra vires* was set up to an action for injuries received by a passenger, on the cars of the defendant, outside the limits of the State which chartered it. The court sustained the right of action on the ground that the corporation had received the consideration of the contract, and was estopped

---

[1] 13 Peters, 519 (1839).
[2] 22 N. Y. 258 (1860).

to set up this defense when redress was sought for its breach.

The validity of such contracts is now well settled, and we see the Pennsylvania Railroad Company practically managing a line of railway from New York to Chicago, extending through seven States. The great telegraph companies extend their lines over a field even wider. And the courts have had no more difficult task than the decision of the question: by what law should contracts for interstate and foreign transportation be interpreted, and the consequences of their breach be determined?

The important question to the consideration of which this chapter is devoted is this: Under what circumstances will a court, sitting in a forum, the public policy of which is opposed to limitations of liability for the negligence of a carrier's servants, enforce such limitations when the contract is made or to be performed in another jurisdiction?

For example: a contract is made in England, between parties domiciled there, by which one agrees to transport to Philadelphia the goods of the other. The contract contains a clause that the carrier shall not be liable to the shipper for any damages caused by the negligence or barratry of the carrier's servants. In England this clause is declared by the courts not to be against the public policy of that country. In Pennsylvania it is declared by the courts to be against the public policy of that State. If loss ensues from the excepted cause, and the carrier is sued in Pennsylvania, shall he have the benefit of the exemption?

We will first consider the general rules which ought to guide courts in determining the validity of particular stipulations in contracts made in one jurisdiction, to be partly or wholly performed in another.

I. A contract which is lawful in the country where it is made and is to be performed is valid everywhere, and the courts of every country in which its enforcement is sought should, therefore, give effect to its provisions.[1]

---

[1] In Hale *v.* N. J. Steam Nav. Co., 15 Conn. 539; s. c. 39 Am. Dec. 398 (1843), which was one of the cases growing out of the loss of the Lexington, the court say: "Contracts are to be construed according to the laws of the State where made, unless it is presumed from their tenor that they were entered into with a view to the laws of some other State. Bartsch *v.* Atwater, 1 Conn. 409, 416 (1815); Smith *v.* Mead, 3 *Id.* 253; s. c. 8 Am. Dec. 183 (1820); Brackett *v.* Norton, 4 *Id.* 517; s. c. 10 Am. Dec. 179 (1823). There is nothing in this case, either from the location of the parties or the nature of the contract, which shows that they could have had any other law in view than that of the place where it was made. Indeed, as the goods were shipped to be transported to Boston or Providence, there would be the most entire uncertainty what was to be the law of the case if any other rule were to prevail. We have, therefore, no doubt that the law of New York, as to the duties and liabilities of common carriers, is to be the law of the case."

Story on Conflict of Laws, section 280, says that, in general, the validity, nature, obligation and interpretation of a contract are to be governed by the law of the place of performance, "in conformity to the presumed intention of the parties." Chancellor Kent, 2 Comm. 461, note c, states the rule differently: "The general principle is, that as to contracts purely personal, their construction is governed by the law of the place where they were made, the consequences of their breach by that of the country where they are enforced." So Lord Langdale, Master of the Rolls, Cooper *v.* Earl of Waldegrave, 2 Beav. 282 (1840).

Knowlton *v.* Erie R. Co., 19 Ohio St. 260; s. c. 2 Am. Rep. 395 (1869). This was an action for injuries caused the plaintiff by the negligence of defendant's servants. By the terms of the contract the plaintiff was to be carried gratuitously, and was to assume all risk of injury arising through the negligence of defendant's servants or otherwise. Held, that the validity of the contract must be determined by the law of New York, and that, as it was valid in that State, the plaintiff could not recover. In this case, however, the contract was wholly to be performed within the State of New York.

In Shuenfeldt *v.* Junkermann, 20 Fed. Rep. 357 (1884), a question arose as to the validity of a contract negotiated in Iowa, which was not to take effect until approved by the principals in Chicago. The contract was valid by the laws of Illinois, but void by the laws of Iowa. The United States Circuit Court for the District of Iowa held that the place of the contract was the place where it was consummated, and not that where it was negotiated. A recovery upon the contract was therefore sustained. It is to be observed that in this case the goods in question were to be delivered in Iowa. That, therefore, was certainly the place of performance. This case must therefore be considered as an authority for the proposition that a court sitting in the State where a contract is to be performed will enforce it, if it is valid by the law of the State where it is made. In other words, its validity is determined by the *lex loci contractus.* Story, Conflict of Laws, sects. 286, 286a.

s. p. Talbott *v.* Merchants' Despatch Trans. Co., 41 Iowa, 247 (1875);

An exception to this first rule may be thus stated. No court is bound to enforce a contract intrinsically wicked (*malum in se*), nor one the enforcement of which is prohibited by the express legislation of the forum (*malum prohibitum*).[1]

II. When a contract is made in one country, to be wholly performed in another, its validity is to be determined by the law of the place of performance, unless the contract expressly provide otherwise.[2]

Malpica *v.* McKown, 1 Louisiana, 248; s. c. 20 Am. Dec. 279 (1830). In Turner *v.* Lewis, 2 Mich. 350 (1852), the court held that in order that a lien might attach under a Michigan statute for the collection of demands against ships for a breach of contract of affreightment, the "contract (*sic*) must arise" in that State, and that a lien did not attach, in case of breach, where the contract, though made in another State, was to be performed in Michigan. Burckle *v.* Eckhart, 3 N. Y. 132 (1849), is directly the reverse, and seems, to the author, to be much more in harmony with the leading authorities.

[1] In Andrews *against* Pond, 13 Pet. 65 (1839), the general rule was held to be that the law of the place of performance is to govern. This does not apply, however, where a contract is made in one State to evade its laws, and in direct violation of its statutes. In *ex parte* Dickinson, 29 So. Car. 453; s. c. *sub nom.* Sheldon *v.* Blauvelt, 7 S. E. Rep. 593 (1888), it was held that an assignment made in New York, and valid by the laws of that State, did not operate to transfer title to property in South Carolina because it contained preferences. The statute of South Carolina provided that an assignment with preferences (except to employees) should be void. On the other hand it is held that a purchase, valid in the State where it was made, transferred a good title to the railway ticket which was the subject matter of the sale, although the ticket was partly to be used in a State where the contract of purchase was prohibited. Sleeper *v.* Penn. R. R., 100 Penn. 259 (1882). Among the cases cited in support of the second rule (*post*, p. 185, n. 2) there are many in which the contract under consideration was invalid by the law of the forum, but was nevertheless enforced. See, also, the cases under the usury laws, *post*, p. 187, n. 2.

[2] "The general principle in relation to contracts made in one place to be performed in another is well settled. They are to be governed by the law of the place of performance." Miller *v.* Tiffany, 1 Wall. 298, 310 (1863); Pritchard *v.* Norton, 106 U. S. 124 (1882); Junction Railroad Co. *v.* Bank of Ashland, 12 Wall. 226 (1870); Bell *v.* Bruen, 1 How. 169, 182 (1843); Le Breton *v.* Miles, 8 Paige, 261 (1840); Osgood *v.* Bauder, 75 Iowa, 550; 39 N. W. Rep. 887 (1888).

The rule thus stated was one of the first to be applied to the solution of the many intricate questions that arose from the conflict be-

The reason given for the decisions to which reference has been had, is that parties are presumed to have contracted with reference to the law of the place of performance. This presumption, in most cases, has been treated

---

tween the laws of different countries, and is expressed with precision by the writers on the civil law.

"*Vulgo quidem ita traditum invenio, observare debere statutum, non loci illius ubi ventilatur restitutionis quaestio, neque etiam regionis illius ubi laedens aut laesus domicilium fovet, sed magis illius territorii in quo contractus seu negotium damnosum celebratum est: nisi contractus implementum ad alium locum sit destinatum, tunc enim hujus loci leges in judicando spectandas esse.*" Voet *ad* Pand. vol. 1, Paris ed., p. 315, lib. 4, tit. 1, sect. 29.

To the same effect is The Digest, Lib. XLIV, tit. VII, 21.

"*Contraxisse unusquisque in eo loco intelligitur in quo, ut solverit, se obligavit.*"

This rule has been carried so far as to sustain the validity of a contract for a loan which was usurious and void by the law of the place where it was made, but valid by the law of the place where the money was payable. Andrews *v.* Pond, 13 Peters, 65, 78 (1839); Miller *v.* Tiffany, 1 Wall. 298, 310 (1863); *post,* p. 187, n. 2.

So in Penobscot & Kennebeck R. R. Company *v.* Bartlett, 12 Gray, 244 (1858), the court say (p. 246), referring to a contract made in Boston, of subscription to stock in a railroad in Maine: "We are of the opinion that the validity, obligation and interpretation of the contract must be governed by the law of the State of Maine. . . . We cannot doubt that the place of performance of the contract was in the State of Maine, and that it was so understood and intended by the parties."

In Burckle *v.* Eckhart, 3 N. Y. 132 (1849), it was held that where a contract was made in Oswego for the manufacture of flour there, to be delivered in Canada, the cause of action arose in Canada, and the performance of the contract was to be regulated according to the law of Canada. In Cox *v.* The United States, 6 Pet. 172, 202 (1832), a bond was executed in Louisiana, conditioned that the principal, who was a government officer, should account at Washington. It was held that, in construing the bond, the law of the place of performance was to govern, and the liability of the sureties was determined by that law.

In Brown *v.* Camden & Atlantic R. R., 83 Penn. 316 (1877), the contract was made in Pennsylvania with a New Jersey railroad company, to transport a passenger and his trunk from Philadelphia to Atlantic City, N. J. The trunk was lost, and it was held that the liability of the carrier was to be determined by the law of New Jersey. The court says (p. 318):

"It is perfectly well settled by a host of authorities, which it would be an affectation of learning to cite, that it is the law of the place of performance by which the mode of fulfilling a contract and the measure of liability for its breach must be determined."

by the courts as a *conclusive* one, and no evidence of the intention of the parties in that regard has been required.[1]

The only exception to this rule just stated, as to the law of the place of performance, is one relating to contracts for the payment of interest for the loan of money. In that case the courts have inclined to allow the parties to stipulate for the rate of interest allowed by the law of either place, and have thus frequently enforced contracts which were void by the positive legislation of the State in which they were made, but which were valid by the law of the place of performance.[2] Nevertheless the rule thus stated is not controlling in our present enquiry, for it is seldom, indeed, that a contract of affreightment is made in one country to be wholly performed in another. The ordinary cases, and those which are difficult, are where a contract is made in one country, partly to be performed in that, partly to be performed in other States—or on the high seas—and partly to be performed in a country other than that of the place of contract.

III. The construction of the language used in a contract is to be determined by the law of the State in which it is made.[3]

---

[1] Prentiss *v.* Savage, 13 Mass. 20 (1816). In this case the court say: "It seems to be an undisputed doctrine, with respect to personal contracts, that the law of the place where they are made shall govern in their construction, except when made with a view to performance in some other country, and then the law of such country is to prevail. This is nothing more than common sense and sound justice, adopting the probable intent of the parties as to the rule of construction. . . . And it is also to be presumed, when the contract is to be executed in any other country than that in which it is made, that the parties take into their consideration the law of such foreign country. The latter branch of the rule, if not so obviously founded upon the intention of the parties as the former, is equally well settled as a principle in the law of contracts." See *ante*, p. 185, n. 2; *post*, pp. 196–199.

[2] Rail Road Co. *v.* Bk. of Ashland, 12 Wall. 226 (1870); Depau *v.* Humphreys, 8 Mart. N. S. (La.) 1 (1829); *ante*, p. 186, note.

[3] 2 Kent Comm. 458, 461, n. c; Story Conf. Law, sect. 272; Scudder *v.* Union Nat. Bank, 91 U. S. 406 (1875). (See this case considered in Dickinson *v.* Edwards, 77 N. Y. 573 [1879].) Aymar *v.* Sheldon, 12

IV. In many cases of maritime contracts courts have held that their validity is to be determined by the law of the flag, that is to say, by the law of the nationality to which the ship belongs.

This rule has been advocated, on the ground that it relieves the court from the difficulties which have been found to attend the application of the rule firstly stated in this chapter, to the case of contracts made in one country, but to be performed in several.[1]

Wend. 439 (1834); Scott *v.* Pilkington, 15 Abb. Pr. 280 (1861); Ferguson *v.* Fyffe, 8 Cl. & Fin. 121, 141 (1841); Waters *v.* Cox, 2 Bradwell (Ill. App.), 129 (1878). In this case the construction of the contract and the rights of the parties under it were held to be fixed by the law of the State where the contract was made, and these rights remained unchanged, notwithstanding the removal of the parties to a State where a different construction would have been given to the contract. Penn. Co. *v.* Fairchild, 69 Ill. 260 (1873); McDaniel *v.* Chicago & N. W. R. Co., 24 Iowa, 412 (1868).

[1] Gaetano & Maria, 7 Prob. Div. 137 (1882); revg. s. c. *Ibid,* 1 (1881); Lloyd *v.* Guibert, 6 Best & Smith, 100 (1865). In this case a British subject, at a Danish island, chartered from its master a ship belonging to a French subject, for a voyage to Havre, London or Liverpool, at the charterer's option. While on its voyage to Liverpool, damage accrued, and the question arose as to whether the Danish, the English or the French law, or the law of Portugal (in which country a bottomry bond was given) should apply. The court held that the law of France governed the case: "And we think that, as far as regards the implied authority of the master of a ship to bind his owners personally, the flag of the ship is notice to all the world that the master's authority is that conferred by the law of that flag; that his mandate is contained in the law of that country, with which those who deal with him must make themselves acquainted at their peril." Affirmed, 6 Best & Smith, 120; s. c., L. R. 1 Q. B. 115 (1865), where the court says that the ship "was, as it were, a floating island, over which France had as absolute, and for all purposes of peace as exclusive a sovereignty, as over her dominions by land, and which, even whilst in a foreign port, . . . was never completely removed from French jurisdiction."

Pope *v.* Nickerson, 3 Story, 465 (1844). In this case a contract was made in Malaga by the master of a vessel for shipment of a cargo from Malaga to Philadelphia. While on the voyage the vessel and cargo were damaged, and sold by the master in Bermuda. The vessel was owned in Massachusetts, and this action having been brought by the owner of the cargo against the owners of the vessel, it was held that the liability of the latter was governed by the laws of Massachusetts, and not by those of Pennsylvania or Spain.

The Woodland, 14 Blatchf. 499 (1878); affg. 7 Ben. 110 (1874).

It seems clear that the authority of the master to bind
his owners, and to hypothecate or sell the ship or the cargo,

---

This was a case where a British vessel, bound from Montevideo to New
York, put into the Danish port of St. Thomas for repairs. The question
arose as to whether the master had authority to create a lien in the foreign port of distress in any other mode than by a bottomry bond. According to the English law, as held in that case, and as since held by
the House of Lords (reversing several prior decisions, The Sara, 14 App.
Ca. 209 [1889]), a lien could only be created by such a bond, while in
the United States that formality was not necessary. The court held that
the law of England applied: "It seems to be settled that the question
is to be determined by the law of the country of which the master was
a citizen, and under whose flag the vessel sailed, and not by the law of
the port where the supplies were furnished, or of the country where the
lien is sought to be enforced." The case was affirmed on another
ground by the Supreme Court. 104 U. S. 180 (1881). The same rule
was applied to the determination of the validity of clauses of exemption
in a bill of lading. The Titania, 19 Fed. Rep. 101 (1883). See, also,
The John Ritson, 35 Fed. Rep. 663 (1888); Force v. Providence Washington Ins. Co., 35 Fed. Rep. 767 (1888).

In Malpica v. McKown, 1 Louisiana, 248 (1830), the court held that
when the law of the country where the contract of affreightment is entered into, and to which the journey is to be made, differs from the law
of the place where the owner resides, the former must govern. And the
same court, in Arayo v. Currel, 1 Louisiana, 528 (1830), again decided
the same point in a similar way. Both of these Louisiana cases are
criticised by Justice Story in the case of Pope v. Nickerson, cited
supra.

In The Montana, reported sub nom. Liverpool & G. W. S. Co. v.
Phenix Ins. Co., 129 U. S. 397 (1889); affg. s. c. 22 Fed. Rep. 715
(1884); affg. 17 Fed. Rep. 377 (1883), contracts of affreightment had
been made, mostly in the State of New York, for the transportation of
goods to Liverpool. Several of them were made by railroad companies,
and were not only for inland transportation to New York city, but also
from New York to Liverpool. The vessel, sailing under the British flag,
was wrecked on the Welsh coast, and this, as the court found, was due
to the negligence of the captain. The Supreme Court held that the law
of the United States must govern the case, and not the law of the flag.

In The Brantford City, 29 Fed. Rep. 373 (1886), it was held the lex
loci contractus must govern and determine the validity of clauses of exemption in a bill of lading, and that such clauses in a bill of lading delivered in Boston, Mass., for transportation on a British ship to England, were invalid.

Re Missouri S. S. Co., 58 Law T. Rep. (N. S.) 377 (1888); s. c. 37
Alb. L. J. 518; affd. Weekly Notes, Notes of Cases, p. 90, May 11,
1889, is directly opposed to The Brantford City, which it quotes.
Foreign ships, while in another country, dealing with its citizens, owe a
temporary allegiance to its laws, and, in respect to such contracts, are
subject to the law of that jurisdiction rather than that of the home

is to be governed by the law of the flag in the absence of express authority. The decisions on this subject are placed solely on reasons springing out of the law of agency. For this very reason it would seem that they are equally applicable to the authority of any agent other than the captain, and therefore to the authority of any agent authorized to contract for the shipment of goods on board a particular vessel.

The rule on the subject has the great merit of simplicity. A party contracting with an agent of a foreign ship can always ascertain the extent of his authority under the law of that country to which the ship belongs. For example: the British law, and the extent of the authority of the agent of a British ship, are well known in the commercial community. And the same is true, to a large degree, of the law of the other commercial countries of Europe.

Some light may be thrown upon this subject of the law of the flag by a consideration of the rule that has, from the necessity of the case, been adopted as to the territorial status of a vessel upon the high seas. No country has exclusive jurisdiction of the part of the earth where she happens to be. Yet she is not, for that reason, beyond the reach of law. It is well settled that a ship on the high seas is to be considered as part of the territory of the nation to which she belongs;[1] and it would seem

---

port. The validity of a maritime lien depends upon the law of the place where it is created, not on that of the flag. The Scotia, 35 Fed. Rep. 907, 910 (1888). Accordingly it has been held in numerous cases that a materialman has a lien for supplies furnished to a vessel in a foreign port, although by the law of her flag her master had no power to create such a lien. The Eliza Jane, 1 Sprague. 152 (1847); Hatton v. The "Melita," 3 Hughes, 497 (1879); The Walkyrien, 11 Blatchf. 241 (1873); affg. 3 Bened. 394 (1869); The J. F. Spencer, 5 Bened. 151 (1871); The Selah, 4 Sawy. 40 (1876). In these, as in most of the cases, the courts have endeavored to support the validity of the contract or enforce the alleged lien.

[1] Crapo v. Kelly, 16 Wall. 610 (1872). At p. 624 the court say: "We are of the opinion, for the purpose we are considering, that the

that the consequences of a tort committed upon or by her, when she is on the high seas, should be determined by those laws.

---

ship Arctic was a portion of the territory of Massachusetts, and the assignment by the insolvent court of that State passed the title to her, in the same manner and with the like effect as if she had been physically within the bounds of that State when the assignment was executed.

"The rule is thus laid down by Mr. Wheaton in his treatise on International Law (8th ed., sect. 106, *et seq*.): 'Both the public and private vessels of every nation on the high seas, and out of the territorial limits of any other State, are subject to the jurisdiction of the State to which they belong. Vattel says that the domain of a nation extends to all its just possessions, and by its possessions we are not to understand its territory only, but all the rights it enjoys. And he also considers the vessels of a nation on the high seas as portions of its territory. Grotius holds that sovereignty may be acquired over a portion of the sea.' As an illustration of the proposition that the ship is a portion of the territory of the State, the author proceeds: 'Every State has an incontestable right to the service of all its members in the national defense, but it can give effect to this right only by lawful means. Its right to reclaim the military service of its citizens can be exercised only within its own territory, or in some place not subject to the jurisdiction of any other nation. The ocean is such a place, and any State may unquestionably there exercise, on board its own vessels, its right of compelling the military or naval services of its subjects.'

"Chancellor Kent, in his Commentaries (vol. i, p. 26), says: 'The high seas are free and open to all the world, and the laws of every State or nation have there a full and perfect operation upon the persons and property of the citizens or subjects of such a State or nation.' 'No nation has any right or jurisdiction at sea, except it be over the persons of its subjects, in its own public and private vessels; and so far territorial jurisdiction may be conceded as preserved, for the vessels of a nation are in many respects considered as portions of its territory, and persons on board are protected and governed by the law of the country to which the vessel belongs.'

"Wharton (Conflict of Laws, § 356) says: 'A ship in the open sea is regarded by the law of nations as a part of the territory whose flag such ship carries.' 'By this (he says) may be explained several cases quoted as establishing the *lex domicilii*, though they are only sustainable on the ground that the ship at sea is part of the territory whose flag she bears. . . . In respect to principle, ships at sea, and the property in them, must be viewed as part of the country to which they belong.'

"The modern German law is to the same point. Bluntschli, in his Moderne Volkerrecht (§ 317), says: 'Ships are to be regarded as floating sections of the land to which they nationally belong, and whose flag they are entitled to carry.'

"Bischof, in his Grundriss des positiven internationalen Seerechts (Graz, 1868; cited in Wharton's Conflict of Laws, § 356. n.), says: 'Every State is free on the seas, so that its ships are to be regarded as

It will be observed that none of the rules already stated, except the last, attempts to solve the difficulty previously suggested, and this rule only applies to maritime con-tracts.

V. A fifth rule which has much support in authority may be thus stated:

The manner in which the contract is to be performed, in all particulars for which it does not expressly provide, is to be determined by the laws of the several States in which it is to be performed, so that the law of each State shall regulate the performance and the consequences of a breach committed in that State.[1]

---

floating sections of its country, *territoria clausa ; la continuation ou la prorogation du territoire*, and those on board such ships in foreign waters are under their laws and protection.   This even applies to chil-dren born to subjects on such ships.' "

The English cases are to the same effect.

In Lloyd *v.* Guibert, L. R. 1 Q. B. 115, 127; 6 Best & Smith, 120, 139 (1865), the court said: " For all purposes of jurisdiction, criminal or civil, with respect to all persons, things and transactions on board, she was, as it were, a floating island, over which France had as abso-lute, and, for all purposes of peace, as exclusive a sovereignty, as over her dominions by land."

The same rule was applied to the case of a child born on a British ship.   Marshall *v.* Murgatroyd, L. R. 6 Q. B. 31 (1870).   To the same effect are Vattel Law of Nations, book I, chap. 19, sect. 216; Wheaton Int. Law, sect. 106.

[1] The rule thus stated found its first application to the law of bills and notes. These are often made or accepted in one place and endorsed in another, and the uniform rule is that the validity and effect of the several contracts of acceptance and endorsement, are to be determined by the law of the respective places where each is to be performed.

In other words, wherever the contract either of the acceptor or en-dorser is to be performed, the law of that place is the measure of his duty and liability. Robinson *v.* Bland, 2 Burr. 1077 (1760); Hibernia Nat. Bank *v.* Lacombe, 84 N. Y. 367 (1881); Everett *v.* Vendryes, 19 N. Y. 436 (1859); Rothschild *v.* Currie, 1 Qu. B. 43 (1841); Cooper *v.* Earl of Waldegrave, 2 Beav. 282 (1840); Boyce *v.* Edwards, 4 Peters, 111 (1830).

The same rule has been frequently applied to carrier's contracts made in one place to be performed in several jurisdictions. In such cases it has been held that: "If a contract is to be performed partly in one country and partly in another country, it admits of a double aspect, nay, it has a double operation, and is, as to the particular parts, to be interpreted distinctively; that is according to the laws of the country

It has, however, been held that any limitation placed by the law of a particular State upon the extent of the re-covery for a breach of such a contract, or for a tort com-mitted in violation of it, is not applicable in a suit brought in another State, if the contract was made in the latter State and the principal portion of the performance was to be within that State, although the tort was committed in the State which enacted the statute.[1]

It is not easy to reconcile the decision in the Dyke case with those previously stated except on the ground that such statutes affect only the remedy and are therefore a part of the *lex fori*.

In a subsequent case, however,[2] where a statute of Pennsylvania, limiting to the amount of $300 the right of a passenger to recover for the loss of baggage, was under consideration by the New York Court of Appeals, this distinction was not alluded to. The contract there was

---

where the particular parts are to be performed or executed." Pope *v.* Nickerson, 3 Story C. C. 465, 484 (1844). In Barter *v.* Wheeler. 49 N. H. 9 (1869), a contract was made in one State, to be performed partly there, partly on the Great Lakes, partly in New York, and partly else-where. Court held that defendant's liability for a loss occurring in New York was governed by the laws of that State. At page 29 the court says: "The original contract was made at Toledo, Ohio, but was to be performed partly in New York, and the loss was altogether in that State. If the contract was to have been performed wholly in New York, it is clear that it would be governed by the laws of that State; . . and if to be executed partially in New York, we perceive no reason why in respect to that part, the law of that State should not govern, and such is the doctrine laid down in Story on Contracts, § 655, where it is said that if a contract is to be performed partly in one country and partly in another country, it has a double operation, and each portion is to be in-terpreted according to the laws of the country where it is to be per-formed. and it is said that the rule applies to a bill of lading of goods, some of which are to be delivered at one port, and some at another, in different countries." Gray *v.* Jackson, 51 N. H. 9, 39; s. c. 12 Am. Rep. 1 (1871); Pomeroy *v.* Ainsworth, 22 Barb. 118, 128 (1856). In the last case the court say: "If a contract is to be performed partly in one country and partly in another, each portion is to be interpreted accord-ing to the laws of the country where it is to be performed."

[1] Dyke *v.* Erie R. Co., 45 N. Y. 113 (1871).

[2] Curtis *v.* Del., Lack. & W. R. R., 74 N. Y. 116 (1878).

13

made in Pennsylvania, to transport a passenger and his baggage from that State through New Jersey to New York. The loss occurred in New York, and it was held that the right of action and the measure of damages must be determined by the law of New York, because delivery was to be made there and the contract was held to be made with reference to the law of that State.[1]

VI. It has been frequently held that liability for a tort is to be determined by the law of the place where the tort was committed.[2]

This question has arisen most frequently in actions for injuries causing death. It is well settled that if the law of the place where the tort was committed does not give a right of action, no action is sustainable.[3]

Having thus stated the general rules which may guide

---

[1] Everett v. Vendryes, 19 N. Y. 436 (1859); Hibernia National Bank v. Lacombe, 84 N. Y. 367 (1881). In both the Dyke and the Curtis cases, it is to be observed that the carrier sought the benefit of statutes limiting his liability in case of loss. In the Dyke case the negligent act complained of was committed in Pennsylvania. The contract was made in the State of New York to carry a passenger through that State, Pennsylvania and New Jersey to New York city. The carrier was held not entitled to the benefit of the limit of liability fixed by the Pennsylvania statute.

[2] Davies v. New York & N. E. R. R., 143 Mass. 301 (1887); Illinois Central R. R. v. Crudup, 63 Miss. 291 (1885); see Re Missouri S. S. Co. 58 Law Times Rep. N. S. 377 (1888); affi'd Weekly Notes, Notes of Cases, May 11, 1889, p. 90, in which the liability for negligence was determined by the law of the place where the tort was committed. But the case was decided on the ground of contract.

The decision in the Dyke case was otherwise, as has been shown.

In Thommasen v. Whitwill, 12 Fed. Rep. 891 (1882); affi'd sub nom. Thommessen v. Whitwill, 118 U. S. 520 (1886); where two colliding vessels were of different nationalities and no foreign law was proved, it was held that the rights of the parties would be determined by the law of the forum.

[3] The Harrisburg, 119 U. S. 199 (1886); Ins. Co. v. Brame, 95 U. S. 754 (1877); Dennick v. R. R. Co. 103 U. S. 11 (1880). In this latter case the court say: "It is indeed a right dependent solely on the statute of the State." In the Scotia, 14 Wall. 170 (1871), this rule was applied to the case of a collision occurring on the high seas.

us in determining the main question, we proceed to consider the question itself.

It is sometimes said that the enforcement by one country of the laws of another is purely matter of comity. In one sense this is true. But the comity, by which the courts of one State respect the rights acquired under the laws of another, is so universal and well established that it has the absolute force of law.[1] When, for example, a contract is made in England, certain rights arise under it. These rights are a species of property. The shipper's right to indemnity under certain circumstances, should certainly be sacred. On the other hand, what good reason can be given for the contention that the carrier's right to exemption under other circumstances, should not be equally sacred. If the laws of Great Britain allow parties dealing there to make a contract for such exemption, and certain rights of property arise by virtue of such contract, how can the courts of America fail to respect those rights if they undertake to enforce the contract at all. Confessedly the contract is not one of those to which the maxim: *Ex turpi contractu non oritur actio* applies. The contract is a legal one. The courts here enforce it. To divest rights acquired under it without compensation is certainly unjustifiable, and no case has yet gone to the length of saying that an express contract for such exemption, which is lawful in the State in which it is made, will not be recognized in other States or countries.

The decisions in the Dyke and Curtis cases already

---

[1] Pritchard *v.* Norton, 106 U. S. 124 (1882). At p. 132, the court say: "Hence it is that a vested right of action is property in the same sense in which tangible things are property, and is equally protected against arbitrary interference. Whether it springs from contract or from the principles of the common law, it is not competent for the legislature to take it away. A vested right to an existing defense is equally protected, saving only those which are based on informalities not affecting substantial rights, which do not touch the substance of the contract and are not based on equity and justice."

cited did not go to this length. The latter was placed by the court partly on the ground that the contract made no mention of exemption or limitation, and that the parties contracted with reference to the laws of New York and not with reference to the statute of Pennsylvania. The reason thus stated could, however, have no application to a case where the contract expressly provides for exemption or limitation of liability. It can hardly be supposed that the parties would make a contract which they thought at the time was invalid, or that they agreed, by implication or otherwise, to import into the contract the laws of a country other than that where it was made, which should annul a part of their own express agreement.[1]

---

[1] In Peninsula O. S. N. Co. v. Shand, 3 Moore, P. C. N. S. 272, 292 (1865), the court say: "Was it intended that the stipulation, in case of an alleged breach of contract, should be construed by the rules of the English law, which would give some effect to it, or by those of the French or any other law, according to which it would have none, but be treated as a merely fruitless attempt to evade a responsibility inseparably fixed upon the appellants as carriers? The question appears to their Lordships to admit of one answer only; but if they take the respondent so to have understood the intention of the appellants, they must take him to have adopted the same intention; it would be to impute want of good faith on his part to suppose that with that knowledge he yet intended to enter into a contract wholly different on so important an article; he could not have done this if the intention had been expressed, and there is no difference as to effect between that which is expressed in terms, and that which is implied and clearly understood." Re Missouri S. S. Co., 58 Law Times (N. S.), 377 (1888); s. c. 37 Albany L. J. 518; affirmed in Court of Appeals, Weekly Notes, Notes of Cases, May 11, 1889, p. 90. The same considerations have led American courts to uphold the validity of similar commercial contracts. "Where the contract is not to be performed in any one State there is difficulty. If from all the circumstances it is reasonable to suppose the parties had in view the law of the place of contract, that must prevail. But where there are no circumstances the safest rule is that which upholds the contract." Ryan v. Missouri, Kansas & T. R. Co., 65 Texas, 13 (1885); s. P., Western & A. R. R. v. Exposition Cotton Mills (Geo.), 7 S. E. Rep. 916 (1888); Bell v. Packard, 69 Me. 105 (1879); Milliken v. Pratt, 125 Mass. 374 (1878). The general rule on this subject is admirably stated in Pritchard v. Norton, 106 U. S. 124 (1882). At p. 137, the court say: " 'The parties cannot be presumed to have contemplated a law which would defeat their engagements.' 4 (Phillimore) Int. Law, sect. dcliv, pp. 470, 471. This rule, if universally applicable, which perhaps it is not, though

But the recent decision of the Supreme Court of the United States in The Montana,[1] holds distinctly that there is no presumption that bills of lading, made in the United States and issued by a British corporation to American citizens for transportation from New York to Liverpool, are issued or accepted with reference to the English law. It did not appear on the face of the bills of lading that the corporation or the ship were British. It was consequently held that the corporation was liable to the shipper for a loss of cargo, caused by the negligence of the master of the steamer, committed on the Irish sea, which resulted in a shipwreck on the British coast.

It will be perceived that this case does not determine

---

founded on the maxim *ut res magis valeat quam pereat*, would be decisive of the present controversy, as conclusive of the question of the application of the law of Louisiana, by which alone the undertaking of the obligor can be upheld.   At all events, it is a circumstance, highly persuasive in its character, of the presumed intention of the parties, and entitled to prevail, unless controlled by more express and positive proofs of a contrary intent."

The Montana is almost the only case in which the court has presumed that a contract was made with reference to a law by which the contract was void.

[1] Reported *sub nom.* Liverpool & G. W. Steam Co. *v.* Phenix Ins. Co., 129 U. S. 397 (1889).   At p. 459, the court say: "The facts that the goods are to be delivered at Liverpool, and the freight and primage therefor payable there in sterling currency, do not make the contract an English contract, or refer to the English law the question of the liability of the carrier for the negligence of the master and crew in the course of the voyage."   To the same effect was the language of the Circuit Court; s. c. 22 Fed. Rep. 715, 728 (1884).   The whole opinion of the court implies that if it had appeared as a fact that the contracting parties looked to the law of England as governing the validity of the contract, it would have been enforced.   The court add, at p. 462: "The present case does not require us to determine what effect the courts of the United States should give to this contract if it had expressly provided that any question arising under it should be governed by the law of England.'

This should be compared with the language of the same court in Watts *v.* Camors, 115 U. S. 353 (1885).   At p. 362, the court say: "Americans and Englishmen, entering into a charter party of an English ship for an ocean voyage, must be presumed to look to the general maritime law of the two countries, and not to the local law of the State in which the contract is signed."

the question as to whether a court in this country would recognize as valid a contract for such exemption, which was valid in the place where the contract was made. In so far as it goes, The Montana would seem to be an authority the other way, for it distinctly applied to the contract under consideration the law of the place where the contract was made. If this be operative to invalidate a contract which would be valid by the law of the place where the performance was to be completed, it would seem equally clear that it should be operative to give validity to a contract, valid in the place where it was made, but invalid by the law of the place where the performance is to be completed.[1]

The authority of the cases previously cited[2] to support the proposition that a contract is presumed to be made with reference to the law of the place of performance, must be considered as seriously impaired by The Montana. The question naturally arises: by what evidence can it be shown that a particular contract was made with reference to the law of a foreign country? This can be shown in several ways:

1. By a positive statement in the contract that it is made with reference to the law of a particular country.[3]

2. By proof of the extrinsic facts in reference to which the contract was made.[4]

---

[1] In Stevens v. Navigazione Gen. It., 39 Fed. Rep. 562 (1889), the court assumed the validity of a clause in a bill of lading, issued and accepted in Shanghai, by the terms of which the carrier was exempted from liability for loss caused by the negligence of his servants. But the point was not definitely decided.

[2] *Ante*, pp. 186, 187.

[3] Such a clause in a "live-stock freight contract" was held valid in The Oranmore, 24 Fed. Rep. 922 (1885). The clause in that case read as follows: "Any questions arising under this contract or the bill of lading, against the steamer or her owners, shall be determined by English law in England."

[4] 1 Greenl. Evid., §§ 288, 289; Brick v. Brick, 98 U. S. 514 (1878); Bank v. Kennedy, 17 Wall. 19 (1872); Bradley v. Wash., A. & G. Co., 13 Peters, 89 (1839); Moore v. Pitts, 53 N. Y. 85, 90 (1873); Phœnix

3. By proof of a custom or usage universally adopted by the mutual agreement of shippers and carriers of the port in which the contract was made. Such proof would be admissible, not to subvert a rule of law, but to show what law it was with reference to which the parties contracted.[1]

One other point relating to this subject requires consideration. The question often arises: how is the law of any particular State to be determined? This question has been most frequently discussed in the Federal Courts, and many of their decisions on this subject are referred to in the first chapter. It is sufficient for our present purpose to briefly state the conclusions to be drawn from these authorities. They hold:

1. The statutory law of any particular State will be enforced in the Federal Courts and the courts of the other States. In construing such statute, those courts will be guided by the construction put upon such statute by the highest tribunals of the State under whose authority the statute was enacted.[2]

Ins. Co. v. Continental Ins. Co., 87 N. Y. 400 (1882); Chartered Merc. Bk. of India v. Netherlands-India S. N. Co., 10 Qu. B. Div. 521 (1883).

[1] Bliven v. New England Screw Co., 23 How. 420 (1859). At p. 431 the court say: "Customary rights and incidents, universally attaching to the subject-matter of the contract in the place where it was made, are impliedly annexed to the language and terms of the contract, unless the custom is particularly and expressly excluded. Parol evidence of custom, consequently, is generally admissible to enable the court to arrive at the real meaning of the parties, who are naturally presumed to have contracted in conformity with the known and established usage." To the same effect is Fabbri v. Kalbfleisch, 52 N. Y. 28 (1873).

So it is well settled with reference to bills of lading, that the custom or usage to carry particular articles on deck may be shown, although parol evidence of consent in the particular case is inadmissible. The Delaware, 14 Wall. 579 (1871).

[2] Elmendorf v. Taylor, 10 Wheat. 152, 160 (1825). In Shelby v. Guy, 11 Wheat. 367 (1826), the court say: "That the statute laws of the States must furnish the rule of decision to this court, as far as they comport with the Constitution of the United States, in all cases arising within the respective States, is a position that no one doubts. Nor is it ques-

2. In questions of the unwritten commercial law the Federal Courts have refused to follow implicitly the decisions of the State courts, and hold distinctly that there is a general commercial law of the United States, of which any local decision is but the evidence, and that the Federal Courts will not follow such local decision if they are satisfied that it is wrong. Numerous State courts have followed the rule thus laid down, and have asserted the right to overrule the decision of the courts of a sister

---

tionable that a fixed and received construction of their respective statute laws in their own courts makes, in fact, a part of the statute law of the country, however we may doubt the propriety of that construction." Township of Elmwood *v.* Marcy, 92 U. S. 289 (1875); Town of South Ottawa *v.* Perkins, 94 U. S. 260, 267 (1876); Peik *v.* Chicago & N. W. R. Co., 94 U. S. 164 (1876); County of Leavenworth *v.* Barnes, 94 U. S. 70 (1876); Adams *v.* Nashville, 95 U. S. 19 (1877); Fairfield *v.* County of Gallatin, 100 U. S. 47 (1879).

The State courts, in like manner, in deciding questions arising under the statutes of another State, adopt the construction put upon them by the courts of that State.   Leonard *v.* Columbia Steam Nav. Co., 84 N. Y. 48 (1881); Jessup *v.* Carnegie, 80 N. Y. 441 (1880); Crum *v.* Bliss, 47 Conn. 592 (1880); Russell *v.* Madden, 95 Ill. 485 (1880).   An important exception has been made to the rule stated in the text.   The Federal Courts have held, where contracts have been made or vested rights acquired upon the faith of a construction given to the Constitution or statute of a State by its highest courts, that the Federal Courts will enforce such contracts and protect such rights although a different construction should subsequently be given by the local courts.   Gelpcke *v.* City of Dubuque, 1 Wall. 175, 206 (1863); Havemeyer *v.* Iowa County, 3 Wall. 294 (1865); Olcott *v.* The Supervisors of Fond du Lac, 16 Wall. 678 (1872).

In Harris *v.* Jex, 55 N. Y. 421 (1874), the Court of Appeals laid down a similar rule in regard to transactions had upon the faith of a decision of the U. S. Supreme Court.   In that case a tender in United States currency was made after the first decision of the Supreme Court in the Legal Tender cases.   Hepburn *v.* Griswold, 8 Wallace, 603 (1869).   This tender was refused, the mortgagee to whom it was made claiming, on the authority of the decision just mentioned, that the tender must be made in gold.   The Court of Appeals held that while the decision was in force, and unreversed, the mortgagee to whom the tender was made had a right to refuse it, and that the lien of the mortgage was not destroyed by such refusal.

This case has gone as far as any in recognizing the fact that a judicial decision is not only evidence of the law, but does actually make the law in all places subject to the authority of the court rendering the decision.

State as to the commercial law, even though the transaction under consideration took place partly in that State.[1]

---

[1] In Faulkner *v*. Hart, 82 N. Y. 413 (1880), a contract of affreightment was made in New York for the transportation of goods from that city to Boston, and for their delivery to the consignee in Boston. He demanded the goods, after their arrival, from the carrier, in whose custody they were; but it was inconvenient for the carrier to make delivery at that time, and delivery was not made. Subsequently, and before they were removed, they were consumed by fire while in the carrier's warehouse, and without fault on his part. The Supreme Court of Massachusetts had held that under such circumstances the carrier was not liable. Rice *v*. Hart, 118 Mass. 201 (1875). The Court of Appeals held that he was. It must be remembered, however, that in this case the contract was made in New York, and was an express contract for delivery to the consignee. The court say: "That the court in Massachusetts had decided the law contrary to what it was is not controlling, for it may be assumed, even if the parties had knowledge of the decision, that they knew it was contrary to the current of authority in similar cases, and contracted having in view the law as it actually existed. Like an unconstitutional law, void of itself, the decision was not the law, and is not to be regarded as authority for that reason." To the same effect is Franklin *v*. Twogood, 25 Iowa, 520 (1868).

In Georgia, however, it was held, in an action brought there for personal injuries received in South Carolina, that the law of the latter State would be applied, and, there being no South Carolina statute regulating the rights of parties in such cases, the Georgia courts, in a liberal spirit of comity, would apply the common law in South Carolina as construed by its court of last resort. Atlanta & C. A. L. R. Co. *v*. Tanner, 68 Georgia, 384 (1882). See, also, Waters *v*. Cox, 2 Bradwell (Ill. App.), 129 (1878); Cubbedge *v*. Napier, 62 Ala. 518 (1878); Ames *v*. McCamber, 124 Mass. 85 (1878); Haywood *v*. Daves, 81 N. C. 8 (1879); Cragin *v*. Lamkin, 7 Allen (Mass.), 395 (1863); Williams *v*. Carr, 80 N. C. 294 (1879); Rorer on Interstate Law, p. 121; Conflict Between Federal and State Decisions, 14 Am. Law Review, 211 (1880); 16 Am. Law Review, 743 (1882).

The conflict between the decisions of the Federal and State Courts on questions of commercial law is referred to by Judge Miller in Faulkner *v*. Hart, 82 N. Y. 413, 419 (1880): "Any other rule would lead to confusion in regard to a principle of general application, for, if the doctrine of the Massachusetts court is to prevail, the right of the aggrieved party might depend upon the fact whether the action was brought in the Federal or the State Court; and if the action in this case had been brought in the Circuit Court of the United States for the State of Massachusetts, the plaintiffs would be entitled to recover, while in the State court a different result would prevail." So the Supreme Court of the United States has held that, in deciding whether a contract was to carry beyond the carrier's line or merely to forward, it was not bound by the decisions of local courts, but would follow its own judgment as to the commercial law on the subject. Myrick *v*. Mich. Cent. R. R., 107 U. S. 102 (1882).

As the logical result of this line of decisions the U. S. Supreme Court held, in Railroad Company *v.* Lockwood,[1] that the Federal Courts would not enforce that portion of the contract of a carrier which stipulated for exemption from liability for the negligence of his servants, although the contract was made in the State of New York, and with a corporation incorporated under the law of that State, and such contracts are held by the courts of that State to be valid. It thus may happen, and has happened, that the determination of the rights of parties depends, not upon the length of the Chancellor's foot, but upon whether the suit is tried on the north or south side of the City Hall Park in the city of New York.

Nevertheless, this apparent anomaly in our jurisprudence (which has existed ever since Swift *v.* Tyson[2] applied to the transfer in New York of negotiable paper, a rule different from that applied by the courts of New York), rests upon solid foundations. From the beginning of our national existence in 1789, the Supreme Court of the United States has endeavored to maintain the national unity. It has labored assiduously to create or preserve uniformity of decision in all commercial questions throughout the Union. In this endeavor its success has been signal, though not complete. And the benefit conferred on the nation by the general uniformity of its system of commercial law far outweighs the evil which flows from the diversities between Federal and local decisions, to which attention has been called.

But the reasons which led the Supreme Court, in the Lockwood case, to overrule the New York decisions as to the validity of stipulations for exemption from liability for negligence in the transaction of interstate commerce,

---

[1] 17 Wallace, 357 (1873).
[2] 1 Peters, 1 (1842).

have no application to contracts for transportation of passengers and freight between this and foreign countries.
The jurisdiction of the court does not extend to these
countries. It is absurd to tell an Englishman that contracts for exemption for negligence are void by the commercial law of England, when the House of Lords has
held otherwise. In Faulkner v. Hart[1] the Court of Appeals could truly say that the commercial law of the
United States was one, because the highest court in the
United States had so held. The Supreme Court of Massachusetts had the opportunity, in Rice v. Hart,[2] to recon-
sider its previous decision on the subject, and put itself
in line with the general current of authority in America
and England. This it had, unfortunately, failed to do.
But still, in the United States Circuit Court for Massachusetts the commercial law had been held to be what the
New York court declared.[3]

If, however, a British ship should be libelled in New
York for failure to deliver merchandise in good order which
had been delivered to it in Liverpool, and the owner should
plead his British bill of lading as a defense to the suit,
no court in this country could say that any British court
would overrule the defense. The most convenient method
of determining all such questions is to apply the law of the
flag. This can readily be ascertained, and the shipper—
if that be the rule—can ship with full knowledge of his
rights and those of the carrier. It has been shown[4] that
this rule is supported by many authorities. While no one
can affirm that it will ultimately be applied by the Fed-

---

[1] 82 N. Y. 413 (1880).

[2] 118 Mass. 201 (1875).

[3] Salmon Falls Manfg. Co. v. Bark Tangier, 1 Clifford, 396 (1860);
Richardson v. Goddard, 23 How. (U. S.) 28 (1859).

[4] *Ante*, pp. 188, 189.

eral Courts to this class of cases upon carrier's contracts, yet for the sake of simplicity and uniformity in the administration of justice it is very much to be hoped that such will be the result, at least in cases where it distinctly appears that such was the agreement of the parties.

The only reasonable alternative, it is respectfully submitted, is to apply the fifth rule before mentioned, and determine the carrier's liability by the law of the place where the injury to the passenger or the cargo is committed. In the case put at the beginning of this chapter, of a contract made in Liverpool for transportation to Philadelphia, the carrier's liability for injuries done in Great Britain would be determined by English law, and for injuries done in Pennsylvania by the law of that State. But what shall we say, in such case, as to the carrier's liability for injuries done upon the high seas? What law but the law of the flag could, in such case, be constantly applied? The right of each country to punish crimes committed upon its own ships is universally recognized.[1]

By parity of reasoning, should not the law of the country to which the ship belongs extend to the consequences of civil as well as criminal wrongs?

---

[1] Grotius, de Jure Belli et Pacis, lib. ii, cap. iii, sect. 13; Rutherforth's Institutes, lib. ii, cap. ix; Vattel, lib. i, cap. xix, sect. 216; Wheaton's International Law (8th ed.), sect. 106; 1 Kent Com. 26; Regina v. Serva, 2 Car. & K. 53 (1845). In Regina v. Bjornsen, 1 Leigh & C. 545 (1865), the court said: "The question is whether an English court has jurisdiction to try a foreigner for an offense committed on the high seas? If the ship was British, so as to be, in law, a part of the British territory, there clearly was jurisdiction; and the point, therefore, is this: Was the ship British, or not?" The court held that the ship was not a British one, and that they consequently had no jurisdiction. U. S. v. Klintock, 5 Wheat. 144 (1820); U. S. v. Holmes, 5 Wheat. 412 (1820), where the court says: "In Klintock's case it was laid down that, to exclude the jurisdiction of the courts of the United States, in cases of murder or robbery committed on the high seas, the vessel in which the offender is, or to which he belongs, must be, at the time, in fact as well as in right, the property of a subject of a foreign State, and, in virtue of such property, subject, at that time, to his control."

It is hardly within the province of a text-book to discuss this subject further. It is hoped that enough has been said to aid, as far as it lies in the author's power, counsel and courts in the examination and decision of the question propounded at the beginning of this chapter.

CHAPTER IX.

CONTRIBUTORY NEGLIGENCE AND FRAUD OF SHIPPER.

The rule as to contributory negligence, so familiar in actions brought to recover damages for personal injuries, has found many curious illustrations in actions against carriers upon the contract to transport freight or passengers.

1. Failure to inform carrier of value or character of articles shipped.—The general rule is well settled that a shipper of freight is not bound to disclose to the carrier the value, or valuable character of goods delivered to the latter for transportation, but that if the carrier desires information on either subject, he should enquire.[1]

It has been questioned whether this rule is applicable to the case of a trunk or other package delivered by a passenger to a carrier of passengers for transportation. It does not fall within the scope of this work to consider what articles accompanying a passenger may be properly termed baggage. But assuming that the articles delivered are baggage, the question has arisen whether the passenger, if there be no inquiry by the carrier, is bound

---

[1] Baldwin *v.* Liverpool & G. W. S. Co., 74 N. Y. 125 (1878); Gorham Man. Co. *v.* Fargo, 35 N. Y. Super Ct. 434 (1873); Shelden *v.* Robinson, 7 N. H. 157 (1834); Merchants' Despatch Trans. Co. *v.* Bolles, 80 Ill. 473 (1875); Baldwin *v.* Collins, 9 Robinson (Louisiana), 468 (1845); Levois *v.* Gale, 17 La. Ann. 302 (1865); Brown *v.* Camden & A. R. R., 83 Penn. St. 316 (1877); Phillips *v.* Earle, 8 Pick. 182 (1829). In McCune *v.* B., C. R. & N. R. R. R. Co., 52 Iowa, 600 (1879), it was held that a shipper was not bound to inform a carrier that a cow shipped by his road was about eight months gone with calf. But for an exception to this rule, in the case of an express company which carries letters, see Hayes *v.* Wells, 23 Cal. 185 (1863); *post*, p. 207, n. 2. In American Ex. Co. *v.* Perkins, 42 Ill. 458 (1867), it was held that the shipper was bound to disclose the fragile nature of goods delivered to the carrier.

to disclose to him the fact that some of them are of special value.

The Supreme Court of the United States has held that the passenger owes the carrier no such duty, and affirmed a judgment recovered against a carrier for $10,000, the value of laces and articles of personal adornment, which were placed by a lady in her trunk and lost by the carrier's negligence.[1]

On the other hand it was held, by the Supreme Court of Illinois, that the rule already stated as to common carriers of freight did not apply to carriers of passengers, and that the passenger was bound to disclose the fact of the presence in his trunk of articles of especial value, and if he did not, could not recover for their loss more than the apparent value of a trunk, containing baggage such as travelers usually carry.[2]

---

[1] Railroad Co. v. Fraloff, 100 U. S. 24 (1879).   To the same effect are Hollister v. Nowlen, 19 Wend. 234 (1838); Brooke v. Pickwick, 4 Bing. 218 (1827).   In the last case gross negligence on the part of the carrier's servants was shown.   See Spooner v. Hannibal & St. Jo. R. R., 23 Mo. App. 403 (1886).

[2] Mich. Cent. R. R. v. Carrow, 73 Ill. 348 (1874).   The court say that the carrier may rely upon the representation, arising by implication, that a trunk contains nothing but baggage.   In this case, however, the articles in question were clearly merchandise, and part of the passenger's stock in trade.   Cincinnati & C. A. L. R. R. v. Marcus, 38 Ill. 219 (1865).

See Orange Co. Bank v. Brown, 9 Wend. 85 (1832), which admits the rule before stated, but holds that it did not apply to a case where the trunk delivered to the carrier contained $11,000 in bank notes.   The decision is placed chiefly on the ground that such a sum of money was not baggage, and that if the carrier was to be responsible for its safe carriage, he was entitled to extra compensation; but the court say that "the conduct of the agent was a virtual concealment of that sum; his representation of his trunk and the contents as baggage was not a fair one, and was calculated to deceive the captain, and it would be a violation of first principles to permit the plaintiffs to recover."   See Weeks v. N. Y., N. H. & H. R. R., 72 N. Y. 50 (1878).

It may be doubted whether a notice, printed on a ticket delivered to a passenger, or otherwise brought to his attention, that the carrier would not be liable for the loss of baggage to more than a specified sum, would not make it the duty of the passenger to state the value of

Indeed, the Supreme Court of Illinois has held that if the appearance of a package delivered to a carrier, does not indicate that it contains articles of value, the shipper is bound to inform the carrier of its real value, and that his omission so to do is a fraud which will prevent a recovery by him, in case of loss, for more than the apparent value of the parcel.[1]

These cases in Illinois, however, admit that under such circumstances the carrier would be subject to the liability of a bailee for hire. But it would seem, on principle, that fraud on the part of the shipper should be a complete bar to his recovery. This question was very much discussed in the New York Court of Appeals, in Magnin v. Dinsmore. That case was three times appealed. The goods delivered to the carrier were watches. A printed receipt limiting the carrier's liability to fifty dollars was given to the shipper. It was held in the New York Superior Court, on the first hearing, that this clause relieved the carrier from liability beyond that amount, even when the loss was occasioned by his negligence. But the Court of Appeals held, on the first appeal,[2] that if the contract did not in express language provide that the carrier should not be liable for the negligence of his servants, the clause limiting the amount for which a recovery could be had should be limited to the case of loss occurring without fault on the part of the carrier.

On the second trial it was shown that the appearance of the package did not indicate the value of the contents.

---

his baggage if he should desire to make the carrier liable for more than the specified amount. See *ante*, p. 180; *post*, Chap. X, sect. 1.

[1] Oppenheimer v. U. S. Express Co., 69 Ill. 62 (1873). In that case the court say that a designed suppression of the value of the goods is unfair conduct on the part of the shipper, and relieves the carrier from his liability as insurer. Chicago & Aurora R. R. v. Thompson, 19 Ill. 578 (1858); Am. Ex. Co. v. Perkins, 42 Ill. 458 (1867).

[2] 56 N. Y. 168 (1874).

The court, on a second appeal, held[1] that, under such circumstances, the omission to disclose the value was a fraud on the shipper's part, even though no artifice was employed by him, and that he could recover only fifty dollars. This rule was adhered to on a third appeal.[2] It must be remembered, however, that in this case the shipper had notice that the carrier intended to limit its liability unless the value was stated by him, and it is on this ground that the court based its decision.[3]

In the absence of such notice it is not perceived why the doctrine of the cases previously stated should not be adhered to. The parties deal on equal terms. One should not be required to disclose value, unless the other in some way gives notice that disclosure is required.

Of course, if the carrier does make enquiry as to the value of the package, or the character of the contents,

---

[1] 62 N. Y. 35 (1875).

[2] 70 N. Y. 410 (1877).

[3] The express receipt is printed in full in the report in 56 N. Y. 168 (1874). It contained the following clause: "If the value of the property above described is not stated by the shipper, the holder thereof will not demand of the Adams Express Company a sum exceeding fifty dollars for the loss." See, also, Batson v. Donovan, 4 B. & Ald. 21 (1820). In this case the carrier gave notice that he would not be liable for more than a certain value on any one parcel. The shipper, knowing this notice, delivered to the carrier a box containing bank notes and other securities to the value of over £4,000. The box had no external indication of the value of its contents, and no information respecting the same was asked or given. It was held that, under the circumstances, the shipper was bound to give information without being asked, and that the carrier was not liable for the loss of* the box. So The Denmark, 27 Fed. Rep. 141 (1886); Gibbon v. Paynton, 4 Burr. 2298 (1769).

Green v. Boston & Lowell R. R., 128 Mass. 221 (1880), held that an express notice that the carrier would not be liable for over $200, unless upon special agreement, was valid, and the shipper could not recover more than that amount. At the same time it was held that another clause, that the company would not be liable for "specie, drafts, bank bills and other articles of great intrinsic or representative value" without disclosure, did not apply to a family portrait.

14

and is not informed correctly by the shipper, the carrier will not be responsible for the loss of the package.[1]

This view would seem to be sustained by the decisions that if a traveler delivers a trunk to a carrier, informs him that it contains merchandise, and pays extra compensation for its carriage, he can recover its full value, although he does not more fully disclose the character of its contents.[2]

So if the appearance of the package delivered by the passenger indicates that it contains merchandise and not baggage, the carrier has the right to demand extra compensation for carrying it, and is liable for its full value should it be lost.[3]

2. Fraudulent concealment of the contents of a package delivered for transportation.—If the shipper use any artifice whatever to conceal from the carrier the true value of the contents of a package delivered to him for transportation, the shipper cannot recover for their loss, unless actual negligence or a conversion by the carrier be shown.[4]

---

[1] Phillips *v.* Earle, 8 Pick. 182 (1829); Charleston & Savannah R. Co. *v.* Moore, 80 Geo. 522; s. c. 5 S. E. Rep. 769 (1888).

[2] Sloman *v.* Great Western R. Co., 67 N. Y. 208 (1876); Camden & Amboy R. R. *v.* Baldauf, 16 Penn. 67 (1851). In the Sloman case the court say: "The fact that the baggage-master charged or received extra pay for their carriage [*i. e.*, of the trunks] is some evidence that they were not regarded as ordinary traveler's baggage, especially as the defendant did not offer any explanation of what the charge was for. From all the circumstances the jury were, we think, authorized to draw the inference that the baggage-master understood that the agent was traveling for the purpose of selling goods, and that these trunks contained his wares; that he was not entitled to have them carried as his ordinary baggage, and therefore the extra charge was made and they were carried as freight." *Cf.* Hellman *v.* Holladay, *post*, page 212, note 1.

[3] Butler *v.* Hudson R. R. R., 3 E. D. Smith (N. Y.), 571 (1854). And see Pfister *v.* Central Pacific R. R., 70 Cal. 170 (1886). But compare Crouch *v.* London & N. W. R. Co., 14 C. B. 255 (1854).

The mere delivery of a valise to a baggage-master is a representation that it contains nothing but personal baggage. If it contains merchandise, the passenger's silence is held to be a fraud. Blumenthal *v.* Maine Cent. R. R., 79 Maine, 550 (1887).

[4] Gibbon *v.* Paynton, 4 Burr. 2298 (1769). In this case the artifice

It is impossible to state accurately what will amount to such concealment. Much will depend upon the circumstances of the case, and the usage of business. For example: an emigrant delivered to a carrier a common packing-box containing bedding and clothing. In the middle the owner had placed some gold. The Circuit Court of the United States for the Northern District of Illinois held that if it were known to the carrier that emigrants frequently placed valuables in boxes of that description, the use of such a box was not a concealment, though ordinarily it might be.[1]

On the other hand the usage of business is not controlling. An express company had in its main office two counters, one for valuable articles and one for ordinary goods. A small parcel, weighing 20 pounds, done up with twine, and sealed, was delivered at the latter counter. It contained silver, and was directed to a well-known dealer in silverware. The N. Y. Superior Court held that the delivery at the wrong counter did not, under the circumstances, amount to a concealment of the character of the goods.[2]

---

used was hiding money in hay in an old nail bag. Phillips *v.* Earle, 8 Pick. (Mass) 182 (1829); Relf *v.* Rapp, 3 Watts & S. (Penn.) 21 (1841). In this case the artifice consisting in marking a box "glass" which really contained jewelry. Magnin *v.* Dinsmore, 56 N. Y. 168 (1874); 62 N. Y. 35 (1875); 70 N. Y. 410 (1877); Warner *v.* Western Trans. Co., 5 Robt. (N. Y.) 490 (1868); Southern Ex. Co. *v.* Everett, 37 Georgia, 688 (1868); Crouch *v.* London & N. W. R. Co., 14 C. B. 255 (1854); Chicago & Alton R. R. *v.* Shea, 66 Ill. 471 (1873); Houston & T. C. R. R. *v.* Burke, 55 Texas, 323 (1881). In this case the rule stated in the text was applied, notwithstanding the Texas statute (Rev. Stat., art. 278) which declares invalid any stipulations limiting the carrier's liability.

[1] Kuter *v.* Mich. Central R. R., 1 Bissell, 35 (1853).

[2] Gorham Man. Co. *v.* Fargo, 35 N. Y. Super. Ct. 434 (1873). In this case the weight of the package and the manner in which it was put up were at least sufficient to put the carrier on enquiry as to its true character. The rule on this subject is well illustrated by a California case. For many years after the settlement of the California coast, the express companies afforded a better service to the public than the United States Mail, and consequently carried many letters. It was held

Any positive misstatement by the shipper as to the character or contents of the package delivered to the carrier, is a bar to an action to recover for its value, unless gross negligence or actual conversion be shown.[1]

Some of the cases on this subject refer to the probability that the motive of the shipper, in using the artifice or deceit, is to get the goods carried at a lower rate of freight.[2]

But it is believed that, on principle, the presence or absence of such a motive must be legally unimportant. The deception or concealment relates to a subject material to the carrier's employment. He may, and generally does, provide especial safeguards for objects of especial value. It is to enable him to use these that he desires to

---

that the company was not liable for the loss of bank-notes enclosed in a letter, unless the sender stated the character of the contents of the envelope. This was for the reason that the character of the package was such as to indicate that the contents had little or no pecuniary value, and its use was, therefore, a deception or concealment. Hayes *v.* Wells, 23 Cal. 185 (1863).

It has been held in Louisiana that the owners of a steamboat, which is in the habit of carrying money for compensation, are not liable for the loss of a package of money handed to the master without informing him of the nature of the contents of the package. In this case no charge was made for the carriage. Mechanics' & Traders' Bank *v.* Gordon, 5 La. Ann. 604 (1850).

[1] Gibbon *v.* Paynton, 4 Burr. 2298 (1769); Phillips *v.* Earle, 8 Pick. (Mass.) 182 (1829); Relf *v.* Rapp. 3 Watts & Serg. (Penn.) 21 (1841); Levois *v.* Gale, 17 La. Ann. 302 (1865); The Ionic, 5 Blatchf. 538 (1867). It is for this reason that a clause in a carrier's contract, that it should not be liable for the loss of goods untruly or incorrectly described, was held reasonable and valid in Lewis *v.* Great Western R. Co., 5 H. & N. 867; s. c. 29 L. J. (Excheq.) 425 (1860). But if, notwithstanding deception by passenger, the carrier in any way learn of the extra value, and charges for it. he is liable for its full value. Hellman *v.* Holladay, 1 Woolw. 365 (1868).

[2] Southern Ex. Co. *v.* Everett, 37 Geo. 688 (1868). In Chicago & Alton R. R. *v.* Shea, 66 Ill. 471 (1873), the court say: "Whilst appellants are willing to admit the law is well settled that it is not the duty of the carrier to inquire as to the contents of packages delivered for shipment, when such contents are not known, yet it is not less a fraud in the shipper to do any act by which such inquiry is avoided or precluded."

know what is the nature of the article delivered to him for carriage.

The weight which has sometimes been given to proof of this sort has led the St. Louis Court of Appeals into a decision opposed to the general current of authorities, and which will, it is believed, hardly be followed in other States. It was held by that court, in Rice *v.* Indianapolis & St. Louis R. R.,[1] that the only effect of artifice or deception used by the shipper to conceal the value or character of the goods shipped was to entitle the carrier to recover the full freight which it would have demanded had it known the facts of the case, and that, in case of loss, this amount should be deducted from the value of the goods; and the carrier would be liable for the balance.

This decision seems to overlook the consideration before referred to respecting the safeguards provided by the carrier, and may possibly yet be reconsidered by the learned court that pronounced it.

3. Errors in direction.—The carrier is not liable for losses caused by errors in direction. For example: goods were marked by the shipper in New York, "Eckley, Iowa," by mistake for Ackley, and were carried by the New York carrier and its connections to Chicago. The Iowa line there refused to receive them. They were deposited in a warehouse, and the carrier telegraphed for further directions. Before these were received the goods were destroyed by fire. It was held that the carrier which received the goods was not liable for the loss.[2] For similar reasons

---

[1] 3 Missouri App. 27 (1876). It was held by the same court that the delivery to a carrier of a trunk containing merchandise, with the fraudulent intent to avoid payment of freight, was no bar to the shipper's right of action for its loss, if the carrier knew that it contained merchandise and allowed it to be carried as baggage. Ross *v.* Missouri, K. & T. R. R., 4 Mo. App. 582 (1877); American Express Co. *v.* Perkins, 42 Ill. 458 (1867).

[2] Erie Railway Co. *v.* Wilcox, 84 Ill. 239 (1876); Southern Express Co. *v.* Kaufman, 12 Heiskell (Tenn.), 161 (1873).

It has, however, been held that the carrier who receives goods which

negligence on the part of the consignor, in omitting wholly to notify the consignee of the shipment of a horse, was held fatal to his recovery for injury to the horse, caused by delay in delivering him.[1]

But in order to exonerate the carrier, it is necessary that the negligence of the shipper should contribute to the loss, and whether or not it does is a question of fact for the jury.[2]

---

are misdirected is liable as carrier for any loss occurring while the goods are in his custody, even though he leaves them at some station along his own line. O'Rourke v. Chicago, B. & Q. R. R., 44 Iowa, 526 (1876). This decision, unless strictly confined to its own peculiar facts, is opposed to the weight of authority, and to the principle of the rule on the subject of concurrent negligence. It certainly imposes rigorous requirements on the agents of the carrier who receives goods for transportation. It would seem that in case of misdirection the carrier, when the fact of misdirection is ascertained, and the transit consequently ceases, should thereupon be liable as warehouseman only. Indeed, the opinion in the O'Rourke case recognizes this as a correct rule.

It is held that if the carrier knows the right direction an error in marking the parcel will not be fatal to the right of the shipper to recover. Mahon v. Blake, 125 Mass. 477 (1878). And in Guillaume v. General Trans. Co., 100 N. Y. 491 (1885), it was held that "if the direction on the bag was of such a character as to advise the defendant's agent of the party for whom it was intended, or to put it on inquiry as to whom that party was or where he resided, then it was either negligence, or a fair question whether it was not such negligence in thus sending the bill of lading" to the wrong address.

[1] Wise v. Great Western R. Co., 1 Hurlst. & N. 63 (1856). In this case the consignor knew the exact time when the train on which the horse was shipped was due, and could have notified the consignee. See, also, cases in Chap. XIV, sect. 3.

[2] Shriver v. Sioux City & St. P. R. R., 24 Minn. 506 (1878); Hutchinson v. Chicago, St. P., M. & O. R. Co, 37 Minn. 524; 35 N. W. Rep. 433 (1887); Viner v. N. Y., Alexandria, G. & W. S. S. Co., 50 N. Y. 23 (1872). In this case there was no direction at all on the packages, and the bills of lading were drawn to the order of the plaintiff. The goods were delivered to the wrong person. A nonsuit was granted on the trial, which the Court of Appeals set aside, and held that the plaintiff's omission to mark the packages, and the writing of an ambiguous letter respecting the delivery did not, as matter of law, constitute negligence which contributed to the loss.

In a case where the goods were marked with the initials of the consignee, and the carrier's agent wrote out the wrong name, it was held that the carrier was liable to the real owner for a delivery to the wrong person. Forsythe v. Walker, 9 Penn. 148 (1848). In these cases there

4. Owner assuming direction.—If the owner under-takes to direct the way in which the goods shall be car-ried, or to manage their transportation, the carrier is not liable for any injuries caused in part by such directions or management.[1] In giving directions, however, as to transportation, the owner has the right to rely on the completion of the transit in the usual and reasonable time.[2] And where he acts according to the directions of the carrier's agent, his acts, even though they incidentally occasion injury, will not be imputed to him for negli-gence. As, for example, where a shipper of live stock asked for tan for bedding, and was directed by the freight agent to get straw; the straw took fire from sparks from the locomotive, and it was held that the carrier was li-able.[3]

If the owner has no control over the transportation, his mere presence will not exonerate the carrier from li-ability for his neglect to provide a suitable car for trans-portation.[4]

---

was no misdirection. The marks were insufficient of themselves to identify the consignee, and no doubt the carrier was entitled to time sufficient to ascertain the true owner. But this insufficient direction clearly did not excuse a delivery to the wrong person. And see cases, *post,* Ch. XI, section 2.

[1] Rixford *v.* Smith, 52 N. H. 355 (1872). So if the shipper directs that the transportation be delayed, the carrier, during the period of de-tention, is liable only as warehouseman. Rogers *v.* Wheeler, 52 N. Y. 262 (1873). Where the contract provides that the shipper's agent shall unload live stock, the carrier is not liable for their negligence in doing so. Owen *v.* Louisville & N. R. R., 9 S. W. Rep. (Ky.) 698 (1888). But the suggestions of passengers to a driver to go out of his road are no excuse to the carrier for injuries caused thereby. His driver should know his business. Anderson *v.* Scholey, 114 Ind. 553 ; 17 North East. Rep. 125 (1888).
Where the carrier failed to deliver at the proper terminus (the reason being unexplained), and the shipper found his cattle in a stable in an adjoining city, and, without consultation with carrier, told the owner of the stable to keep them and take good care of them until further order, and the cattle were burned in the stable, held that the carrier was not liable. Cleveland & P. R. R. *v.* Sargent, 19 Ohio St. 438 (1869).

[2] Phillio *v.* Sanford, 17 Texas, 227 (1858).

[3] Powell *v.* Pennsylvania R. R., 32 Penn. 414 (1859).

[4] Peters *v.* New Orleans, J. & G. N. R. R., 16 La. Ann. 222 (1861).

It often happens that the shipper, at the time of shipment, knows that there is some defect in the equipment of the vessel or vehicle to be used in transporting his goods. It has been much debated whether this knowledge is a bar to his recovery in case loss should occur from this defect. The distinction seems to be whether the defect is of such a character that it can be obviated during the transit. If it can, the shipper has the right to presume that it will be. If it is intrinsic, and not removable during the transit, the shipper cannot complain if a loss should occur in consequence of a defect of which he had notice, and to the transportation, notwithstanding which, he impliedly, if not expressly, consented.[1]

But if a drover, traveling on a free pass with cattle carried at reduced rates, in consideration thereof agrees to take all care of them, the carrier is not liable for injuries resulting from the want of such care, unless there be gross negligence on the part of the carrier. Central R. R. & Banking Co. *v.* Smitha, 85 Ala. 47; s. c. 4 Southern Reporter, 708; 38 Alb. L. J. 298 (1888).

[1] Illinois Central R. R. *v.* Hall, 58 Ill. 409 (1871); Miltimore *v.* Chicago & N. W. R. Co., 37 Wis. 190 (1875). If the car into which the shipper puts his goods is conspicuously unfit for the purpose, the carrier will not be liable for damages caused by such unfitness, although his agent directed the shipper to put the goods there. In this case the agent of the carrier did not know of the particular defect which caused the injury, and the shipper did. Betts *v.* Farmers' Loan & T. Co., 21 Wis. 80 (1866).

To the same effect is Great Western R. Co. *v.* Hawkins, 18 Mich. 427 (1869). In Southern & N. Ala. R. R. *v.* Wood, 66 Ala. 167, 41 Am. Rep. 749 (1880), it was held that knowledge by the shipper that there was no depot nor agent at the station to which the goods were consigned would exonerate the carrier from any liability for failure to provide either. On the other hand the same court has held that knowledge by the shipper that his cotton would be carried on an open car was no bar to his recovery for its destruction by fire, which would not have occurred had the cotton been in a covered car. Montgomery & W. P. R. R. *v.* Edmonds, 41 Ala. 667 (1868).

So, if the shipper agree that goods may be carried on deck, the carrier is not liable for damage, which would not have been done to goods under the hatches. Lawrence *v.* Minturn, 17 How. U. S. 100 (1854). But although the shipper consent that the goods be carried on deck, the carrier is liable for damage done them by rain, from which they could have been protected by a tarpaulin. Schwinger *v.* Raymond, 83 N. Y. 192; 38 Am. Rep. 415 (1880). In this case there was an express

If the negligence relied on to exonerate the carrier be on the part of the shipper's agent, it must have occurred in the course of his employment. A truckman sent to deliver goods to a carrier voluntarily remained and assisted to put them on board the cars. By his negligence, concurring with that of the carrier's agents, the goods were injured. It was held that the carrier was liable.[1]

The same rule is applicable to the delivery of goods. If the negligence of the consignee combine with that of the carrier to cause injury, the latter is exonerated, otherwise not. This is illustrated by two cases, apparently in conflict, but really harmonious.

Goods were delivered at New Orleans at a spot on the levee which was unsafe, owing to the negligence of the municipal authorities. The ship-master knew it was an improper place. The consignee knew of the arrival of the goods, and neglected for several days to take them away. Meanwhile they were injured. Held a case of concurrent negligence, and that the consignee could not recover damages.[2]

---

contract to cover the goods, and the carrier was requested to fulfill it, but neglected so to do.

Where cattle are carried, and the drover fail to examine the cars before loading, but afterwards observes the overcrowding, and that the animals are suffering, and calls attention of the conductor to it, but is told that there are no other cars, and does not insist on unloading, this is contributory negligence. Squire v. New York Cent. R. R., 98 Mass. 239 (1867).

Where a danger, such as a swinging-door in a ferry-house, is clearly obvious to a passenger, he is bound to notice and avoid it, and his not doing so is contributory negligence. Hayman v. Penn. R. R., 118 Penn. 508 (1888).

[1] Merritt v. Old Colony & N. R. Co., 11 Allen (Mass.), 80 (1865). But in Hart v. Chicago & N. W. R. Co., 69 Iowa, 485 (1888), the court said (p. 488): "If the immediate cause of the loss was the act of the owner, as between the parties absolute justice demands that the loss should fall upon him, rather than upon the one who has been guilty of no wrong; and it can make no difference that the act cannot be said to be either wrongful or negligent."

[2] Northern v. Williams, 6 La. Ann. 578 (1851). The reader should not omit to peruse the graphic description at p. 581 of this case.

But where the injury was caused by negligence of the carrier's servants in unloading the goods from its cars, it was held that the carrier was not exonerated by a previous neglect on the part of the consignee to comply with the known rule of the carrier to come and unload the goods himself. The consignee's negligence did not contribute to the injury.[1] But wherever the consignor's negligence does contribute to the loss, he cannot recover.[2]

5. Illegality of voyage or shipment.—The carrier is not liable for injuries to persons who are combined with the carrier in violating the law. This rule was applied in an action brought to recover damages for the death of a negro servant of a Confederate soldier, who was being transported by the carrier to the scene of hostilities. The

---

[1] Kimball *v.* Western R. R., 6 Gray (Mass.), 542 (1856); Shriver *v.* Sioux City & St. P. R. R., 24 Minn. 506 (1878). This is in analogy to the decisions in actions for personal injuries, to the effect that if the defendant, by the exercise of ordinary care and diligence, could have avoided the mischief which happened, prior negligence on the plaintiff's part will be no bar to his recovery. Green *v.* Erie R. Co., 11 Hun (N. Y.), 333 (1877); Kenyon *v.* N. Y. C. & H. R. R. R., 5 Hun, 479 (1875); Radley *v.* London & N. W. R. Co., L. R. 1 App. Ca. 754, 759 (1876); International & G. N. R. Co. *v.* Folliard, 66 Tex. 603 (1886).

Though a consignee delay removal of goods, after notice of arrival by the carrier, beyond the time limited for the purpose by the bill of lading, the carrier will of course be liable if it can be shown that loss or injury occurred after arrival, but before the expiration of such period. The consignee's negligence would not be contributory. See McKinney *v.* Jewett, 90 N. Y. 267, 272 (1882). So where a package was directed to a person at H., who was not there when the coach arrived, nor for some days after, it was held that, as the package never in fact arrived, the absence of the person to whom it was directed did not exonerate the owners of the coach from their liability. Phillips *v.* Earle, 8 Pick. 182 (1829).

Negligent act or omission of plaintiff is no ground of defense unless it contributed to the injury complained of. Haley *v.* Earle, 30 N. Y. 208 (1864); Teall *v.* Barton, 40 Barb. 137 (1863); Savage *v.* Corn Ex. F. & I. N. Ins. Co., 36 N. Y. 655 (1867), aff'g s. c. 4 Bosw. 1 (1858); Hoffman *v.* Union Ferry Co., 47 N. Y. 176 (1872).

[2] Dougherty *v.* Chicago, B. & Q. R. R., 86 Ill. 467 (1877). Where the loss was caused by bad stowage, the shipper who stowed the goods cannot recover. Thomas *v.* Ship Morning Glory, 13 La. Ann. 269 (1858).

action was tried after the termination of the war.   But
the court held that if the servant paid fare as an ordinary
passenger, which the soldier did not, the carrier would be
liable.[1]   A carrier engaged in transporting passengers on
Sunday is liable for injuries caused by the explosion of a
boiler of imperfect construction and negligently managed.[2]   And where goods were shipped with the intent to
smuggle them, but this was unknown to the carrier, and
he took no part in it, it was held that he was liable to the
shipper for the loss of the goods.

The rule deducible from these cases is this: a violation of law by the passenger or shipper does not put him
without the pale of the law.   He is still under its protection, and may recover for the violation by the carrier
of other requirements, which are disconnected from the
violation of law by the passenger or shipper.   But if he
and the carrier are engaged in a common enterprise
which is unlawful, neither will have a remedy against
the other for injuries occurring in the prosecution of the
enterprise.

Thus far the cases referred to have all related to the

---

[1] Redd *v.* Muscogee R. R., 48 Geo. 102 (1873).   Is not this the last
case in the United States in which a recovery was allowed for the
money-value of a slave?

[2] Carroll *v.* Staten Island R. R., 58 N. Y. 126 (1874).   This decision
is based expressly on the ground that the carrier could not and did not
know that the passenger was violating the Sunday law.   But in Merritt *v.* Earle, 29 N. Y. 115 (1864); affg. s. c. 31 Barb. 38 (1859), it was
held that the fact that the contract was made and the property delivered on board the vessel on Sunday did not exempt the carrier from
liability for the loss of the property.   Where the law permits transportation on Sunday, though the carrier is not bound to do business on that
day, yet if he hold himself out as doing so, he is liable for his failure.
Merchants' Wharf-Boat Assn. *v.* Wood, 64 Miss. 661; 2 So. Rep. 76
(1887); s. c. 3 So. Rep. 248 (1887).   Traveling on Sunday was formerly
forbidden, in Massachusetts, by statute.   It was (until a more recent
statute) held that damages could not be recovered against a carrier for
personal injuries caused to a person transported by it on that day.
Bucher *v.* Cheshire R. R., 125 U. S. 555 (1888).

shipper's misconduct or negligence. A similar rule has been applied to the carrier.

Thus it has been held that a notice posted in the baggage room of a steamer, that the carrier would not be liable for the loss of baggage unless it was checked, even if otherwise effectual, constituted no defense in a case where the passenger tried to obtain a check for his baggage, but could not, because the agent whose duty it was to furnish checks was absent.[1]

---

[1] Freeman *v.* Newton, 3 E. D. Smith (N. Y.), 246 (1854).   If the court, in Gleason *v.* Goodrich Trans. Co., 32 Wis. 85 (1873), had been as lenient to the passenger as the Court of Common Pleas was in Freeman *v.* Newton, the decision of the Wisconsin case might have been different.

See *ante*, p. 161, n. 3.

CHAPTER X.

SECTION I.

HOW THE CONTRACT OF LIMITATION MAY BE MADE.

The general rule is clear, that a carrier cannot relieve itself entirely from the liability imposed upon it by the common law, for any particular risk, except by contract. We have already shown that by the law merchant a carrier by sea may discharge itself from liability, by an abandonment of its interest in the ship and her freight. We have also shown that the carrier may say to the shipper orally, or by written or printed notice brought home to him: I will not be liable for this or that risk, beyond a certain amount, unless you comply with my reasonable regulations. But in all these cases the liability is qualified only—not abrogated. We come now to the consideration of the cases in which some particular liability is entirely abrogated. And this can only be done by contract.

Some courts have been more liberal, or if the reader please, more lax than others in their judgment as to the *quantum* of proof necessary to establish the contract. But in no well-considered case has it ever been held that the liability for any particular risk can be abrogated by a mere notice, that is to say by the carrier's own act, not assented to by the shipper.[1]

---

[1] Southern Express Co. *v.* Newby, 36 Georgia, 635 (1867); Bissell *v.* N. Y. Central R. R., 25 N. Y. 442 (1862); Dorr *v.* New Jersey Steam Navigation Co., 11 N. Y. 485 (1854).

The rule is well expressed in Moore *v.* Evans, 14 Barb. 524 (1852): " In this State, carriers have not been allowed to limit their liability by

In the case of the shipment of goods to be transported as freight it is usual for the consignor to receive a bill of lading, expressing the terms and conditions upon which the merchandise is to be carried. He is presumed to assent to its conditions, because he receives it under circumstances which, by the ordinary usages of business, would naturally lead him to infer that the document he receives, which is his muniment of title, *quasi* negotiable and on the faith of which he may borrow money, is a contract and not a mere receipt.[1]

The rule is not changed even though it be shown that the consignor did not read the bill of lading.[2]

---

their own act." New Jersey Steam N. Co. *v.* Merchants' Bank, 6 How. U. S. 343 (1848); Wallace *v.* Sanders, 42 Geo. 486 (1871). In this case the Court say: " The railroad cannot, *by any act of its own,* limit its liability, but if the act have the consent of the other party, then the rule changes, and the stipulation becomes a contract." This is especially clear where the loss arises from negligence. Mann *v.* Birchard, 40 Vt. 326 (1867); Sager *v.* Portsmouth, S. & P. & E. R. R., 31 Maine, 228 (1850); Fillebrown *v.* Grand Trunk R. Co., 55 *Ibid,* 462 (1867); Judson *v.* Western R. R., 88 Mass. 486 (1863).

[1] Huntington *v.* Dinsmore. 4 Hun, 66; 6 Thomps. & C. (N. Y.) 195 (1875); Long *v.* New York Central R. R., 50 N. Y. 76 (1872); Grace *v.* Adams, 100 Mass. 505 (1868); Snider *v.* Adams Ex. Co., 63 Missouri, 376 (1876); Brehme *v.* The same, 25 Md. 328 (1866); McMahon *v.* Macy, 51 N. Y. 155 (1872); Farnham *v.* Camden & Amboy R. R., 55 Penn. 53 (1867); Am. Ex. Co. *v.* Second Natl. Bank, 69 Penn. 394 (1871). In short, a bill of lading is a contract. Logan *v.* Mobile Trade Co. 46 Ala. 514 (1871).

It has been for many centuries usual for the carrier by sea to deliver a bill of lading to the shipper. The delivery of an inland bill of lading was perhaps suggested by the language of Best, C. J., in Brooke *v.* Pickwick, 4 Bing. 218: " If coach proprietors wish honestly to limit their responsibility, they ought to announce the terms to every individual who applies at their office, and at the same time, to place in his hands a printed paper, specifying the precise extent of their engagement. If they omit to do this, they attract customers under the confidence inspired by the extensive liability which the common law imposes on carriers, and then endeavor to elude that liability by some limitations which they have not been at the pains to make known to the individual who has trusted them."

[2] Grace *v.* Adams, 100 Mass. 505 (1868). In this case the Court say : " It is not claimed that the shipper did not know that the receipt was a contract or a bill of lading, It was his duty to read it." Snider

This rule was applied in a case where the shipper tendered a bill of lading, containing an agreement to transport the goods to Detroit. This city was beyond the carrier's line. The freight clerk interlined in red ink before Detroit the words " to Toledo for " and sent it back. The shipper retained the receipt without objection. Held that he must be deemed to have assented to its terms and that the carrier was not liable for a loss by fire occuring at Detroit.[1]

The same rule was applied in a case where the shipper paid more than the usual price for transportation, and might, therefore, naturally have inferred that the carrier's liability was unrestricted.[2]

In this latter case the Court does not appear to have considered the reason of the rule on this subject already stated. This rule is defensible only on the ground that the carrier has a right to charge a higher price for assuming the liability of an insurer, than for the assumption of a restricted liability. He cannot refuse to carry as common carrier and to be liable as such, to the full extent

---

v. Adams Ex. Co., 63 Mo. 376 (1876). In this case the Court say : " The instrument showed on its face that it was not merely a receipt. . . . It was his duty to read it." Mulligan v. Illinois Central R. Co., 36 Iowa, 181 (1873). American Merchants' Union Ex. Co. v. Schier, 55 Ill. 140 (1870), disapproves the decision in the Grace case, and holds that the question whether the shipper assented to the restrictions and conditions in an inland bill of lading is one of fact for the jury.

A contract of exemption, signed by both parties, is different from a notice or receipt given to the shipper, and is not within a statute invalidating the latter, even though the shipper did not read it. Ill. Cent. R. R. v. Jonte, 13 Bradwell (Ill. App.), 424 (1883).

There are certain rules and regulations which a carrier may adopt, of which a passenger is bound to take notice. Ante, p. 178, n. 1.

[1] Muller v. Cincinnati, H. & D. R. R., 2 Cincinnati Superior Ct. Rep. (Ohio), 280 (1872). It is to be observed, however, that this was a case of delivery to a connecting line, and that there is no obligation upon a carrier to transport goods beyond the terminus of his own line.

[2] Huntington v. Dinsmore, 4 Hun, 66 ; 6 Thomps. & Cook (N. Y.), 195 (1875).

imposed by the common law. But he may say, I will carry for less if you will relieve me from this onerous common law responsibility. The real question is this: If the shipper is unwilling to be his own insurer, shall he pay his premium of insurance to the carrier or to an insurance company? In practice so far as marine risks are concerned, the latter plan has proved the more convenient and is that generally adopted.

But if the carrier demand and receive compensation additional to that usually charged for transportation with restricted risk, where is the consideration for the restriction? Clearly the agreement for it would seem to be *nudum pactum.*[1]

The delivery by a carrier to a customer of envelopes, on which is printed an agreement for transportation leaving blanks for the specification of the termini, does not amount to a general contract to carry the money, for containing which the envelopes were adapted, to every point with which the carrier has connections. Under such circumstances the carrier may lawfully, by the delivery of an appropriate bill of lading, limit its liability to its own route.[2]

---

[1] The criticism thus suggested is supported by the reasoning of the Supreme Court of Massachusetts and of Maine in the following cases: Buckland *v.* Adams Ex. Co., 97 Mass. 124 (1867); Perry *v.* Thompson, 98 *Ib.* 249 (1867); Fillebrown *v.* Grand Trunk R. Co., 55 Maine, 462 (1867). In the latter case the consignor, before the special written contract was delivered, had made with the carrier a contract for transportation. This original contract was without restriction as to risk. It was held that there was no consideration for a restriction contained in a bill of lading, delivered upon the specific shipment of a particular lot of goods shipped under this contract, and that the restriction was therefore not binding upon the shipper. In the two former cases there had been a previous general course of dealing, pursuant to which receipts were not given to the shipper, and the Court held that the man to whom the receipt was delivered had no authority to accept it. See, also, Central R. R. *v.* Dwight Mfg. Co., 75 Geo. 609 (1885).

[2] Pendergast *v.* Adams Ex. Co., 101 Mass. 120 (1869); see Chap. XIII, sect. 3.

SECTION II.

REQUISITE EVIDENCE OF THE SHIPPER'S ASSENT TO THE CONTRACT.

There is a large class of cases which hold that evidence is necessary of some affirmative assent on the part of the shipper to the limitations of the proposed contract.

On principle such consent must always be shown in one way or other.   If by the course of business it is customary that the carrier should deliver and the shipper receive a bill of lading or other written contract, and he does receive it, this is evidence of assent.   On this principle the cases already referred to were decided.

There was, however, a time when it was not usual in all the States to deliver such contracts, but the shipper commonly received only a memorandum or receipt specifying the articles shipped, the names of consignor and consignee, and the place of delivery.   When carriers first undertook to add limitations and restrictions to these receipts, it was held that evidence of assent on the part of the shipper should be given, and that the latter could show that he did not read the paper containing the alleged limitations, nor understand their purport, nor know that the paper given him was anything more than a receipt.

This' has been held:

1. In reference to local express companies receiving baggage from travelers for transportation to their immediate destination.   Various circumstances bearing on the question of assent have in such cases been put in evidence, as, for example, that the limitations were printed in small type, and that the printed paper claimed to be a contract was delivered in a dimly lighted car, moving rapidly, in which it was difficult to read.[1]

---

[1] Blossom *v.* Dodd, 43 N. Y. 264 (1870); Madan *v.* Sherrard, 42 N. Y. Superior Ct. Rep. 353 (1877).   MacMahon *v.* Macy, 51 N. Y. 155

The principle of these decisions, to wit, that there is nothing in the nature of the transaction, or the custom of the trade which should naturally lead the shipper to suppose that he was receiving and accepting the written evidence of a contract, is well illustrated by the case of Woodruff *v.* Sherrard.[1]

There a lady, after having given her baggage check to the carrier's clerk at his office, and given directions for delivery, turned to leave the office. At this moment the contract was complete. At the suggestion of a friend she returned and asked for a receipt. The clerk gave her a printed paper containing a form of agreement limiting the carrier's liability to $100. This she did not read, and it was held that she never assented to its terms and was not bound by it. In another case[2] attention was called to the fact that a revenue stamp partly covered the clause by which it was sought to limit the carrier's liability to $100, so that the clause could not be read intelligibly.

2. When express companies first undertook the charge of small parcels, which they transported by means of the

---

(1872), distinguishes Blossom *v.* Dodd, as does also Kirkland *v.* Dinsmore, and Belger *v.* Dinsmore; *post*, p. 228, n. 2.

The burden in such cases is on the plaintiff to show that he did not know the nature of the paper he received.

[1] Woodruff *v.* Sherrard, 9 Hun (N. Y.), 322 (1876). A comparison between this case and that of Long *v.* New York Central R. R., 50 N. Y. 76 (1872), illustrates the text. In the latter there was verbal negotiation which ended in the delivery of the goods. On receiving these the carrier delivered a written instrument called a receipt, which the Court held constituted a valid contract which made the evidence of the prior negotiation incompetent. The Court say: "The evidence in this case accords with what, from experience, may almost be assumed to be the universal custom of common carriers, to wit, that freight is always carried by this defendant under a written contract. . . . The verbal contract was merged in the written agreement, and the latter must be taken as the evidence, and the sole evidence, of the final and deliberate agreement of the parties. . . . By it alone, in the absence of mistake or fraud, the duties and liabilities of the parties must be regulated."

[2] Perry *v.* Thompson, 98 Mass. 249 (1867).

cars or steamboats of other carriers, a like rule was applied to them, and the mere delivery to the shipper of a receipt containing a clause purporting to exempt the express company from liability, either for specified causes or in a specified amount, was held not to amount to a contract unless the terms were read and assented to by the shipper.[1]

But the practice has become general of delivering to the shipper what the express companies style "Domestic Bills of Lading," which obviously contain much more than a receipt.   It is believed that wherever this practice has become general, courts would apply to these documents rules similar to those which for many years have been applied to marine bills of lading, and would hold that they constitute contracts, and that their terms are binding upon both parties.[2]

---

[1] Adams Express Co. *v.* Nock, 2 Duvall (Ky.), 562 (1866); Belger *v.* Dinsmore, 51 Barb. (N. Y.) 69 (1868); reversed 51 N. Y. 166 (1872); Kirkland *v.* Dinsmore, 2 Hun, 46; 4 Thomps. & Cook (N. Y.), 304 (1874); revd. 62 N. Y. 171 (1875).

[2] Farnham *v.* Camden & Amboy R. R., 55 Penn. 53 (1867); Kirkland *v.* Dinsmore, 62 N. Y. 171 (1875); York Co. *v.* Central R. R., 3 Wall. 107 (1865); Westcott *v.* Fargo, 6 Lansing (N. Y.), 319 (1872); Dillard *v.* Louisville & Nashville R. R., 2 Lea (Tenn.), 288 (1879); see Lewis *v.* Great Western R. Co., 5 Hurl. & Norm. 867 (1860).

Collender *v.* Dinsmore, 55 N. Y. 200 (1873), holds that an express receipt delivered at the time of shipment is a contract.   s. p., Magnin *v.* Dinsmore, 56 N. Y. 168 (1874); Steinweg *v.* Erie R. Co., 43 N. Y. 123 (1870); Dorr *v.* New Jersey Steam Navigation Co., 11 N. Y. 485 (1854); Breese *v.* United States Tel. Co., 48 N. Y. 132 (1871); Young *v.* Western Union Tel. Co., 65 N. Y. 163 (1875).   The two latter were telegraph cases, but the Court intimate that the decision that the clauses in the telegraph blank were binding would have been the same had it been a bill of lading.   Hutchinson *v.* Chicago, St. P., M. & O. R. Co., 37 Minn. 524; 35 N. W. Rep. 433 (1887).

The Pacific, Deady Rep. 17 (1861), is an apparent exception, but was decided on its peculiar facts.   The goods shipped were glass.   The carrier's clerk told the carman that the carrier would not be responsible for breakage, and wrote the words "not accountable for contents" across the face of the bill of lading.   This was communicated to the shipper, who at once, and while the glass was on the wharf, notified the clerk that he would not agree to the limitation.   Held that the carrier was liable for breakage, and that the retention of the bill of lading by

The Supreme Court of Illinois, however, must perhaps be excepted from this general statement.   That court has said in several cases, that it was always competent for the shipper to introduce extrinsic evidence to show that he did not understand or did not assent to the terms of the bill of lading, delivered to him or to his agent.[1]

This doctrine seems one-sided.   It imposes a burden on the carrier without holding the shipper to any obligation.   Ordinarily if a man receives a written paper as evidence of the contract between him and the other contracting party, it is his duty to examine it and to notify the other contractor if he does not assent to its terms.   If he fail to do this, the other, in the absence of fraud or mutual mistake, has a right to rely upon the statement of the written contract.   Even a Court of Equity will not relieve against an unilateral mistake, if there be no fraud.[2]

---

the shipper did not under the circumstances constitute an acceptance of the limitation.

[1] Field *v.* Chicago & Rock Island R. R., 71 Ill. 458 (1874); Merchants' Despatch Co. *v.* Leysor, 89 Ill. 43 (1878); *Ibid v.* Joesting, 89 Ill. 152 (1878).

But in Illinois this seems to be governed by the statute of that State, which provides that such "stipulation expressed in the receipt given for the property is not valid."   If, however, the receipt is signed by the shipper or his agent, it is a contract and is valid.   Ill. Cent. R. R. *v.* Jonte, 13 Brad. (Ill. App.) 424 (1883).   And, notwithstanding the statute, if he fully know the contents of the bill of lading and agrees to its terms it is a valid contract.   Merchants' Despatch Co. *v.* Leysor, *supra;* see *post*, p. 231., n. 5.

In Dakota the shipper's signature to the contract is required by statute (Civil Code, § 1261, 1263), except as to the rate of hire, time, place and manner of delivery.   Under this statute a clause in a bill of lading requiring claims to be presented within ninety days is not valid unless signed by the shipper.   Hartwell *v.* Northern Pac. Ex. Co. (Dak.) 3 Lawy. Rep. Ann. 342; 41 N. W. Rep. 732 (1889).   A similar statute, without the exception, has been passed in Michigan. (Laws 1873, No. 198.)   Feige *v.* Michigan Central R. R., 62 Mich. 1; 28 N. W. Rep. 685 (1886).

[2] Jackson *v.* Andrews, 59 N. Y. 244 (1874); Bryce *v.* Lorrillard Fire Ins. Co., 55 N. Y. 240 (1873).   In Belger *v.* Dinsmore, 51 N. Y. 166 (1872), reversing s. c. 51 Barb. 69 (1870), the Court said that the presumption of law was that a party receiving an instrument in any business (in this case an express company's receipt) is acquainted with its

And it should be observed that the statement of the rule in Field *v.* Chicago & Rock Island R. R.[1] was not necessary to the decision of the case. It was shown that the shipper accepted the receipt with knowledge of its contents. And this was held binding on him. The receipt or bill of lading limited the carrier's liability to its own line, and this was held to be a valid limitation. The same court has held that it is not necessary that the shipper should sign a duplicate of the express receipt or inland bill of lading in order to bind him by its terms.[2]

The Supreme Court of Wisconsin has held that though the possession by the shipper of a receipt from the carrier is *prima facie* evidence of his assent to the terms of the receipt, yet parol evidence is admissible to show that he never assented to its terms.[3]

---

contents. In Kirkland *v.* Dinsmore, 62 N. Y. 171 (1875), it is held: (1) that an express company's receipt which the shipper supposed "was to show that the company received the money, and that the money was to be sent," and looked at it to see where it was to be carried, was a contract; (2) that it made no difference that the shipper did not know it was a contract, and did not read it; (3) that the carrier had a right to suppose he read it and assented to its terms.

In Moore *v.* Evans, 14 Barb. 524 (1852), a "memorandum or receipt" specifying the names of consignors and consignees, the amount of freight payable, the description and destination of the goods, and mode of carriage, with the words "owner's risk," was held a special contract binding on the shipper. It does not appear whether he knew its contents.

In Wallace *v.* Sanders, 42 Georgia, 486 (1871), the receipt was in the following form: "Received of Mr. ——— one horse, two mules and one wagon, for shipment to Atlanta, at his own risk. John F. Reynolds, Agt." This was held to be a binding contract, notwithstanding the provisions of the Georgia statute that the carrier cannot limit his liability "by entry on receipts given," provided that the owner had a fair opportunity to understand the terms of the contract. This the Court held should have been left to the jury. It is manifest from these cases that the precise form of the paper is not of so much consequence, nor whether it be called a notice, a receipt, or bill of lading. The circumstances under which it is given and received must control. For other Georgia cases see *post*, p. 231, n. 5.

[1] 71 Ill. 458 (1874).
[2] Adams Ex. Co. *v.* Haynes, 42 Ill. 89 (1866); Chicago & N. W. R. Co. *v.* Montfort, 60 Ill. 175 (1871).
[3] Boorman *v.* Am. Exp. Co., 21 Wis. 152 (1866); Strohn *v.* Detroit &

The sending by the shipper to the carrier, for signature, of printed receipts furnished by the carrier, containing limitations upon his liability, amounts to an assent to the terms of such receipt.[1]

So it has been held that evidence that in previous instances the carrier had delivered to the shipper's teamster a printed receipt for the goods, containing a contract exempting the carrier from liability for loss by fire, and that no objection had been made by the shipper, was sufficient to prove an actual assent on his part to the terms of this contract.[2]   •

For a reason similar to that which controlled the decision of the cases just referred to, no language on a passenger ticket is held to amount to a contract, without proof that the passenger read it and agreed to it. These tickets are vouchers that the passenger has paid his fare, and is entitled to the usual accommodation on the carrier's vehicle. They do not, *per se*, constitute contracts.[3]

And in general it may be said that a notice by the carrier is inoperative to limit the amount or character of

---

Mil. R. Co., 21 Wis. 554 (1867). In a later case, Morrison *v.* Phillips & Colby C. Co., 44 Wis. 405 (1878), the same court say (p. 410): "In most cases it may be absolutely conclusive."

[1] Falkenan *v.* Fargo, 44 How. Pr. Rep. (N. Y.) 325 (1872); Westcott *v.* Fargo, 6 Lansing (N. Y.), 319 (1872); Wallace *v.* Matthews, 39 Georgia, 617 (1869).

[2] Van Schaack *v.* Northern Trans. Co., 3 Biss. 394 (1872); compare Adams Ex. Co. *v.* Stettaners, 61 Ill. 184 (1871).

[3] Nevins *v.* Bay State Steamboat Co., 4 Bosw. (N. Y.) 225 (1859); Verner *v.* Sweitzer, 32 Penn. St. 208 (1858). A commuter on whose ticket a notice is printed purporting to limit the carrier's liability is still a passenger, and the carrier is indictable for negligently causing his death. Commonwealth *v.* Vt. & Mass. R. R., 108 Mass. 7 (1871).

The ticket for a berth in a sleeping-car does not express all the terms of the contract. Lewis *v.* New York Sleeping-Car Co., 143 Mass. 267 (1887).

In St. Louis, A. & T. R. R. *v.* Mackie, 1 Lawyers' Rep. 667 (Supreme Ct., Texas, 1888), the court held that a passenger who paid for first-class tickets and, without negligence on his part, received second-class tickets, had a valid cause of action against the carrier for the conductor's refusal to allow him to travel on first-class cars.

his liability, unless brought home to the shipper and expressly or impliedly assented to by him. In this case it becomes a contract, and in strictness of terms ought not to be styled a notice at all.[1]

The same rule applies although the shipper paid the carrier for the transportation of his goods at a reduced rate, and the printed table of the rates of freight stated that the carrier would assume no responsibility for the loss, damage or delay of goods carried at this reduced rate. Even though the shipper pays only this reduced rate of freight, evidence must, in the absence of a written contract, be given that the shipper knew of the restriction and assented to it.[2]

In making proof of such a contract, a railway ticket delivered to a passenger[3] or a check for baggage[4] are admissible in evidence.

The real distinction is this: If the paper delivered to the shipper by the carrier contains the terms of the contract between them, and is accepted by the shipper, it is conclusive evidence of the contract, in the absence of fraud or mutual mistake. But if it is a notice only, and does not purport to be a contract, or does not contain language sufficient to constitute a contract, it is no more than a parol statement, and proof must be given of actual assent by the shipper to its terms.[5]

---

[1] Camden & Amboy R. R. Co. v. Baldauf, 16 Penn. St. 67 (1851); Southern Express Co. v. Crook, 44 Ala. 468 (1870); Fibel v. Livingston, 64 Barb. (N. Y.) 179 (1872); Brown v. Adams Ex. Co., 15 W. Va. 812 (1879); Gott v. Dinsmore, 111 Mass. 45 (1872); Farmers' Bank v. Champlain Trans. Co., 23 Vt. 186 (1851).

[2] Balt. & Ohio R. R. v. Brady, 32 Md. 333 (1869). See Thomas v. The Morning Glory, 13 La. Ann. 269 (1858). That such a reduced rate was a sufficient consideration for a limitation of liability, was held in Dillard v. Louisville & N. R. R., 2 Lea (Tenn.), 288 (1879).

[3] Barker v. Coflin, 31 Barb. 556 (1860).

[4] Wilson v. Chesapeake & Ohio R. R., 21 Gratt. (Va.) 654 (1872).

[5] In Rome R. R. v. Sullivan, 32 Geo. 400 (1861), it was said: "The jury may consider the receipt, together with all the facts in the case, to show that there was a special contract." See Geo. R. R. v. Spears, 66 Geo. 485 (1881); Geo. Code, sect. 2068.

In Judson v. Western R. R., 88 Mass. 486 (1863), the rule in Massa-

In some cases, like that of the Southern Ex. Co. *v.* Crook,[1] the further qualification is annexed that the terms of this notice must be just and reasonable. No well-considered case, however, holds that if the notice, by agreement of the shipper, is transformed into a contract, the justice or reasonableness of its terms, if not opposed to public policy, are a proper subject for the consideration of the court.

It cannot be denied that the earlier English, and some of the American decisions recognize and maintain the right of the carrier to limit the amount of his liability by a notice posted conspicuously in his office, or advertised generally, or contained on the face of a receipt given to the shipper or passenger, even though the latter does not read or know of this notice.[2]

But the distinction thus taken is not supported in its full extent by the later authorities. As far as there was reason and good sense in it, the cases cited and commented upon in the ninth chapter adopt it. That is to say, a shipper cannot lawfully mislead a carrier by imposing upon him the carriage of goods of great intrinsic value, contained in a package or wrapping calculated to deceive

---

chusetts is laid down that "a notice by the carrier that he will not assume the ordinary responsibility imposed by law, if brought home to him and assented to clearly and unequivocally, will be binding, because tantamount to an express contract."

This leaves open the question whether placing such a notice in his hands will amount to "bringing it home to him," whether he reads it or not. As to what constitutes assent, it is said that "mere silence cannot be said to amount to assent." Buckland *v.* Adams Ex. Co., 97 Mass. 124 (1867).

Redfield on Railways, vol. 2, pt. 8, sect. 11, p. 88, thus states the rule: "At all events the carrier must show that the owner . . . acquiesced by making no remonstrance."

See cases *ante*, p. 228, n. 2.

[1] Southern Ex. Co. *v.* Crook, 44 Ala. 468 (1870).

[2] Cowen, J., in Cole *v.* Goodwin, 19 Wend. 251 (1838), and cases cited. Hopkins *v.* Westcott, 6 Blatchf. 64 (1868); Whitesell *v.* Crane, 8 Watts & S. (Penn.) 369 (1845); Barney *v.* Prentiss, 4 Harr. & Johns. (Md.) 317 (1818).

him as to the character of the contents.   Farther than this no recent cases of authority have gone.

The change in the current of decisions began when it was held that a notice was of no avail unless brought home to the shipper, no matter how widely it had been advertised.[1]   Then followed the decisions that even if notice were brought home to the shipper, it would not be binding upon him unless he assented to its terms, and if he did so assent it would cease to be a mere notice and become a contract.[2]

Merely marking a package C. O. D. does not constitute a contract with the carrier to collect the price.   An agreement by him so to do must be proved, either by positive evidence or by proof that it is customary for the carrier to collect the price on receiving parcels so marked.[3]

SECTION III.

CONSTRUCTION OF CONTRACTS CLAIMED TO EXEMPT FROM NEGLIGENCE.

It has been shown in Chapter IV that the Federal Courts and courts of many States, deny the validity of

---

[1] Peck v. Weeks, 34 Conn. 145 (1867); Bean v. Green, 12 Maine, 422 (1835); Sager v. Portsmouth & S. & P. & E. R. R., 31 Maine, 228 (1850); Fillebrown v. Grand Trunk R. Co., 55 Ib. 462 (1867); Hollister v. Nowlan, 19 Wend. (N. Y.) 234 (1838); Cole v. Goodwin, Ibid, 251 (1838); Clark v. Faxton, 21 Ibid, 153 (1839); Camden & Amboy R. R. & Trans. Co. v. Belknap, 21 Ibid, 354 (1839); Jones v. Vorhees, 10 Ohio, 145 (1840); Moses v. Boston & Maine R. R., 24 N. H. 71 (1851); Sanford v. Housatonic R. R., 11 Cushing (Mass.), 155 (1853). This same rule was applied, even to a reasonable regulation of the carrier, in Macklin v. N. J. Steamboat Co., 7 Abb. Pr. N. S. (N. Y.) 229 (1869).

[2] Blomenthal v. Brainerd, 38 Vermont, 402 (1866); Western Trans. Co. v. Newhall, 24 Ill. 466 (1860); Derwort v. Loomer, 21 Conn. 244 (1851); Moses v. Boston & Maine R. R., 32 N. H. 523 (1856); Dorr v. N. J. Steam Nav. Co., 11 N. Y. 485 (1854); Rawson v. Penn. R. R., 2 Abb. Pr. N. S. (N. Y.) 220 (1867); Kimball v. Rutland & B. R. R., 26 Vt. 247 (1854); Farmers' & Mechanics' Bank v. Champlain Trans. Co., 23 Vt. 186 (1851); Hale v. N. J. Steam Nav. Co., 15 Conn. 539 (1843).

[3] Chicago & N. W. R. Co. v. Merrill, 48 Ill. 425 (1868).

contracts which purport to exempt the carrier from liability for the negligence of its servants. But in England and in those States which admit the validity of such contracts, the question has been frequently considered, whether it was the intention of the particular clause under consideration, to exempt the carrier from liability, either for an intentional or willful act or for negligence on the part of its servants. In those States it is well settled that the "contract will not be deemed to except losses occasioned by the carrier's negligence unless that be expressly stipulated."[1]

The English courts state this rule of construction substantially in the form in which it is laid down in America. But in the application of the rule there is a difference between the courts of the two countries. If the language of the bill of lading is so general as in terms to exclude "*all* risks," of whatever kind, a loss from negligence is held in England to be included, although a loss from negligence be not specified.[2]

---

[1] The quotation in the text is from Magnin *v.* Dinsmore, 56 N. Y. 168 (1874). In Mynard *v.* Syracuse, B. & N. Y. R. R., 71 N. Y. 180 (1877), revg. s. c. 7 Hun, 399 (1876), the contract under consideration purported to release the carrier from all claims for injury to the stock transported "from whatsoever acts arising." The Court held that this general language was not sufficient to include a loss occasioned by the negligence of the carrier's servants. To the same effect are Steinweg *v.* Erie R. Co., 43 N. Y. 123 (1870); Wells *v.* Steam Nav. Co., 8 N. Y. 375 (1853); Nicholas *v.* N. Y. Central & H. R. R. R., 89 N. Y. 370 (1882); Holsapple *v.* Rome, W. & O. R. R., 86 N. Y. 275 (1881); Schieffelin *v.* Harvey, 6 Johns. 178 (1810).

The language of Nelson, J., in New Jersey Steam Nav. Co. *v.* Merchants' Bank, 6 How. (U. S.) 344 (1848), is to the same effect. See The New Orleans, 28 Fed. Rep. 44 (1885).

The words "at owner's risk" will not be held to exempt the carrier from liability for loss caused by negligence. Canfield *v.* Baltimore & O. R. R., 93 N. Y. 532 (1883); Alexander *v.* Greene, 7 Hill (N. Y.), 533 (1844); Baltimore & Ohio R. R. *v.* Rathbone, 1 W. Va. 87 (1865); Western & A. R. Co. *v.* Exposition Cotton Mills (Ga.), 7 S. E. Rep. 916 (1888).

[2] The general rule of construction stated in the text is supported by Hayn *v.* Cullifor, 3 C. P. Div. 410 (1878); s. c. on appeal, 4 C. P. Div. 182 (1879); Chartered Merc. Bk. of India *v.* Netherlands India S. N.

A clause exempting the carrier from liability for loss by fire does not cover the case of a loss from fire, occasioned by negligence of the carrier's servants, or his failure to provide reasonable precautions against danger, unless the intention to provide for such exemption appears distinctly in the contract.[1]

Where a loss occurs from an excepted risk, but the negligence of the carrier or his breach of contract contributes to the loss, the question has frequently been raised whether the carrier is entitled to the benefit of the limitations of liability contained in the bill of lading. The decisions on this subject are not uniform. In New York, where the bill of lading exempted the carrier from liability for loss by fire, it was held that he was liable for destruction, caused by fire which consumed the goods while awaiting transportation, because the omission to transport was attributable to the carrier's neglect to provide proper means for transportation.[2] This case is supported by others of authority.[3]

Co. (The Kron Prinz), 9 Qu. B. Div. 118 (1882); s. c., reversed in part, 10 *Ib.* 521 (1883). Its application by the English courts is illustrated by Austin *v.* Manchester R. Co., 10 C. B. 454 (1850); Carr *v.* Lancashire & Yorkshire R. Co., 7 Excheq. 707 (1852). In this latter case the language of the contract was, "subject to the owner's taking all risk of conveyance whatsoever, as the company will not be responsible for any injury or damage (however caused)." It was held that the carrier was not liable for a loss caused by the negligence of his servants. Phillips *v.* Edwards, 28 L. J. Excheq. 52 (1858); Peek *v.* North Staffordshire R. Co., 10 House of Lords Cases, 473, 499, 511 (1862).

Since the passage of the English statute authorizing the courts to determine what clauses in contracts for conveyance by land are unreasonable, the courts have held that general clauses of exemption like these in such contracts are unreasonable. McManus *v.* Lancashire R. Co., 4 H. & N. 327 (1859); Gregory *v.* West Midland R. Co., 33 L. J. Excheq. 155 (1864).

[1] Erie R. Co. *v.* Lockwood, 28 Ohio St. 358 (1876); U. S. Express Co. *v.* Backman, *Ibid*, 144 (1875); Gaines *v.* Union Trans. Co., *Ibid*, 418 (1876); Chicago, St. L. & N. O. R. R. *v.* Moss, 60 Miss. 1003 (1883); Montgomery & W. P. R. R. *v.* Edmonds, 41 Ala. 667 (1868); New Orleans, St. L. & C. R. R. *v.* Faler, 58 Miss. 911 (1875).

[2] Condict *v.* Grand Trunk R. Co., 54 N. Y. 500 (1873); see s. c., 4 Lansing 106 (1871).

[3] McDaniel *v.* Chicago & N. W. R. Co., 24 Iowa, 412 (1868). In

So, it is well settled that if the carrier does not forward the goods by the conveyance named in the bill of
lading, or by the ordinary route, he is liable for a loss,
although it occur from an excepted peril.[1]

Where the contract is to transport "all rail," these
words should receive a reasonable construction. The
carrying of goods in the ordinary cars of the railroad,
from the terminus of the railroad over a ferry would not
be a violation of such stipulation. But if the carrier
under such a contract, without necessity, transports the
goods over a part of the route by water, even though such
transportation be common, and over one of his regular
routes, he loses the benefit of the limitation. This was
held in a case where the contract was made at one end
of a route formed of several connecting lines, and the carrier at the other end transported the goods in his usual
way for 20 miles by water—from Perth Amboy to New
York. The goods were destroyed by fire before delivery
at the latter place. The contract exempted the carrier

---

this case the immediate cause of the injury was defective cars. Whit-
worth v. Erie R. Co., 45 N. Y. Superior Ct. 602 (1879); Michaels v. N.
Y. Central R. R., 30 N. Y. 564 (1864); Bostwick v. Baltimore & Ohio
R. R., 45 N. Y. 712 (1871); Heyl v. Inman S. S. Co., 14 Hun (N. Y.),
564 (1878). This was a case of loss by fermentation. Dunson v. New
York Central R. R., 3 Lans. (N. Y.) 265 (1870), and Read v. Spaulding,
30 N. Y. 630 (1864), were cases of loss by a flood. Wing v. New York
& Erie R. R., 1 Hilton, 235 (1856), was a case of damage by freezing.
So was The Aline, 25 Fed. Rep. 562 (1885); affg. s. c. 19 Fed. Rep.
875 (1883). So was Siordet v. Hall, 4 Bing. 607 (1828). New Bruns-
wick Steamboat Co. v. Tiers, 24 N. J. Law, 697 (1853), was a case of
loss by a storm. Campbell v. Morse, 1 Harper Law (S. C.), 468 (1824),
was a case of loss by flood. In all these cases, though the immediate
cause of the injury or loss was an excepted peril, it was held that the
carrier was liable, because his negligence contributed to the result.

[1] Express Co. v. Kountze, 8 Wall. 342 (1869). In this case the loss
was by capture. The carrier had a route by which the goods might
have been forwarded and which was safe. *Held*, the carrier was liable.
Marckwald v. Oceanic Steam. Nav. Co., 11 Hun (N. Y.), 462 (1877);
Goddard v. Mallory, 52 Barb. (N. Y.) 87 (1868); Merchants' Despatch
Trans. Co. v. Kahn, 76 Ill. 520 (1875); Hand v. Baynes, 4 Whart. (Pa.)
204 (1838); Lamb v. Camden & Amboy R. R., 2 Daly (N. Y.), 454
(1869); Simon v. The Fung Shuey, 21 La Ann, 363 (1869).

from liability for loss by fire. It was nevertheless held that he was liable.[1]

The Supreme Court of the United States, and also that of Massachusetts, has declared a somewhat different rule. Those courts cited the maxim familiar in insurance law, *causa proxima, non remota, spectatur,* and held the carrier not liable if the immediate cause of the loss was a peril for which the carrier was not liable, although delay on the carrier's part brought the goods into the place and time at which the peril occurred.[2]

If the carrier has good reason for declining to receive goods or passengers, he should state it at the time the application for transportation is made. If not stated then he cannot set it up afterwards.[3]

---

[1] Maghee *v.* Camden & Amboy R. R., 45 N. Y. 514 (1871).

[2] Railroad Co. *v.* Reeves, 10 Wall. 176 (1869); Hoadley *v.* Northern Trans. Co., 115 Mass. 304 (1874); Denny *v.* New York Central R. R., 13 Gray (Mass.), 481 (1859); Morrison *v.* Davis, 20 Penn. 171 (1852). See another case where this maxim was applied to the liability of a carrier for injuries caused directly by a storm but remotely by his negligence: Gillespie *v.* St. Louis, Kansas City & N. R. R., 6 Mo. App. 554 (1879). No doubt these cases are supported by analogous decisions in reference to contracts of a different species. But they appear to overlook the well-established policy of the law to confine within the narrowest limits exemptions for losses by negligence or omission of duty. In the recent case of Fox *v.* Boston & Me. R. R., 1 Lawyers' Rep. 702 (Supreme Court, Mass.), the loss occurred by freezing. If the apples had been forwarded without delay they would not have been frozen. The court held the carrier liable, and distinguished the case from the Denny and Hoadley cases thus: "In each of these cases, the loss to the plaintiff was caused by an extraordinary event, a fire and a freshet; and the Court held that the defendants, although guilty of negligent delay, were not responsible, because the event was not one which would reasonably be anticipated. In the case at bar the event which caused the loss was contemplated by the parties when they made their contract, as a probable consequence of the breach of it." In the Reeves case, cited in this note, the connection of the negligence of the carrier with the loss was very remote. The general doctrine in the Federal courts is the same as that of the cases cited in notes 4 and 5. See cases cited Chap. XIV. sect. 6, note 2; sect. 7, notes 1, 2; sect. 8, notes 3, 5, 6.

[3] Hannibal R. R. *v.* Swift, 12 Wall. 262 (1870); Phelps *v.* Ill. Cent. R. R., 94 Ill. 556 (1880).

When the language of the contract was that "the company would not be responsible for articles conveyed upon its road, unless," &c., it was held that this limitation applied only to the transportation, and did not limit the carrier's liability for injuries to the goods while in his possession waiting to be transported.[1]

Like all other contracts, the carrier's contract with the shipper must be construed as a whole, and effect, if possible, be given to every clause.[2]

Contracts with carriers are generally drawn by the carrier himself, and should, therefore, be construed strictly as against him.[3]

---

[1] Detroit & Milwaukee R. R. *v.* Adams, 15 Mich. 458 (1867).

[2] In Sisson *v.* Cleveland & Toledo R. R., 14 Mich. 489 (1866), the language of a subsequent clause of the contract was held to limit that of a prior clause. The first provided that the owner of the live stock transported should assume " all and every risk of injuries which the animals, or either of them, may receive," &c., and " risk of any loss or damage which may be sustained by reason of any delay or from any other cause or thing, in or incident to or from or in loading or unloading the stock." It was held that the limitation applied wholly to injuries to the stock caused by delay and not to injury done the owner by the delay which occurred and which brought the stock to market after prices had declined.

[3] Hooper *v.* Wells, 27 Cal. 11 (1864).   Sawyer, J., at p. 27, said : "The language must be taken most strongly against the defendants. . . . The instrument is executed by them alone. It was drawn up with care, in language selected by themselves, the blank form having been printed in advance ready to be presented to all persons offering property for transportation by their express. The restrictions were for their benefit." Cream City R. R. *v.* Chicago, M & St. P. R. Co , 63 Wis. 93 (1885).

In Keeley *v.* Boston & Me. R. R., 67 Maine, 163 (1878), the contract was construed strictly against the passenger. It was held that a ticket from Portland to Boston meant precisely what it said and would not authorize the holder to ride the reverse way. See Downs *v.* N. Y. & N. H. R. R., 36 Conn. 287 (1869).

CHAPTER XI.

USAGE OF BUSINESS.

SECTION I.

EFFECT OF THE CARRIER'S USAGE, WITH ESPECIAL REFERENCE
TO THE QUESTION OF NOTICE TO THE SHIPPER.

Evidence of uniform usage in the transaction of business between carrier and shipper is material in one of two ways :

1. As bearing on the question of actual notice to the shipper, and of assent by him to the transportation of his goods in accordance with the usage.

2. As establishing a reasonable regulation for the conduct of the carrier's business, pursuant to which it may be done, on the whole, with greater facility and convenience both to the public and carrier, whose real interests will, in the end, always be identical, however diverse they may appear upon a superficial view.

The general rule is that custom cannot be set up to contradict the agreement contained in the bill of lading. For example: it was held that a carrier who agreed to transport freight from San Francisco to New York *via* Panama, could not show the existence of a custom that the carrier should not be liable for loss on the Isthmus.[1]

---

[1] Simmons *v.* Law, 4 Abb. Ct. App. (N. Y.) 241 (1866). In this case the bill of lading provided against perils of "navigation, land carriage, &c.," and the carrier endeavored to support the exception by showing that it was the custom of the trade for shippers to assume all the risk of transportation of gold across the Isthmus. Held that, as against the positive agreement to deliver safely in New York, evidence of such cus-

Evidence of the usage of business is always admissible to explain the meaning of ambiguous terms in a bill of lading.[1]

Usage cannot add to a contract an independent clause. If there be an express contract for the carriage of goods, which contains no clause exempting the carrier from liability for the loss in question, evidence is not admissible that a clause providing for such exemption is usual in the carrier's bill of lading.[2]

When no express contract is made, the same rule applies to the contract implied by law from delivery of goods to a carrier for transportation.[3] Proof of the usage of the carrier in the conduct of its business is not, of itself, sufficient in any case to exempt the carrier from liability for any particular species of injury or loss; as, for example, loss by fire,[4] or by overloading a vehicle.[5]

The fact that the shipper has, in the case of previous shipments, accepted from the carrier bills of lading con-

---

tom was not admissible, even under this somewhat ambiguous bill of lading. On the other hand it has been held that a usage to carry passengers' trunks of a peculiar construction, containing samples of merchandise, would not render the carrier liable for the merchandise contained in them. And see p. 210, n. 2, *ante*. Alling *v.* Boston & Albany R. R., 126 Mass. 121 (1879).

[1] Balfour *v.* Wilkins, 5 Sawyer, C. C. 429 (1879). In this case it was also held that evidence of the facilities for loading at the port of lading was admissible to explain the language of the bill of lading; as, for instance, to show what was meant by "rainy days." See, also, Fabbri *v.* Mercantile Mutual Ins. Co., 6 Lansing (N. Y.), 446 (1872); Vose *v.* Morton, 5 Gray (Mass.), 594 (1856); Houghton *v.* Watertown Fire Ins. Co., 131 Mass. 300 (1881).

[2] Clyde *v.* Graver, 54 Penn. 251 (1867). The rule which excludes parol evidence to vary or contradict a written contract, is as applicable to carrier's contracts as to any others. Long *v.* New York C. R. R., 50 N. Y. 76 (1872).

[3] McMillan *v.* Michigan S. & N. I. R. R., 16 Mich. 79 (1867); Browning *v.* Long Id. R. R., 2 Daly (N. Y.), 117 (1867).

[4] Coxe *v.* Heisley, 19 Penn. 243 (1852). But see Patton *v.* McGrath, Dudley (S. C.), 162 (1838); Swindler *v.* Hilliard, 2 Rich. Law (S. C.), 286 (1846), and Singleton *v.* Hilliard, 1 Strob. (S. C.) 203 (1847).

[5] Derwort *v.* Loomer, 21 Conn. 245 (1851).

taining clauses restricting the carrier's liability, affords no ground for the inference that when no bill of lading was delivered or accepted he agreed to similar limitations. The inference that he was unwilling to agree to them is at least equally consistent with his conduct and that of the carrier.[1] But evidence of usage is admissible as bearing on the question of assent by the shipper to the proposed limitation.[2]

It has been very much debated whether, in order to make the usage effectual to modify or restrict the carrier's liability in reference to the delivery of goods intrusted to

---

[1] McMillan v. Michigan S. & N. I. R. R., 16 Mich. 79, 111 (1867). The rule that "the common-law liability of a common carrier is not limited by a general notice that he will not accept or carry goods except under a restricted responsibility, although the notice is known to the shipper when he delivers them for shipment," Kirkland v. Dinsmore, 62 N. Y. 171 (1875); Bean v. Green, 3 Fairfield (12 Me.), 422 (1835), ought, on principle, to decide all these questions that have been mooted concerning the effect of the carriers' usage. As the court in Kirkland v. Dinsmore well said (p. 175): "It is presumed, under such circumstances, that the shipper delivers the goods under the contract which the law creates, and not upon the terms stated in the notice." Hollister v. Nowlen, 19 Wend. 234 (1838); Dorr v. N. J. S. Nav. Co., 11 N. Y. 485 (1854). See ante, pp. 225, 230, 231.

[2] Cooper v. Berry, 21 Georgia, 526 (1857); Hinkley v. N. Y. Central R. R., 3 Thomps. & Cook (N. Y.), 281 (1874); Nevins v. Bay State S. B. Co., 4 Bosw. 225, 238 (1859), per Woodruff, J.

Cooper v. Berry was a case where cotton delivered to a carrier was burned. The evidence tended to show that, by the usage of the business, the carrier was not liable for loss by fire. There was no written contract in the case, and the court held that a contract to limit the carrier's liability might be proved by the acts from which a contract is to be implied, such as public notice known to the person for whom he carries that he will not be answerable for loss of goods committed to his care. Any other acts or facts from which such a contract is to be implied must stand on the same footing. Gibbon v. Paynton, 4 Burr. 2298 (1769); Hyde agst. Trent & Mersey Nav. Co., 5 Term Rep. 389 (1793); Angell on Carriers, 106, 179, 301, 355.

Browning v. L. I. R. R., 2 Daly, 117 (1867). At page 121 the court say: "This general obligation (as to delivery and notice to the consignee) may be varied by an express contract between the parties; or a uniform and well-known usage may be shown, establishing a mode of delivery in certain cases or at particular places, in conformity with which the parties may be presumed to have contracted." Gibson v. Culver, 17 Wend. 305 (1837).

16

him, it is necessary to prove that the consignee had notice
of such usage. On the one hand some courts have held
that the consignee or owner of the goods is bound to ac-
quaint himself with the usages of business of the carrier
with whom he deals, and is bound to take notice of them
and act in accordance with them.[1] And it has even been
held that a reasonable regulation of a railroad company
as to the transportation of passengers—to wit, requiring
the trip to be continuous—was binding on a passenger, although he had no notice of it, and the usage had been to
disregard it.[2] And it is held that passengers are bound
to enquire and take notice at what stations a particular
train usually stops.[3]

On the other hand it has been held in numerous cases
that a usage is of no effect to limit the carrier's liability
unless notice of it is brought home to the shipper or owner of the goods in question.[4] Notice of such a usage

---

[1] Farmers' & Mechanics' Bank v. Champlain Trans. Co., 18 Vermont, 131 (1846); s. c. 23 Vt. 186 (1851); Beebe v. Ayres, 28 Barb. (N.
Y.) 275 (1858).

[2] Johnson v. Concord R. R., 46 N. H. 213 (1865). But this decision
would seem, on principle, indefensible. The power that makes a rule
can change it. To suffer it to become obsolete is practically to change
or repeal it. And a carrier, having thus dealt with its own rules, ought
not to be allowed suddenly to revive them. This would make them a
trap to the unwary, rather than a source of safety to the public. The
Supreme Court of Louisiana held the reverse in Leisy v. Buyers, 36 La.
Ann. 705 (1884). Still it may be just to require, as the Supreme Court
of Iowa did in O'Neill v. Keokuk & D. M. R. Co., 45 Iowa, 546 (1877),
that some evidence should be given that this customary disregard of the
rule was known to the officer charged with its enforcement.

[3] Fink v. Albany & Susquehanna R. R., 4 Lansing (N. Y.), 147
(1871). See Chap. VII, sect. 11.

[4] Cantling v. Hannibal & St. Joseph R. R., 54 Mo. 385 (1873).
(This case was similar to Mayal v. B. & M. R. R., infra.) Minter v.
Pacific R. R., 41 Mo. 503 (1867); Gleason v. Goodrich Trans. Co., 32
Wis. 85 (1873).

As to the trains on which passengers may ride, see Marony v. Old
Colony R. Co., 106 Mass. 153 (1870). As to notice to the consignee of
the arrival of the freight, see Judson v. Western R. R., 6 Allen, 486
(1863); The Mary Washington, 1 Abb. (U. S.) 1; s. c. Chase Dec. 125
(1865). As to the requirement that a ticket must be purchased by the
passenger on a freight train, where the rule was new and the passenger

may, perhaps, be implied from its notoriety and long continuance.[1] And the weight of authority is that if proof is not given of actual notice of the usage to the party sought to be affected by it, evidence must be adduced that it has been so uniform, well settled, and of long duration, that it may reasonably be inferred that he had notice of it.[2] In other words, it must be so general and well known that the court may fairly presume that it was within the contemplation of the parties when the contract was made, and thus formed a part of it. Thus it was held that a custom on the part of a carrier by rail, to deliver to a carter those goods for which the consignee did not call, was not sufficient to impose an obligation on the carrier to deliver at the consignee's place of business.[3]

---

had been in the habit of riding without a ticket, see Lake Shore & M. S. R. Co. *v.* Greenwood, 79 Penn. 373 (1875). As to contracts between the carrier and one of its agents, by which the latter is to transport a certain class of goods, and be alone responsible for loss or injury to them, see Mayall *v.* Boston & Maine R. R., 19 N. H. 122 (1848).

[1] See St. John *v.* Southern Express Co., 1 Woods, 612 (1871). In this case the question was considered, but not definitely decided.

[2] Duling *v.* Phil., W. & B. R. R., 66 Md. 120; 5 Central Rep. 570 (1886). In this case a passenger sought to bind a railroad company by the usage of its ticket agent, and the rule stated in the text was applied. Illinois Central R. R. *v.* Smyser, 38 Ill. 354 (1865); Bissell *v.* Price, 16 Ill. 408 (1855); Macklin *v.* New Jersey S. Co., 7 Abb. Pr. N. S. 229 (1869); Cooper *v.* Berry, 21 Geo. 526 (1857). The same rule was applied in a case where it was sought to prove a usage as to the meaning of words in a contract. Miller *v.* Burke, 68 N. Y. 615 (1877).

[3] Cahn *v.* Michigan Central R. R., 71 Ill. 96 (1873). An illustration of this rule is to be found in the case of Wiltse *v.* Barnes, 46 Iowa, 210 (1877). The court in that case treat a usage of the carrier as to delivery, known to the consignor, as a part of the contract and equivalent to a direction from the consignor to follow such usage. It was to require prepayment of the charge for transportation before the consignee should be allowed to examine the goods. He refused to make such prepayment, and the goods were consequently returned to consignor. It was held that the consignee had no right of action against the carrier for the refusal to deliver. (*Post*, pp. 244, 245).

The contradiction between the cases as to whether proof must be made of actual notice to the shipper or passenger of the existence of a usage, may be explained by a reference to the nature of the rule which may be under consideration. A rule may be reasonable if notified to

SECTION II.

USAGE AS REGULATING THE CARRIER'S MODE OF TRANSACTING BUSINESS.

There are some matters relating to and modifying the carrier's common law liability, which in the absence of express contract are determined by the usage of the business. One of these is the manner of delivery of the goods intrusted to him. It is well settled that this should be according to the usages of the place where the delivery is to be made, or the usual exigencies of business there.[1]

These usages in reference to the manner in which delivery should be made are binding upon both parties and may be shown by either.[2] For example, where it was the usage that vessels bound to the port of Cleveland should deliver their cargoes at an elevator, each vessel awaiting its turn, the Court held that this usage formed a part of the contract, and that the carrier was responsible for injury to the goods which occurred while the vessel was waiting its turn, and could not recover demurrage for delay caused by such injury.[3] In another elevator case, however, the

---

the passenger, which he would not be bound to inquire for or expect. On the other hand there are some matters on which shippers and passengers are bound to inform themselves, as, for example, where a particular train will stop. *Ante*, Chap. VII, sect. 11.

[1] Richmond *v.* Union Steamboat Co., 87 N. Y. 240 (1881); Homesly *v.* Elias, 66 N. C. 330 (1872); Adams Ex. Co. *v.* Darnell, 31 Ind. 20 (1869); Salter *v.* Kirkbride, 4 N. J. Law Rep. 223 (1818); McMasters *v.* Penn. R. R., 69 Penn. 374 (1871); *post*, Chap. XIV, sect. 8.'

[2] The Tybee, 1 Woods, 358 (1870); Hooper *v.* Chicago & N. W. R. Co., 27 Wis. 81 (1870); Whitehouse *v.* Halstead, 90 Ill. 95 (1878); Hodgdon *v.* N. Y. New Haven & H. R. R., 46 Conn. 277 (1878). In New Orleans, J. & G. N. R. R. *v.* Hurst, 36 Miss. 660 (1859), it was held that a usage as to the place at which a particular train should stop was binding upon the carrier. But delivery to the holder of the invoice is not justified by a previous course of dealing between him and the carrier, unknown to the shipper, the bill of lading being to the order of the latter. Penn. R. Co. *v.* Stern, 119 Penn. 24 (1888); Weyand *v.* Atchinson, T. & S. F. R. Co., 39 N. W. Rep. (Iowa), 899 (1888); North Penn. R. R. *v.* Commercial Bk. of Chic., 123 U. S. 727 (1887).

[3] The Glover, 1 Brown Adm. 166 (1872).

Court held that a custom to moor along side an elevator barges containing cargo consigned to its owner, leaving him to take care of them, would not relieve the carrier, nor justify the Court in finding that there had been a delivery to the consignee.[1]

The rule already stated as to the effect of the usage at the port of delivery has been applied to the delivery by a carrier to the next connecting line. The customary method of forwarding the goods from the terminus of the first carrier's line is presumed to have entered into and formed part of the contract.[2] But a mere practice established by a carrier for its own convenience, in reference to delivering goods to a connecting line, will not excuse delay on the part of the carrier in forwarding the goods, although justified by the custom.[3]

The custom in reference to the part of the vessel on which goods of a particular kind are to be stowed is binding upon both parties.[4] The usage of business as to the

---

[1] Germania Ins. Co. v. La Crosse & Minn. Packet Co., 3 Bissell, 501 (1873). The carrier in this case was a tug, and moored her tow while a gale was raging, which caused the damage.

[2] The Convoy's Wheat, 3 Wallace, 225 (1865); Simpkins v. Norwich & N. L. Steamboat Co., 11 Cushing, 102 (Mass.) (1853); Van Santvoord v. St. John, 6 Hill (N. Y.), 157 (1843), revg. s. c., 25 Wend. 660 (1841); Mich. Cent. R. R. v. Curtis, 80 Ill. 324 (1875). For example, where a carrier by rail received goods for transportation to Albany, there to be delivered to the People's line of steamboats for transportation to New York, and the People's line refused to take the goods, and the carrier thereupon delivered them to another line, to which such goods were customarily delivered, it was held that this was a good delivery and relieved the carrier from further responsibility. Johnson v. N. Y. Central R. R., 31 Barb. (N. Y.) 196 (1857).

[3] Lawrence v. Winona & St. Peter R. R., 15 Minn. 390 (1870). This decision is sustainable on the ground that the usage under which the railroad company sought to excuse its delay was not a general use, and there could be no presumption that it was known to the shipper, or that it entered into the contract so as to form part of it.

[4] Baxter v. Leland, 1 Abb. Adm. 348 (1848); The Colonel Ledyard, 1 Sprague, 530 (1860). In The Delaware, 14 Wallace, 579 (1871), it was held that parol evidence of the shipper's consent that his goods might be carried on deck was inadmissible, but the Court ad-

mode or time of transportation is binding upon the parties.[1] This statement is subject, however, to the limitation that the usage must not be in conflict with the carrier's obligation, imposed by law, or created by contract.[2]

Evidence of usage has been admitted to extend or amplify the language of the bill of lading.[3] It may regulate

---

mitted "that where there is a well-known usage in reference to a particular trade to carry the goods as convenience may require, either upon or under deck, the bill of lading may import no more than that the cargo shall be carried in the usual manner." Sproat *v.* Donnell, 26 Me. 185 (1846); and see *post*, Ch. XIV, sect. 8; Lapham *v.* Atlas Ins. Co., 24 Pick. (Mass.) 1 (1833).

[1] Cooper *v.* Kane, 19 Wend. 386 (1838); Peet *v.* Chicago & N. W. R. R., 20 Wis. 598 (1866); Lowry *v.* Russell, 8 Pick. (Mass.) 360 (1829); Sproat *v.* Donnell, 26 Me. 185 (1846); Broadwell *v.* Butler, 1 Newb. Adm. 171; 6 McLean, 296 (1854); see Hatchell *v.* The Compromise, 12 La. Ann. 783 (1857). In Tierney *v.* N. Y. Central R. R., 76 N. Y. 305 (1879), the Court say, p. 314: "The freight in question was not only perishable, but known to be so by both parties, and was shipped as such, and with knowledge on the plaintiff's part of the custom of the defendant to give a preference in transportation of such goods, and the parties, though silent, may be regarded as adopting the custom as part of the contract." The rule stated in the text was applied to a case where the carrier's custom was to seal valuable packages, and its omission to do this was held to be negligence. Overland Mail & Express Co. *v.* Carroll, 7 Col. 43 (1883).

[2] Coxe *v.* Heisley, 19 Penn. 243 (1852); Missouri Pac. R. Co. *v.* Fagan (Texas), 9 S. W. Rep. 749 (1888); Leonard *v.* Fitchburg R. R., 143 Mass. 307; 3 New England Rep. 342 (1887). In this case the Court say: "If it was an unsafe method of transportation, the fact that it was usual with the defendant cannot exonerate it from its contract to safely transport, and its own usage would not have any tendency to show that it had adopted a safe method." The contract was to transport cattle, and the defects proved were insufficient ventilation and failure to nail cleats to the floor of the car, to enable cattle to maintain their footing. The principle stated in the text is in accordance with the general law as to all customs—that they must be lawful. In Lawrence *v.* Maxwell, 64 Barb. 102 (1872), which was an action for conversion of stock, the court said: "A long continued course of wrong doing or violation of law will never prove a valid custom to continue it."

[3] Sullivan *v.* Thompson, 99 Mass. 259 (1868). In this case the contract provided that the goods were "to be forwarded to our agency nearest or most convenient to destination only." The custom of the carrier was to deliver parcels marked with a particular street, number and address, at the place of such address. Held that the carrier was liable for a failure to deliver a parcel so marked according to his custom, although he did deliver it at his own office or agency. The same case,

the manner of transportation and relieve the carrier from liability for injuries incidental to the usual method of conveyance. In this case cotton was transported in open boats, which was the usual and only available way, and was injured by rain. Held that the carrier was not liable.[1]

The strict language of the contract will be adhered to though it be shown that in some previous instances the carrier has waived compliance with the requirement in question.[2] But if the usual course of dealing between the carrier and the charterers has led the shipper to believe that a condition in the printed contract of charter-party would not be insisted upon, it has been held that the carrier cannot interpose it as a defense.[3]

But the carrier may waive the benefit of a regulation, established by itself, e. g., that it will only receive fruit on certain days.[4]

---

however, sustained the validity of usage regulating the method of delivery. It held that a usage to deliver parcels to the clerk of the consignee, without giving personal notice to the latter, was reasonable, in reference to parcels of ordinary character and value. But custom will not require a carrier to deliver at the usual place, if there be good reason for his not doing so. Arnold v. National S. S. Co., 29 Fed. Rep. 184 (1886). In this case the usage was not universal, and the "good reason" was that the wharf was full. The bills of lading merely required discharge at the port of New York, but it is well settled this means at a wharf or pier. It is easy to see that good reasons might arise to justify a carrier in not landing at a pier where he had always before been in the habit of landing. For a further consideration of usage as affecting delivery, see Chap. XIV, sect. 8, *post*.

[1] Chevellier v. Patton, 10 Texas, 344 (1853); Sproat v. Donnell, 26 Me. 185 (1846); The William Gillum, 2 Lowell, 154 (1872); The Delaware, 14 Wall, 579 (1871); *contra*, The Wellington, 1 Biss. (U. S.) 279 (1859).

[2] Keeley v. Boston & Maine R. R., 67 Maine, 163 (1878); *ante*, p. 163.

[3] Leisy v. Buyers, 36 La. Ann. 705 (1884). This is analogous to the well-settled exception to the rule which prohibits the introduction of parol evidence to contradict or vary a written contract, to wit, that such evidence is admissible when the suit on which it is offered is not between the parties to the contract. Tyson v. Post, 108 N. Y. 217 (1888); Dempsey v. Kipp, 61 N. Y. 462 (1875); 1 Greenl. Evid., sect. 279.

[4] Reed v. Philadelphia, W. & B. R. R., 3 Houston (Del.), 176

If the usage of business or the regulations made by the carrier are relied upon to relieve him from liability he must show strict compliance with them.[1]

The usage of the business will form a part of the contract so far as to limit the class of goods which the carrier holds himself out to carry. A man may be a common carrier of some kinds of merchandise only, and if it is not his custom to carry other kinds he is not liable for their loss, should they be entrusted to his agents. This was held in reference to packages of money entrusted to the officers of steamboats for transportation.[2]

But if it be his custom to carry money packages he is liable for their loss, though the custom was to carry them without compensation.[3]

Custom also may be shown as to what precautions the carrier should take against danger to the goods which are

---

(1869). All the cases agree that the usage must be reasonable. Johnson v. 318 Tons of Coal, 44 Conn. 548 (1877), is a curious instance of a regulation held to be unreasonable, to wit, that parties receiving coal from the carrier's cars should employ shovellers designated by the carrier and at wages fixed by it.

[1] Angle v. Miss. & Mo. R. R., 18 Iowa, 555 (1865).

[2] Whitmore v. The Caroline, 20 Mo. 513 (1855); Chouteau v. The "St. Anthony," 16 Mo. 216 (1852); Sewall v. Allen, 6 Wend. 335 (1830). The legislature may prohibit a common carrier from limiting itself to the carriage of a particular kind of freight. If such a statute be in existence, a custom in contravention of it, e. g., not to carry blooded live stock except upon receiving a release from liability for damage, is void. McCune v. B. C. R. & N. R. Co., 52 Iowa, 600 (1879).

[3] Garey v. Meagher, 33 Ala. 630 (1859). See this subject more fully treated in Chap. IV, sect. 4. Hosea v. McCrory, 12 Ala. 349 (1847). Under such circumstances a delivery to the clerk is a delivery to the master if the clerk is the person who usually receives such packages of money. (Ibid.) And if a carrier is accustomed to carry live stock under certain conditions, he is under those conditions a carrier of live stock, and bound to furnish cars and receive and transport them upon receiving reasonable notice to do so. If from any sudden emergency he cannot transport the stock, he is bound to use diligence in notifying any person giving such notice. Ayres v. Chicago & N. W. R. Co., 37 N. W. Rep. (Wis.) 432 (1888).

being transported, and as to what is the usual method of stowage.[1]

---

[1] Chicago, St. L. & N. O. R. R. *v.* Moss, 60 Miss. 1003 (1883); Lamb *v.* Parkman, 1 Sprague, 343 (1857). But if the manner of stowage is unsafe, the usage, to justify the carrier, must be a general one. Leonard *v.* Fitchburg R. R., 143 Mass. 307 (1886).

CHAPTER XII.

BURDEN OF PROOF OF THE CONTRACT.

The burden of proof is a question that sometimes becomes important in determining whether a case shall be submitted to the jury, or disposed of by the Court, by a non-suit or direction to find a verdict.

It is clear that the carrier who alleges that he has made a contract which limits his common law liability must establish its existence and terms by the preponderance of evidence. The burden of proof in such cases is upon him.[1]

---

[1] Western Transp. Co. v. Newhall, 24 Ill. 466 (1860); Baltimore & Ohio R. R. v. Brady, 32 Md. 333 (1869); Am. Trans. Co. v. Moore, 5 Mich. 368 (1858); Gaines v. Union Trans. & Ins. Co., 28 Ohio St. 418 (1876); Southern Express Co. v. Newby, 36 Geo. 635 (1867); Verner v. Sweitzer, 32 Penn. 208 (1858). In Gaines v. Union Transportation Co., 28 Ohio, 418 (1876), the Court state the rule even more strongly against the carrier, holding that where the action against the carrier is to recover on his common law liability, for losses occurring at the point of delivery, after the transit is ended, but before notice of delivery to the consignee, and the defendant claims exemption from such loss by virtue of a condition in the bill of lading to that effect, he must aver and prove, not only that this condition was assented to, but that the loss happened without any fault or neglect on his part, and the failure to establish such assent or show due and proper care to prevent the loss entitles the plaintiff to recover. Kallman v. U. S. Express Co., 3 Kans. 205 (1865); Adams Express Co. v. Guthrie, 9 Bush (Ky.), 78 (1872).

When a carrier has received goods marked for a station on a connecting line and they are delivered at that point injured, *quære*, whether that is *prima facie* proof of the carrier's liability. Irwin v. N. Y. Central R. R., 1 Thomps. & C. (N. Y.), 473 (1873), *post*, p. 253, n. 1. In the same case, the question is considered as to what proof will rebut the presumption of his liability, if in such a case it exists. See Chap. XIII, sect. 3.

The contract need not be in writing.[1]   An examination of the cases cited in the notes to this section will show that the disposition to establish more rigid rules as to the proof of such contracts between a carrier and shipper than would be applied in ordinary cases no longer exists, and that the recent authorities apply in such cases the same rules that govern the proof of ordinary contracts. No good reason is perceived for a distinction.

If the carrier makes *prima facie* proof of a contract limiting his liability, and there is nothing in the circumstances disclosed by the evidence indicating a want of fairness or good faith in the making of the contract, the burden of proof is shifted, and it is for the shipper to establish that it was obtained by duress or made under a mutual mistake.[2]   Where the shipper himself tenders the

---

[1] Am. Trans. Co. *v.* Moore, 5 Mich. 368 (1858); Roberts *v.* Riley, 15 La. Ann. 103 (1860).

Roberts *v.* Riley was an action for damages occasioned to horses shipped on board defendant's steamboat. The defendant pleaded an agreement between the parties, that the horses were to be under the exclusive management and control of the plaintiff during the voyage. Parol evidence was offered to prove the special agreement. The Court held that in the absence of a bill of lading oral evidence was properly admitted, and that there is no law that requires a contract of affreightment to be in writing.

In the American Transportation Co. *v.* Moore, the Court say that "although it devolves upon a carrier to show affirmatively the terms of any contract which lessens his common law liability, yet that fact is to be proved like any other, by any pertinent evidence. If in writing, the writing must be shown; but if by parol, there is no rule which requires different proof from that which would establish any other contract." See also sect. 4, *post.*

[2] Adams Ex. Co. *v.* Guthrie. 9 Bush (Ky.), 78 (1872); see Louisville, C. & L. R. R. *v.* Hedger, *Ibid,* 645 (1873).   In Adams Ex. Co. *v.* Guthrie, the Court say : "If the contract was actually made, it is binding upon both parties, and appellee cannot escape from its consequences, unless it appears that he acted under duress, or that it was imposed upon him or his agent under circumstances which probably prevented them from examining the writing and understanding its nature.   Ordinarily written contracts cannot be contradicted or essentially modified by oral testimony without proof of fraud or mistake; and it would be carrying the innovation, made upon this salutary rule in this class of contracts, to a most unreasonable extent to allow the shipper to avoid

bill of lading for signature, and especially where the instrument is one which he has himself caused to be printed, the evidence is conclusive that the contract was not procured by duress.[1]

SECTION II.

BURDEN OF PROOF OF NEGLIGENCE AND LOSS.

In many cases the question of burden of proof of negligence and of loss is of considerable importance. The loss or injury for which compensation is sought sometimes happens from causes which it is difficult to trace. The doctrine which on the whole is established by the preponderance of authority is this: The shipper in the first instance makes out his case by proving his contract and the non-delivery of the goods. The burden of proof is then on the carrier to bring himself within the exemption clauses of the bill of lading, or, in other words, to show that the loss happened by one of the excepted perils. The reason is obvious. The goods were in his custody, and he is bound like all other bailees to account for their loss, if they are lost.[2] The rule is the same where the

---

them on account of duress, misfortune, delusion or failure to understand their effect, and also to presume the existence of one or all of these grounds of avoidance and compel the carrier by proof to rebut the presumption."

[1] Lawrence v. N. Y., Prov. & Boston R. R., 36 Conn. 63 (1869).

[2] Western Transportation Co. v. Downer, 11 Wall. 129 (1871); Hooper v. Rathbone, Taney, 519 (1853); Hunt v. The Propeller Cleveland, 6 McLean, 76; s. c. 1 Newb. Adm. 221 (1853); Bazin v. Steamship Co., 3 Wall. Jr. 229 (1857); Lewis v. Smith, 107 Mass. 334 (1871); Hill v. Sturgeon, 35 Mo. 212 (1864); Lamb v. Camden & Amboy R. R. 46 N. Y. 271 (1871); Newstadt v. Adams, 5 Duer (N. Y.), 43 (1855); American Ex. Co. v. Sands, 55 Penn. 140 (1867); Adams Ex. Co. v. Holmes, 8 Central Rep. (Penn.) 155 (1887); Camden & Amboy R. R. v. Baldauf, 16 Penn. 67 (1851); Adams Ex. Co. v. Stettaners, 61 Ill. 184 (1871); Atchinson, Topeka & S. F. R. R. v. Brewer, 20 Kansas, 669 (1878). In this case the demand was made by a passenger for baggage for which he held a check, and was made at a reasonable time, and at

goods are delivered in a damaged condition.   The carrier must show that the damage was caused by one of the excepted causes or perils.[1]   In like manner where the carrier seeks to escape liability by showing a delivery to

---

the point of destination.   It was held that the failure to produce the baggage under such circumstances or to account for its loss raised a presumption of negligence.   In Penn. R. R. *v.* Miller, 87 Penn. 395 (1878), the Court held that failure to account for the loss raised a presumption of negligence, which was not repelled by general proof of ordinary care in the management of the road.   In this case the loss was by fire.   So proof that carboys were broken while the car containing them was being switched, does not rebut the presumption of negligence, but rather tends to support it.   Kirst *v.* Milwaukee, L. S. & W. R. Co., 46 Wis. 489 (1879); Alden *v.* Pearson, 3 Gray (Mass.), 342 (1855); Adams Ex. Co. *v.* Stettaners, 61 Ill. 184 (1871); Finn *v.* Timpson, 4 E. D. Smith (N. Y.), 276 (1855); Hall *v.* Cheney, 36 N. H. 26 (1857); Angle *v.* Miss. & M. R. R., 18 Iowa, 555 (1865); M'Call *v.* Brock, 5 Strob. Law (S. C.), 119 (1850); Smyrl *v.* Niolon, 2 Bailey (S. C.), 421 (1831).

[1] Clark *v.* Barnwell, 12 How. (U. S.) 272 (1851); Rich *v.* Lambert, 12 How. (U. S.) 347 (1851); Tygert Co. *v.* The Charles P. Sinnickson, 24 Fed. Rep. 304 (1885); Zerega *v.* Poppe, 1 Abb. Adm. 397 (1849); Bearse *v.* Ropes, 1 Sprague, 331 (1856); The Schooner Emma Johnson, 1 Sprague, 527 (1860); Hunt *v.* The Propeller Cleveland, 1 Newb. Adm. 221; s. c. 6 McLean, 76 (1853); Mahon *v.* Steamer Olive Branch, 18 La. Ann. 107 (1866); Grogan *v.* Adams Ex. Co., 114 Penn. 523; s. c. 5 Cent. Rep. 300 (1887); American Ex. Co. *v.* Second National Bk., 69 Penn. 394 (1871); Arend *v.* Liverpool, N. Y. & P. S. S. Co., 6 Lans. (N. Y.) 457 (1872).   And where a vessel takes the ground while at dock in a storm, the burden is on the carrier to show that this could not have been foreseen and prevented.   Ewart *v.* Street, 2 Bailey (S. C.), 157 (1831).   But when the carrier has shown delivery in apparent good condition and it appears afterwards that part of the contents has been stolen, the burden is on the owner to prove that it was done before delivery.   Canfield *v.* B. & O. R. R., 75 N. Y. 144 (1878); s. c. 93 N. Y. 532 (1883).

A box which has been through the hands of several carriers and found opened at the end of the route, may be presumed to have been opened in the hands of the last carrier.   Laughlin *v.* Chicago & N. W. R. Co., 28 Wis. 204 (1871); Shriver *v.* Sioux City & St. P. R. R., 24 Minn. 506 (1878).

The rule is thus stated in Inman *v.* South Carolina R. Co., 129 U. S. 128 (1889): "As in case of loss the presumption is against the carrier, and no attempt was made here to rebut that presumption, the defendant's liability, because in fault, must be assumed upon the evidence before us."

a connecting carrier, he must prove that this delivery was pursuant to the contract of affreightment.[1]

The proof on the part of the carrier must be clear and explicit. It is not enough for him to show that the loss might have occurred by one of the excepted perils.[2] In a case in which this rule was laid down with as much strictness as in the "Compta" it was, however, held that the mistake of a light made by the captain on a dark and stormy night at the entrance of a harbor, which was difficult of access, was excusable. It was shown that vigi-

---

[1] Schutter v. Adams Ex. Co., 5 Mo. App. 316 (1878).

[2] The Ship "Compta," 4 Sawyer, 375 (1877); The Live Yankee, Deady, 420 (1868). In the Compta the damage to the goods was occasioned by leaks in the ship's deck. The defence relied on was perils of the sea. The Court held that it was not enough for the carrier to prove the occurrence of sea peril which might have caused the leak ; he must show that they did. This he may do by showing that the peril was of such a character that injury to the vessel was its natural and necessary consequence; or he may prove that the vessel was in fact injured, by the testimony of those who observed the effect of the peril at the time of its occurrence ; or he may prove the fact by showing her condition on her arrival; or he may exclude any other hypothesis by satisfactory proof that her decks were sound, staunch and well caulked at the commencement of the voyage.

In Kirby v. Adams Ex. Co., 2 Mo. App. 369 (1876), the Court say that the presumption from the fact of loss is that it was occasioned by negligence. This is true where the loss is unexplained. But if more than this was intended by the Court the proposition is against the weight of authority.

In Roberts v. Riley, 15 La. Ann. 103 (1860), it was agreed that the goods shipped should be in the exclusive custody of the shipper or his servants. Yet the Court held that in case of loss the burden of proof was on the carrier to show that the loss was caused by the negligence of the shipper's servants. This is construing the rule literally, but the Court would seem to carry it further than the circumstances of the case required. The rigid common law doctrine as to the carrier's liability rested on the assumption that the goods were in his custody. Where the consignee of a package of money refused to receive it, and consequently the package was returned to the consignor, it was held that the carrier was not bound to account for the loss of part of the contents of the package, or to show when, where or how it occurred. But this was put on the ground that part of the transit was over a connecting line, and as to this part of the route the connecting carrier, under the terms of the contract, was liable only as forwarder. American Ex. Co. v. Second National Bank, 69 Penn. 384 (1871).

lance was used, and that the loss was really caused by the darkness and storm, and not by the captain's negligence.[1]

When the carrier has proved that the loss was caused immediately by one of the excepted perils, the burden of proof again shifts to the plaintiff, and it is incumbent on him to show that its real cause was the negligence of the carrier or his agents.[2]

---

[1] The Juniata Paton, 1 Biss. 15 (1852).   In this case the bill of lading contained the clause, "dangers of navigation excepted."   The carrier was held to bring himself within this clause by proving that on a dark and stormy night, at the entrance of a harbor, difficult of access, he mistook a light on shore in a line with the pier light for the latter, in consequence of which mistake he steered wrongly, and the vessel went ashore and damaged a portion of the cargo.   The Court said that in order to avail himself of the benefit of this restrictive clause he must bring his case strictly within the words of the exception, and for this purpose the burden of proof is upon him.

[2] Harris v. Packwood, 3 Taunt. 264 (1810); Marsh v. Horne, 5 Barn. & Cress. 322 (1826); Western Transportation Co. v. Downer, 11 Wall. 129 (1871); Clark v. Barnwell, 12 How. (U. S.) 272 (1851); The Adriatic, 16 Blatch. 424 (1879); The Saratoga, 20 Fed. Rep. 869 (1884); Marx v. The Britannia, 34 Fed. Rep. 906 (1888); The Barracouta, 39 Fed. Rep. 288 (1889); The New Orleans, 26 Fed. Rep. 44 (1885); French v. Buffalo & Erie R. R., 2 Abb. Ct. App. Dec. (N. Y.) 196; s. c. 4 Keyes, 108 (1868); Lamb v. Camden & A. R. R. & T. Co., 46 N. Y. 271 (1871); Kallman v. U. S. Express Co., 3 Kans. 205 (1865); Kansas Pacific R. Co. v. Reynolds, 8 Kans. 623 (1871); Sager v. Portsmouth, S. & P. & E. R. R., 31 Me. 228 (1850); Patterson v. Clyde, 67 Penn. 500 (1871); Price v. The Ship Uriel, 10 La. Ann. 413 (1855); Little Rock, M. R. & T. R. R. v. Corcoran, 40 Ark. 375 (1883).   See Childs v. Little Miami R. R., 1 Cinc. (Ohio), 480 (1871).

In Clark v. Barnwell the Court say: "If it can be shown that it (the loss) might have been avoided by the use of proper precautionary measures, and that the usual and customary methods for this purpose have been neglected, they (the carriers) may still be held liable.   Hunt v. The Propeller Cleveland, 1 Newb. Adm. 221; 6 McLean, 76 (1853); Slater v. So. Car. R. Co., 29 S. Car. 96; s. c. 6 S. E. Rep. 936 (1888).

In French v. Buffalo & Erie R. R., it was held that it was enough for the shipper, when the loss was shown to have been caused by an excepted peril, to prove that the injury resulted from a railroad accident, the causes of which were not explained, and which did not appear affirmatively not to have been preventible by the exercise of ordinary care and diligence on the part of the company and its servants.

The proposition in the text is also sustained by Canfield v. Balt. & Ohio R. R., 93 N. Y. 532 (1883); Cochran v. Dinsmore, 49 N. Y. 249 (1872); Sutro v. Fargo, 41 N. Y. Super. Ct. 231 (1876); Smith v. N.

This is especially so when the contract of shipment is that the carrier shall not be liable for loss arising from certain specified risks, unless it shall be proved that such loss occurred through the negligence or default of the carrier's agents.[1]

It is not enough to show an error in judgment on the part of the carrier's servants. It is incumbent on the shipper to prove actual negligence in order to deprive the carrier of the benefit of the clauses of exemption in his contract.[2]

This proposition is well illustrated by the litigation that arose in consequence of the fire at the pier of the Camden & Amboy R. R. Co. in the city of New York in 1864. The fire broke out on the defendant's steamboat, which was lying at the pier. The crew were on board and watchmen were on duty at the warehouse on the pier. The fire extended to this warehouse, which was consumed

---

Car. R. R., 64 N. C. 235 (1870); Bankard v. Balt. & O. R. R., 34 Md. 197 (1870).

By statute in Utah (Comp. Laws, sect. 503, p. 217, ed. 1876 ; sect. 2359, ed. 1888), proof that property is set on fire by sparks from an engine raises a *prima facie* presumption of negligence on the part of the carrier. Anderson v. Wasatch & J. V. R. R., 2 Utah, 518 (1880). It was held in this case that where the sparks set fire to grass which in turn set fire to the plaintiff's property, there was a "communication" of fire from the engine within the statute. See Turney v. Wilson, note 4, p. 257, *post.*

Where there was a contract limiting the amount for which the carrier was liable, an Alabama Court held that the burden was on him to show that the loss occurred without negligence. Ala. Gt. So. R. R. v. Little, 71 Ala. 611 (1882). But where the proof showed very heavy weather and the damage was such that it might have been caused by the storm, there should be some rebutting proof of negligence in order to charge the carrier. The Fern Holme, 24 Fed. Rep. 502 (1885); Giglio v. The Britannia, 31 Fed. Rep. 432 (1887); The Thomas Melville, 31 Fed. Rep. 486 (1887); The Jefferson, 31 Fed. Rep. 489 (1887); Louisville & N. R. R. v. Oden, 80 Ala. 38 (1885); Czech v. Gen. Steam N. Co., L. R., 3 C. P. 14 (1867); Platt v. Richmond, Y. R. & C. R. R., 108 N. Y. 358 (1888).

[1] Wertheimer v. Penn. R. R., 17 Blatchf. 421 (1880). The loss in this case was caused by fire during the Pittsburgh riots of 1877.

[2] The "Montana," 17 Fed. Rep. 377 (1883).

with its contents. Actions were brought against the carrier, in the New York Common Pleas. The plaintiff proved his loss. The defendant then proved that this was caused by fire, which was one of the risks excepted in the bill of lading. The plaintiff then gave evidence tending to show that the cause of the fire was defendant's negligence. The carrier gave rebutting proof. The trial Court refused to charge that the burden was on the plaintiff to prove that the real cause of the fire was the carrier's negligence. The New York Court of Appeals held that this was error and reversed the judgment.[1] The same rule was laid down by the Supreme Court of Pennsylvania in a case growing out of the same fire.[2] All the authorities concede that the carrier is bound to use diligence, skill and foresight to guard against loss by the excepted perils,[3] and it has been held that the burden is on him to prove that he complied with the requirements of law in each particular.[4] But the weight of authority is otherwise.

---

[1] Lamb v. Camden & Amboy R. R., 46 N. Y. 271 (1871); revg. s. c. 2 Daly, 454 (1869).

[2] Farnham v. Camden & Amboy R. R., 55 Penn. 53 (1867). To the same effect are Little Rock, M. R. & T. R. R. v. Corcoran, 40 Ark. 375 (1883); Little Rock, M. R. & T. R. R. v. Harper, 44 Ark. 208 (1884); Denton v. Chicago, R. I. & P. R. Co., 52 Iowa, 161 (1879); Whitworth v. Erie R. Co., 45 N. Y. Super. Ct. 603 (1879).

[3] In The Saratoga, 20 Fed. Rep. 869 (1884), the goods were stolen. Loss by thieves was one of the excepted perils. The Court held that no ordinary and reasonable precaution must be neglected by the carrier, and that the omission to use a precaution provided by the owner and to observe a suspicious person was negligence.

The Maggie M., 30 Fed. Rep. 692 (1887). The carrier must also prove that he used diligence in furnishing means of transportation, and if he excuses his failure to do so he must prove diligence in notifying the shipper of his inability. Ayres v. Chicago & N. W. R. Co., 71 Wis. 372 ; s. c. 37 N. W. Rep. 432 (1888).

[4] Turney v. Wilson, 7 Yerger (Tenn.), 340 (1835); Mobile & Ohio R. R. v. Jarboe, 41 Ala. 644 (1868); U. S. Express Co. v. Backman, 28 Ohio St. 144 (1875); Baker v. Brinson, 9 Rich. Law (S. C.), 201 (1856); Levering v. Union Trans. & Ins. Co., 42 Mo. 88 (1867). In this case the loss was by fire, an excepted peril, but the Court held that the car-

17

No doubt the circumstances attendant upon the loss or injury in question may be such as to justify a Court or a

---

rier must show that the loss was not caused by any want of care, skill and diligence on its part.   Still, if in such case the persons in charge of the train took all reasonable care and used all reasonable precautions, and the car containing the goods was reasonably tight and suitable for the transportation of the goods, the carrier will not be liable.

In Turney *v.* Wilson, the carrier by contract exempted himself from liability from loss occasioned from "dangers of the river." It was held that he would be responsible, except for losses which could not have been prevented by human skill and foresight, and it was incumbent on him to prove that the loss did occur from such cause.   In Mobile & Ohio R. R. *v.* Jarboe, the bill of lading contained an exception in these words: "taken at the owner's risk." It was held that the carrier must at least show *prima facie* that the loss was not caused by negligence. The contract was made during the late war.   The railroad was at that time frequently used by the military authorities in the transportation of troops and supplies, and in consequence of the condition of the country there was a great want of safety and certainty in the transporting of freight over the road.   It was held that these facts were insufficient to make out a *prima facie* case of absence of negligence.   It is to be observed that in this case no specification was made of any particular kind of loss for which the carrier would not be responsible.   This constitutes a distinction between this case and those cited *ante*, p. 255, note 2.

In Chicago, St. L. & New Orleans R. R. *v.* Moss, 60 Miss. 1003 (1883); s. c. 45 Am. Rep. 428, the Court, commenting upon the question of the burden of proof of the carrier's negligence, say : " It is no uncommon thing in this age to see under one management a line of railroads extending from the lakes of the North to the Gulf of Mexico, or from the Atlantic to the Pacific ocean.   To hold that a shipper in New York or Chicago shall be required to establish the negligence of the carrier by proof of the circumstances of a fire in California or New Orleans, would in a great number of cases result in a verdict for the carrier, even though there was in fact negligence.   In a great majority of cases the facts rest exclusively within the knowledge of the employees, whose names and places of residence are unknown to the shipper.   In many cases the witnesses are the employees whose negligence has caused the loss, and if known to the shipper it may be dangerous for him to rest his case upon their testimony.   .   .   .   All the authorities hold that it devolves upon the carrier to show the loss to have occurred by the excepted cause.   In doing this it will add but little to his burden to show all the attending circumstances, and that the burden rests upon him to do so and disprove his own negligence, we think arises from the terms of the contract, from the character of his occupation, and from that rule governing the production of evidence which requires the facts to be proved by that party in whose knowledge they peculiarly lie."

And in Chicago, St. L. & N. O. R. R. *v.* Abels, 60 Miss. 1017 (1883), the same Judge said : " The burden is on the carrier   .   .   .   to show that the injury complained of resulted, without fault of the carrier,

jury in finding negligence on the part of the carrier, without other proof.[1] Still it is equally true that "negligence

from some cause excepted by the contract. The carrier in such case must show at least *prima facie* that the injury did not result from neglect. It would then devolve on the other party to produce evidence to fasten blame on the carrier for the injury. . . . The carrier must show a full performance of duty with respect to what was shipped, according to its nature, and when that showing is made, and that the injury was from an excepted cause in the contract, liability cannot be fixed on the carrier, except by proof of a want of due care and diligence." Ryan *v.* Mo. & K. & T. R. Co., 65 Texas 13 (1885).

It has been held that under a clause exempting the carrier from liability for loss by fire, the burden of proof is on the carrier to show that the fire was not caused by his own negligence. Grey's Executors *v.* Mobile Trade Co., 55 Ala., 387 (1876). In this case a cargo of cotton was transported on a steamer under a bill of lading which excepted "dangers of the river and fire." The cotton was burned. It was held that the carrier must show that he employed that degree of diligence which very careful and prudent men take of their own affairs; and that his failure to have the cotton upon the steamer's deck "protected by a complete and suitable covering of canvass, or other suitable material, to prevent ignition from sparks," as required under penalty by act of Congress approved July 25, 1866 (14 U. S. Stat. at Large, 227), was a lack of that extraordinary care and diligence which the law requires in such cases, and rendered the carrier liable for the loss. These cases of loss by fire may possibly be harmonized with those previously referred to, on the ground that the carrier has better means of information than the shipper as to the origin of a fire, and ought, therefore, to be able to explain it, and that his failure to do so raises a presumption of negligence. Penn. R. R. *v.* Miller, 87 Penn. 395 (1878); Berry *v.* Cooper, 28 Geo. 543 (1859).

Where delay was shown to have been caused by high water, this was held not enough to excuse the carrier, because it might have been possible to anticipate and ship by another line. Chicago, B. & Q. R. R. *v.* Manning, 23 Neb. 552; s. c. 37 N. W. Rep. 462 (1888).

[1] Caldwell *v.* N. J. Steamboat Co., 47 N. Y. 282 (1872); Mullen *v.* St. John, 57 N. Y. 567 (1874); Blanchard *v.* W. U. Tel. Co., 60 N. Y. 510 (1875); Marckwald *v.* Oceanic Steam Nav. Co., 11 Hun (N. Y.), 462 (1877). So where a bad condition of the vessel developes during the voyage, and no adequate cause from stress of weather or otherwise appears, it becomes a presumption of fact that the vessel was unseaworthy when she sailed. Cameron *v.* Rich, 4 Strobh. (S. C.) 168 (1850).

The character of the evidence which will or will not establish that damage to cargo, occurring during a voyage, was due to an excepted peril is considered in The Bark Vivid, 4 Bened. 319 (1870); The Ship Delhi, 4 Bened. 345 (1870); The Steamship Bellona, 4 Bened. 503 (1871); The Steamship Pereire, 8 Bened. 301 (1875); Six hundred and thirty casks of wine, 14 Blatchf. 517 (1878). If the cargo is damaged, and the proof is that the weather was heavy enough to cause damage, it is never presumed."[1] In the case of live stock, the mere fact of sickness at the journey's end is not evidence of negligence on the part of the carrier, if there be no external injuries.[2]

In Western Transportation Co. v. Downer,[3] it was shown that the carrier's vessel was staunch and well equipped. The Court held that negligence would not be presumed from the fact that she grounded on a dark night at the entrance of a well-known harbor on the lake.[4]

---

is for the shipper to show bad stowage. Proof that other cargo of like character adjoining that injured was not itself injured is not enough. The Polynesia, 30 Fed. Rep. 210 (1887). On the other hand, in The Black Hawk, 9 Bened. 207 (1877), it was held that the fact that a cask of wine had its head crushed in was evidence of either negligent stowage or handling, which the carrier must rebut; and that proof of careful stowage did not rebut the presumption of negligent handling. In The Adriatic, 16 Blatchf. 424 (1879), the bales in question when unpacked were found to have been injured by sea water. The carrier showed that the goods were properly stowed, that no other goods came out wet, and that there was no sign of a leak in the ship; and the appearance of the goods indicated that they might have been injured before delivery to the carrier. It was held that the burden was on the shipper to show the injury occurred on board that ship.

[1] Memphis & Charleston R. R. v. Reeves, 10 Wall. 176 (1869); New Jersey Steam Nav. Co. v. Merchants' Bank, 6 How. (U. S.) 344 (1848); Curran v. Warren Chemical & M. Co., 36 N. Y. 153, 156 (1867); Curtis v. Rochester & Syr. R. R., 18 N. Y. 534 (1859); Schmidt v. Blood, 9 Wend. (N. Y.) 268 (1832); Sherman v. Western Trans. Co., 62 Barb. 150 (1861); Gandy v. Chicago & N. R. R., 30 Iowa, 421 (1870); Laing v. Colder, 8 Penn. St. 479 (1848); Bankard v. Baltimore & Ohio R. R., 34 Md. 197 (1870).

[2] Hussey v. The Saragossa, 3 Woods, 380 (1876). No doubt the decision would have been otherwise had any circumstances been in evidence tending to show that the horses in question had been negligently stowed. In a fruit case, where there was evidence of defective ventilation, the shipper recovered, and it was held that he was not bound to prove that there was no inherent deterioration. The Steamship America, 8 Bened. 491 (1878). Where by the contract the shipper was to have the care of the stock, and the horse was found dead at the end of the journey, without explanation, the carrier was not liable; and *semble* that there being no evidence of negligence, the special contract was not necessary to protect the carrier. Penn. R. R. v. Riordan, 13 Atl. Rep. (Penn.) 324 (1888).

[3] 11 Wall. 129 (1871); compare The Juniata Paton, *ante*, p. 255, n. 1.

[4] The Court, however, expressly admitted the soundness of the doctrine laid down in Scott v. London & St. K. Docks, 3 Hurlst & Colt

The inference of negligence from the circumstances attendant upon the disaster would be made less readily in case of a marine disaster than in that of one on land. Man has done much to control the winds and currents of the ocean, but their forces are much less subject to his skill than the agencies by which transportation on land is effected. The question is really one of fact, and must be determined by the circumstances of each case.[1]

---

596 (1865), as follows: "Where the thing is shown to be under the management of the defendant or his servants, and the accident is such as in the ordinary course of things does not happen if those who have the management use proper care, it affords reasonable evidence in the absence of explanation by the defendants that the accident arose from want of care." In this action the plaintiff proved that he was an officer of the customs, and that whilst in the discharge of his duties he was passing in front of a warehouse in the dock, when six bags of sugar fell upon him. Held evidence of negligence sufficient to be left to the jury.

So in Ketchum *v.* American Merchants' Union Ex. Co., 52 Mo. 390 (1873), it was held that the breakage of goods while in the carrier's possession was *prima facie* evidence of negligence, and the burden was on him to explain it. On the other hand, in Forbes *v.* Dallett, 9 Phila. (Penn.) 515 (1872), the Court held that leakage of petroleum from the barrels in which it was shipped raised no presumption of negligence. In that case the contract was to pay freight "on each and every barrel, delivered full, not full, or empty." This case is not really inconsistent with Adams Ex. Co. *v.* Stettaners, 61 Ill. 184 (1871), although at first sight it may appear to be. The Court do say in the latter case that no special contract can change the law as to the burden of proof. But this must be understood with reference to the facts which showed a loss wholly unexplained. In Forbes *v.* Dallett, the nature of the substance transported tended of itself to explain the loss, and the language of the contract showed that this was within the contemplation of the parties. In Adams Ex. Co. *v.* Loeb, 7 Bush (Ky.), 499 (1870), the contract was that the carrier should not be liable for loss caused by certain specified causes, unless it was caused by the carrier's fraud or gross negligence, and it was held that the burden was on the plaintiff to show that the loss was caused by fraud or negligence.

And where a bulkhead, which had been well tested, had shown itself sufficient on previous occasions, had been carefully inspected and showed no signs of weakness, did burst, held that the fact of its bursting was not of itself proof of negligence. New York Bal. Dry Dock Co. *v.* Howes, 9 Bened. 232 (1877). Where a swinging door in a ferry house, of a kind in ordinary use, had caused injury to a passenger, held that the burden was on the plaintiff to show defective construction. The character of the door should have been observed by plaintiff. Nayman *v.* Penn. R. R., 118 Penn. 508 (1888).

[1] For example: In Central Passenger R. Co. *v.* Kuhn, 86 Ky. 578

What has been said must be understood with this restriction. The negligence for which a recovery is claimed must be such as contributed to the loss.[1] The burden of showing that the negligence did not contribute to the loss is on the carrier. If, on the evidence, it appears that there was negligence on his part, and it is doubtful whether this did or did not contribute to the loss, his defence is not established.[2] The same rule applies

---

(1888), a passenger in a horse car injured by a collision with an engine at a railway crossing sued both companies. Held that the passenger not being in fault, there was a presumption that the accident was due to the negligence of the servants of the horse car company, but that the burden was on plaintiff to show negligence on the part of the steam railway company. In Falvey *v.* Northern Trans. Co., 15 Wis. 129 (1862), the vessel in which the goods were being transported from Buffalo to Racine was wrecked. The agreement was made in New York late in the season, when the risk of navigation on the lake was greater than earlier in the year. Held that delay in transporting goods to the vessel was *prima facie* evidence of negligence.

In The Bark Wilhelmina, 3 Bened. 110 (1868), the goods were injured by the rolling of the vessel in rough weather. Held that the burden of proof was on the shipper to show that proper precautions were not taken to guard against the danger. When a shaft which had stood service for many years breaks in heavy weather, the burden is still on the shipper to show defective construction. The Rover, 33 Fed. Rep. 515 (1887).

[1] Hill *v.* Sturgeon, 35 Mo. 212 (1864). In this case the Court held that it was not sufficient to entitle a shipper to recover against a carrier to show that there was a defect about the vessel or want of skill in the carrier, but it must also appear that such defect or want of skill contributed or may have contributed to occasion the loss. Where the loss is caused by perils of navigation within the exceptions of the bill of lading, it is not incumbent upon the carrier to show affirmatively the particular and identical cause of loss.

[2] Speyer *v.* The Mary Belle Roberts, 2 Sawyer, 1 (1871); Collier *v.* Valentine, 11 Mo. 299 (1848); and see opinion Andrews, J., in Maghee *v.* Camden & Amboy R. R., 45 N. Y. 514, 523 (1871). The question whether the negligence did or did not contribute to the injury is one of fact for the jury. Canfield *v.* Balt. & O. R. R., 93 N. Y. 532, 537 (1883). In Collier *v.* Valentine it appeared that the carrier's boat was not seaworthy, but the Court held that he could show that the loss was in fact occasioned by the excepted perils of the river, and not by the unseaworthiness of the boat. Although a carrier may be in default, yet if the loss were not occasioned by his default, but must have happened without such default, he is not liable. The rule which imputes carelessness to the captain whose boat strikes a known rock or shoal, unless driven

where the injury is occasioned by delay in transportation, unless the carrier can discharge himself by a proper excuse for the delay.[1] In like manner, if the goods are destroyed by one of the excepted perils, but the destruction takes place after the time within which, according to the usual course of business, the goods could reasonably have been delivered, the carrier is liable.[2]

SECTION III.

WHAT WILL BE TREATED AS A PART OF THE CONTRACT.

A notice or memorandum, even though printed upon the bill of lading or other contract with a carrier, unless referred to in the body of the contract and thus made a part of it, is no more than a notice, and does not form a part of the contract between the shipper and the carrier.[3]

---

by a tempest, is only applicable to navigation where the rocks and shoals are marked upon maps. It does not apply to the navigation of those rivers of which no accurate charts exist. In such navigation each case must be governed by its own circumstances, and be tested by the care usually pursued by skilfull pilots in such cases. The qualification thus stated is certainly reasonable. In Whitesides v. Russel, 8 Watts & S. (Penn.) 44 (1844), it was, however, held it was not enough for a carrier to show that his steamboat ran on a rock in the Ohio river, and thereby caused the loss, but that he must prove that diligence and skill were used to avoid the accident, and that it was unavoidable. To the same effect are Graham v. Davis, 4 Ohio St. 362 (1854); Davidson v. Graham, 2 Ohio St. 131 (1853); Swindler v. Hillard, 2 Rich. (S. C.) 286 (1845).

[1] Galena & Chicago Union R. R. v. Rae, 18 Ill. 488 (1857).

[2] Whitworth v. Erie R. Co., 45 N. Y. Super. Ct. 602 (1879).

[3] Michigan Central R. R. v. Mineral Springs Mfg. Co., 16 Wall. 319 (1872); Ayres v. Western R. R., 14 Blatchf. 9 (1876); Prentice v. Decker, 49 Barb. (N. Y.) 21 (1867); Limburger v. Westcott, Ibid, 283 (1867); Southern Ex. Co. v. Purcell, 37 Georgia, 103 (1867); Ormsby v. Union Pac. R. Co., 4 Fed. Rep. 706 (1880). In Railroad Co. v. Manf. Co., the following notice was printed on the back of the railroad company's receipt : " The company will not be responsible for damages occasioned by delays from storms, accidents or other causes, . . . and all goods and merchandise will be at the risk of the owners thereof while in the company's warehouses, except such loss or injury as may

Much less would a notice posted in a steamboat form a part of such contract.[1]

The same rule has been applied to a notice on the back of a check for baggage,[2] and to a notice on back of a railway ticket.[3] If, however, the notice printed on the back of the receipt be referred to upon its face, and thus incorporated therein, it will be taken to form a part of the contract.[4] This would be especially clear if the printed

---

arise from the negligence of the agents of the company." Held that this formed no part of the contract.

In Prentice v. Decker, plaintiff's daughter delivered her baggage check at defendant's office and received their card, on one side of which was printed, "Westcott's Express for the delivery of freight and baggage, &c." At the bottom of the card the following statement was printed: "Delivery of baggage to railroads and steamboats to be made to the baggage agent thereof, liability limited to $100, except by special agreement to be noted on this card." The baggage was lost while in defendant's charge. Held that the mere manual delivery and acceptance of the card was not evidence of the daughter's assent to the terms thereon, and that this notice was no part of the contract with the carriers. In Mauritz v. N. Y. Lake Erie & W. R. Co., 23 Fed. Rep. 765 (1884), a statement purporting to limit the amount of the carrier's liability for loss of or injury to baggage was printed on the face of a railway ticket. It was held inoperative unless it was actually called to the attention of the passenger, or unless it was negligent, under the circumstances, not to read it.

[1] Freeman v. Newton, 3 E. D. Smith (N. Y.), 246 (1854). In this case, however, the steamboat owners failed to give the plaintiff an opportunity to comply with the requirements of the notice. This purported to exempt them from liability for loss of baggage which had not been checked; but the person whose duty it was to give checks was not at his post when plaintiff's baggage was received, and for this reason no check was given.

[2] Malone v. Boston & Worcester R. R., 12 Gray (Mass.), 388 (1859).

[3] Brown v. Eastern R. R., 11 Cush. (Mass.) 97 (1853).

[4] Myrick v. Michigan Central R. R., 107 U. S. 102 (1882). In this case the Court gave effect to the printed matter on the back of the receipt. At the same time it must be observed that the form of the receipt in that case was not sufficient to constitute a contract in itself. The reference to the matter on the back was in this form: "Notice. See rules of transportation on the back hereof." The Court say: "Though this rule, brought to the knowledge of the shipper, might not limit the liability imposed by a specific through contract, yet it would tend to rebut any inference of such a contract from the receipt of goods marked for a place beyond the road of the company."

matter claimed to be a part of the contract should be signed by the carrier, and be sufficient in form to constitute a contract as to the terms of carriage. The decisions as to railway tickets are not entirely harmonious. The weight of authority is that printed matter upon such a ticket does not constitute a contract, and that the ticket is a mere voucher showing that the passenger has paid his fare.[1]

The printed matter upon it is, however, notice to the passenger. There are many cases fully considered in Chapter VII, in which notice of the carrier's rules and regulations has the effect of making them binding upon the passenger. In all such cases the notice may be given by printing it upon the ticket delivered to the passenger.[2]

It was said in Pier v. Finch[3] that the railway ticket was evidence of the contract to carry the passenger. No doubt it is admissible in evidence for this purpose, just as parol proof of the payment of fare would be, but its force should not be further extended.[4]

A pass issued to a drover and a written contemporaneous agreement referring to the holder of the pass

---

[1] Michigan Central R. R. v. Harris, 12 Wallace, 65 (1870); Frank v. Ingalls, 41 Ohio, 560 (1885). But notice on the ticket that a coupon is not good if detached is binding; and perhaps the same rule will apply in regard to other reasonable rules which a carrier may make without the assent of the shipper or passenger. Boston & M. R. R. v. Chipman, 146 Mass. 107 (1888); see *ante*, Chap. X, sect. 2, pp. 225–233.

[2] See cases cited in Chap. VII, sect. 11, *ante*, pp. 177–180.

[3] Pier v. Finch, 24 Barb. (N. Y.) 514 (1857). In this case the Court held that the words "good for this trip only" upon a passage ticket will not limit the undertaking of the company to any particular day or any specific train of cars. They do not relate to time, but to a journey; and if the ticket has not been previously used, it entitles the holder to a passage on a subsequent day, as well as on the day it bears date.

[4] Wilson v. Chesapeake & Ohio R. R., 21 Gratt. (Va.) 654 (1872). In this case the Court say: "At all events, it seems to be well settled that a carrier cannot be released from the legal responsibilities of his undertaking, unless the knowledge of the notice is brought home to the passenger in time to leave the car and have his baggage removed before the train leaves." See also Chap. X, sect. 2, *ante*, pp. 225–233.

must be construed together.[1]   So a shipper who relies on a notice given by a carrier must take it as a whole, and the carrier in such case is entitled to the benefit of any exemptions contained in it.[2]

SECTION IV.

ADMISSIBILITY OF PAROL EVIDENCE.

The bill of lading or other carrier's contract of shipment generally consists of two parts: a receipt for the goods, and a contract with reference to their carriage. The admissions in the receipt are evidence against the carrier and the shipper, but not conclusive against either, and may be contradicted by parol evidence.[3]   Thus, for

---

[1] Cleveland P. & A. R. R. v. Curran, 19 Ohio, 1 (1869).   As between charterer and carrier, the charter controls the bill of lading issued by the latter.   Ardan S. S. Co. v. Theband, 35 Fed. Rep. 620 (1888).

[2] Burroughs v. Norwich & Worcester R. R., 100 Mass. 26 (1868).

[3] The Lady Franklin, 8 Wall. (U. S.) 325 (1868); The Nith, 36 Fed. Rep. 86 (1888); Meyer v. Peck, 28 N. Y. 590 (1864); Abbe v. Eaton, 51 N. Y. 410 (1873); Long v. N. Y. Central R. R., 50 N. Y. 76 (1872); Bissel v. Price, 16 Ill. 408 (1855); Bond v. Frost, 6 La. Ann. 801 (1851); Tarbox v. Eastern Steamboat Co., 50 Me. 339 (1861).

In Nelson v. Woodruff, 1 Black (U. S.), 156 (1861), it was held that a bill of lading which stated that a cargo of lard in casks had been shipped in "good order and condition" was but *prima facie* evidence of their condition, and did not preclude the carrier from showing that the loss by leakage proceeded from causes which existed but were not apparent at the time of shipment.   In Ellis v. Willard, 9 N. Y. 529 (1854), it was stated that parol evidence of condition was admissible even though the goods were open to inspection when the bill of lading was given.   So also in Abbe v. Eaton, 51 N. Y. 410 (1873), where the bill of lading contained this clause: "All damages caused by boat or carrier, or deficiency of cargo from quantity, as herein specified, to be paid by the carrier and deducted from the freight."   Held that this was not a guaranty of the quantity specified, or an agreement that the bill of lading should furnish the only evidence of the quantity.   In Glass v. Goldsmith, 22 Wis. 488 (1868), it was held that the fact that the shipper had surrendered to the warehouseman, after the execution of the bill of lading, his warehouse receipt for the full amount named in such bill, would not preclude the shipowner from disputing the correctness of the admission in the bill of lading that the full amount had been received by the carrier.

example, the statement therein that the package shipped was valued at fifty dollars was held subject to explanation by parol evidence. The shipper proved that he stated to the carrier's agent at the time of delivering the package to him that it contained a much larger sum. It was held that he could recover the full value of the package.[1] On the other hand, the indorsement by the company's agent upon the package of the words " said to contain $300 " has been held to be evidence of the value of the package.[2]

That portion of the bill of lading which expresses the agreement of the parties cannot be contradicted by parol evidence.[3]

The carrier may, however, relieve himself from liability for delay in transportation by showing that the shipper verbally consented to the manner of navigation which caused it.[4] This case is not opposed to the general

---

[1] Kember v. Southern Express Co., 22 La. Ann. 158 (1870).

[2] Weil v. Express Co., 7 Phila. (Penn.) 88 (1868).

[3] White v. Van Kirk, 25 Barb. (N. Y.) 16 (1856); Wolfe v. Meyers, 3 Sandf. S. C. R. (N. Y.) 7 (1849); O'Rourke v. Tons of Coal, 1 Fed. Rep. 619 (1880).

In Fitzhugh v. Wiman, 9 N. Y. 559 (1854), the Court say : " As to the contract for transportation, a bill of lading is like any other contract in writing, and cannot be altered or contradicted by parol. As to the quantity or property acknowledged by it to have been received, it has been sometimes held to be open to explanation, as a receipt. But the cases have never gone to the extent of holding that the agreement between the parties as to the destination of the property, or the freight to be paid, or any other of the terms of the contract for carriage, could be varied by parol." In Camden & Atl. R. R. v. Bausch, 6 Central Rep. 121 (1887), the Court was equally divided as to the admissibility of parol evidence to contradict the recital in a pass, that the transportation of the person receiving it was without consideration. In Hostetter v. B. & O. R. R., 11 Atl. Rep. 609 (Penn.) (1887), it was held that parol evidence was inadmissible to show that the contract was for transportation wholly by rail. The contract was silent on this subject. Parol evidence cannot be used to add to a bill of lading a verbal agreement to deliver before a particular day. Petrie v. Heller, 35 Fed. Rep. 310 (1888). Where the bill of lading gives the ship leave to call at any port or ports, one of its usual ports being known to both parties to be under quarantine, a verbal agreement not to call there cannot be shown. The Sidonian, 34 Fed. Rep. 805 (1888); aff'd, 35 Fed. Rep. 534 (1888).

[4] Johnson v. Lightsey, 34 Ala. 169 (1859).

rules of evidence. After a written contract is made any of its stipulations may be waived or modified by an executed parol agreement.[1] But there are decisions in reference to carrier's contracts which go farther than this, and are irreconcilable with the rules which are applied to other species of contracts. These illustrate the readiness with which the courts have taken hold of any circumstances to show that the printed receipt given to the shipper did not contain the real contract of the parties. Thus it was held in Union R. R. & Trans. Co. v. Riegel,[2] that although the printed contract required that the consignee's name should be marked on each package, evidence was admissible to show that this was waived by oral agreement between the shipper and the carrier's agent. This oral agreement further stipulated that the goods were not to be delivered without special directions. The carrier was consequently held liable for a loss caused by the delivery to the consignee in violation of this oral agreement.

The Court of Appeals of the State of New York in a case somewhat similar held directly the reverse, and that evidence of verbal directions to the carrier in contradiction of the printed receipt was inadmissible.[3] This doctrine is more in accordance with the general rule, and must be considered as preferable, on principle, to the Pennsylvania decision just cited.

The meaning which the law implies from the language of a contract is just as much a part of it as if this meaning were expressed. It, therefore, follows that one party to it should not be permitted to show by parol that an agreement was made which differed from that which the

---

[1] Taylor v. Seaboard & R. R. Co., 5 S. E. Rep. 750 (1888).

[2] Union R. R. & Trans. Co. v. Riegel, 73 Penn. 72 (1873). In this case there were marks on the packages, which the Court held were to be construed in connection with the contract.

[3] Hinckley v. N. Y. Central R. R., 56 N. Y. 429 (1874).

law would imply from the terms of the written contract.[1] But a contract collateral to the written contract may be shown by parol.   Of this exception to the general rule of exclusion of parol evidence to contradict or vary a written contract, the most familiar instance is that of a parol warranty, collateral to a written bill of sale.[2]

To draw the line exactly between the rule and the exception is difficult, and to pursue the subject further is not within the scope of this work.

A bill of lading, like other contracts, if obscure, may be explained by parol evidence.[3]

---

[1] Martin v. Cole, 104 U. S. 30 (1881); Brown v. Spofford, 95 U. S. 474 (1877); Brown v. Wiley, 20 How. (U. S.) 442 (1857); Renard v. Sampson, 2 Duer, 285 (1853); aff'd, 12 N. Y. 561 (1855).   In White v. Boyce, 21 Fed. Rep. 228 (1884), at p. 232, the Court say : "The legal effect of a written contract is as much within the protection of the rule which forbids the introduction of parol evidence as its language."   This is quoted from Barry v. Ransom, 12 N. Y. 462, 464 (1855).   In The Delaware, 14 Wall. 579 (1871), it was held that the usual clean bill of lading, containing no consent that the goods might be carried on deck, imported an agreement that they should not be carried there, and that parol evidence that the parties agreed that the goods might be carried on deck, was inadmissible.   Under somewhat peculiar circumstances, such evidence was held to be admissible in Doane v. Keating, 12 Leigh (Va.), 391 (1841); Missouri Pacific Ry. Co. v. Fagan, 9 S. W. Rep. (Texas), 749 (1888).

[2] Morrison v. Davis, 20 Penn. 171 (1852).   Parol proof of an agreement that the carrier would be liable for losses caused by the "act of God" was held admissible.   This case may be sustained under the distinction mentioned in the text.   And see West v. The Berlin, 3 Iowa, 532 (1856); Hamilton v. Western N. C. R. R., 96 N. C. 398 (1887).

[3] The Wanderer, 29 Fed. Rep. 260 (1886).   It has been held that conversation as to the probable duration of the voyage, taking place at the time the contract is made, may have formed an inducement to making the contract, and may be shown.   Blodgett v. Abbott, 40 N. W. Rep. (Wisc.) 491 (1888).

CHAPTER XIII.

SECTION I.

TIME WHEN CONTRACT MADE, AS AFFECTING ITS CONSIDERATION AND VALIDITY.

The contract between the shipper and the carrier is complete, when the goods are delivered by the former and accepted by the latter, so that the shipper has no longer the custody or control of them. If after this a written or printed receipt, containing stipulations limiting the carrier's liability, is sent by the carrier to the shipper, it has no force as a contract, unless it appears that it was accepted by him as such.[1]

---

[1] German *v.* Chicago & N. W. R. R., 38 Iowa, 127 (1874). In this case the shipper was to send some one with the cattle, and there was a custom known to him that the road would not take cattle until a contract was signed. The cars were sent off with the first load of cattle before the contract was signed, and without giving him the opportunity to send a drover with them. Held that he had a right to expect the cars would wait and that the contract which was afterwards signed was without consideration. The case is put also on the ground that the carrier failed to keep his part of the contract.

Bostwick *v.* Baltimore & O. R. R., 45 N. Y. 712 (1871). In this case goods were shipped and freight paid under a verbal agreement, for an all rail route. It was held that the verbal agreement was not merged in a bill of lading subsequently sent to the shipper. The court say: "Conditions in a bill of lading not delivered until after the shipment and loss of the goods, before the loss was known, did not control the rights of the shippers." Lamb *v.* Camden & Amboy R. R., 4 Daly (N. Y.), 483 (1873); Coffin *v.* N. Y. Central R. R., 64 Barb. 379 (1872); Schiff *v.* New York C. & H. R. R. R., 52 How. Pr. (N. Y.) 91 (1876). The Illinois Supreme Court held that such was the law in Massachusetts. Michigan Central R. R. *v.* Boyd, 91 Ill. 268 (1878); s. P. Gage *v.* Tirrell, 91 Mass. 299 (1864). And such is the law in Illinois. American Ex. Co. *v.* Spellman, 90 Ill. 455 (1878). The point was considered but not decided in Merchants' Despatch Co. *v.* Cornforth, 3 Col. 280 (1877).

In Strohn *v.* Detroit & Mil. R. R., 21 Wis. 554 (1867), the court

If an agent authorized to ship goods, receives and accepts a bill of lading for them subsequently to their delivery to and acceptance by the carrier, the stipulations of the bill of lading are not binding upon the principal.[1]

The receipt of a bill of lading and even its acceptance by the shipper after the goods are lost, will not operate either to increase or diminish the carrier's liability.[2]

said that it would be a fraud on the part of the carrier to insert in a bill of lading, delivered after the completion of the oral agreement, any stipulations not included in the latter.

So where there has been an express oral contract to carry goods to a place beyond the carrier's line, and the goods are received and placed on the cars, the shipper is not bound by a bill of lading or receipt, subsequently given him, and containing only a contract to carry to the end of the route.   Missouri, Pa., R. Co. *v.* Beeson, 30 Kans. 298 (1883).   The same rule was applied where the bill of lading was not delivered at the time the goods were received, but was sent by mail to the place of their destination.   Louisville & Nashville R. R. *v.* Meyer, 78 Ala. 597 (1885). So where the bill of lading was issued by mistake ,contradicted itself as to the freight to be paid by the shipper, and covered only a portion of the goods shipped, it was held that it did not control a prior oral agreement pursuant to which all the goods were shipped. Mehrbach *v.* Liverpool & G. W. S. Co., 12 Fed. Rep. 77 (1882).

In Detroit & Milwaukee R. Co. *v.* Adams, 15 Mich. 458 (1867), part of a lot of wool was delivered to the defendant by the plaintiff, and received for transportation, with the understanding that the balance should be sent to the depot as soon as defendant should give notice that it had cars sufficient for the shipment.   This notice was given, and the rest of the wool was delivered to and accepted by defendant.   Thereupon the owner signed a shipping request, to the effect that the company would forward all the wool, according to certain special conditions limiting the carrier's liability, which were endorsed upon the request. Part of the wool was lost before the residue was shipped.   Held, that whatever might have been the effect of such an agreement, if made before the delivery of the property at the depot, it did not affect the company's liability as common carrier by reason of the prior delivery to and acceptance by it; and that plaintiff had a right to consider the contract as referring only to the carrier's liability in respect to the *carriage* of the property, not its safe keeping in the depot before shipping.

See cases cited under Chapter X, sect. 2, *ante* pp. 227–233.

[1] Shelton *v.* Merchants' Trans. Co., 36 N. Y. Superior Ct. Rep. 527 (1873); Lamb *v.* Camden & Amboy R. R., 4 Daly (N. Y.), 483 (1873); Perry *v.* Thompson, 98 Mass. 249 (1867).   In this case attention is drawn to the fact that the clauses of exemption were partly concealed by a revenue stamp pasted over them.

[2] Gott *v.* Dinsmore, 111 Mass. 45 (1872); The Edwin, 1 Sprague, 477 (1859).

A similar rule was applied to a notice on a railway ticket, relating to liability for the loss of baggage, which was read by the passenger, but not until after he had taken his seat in the cars.[1]

The subsequent receipt of a bill of lading by the consignor, his sending it to the consignee, and the use of it by the latter as a voucher to obtain a portion of the goods shipped, do not establish its validity as a substituted contract, if it be shown that its conditions were not known to the consignor and never assented to by him.[2]

But if there be a consideration for the change in the original contract it is valid. The payment of the freight in advance in lieu of paying it on delivery would constitute such a consideration.[3]

And it cannot be denied that the possession of a bill of lading is of value to the shipper, especially in shipments by sea. It is a quasi-negotiable instrument, and constantly used as collateral security for the loan of

---

[1] Rawson v. Penn. R. R., 48 N. Y. 212 (1872). Earl C. at p. 217, said: "The contract between these parties was made when the plaintiff bought her ticket and the rights and duties of the parties were then determined. Hence, even if the plaintiff had read what appears upon her ticket after she had entered upon her journey, it would have made no difference with her rights. She was not then obliged to submit to a contract which she never made, or leave the train and demand her baggage."

[2] In Bostwick v. Baltimore & Ohio R. R., 45 N. Y. 712 (1871), the Court said: "After the verbal agreement had been consummated and rights had accrued under it, the mere receipt of the bill of lading, inadvertently omitting to examine the printed conditions, was not sufficient to conclude the plaintiff from showing what the actual agreement was under which the goods had been shipped."

Where there was a previous contract by letter and the carrier obtained the goods from the ship where they were, and issued a bill unknown to the owner exempting itself from perils of navigation, the owner was not bound thereby. Park v. Preston, 108 N. Y. 434 (1888).

[3] Baker v. Steamboat Milwaukee, 14 Iowa, 214 (1862). In this case Baldwin, C. J. (p. 225), used the following language: "The freight was paid as it is claimed upon the new agreement, and if the jury found this to be the fact, then we think the defendant was bound to take notice of the conditions of the new contract, and should have acted accordingly."

money. This will more distinctly appear if we consider the nature of a bill of lading. It is in the form of a contract on the part of the carrier to carry and deliver goods. It is signed by the officer or agent of the carrier and states the terms and conditions of the contract of affreightment. The acceptance of a bill of lading, knowing that it purports to represent and contain the contract, makes the contract just as binding on the shipper as his signature would, even though it is delivered subsequently to the shipment. It is not a case where a signature is necessary, and the acceptance on the one hand and the signature on the other are simply modes of indicating that the consignor contracts with the carrier on the terms stated in the bill of lading.[1]

The course of business and the consequent growth of the law on this subject is this: It became convenient for carriers not to deliver bills of lading when goods were received at the pier or station, but to deliver to the carter

---

[1] York Company v. The Central Railroad, 3 Wall. 107 (1865). In that case it was proved (p. 108) "that the cotton was shipped on the steamer before the bills of lading were signed; that the shipper had not examined the bills; that his attention was not called to the fire clause, and that his firm had no authority to ship for their principals with that exemption." It was also argued that there was no consideration for the exemption. But the court overruled all the objections, and held that the plaintiff, who was the owner of the goods, was bound by the exemption in the bill of lading. St. Louis, K. and N. R. Co. v. Cleary, 77 Mo. 634 (1883). Bostwick v. Baltimore & Ohio R. R., 45 N. Y. 712 (1871).

In The Alene, 25 Fed. Rep. 562 (1885), this precise question was argued fully; but the court did not pass upon it, because the acceptance of the bill of lading was in that case admitted by the pleadings. It appeared that when the goods were delivered to the steamer, receipts were given for them, and that the bills of lading were not delivered until after the steamer had sailed. It also appeared that it had been customary practice to send bills of lading under such circumstances, and that the shippers duly accepted them. Nothing could better illustrate the way in which this practice was understood than the fact that the libel in that case alleged the receipt and acceptance of the bill of lading, and it was not until the case was in the Circuit Court that an attempt was made to avoid its exemptions by proving the facts before stated, as to the receipt.

a paper expressing merely the receipt of the goods. Bills of lading were afterwards made out at the carrier's office, and forwarded to the shipper, or occasionally to the consignee. It was contended that bills of lading, so forwarded, were ineffective, because the contract was complete when the goods were delivered and the receipt given. In reply the carrier proved that the usage of business was to treat these receipts as mere vouchers which entitled the shipper to receive bills of lading for the goods mentioned in the receipt. On proof of such usage it was held that the carrier had received the goods upon the terms specified in the usual bills of lading.

When this question first arose, in order to guard against the allegation by the shipper that the bill of lading was not accepted by him, and also to avoid delay and facilitate the transaction of business, many carriers adopted the practice of delivering a shipping receipt at the time of shipment stating that the goods would be forwarded subject to the conditions in bills of lading, to be afterwards delivered. In such case the shipper is bound by the conditions and terms of the bill of lading.[1]

SECTION II.

AUTHORITY SHIPPING AGENT.

An agent who is employed by the owner of goods to procure them to be transported by a common carrier has general and implied authority to make an agreement with

---

[1] Wilde v. The Merch. Despatch Trans. Co., 47 Iowa, 272 (1877); Chicago & N. W. R. Co. v. Montfort, 60 Ill. 175 (1871), appears opposed to the statement in the text; but the circumstances there were peculiar. The drayman, to whom the original receipt was delivered, two or three days after the goods were shipped, asked for a duplicate receipt to send to the consignee. The court held that the shipper was not bound by limitations inserted in a paper, not a duplicate of the original, thereupon delivered to the drayman. See further cases in Chapter X, sect. 2, pp. 225–233.

the carrier as to the terms upon which the goods are to be transported.[1]

If the carman employed to deliver the goods to the carrier, signs a contract limiting the carrier's liability and providing that any objection to the contract should be immediately made to the freight agent, and further agrees that the goods shall be retained for a day in order to give opportunity for such dissent, if none is made acceptance by the carman's employer is established.[2] It is apparent, however, that the circumstances under which the authority was given and the extent of this authority may modify the general rule. Thus, when at the shipper's request the agent of the carrier went to another town, procured government orders on the warehouse where the goods were stored, obtained the goods and shipped them without issuing any bill of lading, it was held that he was not

---

[1] York Co. v. Central R. R., 3 Wall. 107 (1865) ; Squire v. N. Y. Central R. R., 98 Mass. 239 (1867); Nelson v. Hudson R. R. R., 48 N. Y. 498 (1872) ; Meyer v. Harnden's Ex. Co., 24 How. Pr. (N. Y.) 290 (1862) ; s. c. sub nom. Moriarty v. The Same, 1 Daly (N. Y.), 227 (1862); Shelton v. Merchants' Trans. Co., 36 N. Y. Superior Ct. 527 (1873). In the latter case, however, it was held that after the shipment was completed the authority of the agent terminated, and he could no longer bind the owner by the acceptance of a contract limiting the carrier's liability. It has been held otherwise in Illinois, and that the authority to contract for a limitation of the carrier's liability must be express. Merchants' Dispatch Co. v. Joestings, 89 Ill. 152 (1878).

See, however, Illinois Central R. R. v. Jonte, 13 Bradw. (Ill. App.) 424 (1883), in which the rule stated in the text is laid down distinctly by the court.

[2] Nelson v. Hudson R. R. R., 48 N. Y. 498 (1872). In this case the provisions of the contract excluded all liability for injury, except that caused by the carrier's negligence. These provisions though usual in the case of goods of the description shipped (a large mirror) were unusual in relation to other goods, and for this reason, no doubt, the evidence as to acceptance was so full. But in The May Queen, 1 Newb. Adm. 464 (1854), when the manufacturer of glass show cases himself delivered them on board, and was told that the ship was not responsible for breakage, he being neither the shipper, owner or consignor of the goods, it was held that he was not an agent authorized to make a special contract, or at least that this proof did not establish an authorized contract of limitation.

the agent of the shipper to bind the latter by the terms of the bill of lading ordinarily issued by the carrier.[1]

So, too, a shipper is not bound by the conditions in a bill of lading issued to a mere drayman, if the shipper protests against them as soon as known.[2] But the drover who is in charge of stock, and the only person with whom a connecting carrier can make terms, is authorized to make a contract of limitation to bind the owner.[3] Again where goods are shipped to market for sale pursuant to a custom by which the carrier returns empty tubs and baskets free, a local carrier at the market place, employed by both shipper and carrier, who collects the empty tubs, &c., is authorized to sign a contract limiting the liability of the carrier for injuries to the tubs.[4]

SECTION III.

CONTRACTS WITH CONNECTING LINES.

Contracts are constantly being made under which a carrier receives goods for transportation beyond the limits of his own line. In some cases the first carrier agrees that the goods shall be transported to their place of destination. In others the carrier's contract is simply to deliver the goods to the next connecting line, in order that this line may transport them. In the latter class of cases the question has arisen whether the first carrier has authority to contract with the second that the second be exempt from any part of his common law liability. Allen,

---

[1] Clyde v. Graver, 54 Penn. 251 (1867).

[2] Seller agst. The Pacific, 1 Oregon, 409 (1861) ; s. c. 1 Deady's Adm. Rep. 17.

[3] Squire v. N. Y. Central R. R., 98 Mass. 239 (1867).'

[4] Aldridge v. The Great Western R. Co., 15 C. B. (N. S.) 582 (1864)' In this case the shipper had little choice in the selection of the local carrier who was held to be his agent. But this was really immaterial. He adopted and recognized the employment.

J., in Babcock *v.* Lake Shore & Mich. S. R. Co.,[1] said that the first carrier had no such authority.   But the facts of that case did not require this proposition to be adjudged. No special contract was made by the first carrier with the second.   There was a provision in the shipper's contract with the first carrier limiting its liability, by excepting loss by fire.   There were general words in the printed form which would have extended the benefit of this exemption to all connecting lines.   The court held that these were controlled by the written part of the contract which was plainly for transportation over the first carrier's line and for delivery to the second carrier, and no more.[2] No reason is perceived why the rule that the agent to ship has an implied authority to contract respecting the terms of shipment, which was laid down in Nelson *v.* Hudson R. R. R.,[3] would not be applicable to the case of a contract made by the first carrier with the connecting carrier limiting the latter's liability.   The first carrier is certainly employed by the owner to deliver the goods to the second carrier, just as plainly as a carman is employed by the merchant, and if one can assent to the terms of a contract of limitation, why not the other?

In Lamb *v.* Camden & Amboy R. R.,[4] the same court held that the first carrier, who received goods in Illinois to be transported to New York, but did not contract for their transportation beyond its own line, could make a

---

[1] Babcock *v.* Lake Shore & M. S. R. Co., 49 N. Y. 491 (1872).

[2] There was no agreement for a through rate of freight.   The court say, at p. 497: "There was no consideration for an agreement by the plaintiff to relieve the carriers who should thereafter receive the property for transportation, from the common law liabilities, *and no such agreement was made.*"   Taylor *v.* Little Rock, M. & T. R. R., 39 Ark. 148 (1882).   In the latter case also, no through rate of freight was agreed upon.   The court said that if there had been, the exemption might have been valid.

[3] Nelson *v.* Hudson R. R. R., 48 N. Y. 498 (1872).

[4] Lamb *v.* Camden & A. R. R., 46 N. Y. 271 (1871).

contract with the second carrier, containing the same exceptions as those in the original contract and no other. It was also held that on the proper construction of the original contract which fixed the rate for the through freight, it was the shipper's agreement that the carriers throughout should be exempted from loss by fire. In this case the words " not liable for fire " were written across the face of the receipt.[1]

It may justly be said that the terms of the original contract express the terms on which the shipper is willing to contract with connecting lines, and thus constitute a limitation to which these lines assent by receiving the goods, and to which the shipper assents by accepting the contract. The proposition thus stated is supported by authority of weight,[2] and is believed to rest on the sound foundation of principle.

---

[1] See Lamb v. Camden & A. R. R., in Common Pleas, 2 Daly, 454 (1869).

[2] Railroad Co. v. Androscoggin Mills, 22 Wall. 594 (1874); Levy v. Southern Express Co., 4 S. Car. 234 (1872). See Manhattan Oil Co. v. Camden & Amboy R. R., 52 Barb. (N. Y.) 72 (1872); aff'd. 54 N. Y. 197 (1873); Whitworth v. Erie R. Co., 45 N. Y. Superior Ct. 602 (1879); aff'd 87 N. Y. 414 (1882). In this latter case it was distinctly held that the contract was several and not joint, each carrier being liable only for transportation over its own line and delivery to the next. But the connecting carrier was nevertheless held entitled to the benefit of the clauses of exemption contained in the contract. These, by the terms of the contract, were applicable to the connecting carriers. In the Androscoggin case the carrier delivered to the shipper a through bill of lading, containing the words: "The Evansville and Crawfordsville Railroad Company will not be liable for loss or damage by fire from any cause whatever." The goods were destroyed by fire, but not upon the line of the contracting carrier. In a suit against that carrier, it was held that the exemption applied to the whole route, and was valid.

In the Levy case there was an express authority contained in the contract with the first carrier to deliver to a connecting carrier, and an express agreement that all the stipulations in the contract should enure to the benefit of connecting lines. The Court said: "As between the Adams Express Co. (the first carrier) and the owner, the terms of the bill of lading are to be regarded as modifying in certain particulars the common law liability of the company as common carriers. The shipper having authority to ship must be regarded as authorized to bind the owner by a contract containing special terms of shipment. Adams Ex-

It has been held in analogy to the rule stated in a previous chapter[1] that a notice from the second carrier to the first, as to the terms on which it would accept goods for transportation, is not sufficient to limit its liability for goods received by it from the first carrier, and generally accepted without any contract at the time of such receipt, other than that implied by law.[2] This was on the ground that a mere notice was insufficient to limit the carrier's liability. But, no doubt, a general contract between the two carriers as to the terms upon which all shipments would be made and received would be as effective as a special contract at the time of each delivery. In the absence of a contract between the two carriers, if the agreement with the first carrier provides only for transportation to the terminus of his line and delivery to the second, and has no stipulation which can be construed to apply to the entire transit, the second carrier cannot avail himself of limitations in the contract with the first.[3]

---

press Co. had express authority to employ the defendants as common carriers, and to fix the terms of the contract in conformity with the terms stipulated between the shipper and themselves. It is to be presumed, as the case stands, that the defendants accepted the trunk on the terms of the original bill of lading, and such acceptance is accordingly special and subject to such terms."

[1] *Ante*, Chap. X, p. 221.

[2] Judson *v.* Western R. R., 6 Allen (Mass.), 486 (1863); Adams Ex. Co. *v.* Harris (Ind.), 21 N. E. Rep. 340 (1889).

[3] Camden & Amboy R. R. *v.* Forsyth, 61 Penn. 81 (1869); Ætna Ins. Co. *v.* Wheeler, 49 N. Y. 616 (1872); aff'g. s. c. 5 Lansing, 480 (1871); Babcock *v.* Lake Shore & M. S. R. Co., 49 N. Y. 491 (1872); Merchants' Trans. Co. *v.* Bolles, 80 Ill. 473 (1875); Southern Express Co. *v.* Urquhart, 52 Ga. 142 (1874); Ed-all *v.* Camden & A. R. R., 50 N. Y. 661 (1872). In The Forsyth case the rate for through freight was noted on the margin of the contract, but this was held not to make it a through contract. The connecting carrier gave a receipt to the first carrier, but issued no bill of lading and made no special contract. In The Ætna Ins. Co. case, the agreement with the first carrier was in terms to deliver "unto consignees at Ogdensburgh" (the terminus of its line). The goods were marked for Boston and a through rate of freight agreed upon, but the contract in all other respects was silent as to the terms upon which the goods should be carried by the connecting line.

In The Bolles case the Court say: "It is only where the contract is

The rule on this subject is further illustrated by reference to a New York decision. A shipper delivered oil to a carrier to be transported to a point beyond its line. No agreement limiting the carrier's liability was made. The connecting carrier on receiving the oil gave to the first carrier a receipt with the clause appended, "Owners' risk F. and L." The goods were destroyed by fire while being transported by the second carrier. It was shown that these letters were commonly understood in the trade to mean fire and leakage, and the court held this evidence admissible, and that the first carrier was the shipper's agent to deliver the oil to the connecting carrier; that the latter had a right to contract with such agent for the limitation of its own liability, and that the delivery of the receipt in question effected such limitation.[1]

It must be admitted that the authority of this case is somewhat impaired by the dictum of Allen, J., before referred to. It cannot be claimed that the result of these cases is to leave the law on this important subject in a very satisfactory condition.

So far as through contracts for the transportation of goods are concerned, there is no question that the last carrier is entitled to all the benefits of the exemptiom from liability contained in the through bill of lading under which the goods are transported, even though the bill of

---

for through transportation that each connecting carrier will be entitled to the benefits and exemptions of the contract between the shipper and the first carrier."

In The Urquhart case the court held that in the absence of proof as to the terms upon which the connecting carrier received the goods from the first carrier, the connecting carrier should be presumed to have received them for transportation to the owner under such obligations as to diligence, &c., as the law imposes on common carriers, who do not, by contract, limit their liability.

[1] Hinkley v. N. Y. Central & H. R. R. R. 3 Thomps. & Cook (N. Y.), 281 (1874); Alabama & Gt. S. R. Co. v. Thomas, 3 So. Rep. 802 (1888), Ala.

lading expressly provides that each carrier shall be liable
only for losses occurring on its own line.[1]

---

[1] Bristol & Exeter R. Co. *v.* Collins, 7 House of Lords, 194 (1859),
rev'g. s. c. 1 Hurlst. & N. 517 (1856); Maghee *v.* Camden & Amboy
R. R., 45 N. Y. 514 (1871); Manhattan Oil Co. *v.* Camden & Amboy
R. R., 54 N. Y. 197 (1873); aff'g. s. c. 52 Barb. 72 (1868). In this case
a through contract for the transportation of goods was made by a carrier, containing a clause exempting it from liability "for loss or damage
by fire or other casualty while in depots or places of transhipment."
Certain other exemptions were contained therein in reference to which
the contract made express provision for exemption in favor of connecting lines. The goods were received by defendant, a connecting carrier,
and it received from the contracting carrier a portion of the freight.
While in its depot the goods were destroyed by fire. The court said:
"The oil destroyed by fire, the value of which is the subject of the present controversy, was received by the Union Transportation and Insurance Company, at Cincinnati, to be transported by that company to
New York at a stated price for the whole route, and upon certain conditions, one of which was that the company should not be liable for
damages or loss by fire, or other casualty which should occur to the oil
while in depots or in places of transhipment. Under this contract that
company would undoubtedly have been liable had the oil been damaged or destroyed while on defendant's road or boat, by any of the perils
hazarded by common carriers not excepted in the contract for its transportation; and it is equally clear that if the action had been brought
against that company to recover the value of the oil, it would have been
shielded by the exception in the bill of lading. . . . The plaintiff
insists that the defendant, who was the last carrier on the route to New
York, to which the Union Company had agreed to transport it, is not entitled to the benefit of the condition referred to, upon which the Union
Company agreed to carry it to that city. The contract made by the
Union Company was for a service to be performed, not only for a compensation to which it would not have been entitled until the property
had been transported to and ready for delivery in New York, but by it
that company would have incurred a liability for damage to, or a loss
of it, had not the loss occurred in a depot or place of transhipment.
The contract having been made by that company for the transportation
of the oil from Cincinnati to New York was, including the condition
referred to, commensurate with the undertaking to transport it over the
whole and every part of the route. Had it been a contract which did
not carry the liability of the first carrier beyond the distance traversed
by its cars, the condition could not avail the defendant; but as it is,
the defendant, instead of being the party who contracted with the
plaintiff, was aiding the first carrier in performing its contract, and for
a compensation to be equally apportioned and paid by that carrier, to
whom the defendant was but a subordinate, and shielded by the condition made by that company against a liability for loss by fire." To the
same effect are Oakey *v.* Gordon, 7 La. Ann. 235 (1852); Whitworth *v.*
Erie R. Co., 45 N. Y. Superior Ct. 602 (1879); aff'd. 87 N. Y. 414
(1882); U. S. Express Co. *v.* Harris, 51 Ind. 127 (1875); Kiff *v.* Atchi-

It does not fall within the scope of this work to consider in detail the law as to when the liability of the first carrier ceases, nor as to when he is liable for injuries occurring on a connecting line.

In general it may be said that in order to discharge himself he must make such a delivery to the connecting line as he should make if the place of consignment was on his own route.[1]   And when he has made such delivery

son T. & S. R. R., 32 Kans. 263 (1884).   In this case the limitation was effected by the words "owner's risk."

In Oakey v. Gordon, the carrier owned a railroad and ran a steamboat in connection with it.   Cotton was shipped under a bill of lading given by the captain of the boat, binding him to deliver the cotton at a station on the railroad, "unavoidable dangers of navigation and fire" only excepted.   The cotton was destroyed by fire issuing from the chimney of the locomotive, in transit to New Orleans.   Held, that the contract to carry the cotton was entire, and the exception in the bill of lading against loss by fire extended as well to loss on the cars as on the boat.

On the other hand, if there be no exemption provided for in the through contract, the contracting carrier is liable for the default of the connecting line.   Toledo, W. & W. R. Co. v. Lockhart, 71 Ill. 627 (1874).

In Owen v. Louisville & Nashville R. Co., 9 S. W. Rep. 698 (1888), it was held that the last carrier was the agent of the first, so far as to bind the latter by a waiver of a condition requiring the claim to be presented within a given time.

[1] In re Peterson, 21 Fed. Rep. 885 (1884); Eaton v. Neumark, 33 Fed. R. 891 (1888); Reed v. U. S. Ex. Co., 48 N. Y. 462 (1872); Mills v. Mich. Central R. R., 45 N. Y. 622 (1871); Dunson v. N. Y. Central R. R., 3 Lansing (N. Y.), 265 (1870); Wahl v. Holt, 26 Wis. 703 (1870); Mobile & Ohio R. R. v. Hopkins, 41 Ala. 486 (1868); Lewis v. Western R. R., 11 Metc. (Mass.) 509 (1846); Louisville & N. R. R. v. Campbell, 7 Heiskell (Tenn.), 253 (1872); Lawrence v. Winona & St. P. R. R., 15 Minn. 390 (1870); Wood v. Milwaukee & St. Paul R. Co., 27 Wis. 541 (1871).   This latter case was, however, expressly overruled by Conkey v. Milwaukee & St. P. R. R., 31 Wis. 619 (1872) in the same court, and arising out of the same occurrence.   In the former it was held that if the second carrier fail to accept the goods after a reasonable time, the first carrier is liable only as warehouseman.   In the Conkey case, it was held, however, that the carrier's liability as such continued till the goods were delivered to the consignee.   It was said that the carrier, in whose possession the goods were injured or lost, suffered from delay in receiving them by a succeeding carrier, he might have a remedy against the latter.

In Mills v. Michigan Central R. R., 45 N. Y. 622 (1871), it was held that where goods are received by a carrier for transportation, his liability ceases.   If he notify the next connecting carrier that he is ready to deliver the goods to him, and the latter, after a reasonable time, neglects to receive and remove the goods from the custody of the first carrier; they may then be warehoused and the liability of the first carrier as such will thereupon cease, and he will be liable as warehouseman only.[1]   In such case the first carrier should notify the shipper.[2]

---

marked for a destination beyond the terminus of such carrier's route, the manner of giving notice to the next carrier of their arrival and readiness for delivery, and the length of time which is reasonable and must elapse before the first carrier is relieved from his carrier's liability, are regulated by existing custom between them.

Where there was an agreement between two connecting lines that goods should not be regarded as transferred until the freight charges of the second carrier were paid or secured, held that although the goods had actually been placed in the second carrier's warehouse, the first carrier was not discharged, payment not having been made.   Palmer v. Chicago B. & Q. R. Co., 13 Atl. Rep. (Conn.) 818 (1888); compare Alabama G. S. R. R. v. Mt. Vernon Co., 4 So. Rep. 356 (1887); 84 Ala. 173.   If cattle are delivered safely to connecting line, their delivery is good though they are transferred to unsafe cars.   Alabama G. S. R. R. v. Thomas, 3 So. Rep. 802 (1888).

[1] Rawson v. Holland, 59 N. Y. 611 (1875); s. c. 47 How. Pr. (N. Y.) 292 (1874); Inhabitants v. Hall, 61 Me. 517 (1873); Devillers v. Bell, 6 La. Ann. 544 (1851); Dalzell v. The Saxon, 10 Ib. 280 (1855). See Condon v. Marquette, H. & O. R. R., 55 Mich. 218 ; 21 N. W. Rep. 321 (1884).   The general rule as to delivery to the consignee is the same.   Faulkner v. Hart, 82 N. Y. 413 (1880); See, also, the cases cited in Faulkner v. Hart, and the Massachusetts cases to the contrary, also therein cited.   Fenner v. Buffalo & State Line R. R., 44 N. Y. 505 (1871), does not conflict with the rule stated in the text.   In that case the Court say (p. 507): " It is well settled in this State that an intermediate carrier, one who receives goods to be transported over his route, and thence by other carriers to their place of destination, generally remains liable as a common carrier until he has delivered the goods to the

---

[2] Louisville & N. R. R. v. Campbell, 7 Heisk. 253 (1872); Lesinsky v. Great W. Disp., 10 Mo. App. 134 (1881).   In *In re* Peterson, 21 Fed. Rep. 885 (1884), it was held that where the second carrier notifies the first carrier that on account of a freight blockade it cannot receive the goods, the liability of the first carrier will not become that of a warehouseman if the first carrier fails to notify the shipper and give the latter opportunity to preserve property.   And as to delivery to consignee, see Chap. XIV, sect. 8, *post*.   See Dunn v. Hannibal & St. J. R. R., 68 Mo. 268 (1878).

Depositing goods in its own depot is not sufficient to relieve the carrier from its common law liability.[1]   It is liable for injuries done to person or property on a connecting line when it has made a contract for through transportation, and not otherwise.[2]

---

next carrier." McDonald *v.* Western R. R., 34 N. Y. 497 (1866); Ladue *v.* Griffith, 25 N. Y. 364 (1862); Goold *v.* Chapin, 20 N. Y. 266 (1859); Miller *v.* Steam Nav. Co., 10 N. Y. 431 (1853). In none of these cases except Goold *v.* Chapin had a reasonable time elapsed for the connecting carrier to receive and remove the goods. In Goold *v.* Chapin the connecting carrier had notice and a reasonable time to remove them, and had failed so to do; but the carrier still retained them on the float on which they had been discharged. The court held that the liability of the carrier as such still continued. In both the prevailing opinions it is conceded that if the goods had been removed to a warehouse, because of the delay on the part of the next carrier, the liability of the preceding carrier as such would have terminated. See pp. 264, 267. It was, however, held otherwise in Bancroft *v.* Merchants' Desp. Co., 47 Iowa, 262 (1877); Illinois Central R. R. *v.* Mitchell, 68 Ill. 471 (1873).

[1] Railroad Company *v.* Manufacturing Co., 16 Wall. 318 (1872); See cases cited, *ante,* p. 283, n. 2.

[2] Myrick *v.* Michigan Central R. R., 107 U. S. 102 (1882); Insurance Co. *v.* R. R. Co., 104 U. S. 146 (1881); Barter *v.* Wheeler, 49 N. H. 9 (1869); Parmelee *v.* Western Trans. Co., 26 Wis. 439 (1870); Green *v.* N. Y. Central R. R., 12 Abb. N. S. (N. Y.) 473 (1872); Root *v.* Great Western R. R., 45 N. Y. 524 (1871); rev'g. s. c. 2 Lans. 199 (1869); Hunt *v.* N. Y. & Erie R. R., 1 Hilt. (N. Y.) 228 (1856); Dillon *v.* N. Y. & Erie R. R., Ibid, 231 (1856); Weil *v.* Merchant's D. & T. Co., 7 Daly (N. Y.), 456 (1878); Jacobs *v.* Hooker, 1 Edmonds (N. Y.), 472 (1847); Manhattan Oil Co. *v.* Camden & Amboy R. R., 52 Barb. (N. Y.) 72; s. c. 5 Abb. Pr. R. (N. S.) 289 (1868); aff'd. 54 N. Y. 197 (1873); Babcock *v.* Lake Shore & M. S. R. Co., 49 N. Y. 491 (1872); Rawson *v.* Holland, 59 N. Y. 611 (1875); Toledo, W. &. W. R. Co. *v.* Lockhart, 71 Ill. 627 (1874); Cutts *v.* Brainerd, 42 Vt. 556 (1870); Ill. Central R. R. *v.* Copeland, 24 Ill. 332 (1860); Illinois Central R. R. *v.* Frankenberg, 54 Ill. 88 (1870); Adams Ex. Co. *v.* Wilson, 81 Ibid, 339 (1876); McCann *v.* Baltimore & Ohio R. R., 20 Md. 202 (1863); Baltimore & Ohio R. R. *v.* Schumacher, 29 Md. 168 (1868); McMillan *v.* Mich. S. & N. I. R. R., 16 Mich. 79 (1867); Lowell Wire Fence Co. *v.* Sargent, 8 Allen (Mass.), 189 (1864); Hill Manufacturing Co. *v.* Boston & L. R. R. Co., 104 Mass. 122 (1870); Newell *v.* Smith, 49 Vt. 255 (1876); Hadd *v.* U. S. & Canada Express Co., 52 Vt. 335 (1880); Crawford *v.* Southern R. R. Ass'n, 51 Miss. 222 (1875); Skinner *v.* Hall, 60 Me. 477 (1872); Halliday *v.* St. Louis, K. & N. R. Co., 74 Mo. 159 (1881); s. c. 41 Am. Rep. 309 ; Ortt *v.* Minneapolis & St. L. Ry. Co., 36 Minn. 396 (1887).

The making of a through contract will not be inferred from the re-

The validity of contracts for the transportation of freight beyond the terminus of the contracting carrier's

ception by the first carrier of goods marked for a place beyond the terminus of its own line. Myrick *v.* Michigan Central R. R.. 107 U. S. 102 (1882). Where the bill of lading contains a stipulation that no one of the connecting carriers composing a through line shall be liable for any injury not occurring on his portion of the entire route, this is binding on the shipper, and he cannot recover against the first carrier for a loss occurring on the line of another, if the occurrence of the loss is not due to delay on the part of the first carrier. Schiff *v.* New York Central & H. R. R. R., 52 How. Pr. (N. Y.) 91 (1876); Tardos *v.* Chicago, S. & L., & N. O. R. R., 35 La. Ann. 15 (1883). In this latter case the first carrier guaranteed the through rate, and the connecting line refused to recognize this. It was held that the contracting carrier was entitled to notice of this refusal, and in the absence of such notice was liable to the shipper only for the difference between the rate exacted and the guaranteed rate.

In Sumner *v.* Walker, 30 Fed. Rep. 261 (1887), Brown, J., thus states the law : "Each carrier on a through bill of lading or on connecting lines is liable only for the negligence that arises on his own line, unless some different understanding be shown or circumstances from which such an understanding should be inferred." Railroad *v.* Androscoggin Mills, 22 Wall. 594 (1874); Railroad *v.* Pratt, 22 Wall. 123 (1874); s. c. 95 U. S. 43 (1877); Harding *v.* International Nav. Co., 12 Fed. Rep. 168 (1882). In Darling *v.* Boston & Worcester R. R., 93 Mass. 295 (1865), it was held that in the absence of usage or contract the carrier is bound only to carry goods over its own route. If it deliver to a customary or prescribed connecting carrier its liability is discharged. It may contract to carry further ; otherwise the arrangement between connecting lines would control. In the same case it was also held that the last carrier who delivers the goods and collects all the freight is not, in the absence of agreement, liable for damages on previous lines.

A carrier which agrees to transport goods beyond its line undertakes to transport them to their destination by itself or competent agents, and if they are lost beyond its line, it is liable. A statute provided that each company should be responsible only to its own terminus, and that the last company which received the goods "in good order" should be responsible to the consignee. It was held that this did not change this common law rule except by giving a remedy against the last carrier. Falvey *v.* Georgia R. R., 76 Ga. 597 (1886); overruling Baugh *v.* McDaniel, 42 Ga. 641 (1871). Where the evidence showed that damage occurred before the goods reached the last carrier, it is error to charge in the language of this statute. Columbus & W. R. Co. *v.* Tillman, 5 S. E. Rep. 135 (1888).

A statute prescribed that "where two railroads are connected together, the first railroad receiving freight should be liable for loss or injury on the route." It was held that a mere mechanical connection was not meant—that it must be a business connection. Laws of N. Y., 1847, chap. 270; Colby's New R. R. Laws, p. 270, Root *v.* Great Western R. R., 45 N. Y. 524 (1871).

route was at one time doubted, but is now well settled,[1] and the shipper may always affirm a contract with a connecting carrier.[2]

The previous observations in this section refer only to contracts for the tranportation of freight. In reference to contracts for the transportation of passengers, it is held that a carrier who is authorized by connecting lines to sell through tickets for transportation over the several lines is the agent of the several lines for the purpose of making the contract of transportation. It follows that each company, for transportation over whose line the contract is made, is bound to transport the person to whom the through ticket is sold, upon his presenting the ticket in accordance with its terms, and that each line is bound by the representations of the line selling the ticket as to privileges of breaking the journey ;[3] and if the first carrier makes a contract to transport a passenger through to a point beyond the terminus of its own line, the liability of the contracting carrier will not be limited by agreements with the connecting lines of which the passenger has no notice.[4]

A statute provided that the last of several connecting carriers should be liable for loss of goods delivered to the first for transportation. Goods being billed from Boston to Atlanta, the railroad running into Atlanta was held to be the last carrier, and to be liable for the loss of the goods, although it had delivered them to another local railroad for delivery in the city. Georgia Code, sect. 2084 ; Western & A. R. Co. v. Exposition Cotton Mills, 7 S. E. Rep. 916 (1888); Central R. R. v. Avant, 5 S. E. Rep. (Ga.) 78 (1888); Washington v. Raleigh & G. R. Co., 7 S. E. Rep. (N. C.) 789 (1888); Block v. Merch. Desp. Trans. Co., 6 S. W. Rep. 881 (1888).

[1] Swift v. Pacific Mail S. S. Co., 7 Central Rep. (N. Y.) 811 (1887); s. c. 106 N. Y. 201 ; Railroad Co. v. Pratt, 22 Wall. (U. S.) 124 (1874).

[2] Sanderson v. Lambertson, 6 Binn. (Pa.) 129 (1813).

[3] Young v. Penn. R. R.; 5 Central Rep. 848 ; s. c. 115 Penn. 112 (1887).

[4] Little v. Dusenberry, 46 N. J. (Law). 614 (1884). In Central R. R. v. Combs, 70 Ga. 533 ; s. c. 48 Am. Rep. 582 (1883), it was held that the liability of the contracting carrier who has made such a through contract, is not limited by a provision printed upon the ticket that each

And a carrier selected by the person to whom the goods are addressed, to receive the goods, is not a connecting carrier and not liable to the holder of the bill of lading, though the person employing him had no title to the goods.[1]

---

of the carriers composing the through line should be liable only for injuries occurring upon its own route. But the circumstances of this case were peculiar. The damage sued for was occasioned by the failure of the connecting line to transport the passenger at all. It had stopped running its cars, owing to the prevalence of yellow fever. The carrier selling the through ticket was held liable for the expense and trouble caused to the passenger by his detention at the connecting point. The view taken by a court of this general question would in part depend upon whether it treated the ticket as a contract, or merely a voucher for the payment of fare. See Chap. X, sect. 2, p. 230.

[1] Nanson *v.* Jacob, 6 S. W. Rep. 246; s. c. 93 Mo. 331 (1887).

CHAPTER XIV.

CONSTRUCTION OF PARTICULAR CLAUSES IN BILLS OF LADING.

SECTION I.

RECEIVED IN GOOD ORDER.

Contracts between the carrier and the shipper almost invariably begin with an acknowledgment that the carrier has received certain merchandise. Then follow the stipulations expressing the contract between the parties. But whatever the form, if the instrument delivered by the carrier to the shipper contain language sufficient to show that the carrier agrees with the shipper to transport certain goods therein described from one place to another for a consideration therein specified, the instrument will be a bill of lading.[1]

Where the bill of lading contains the usual acknowledgment that the goods were received in good order, and the words "contents and value unknown," are omitted, the presumption is that not only the package but the goods themselves were in good order when received. The burden of proof in such case, if they fail to arrive at the port of destination in good condition, is upon the carrier, and he must show that the injury happened before the goods came to his hands.[2]

---

[1] Dows v. Perrin, 16 N. Y. 325 (1857); Dows v. Rush, 28 Barb. (N. Y.) 157 (1858); *ante*, p. 231.

[2] The Historian, 28 Fed. Rep. 336 (1886); The Zone, 2 Sprague, 19 (1860); The Martha, Olcott, 40 (1845); Price v. Powell, 3 N. Y. 322 (1850); Nelson v. Stephenson, 5 Duer (N. Y.), 538 (1856). In West v.

RECEIVED IN GOOD ORDER.

This admission, however, does not preclude the carrier from introducing evidence to rebut it. It is *prima facie* only;[1] and the condition of the package itself may be such as to rebut the presumption. This was so held when the package was found to be perforated by nail holes and the water had thereby been admitted to the interior.[2]

It was said in one case that in order to rebut this presumption derivable from the admission in the bill of lading, the carrier's proof must amount to a certainty.[3] It may fairly be questioned, however, whether the learned court did not go too far in this statement. There would seem to be no good reason why any rule of evidence should be applied in this class of cases different from that which prevails in ordinary civil cases. The jury or the court must always be satisfied that the preponderance of evidence is in favor of the party upon whom the law casts the burden of proof. To go further than this and say that he must establish his case with certainty, would seem rather to obscure than to elucidate the question under discussion.

In a previous case in the same court, this question of

The Berlin, 3 Iowa, 542 (1856), this rule was held not to apply to the case of pork packed in barrels, because the carrier was not bound to open or inspect them.

[1] The Oriflamme, 1 Sawyer, 176 (1870); The Black Warrior, 1 McAllister, 181 (1856); Gowdy *v.* Lyon, 9 B. Monr. (Ky.) 112 (1848); Carson *v.* Harris, 4 Green (Iowa), 516 (1854); Barrett *v.* Rogers, 7 Mass. 297 (1811); The Nith, 36 Fed. Rep. 86 (1888); Bissell *v.* Price, 16 Ill. 408 (1855); Seller *v.* The Pacific, 1 Oregon, 409 (1861); s. c. Deady, 19. It was held in The Martha, Olcott, 140 (1845), that this presumption was not rebutted by proof that the iron in question, which was stained, was well stowed ; that the ship came in tight and dry, and that the iron was taken on board in dry weather, and had not been exposed to water. So in Arend *v.* Liverpool S. S. Co., 6 Lans. (N. Y.) 457 ; s. c. 64 Barb. 118 (1872), where the claim was for loss of wine shipped in a cask, it was held that this presumption was not rebutted by proof that the voyage was tempestuous, the cargo well stowed, and the hatches properly secured.

[2] Richards *v.* Doe, 100 Mass. 524 (1868).

[3] Bond *v.* Frost, 8 La. Ann. 297 (1853).

19

evidence was considered, and the court examined the various facts and circumstances which went to show that the master stowed cargo, which he knew to be peculiarly liable to injury, in a place near the deck, where it was more exposed to such injury, and held that this rendered the carrier liable for an injury apparently resulting from that cause, which was discovered when the goods arrived.[1]

The admission under consideration, so far as it relates to the external cover, refers only to its apparent good condition and not to its intrinsic soundness and sufficiency.[2] And even if the goods were visibly in bad condition when delivered to the carrier, yet if he receipt for them as being in good order and well conditioned, he cannot recover his freight from consignees who had made advances upon the faith of the statement in the bill of lading.[3] It was said in the same case that the language of the clause under consideration extended only to the external and apparent condition of the goods, and did not refer to or warrant the internal quality or condition of the contents of the package.[4]

The weight of authority, however, is against the proposition that the admission in question, if not qualified, relates only to the external appearance of the goods. The cases just cited in support of this proposition, which were

---

[1] Montgomery v. The "Abby Pratt," 6 La. Ann. 410 (1851).

[2] The Olbers, 3 Bened. 148 (1869). In both cases cited by the learned court, the bills of lading contained the qualification "Weight and contents unknown." See *post*, p. 291. It is possible that these words may have been contained in the bill of lading in The Olbers, but the report does not so state.

[3] Bradstreet v. Heran, 2 Blatch. 116 (1849). Nelson, J., begins his opinion by saying: "It is admitted." The proposition stated in the text was certainly therefore not argued before him.

[4] To the same effect are the following cases: Keith v. Amende, 1 Bush (Ky.), 455 (1866); West v. Steamboat "Berlin," 3 Iowa, 532 (1856); Gauche v. Storer, 14 La. Ann. 411 (1859); *Cf.* Nelson v. Stephenson, 5 Duer (N. Y.), 538 (1851); Goudy v. Lyon, 9 B. Monr. (Ky.) 112 (1848).

determined in the Federal Courts, must be considered as overruled by the Supreme Court.[1]

The clause " Value and contents unknown," and similar clauses were undoubtedly introduced into bills of lading to protect the carrier from the presumption referred to, and it is certainly going a great way to maintain that when the carrier receipts for the goods in good order, without any clause of limitation, he can claim that all this means is that the box was in good order.

SECTION II.

LIMITATIONS RELATING TO QUANTITY, CHARACTER OR QUALITY.

When the words " Value and contents unknown," or their equivalent, are added to a bill of lading, they qualify the language with which it usually begins : " Received in good order and well conditioned ; " and shift the burden of proof as to the condition of the contents when shipped.

The admission implied from the two clauses construed together refers to the condition of the package or wrapper itself, and not to that of its contents. Thus, for example, in a case where a box of dry goods was found on arrival at its destination to be only partly filled, it was held that no admission that the box was full when received by the carrier could be inferred from a bill of lading containing both these clauses, there being no defect observable in the external condition of the box.[2] In other words, the ad-

---

[1] The Ship Howard v. Wissman, 18 How. (U. S.) 231 (1855). The Court say: "The owner having been committed to the *prima facie* facts of soundness and good condition by his contract of affreightment, it was properly imposed on him by the District Court to establish the contrary by due proof." See *ante*, p. 253, n. 1.

[2] The "California," 2 Sawyer, 12 (1871). In this case the words used were " in apparent good order." Matthiessen & W. S. Ref. Co. v.

mission by the carrier is limited to that which can be ascertained from looking at or handling the package containing the goods, and does not extend to the quantity, character or quality of the contents.[1]

Gusi, 29 Fed. Rep. 794 (1887); St. Louis, Iron Mountain & S. R. Co. *v.* Knight, 122 U. S. 79 (1886). In this case the bills of lading acknowledged the receipt of cotton bales " marked and numbered as in margin," " contents unknown." The carrier tendered to the consignee, who had in good faith advanced money on the bills, bales so marked but not corresponding to the quality called for by the marks. Held that this was a good tender.

In Seller *v.* The Pacific, 1 Oregon, 409; Deady, 17 (1861), however, the court gave effect to the words "in good order" in a bill of lading, and refused to modify them by the clause " not responsible for the contents " in the same bill, on the ground that it would be a contract that the person who in that case received the bill had no authority to make.

[1] Clark *v.* Barnwell, 12 How. U. S. Rep. 272 (1851); Eaton *v.* Neumark, 33 Fed. Rep. 891 (1888); Abbott *v.* National S. S. Co., Ibid, 895 (1888); The Columbo, 3 Blatch. 521 (1856). These two authorities also hold that in such cases the burden is on the shipper to show that the contents were in good condition when delivered to the carrier. The " Adriatic," 16 Blatch. 424 (1879). In the latter case a bill of lading for Coir Yarn in bales, receipted for them as " in good order and well conditioned," and described them as " in transit " from another steamer. They were apparently in good external order. When the bales were landed in New York, one hundred were found to have been wet at some time with sea water. On cutting the wrappers the yarn was found to be damp to the touch, but not enough to drip, and was to some extent discolored and unfit for the manufacture of fine goods, for which it had been intended. The bales were proved to have been properly stowed. No other part of the cargo was wet. There was no appearance of a leak, and the hatches were all in good order and well secured when the vessel arrived. There was no evidence as to the condition of the bales when shipped, other than that contained in the bill of lading. It was not shown how long they had been " in transit " when the shipment was made, nor from what place the original consignment was made, nor whether the bales had been specially exposed to sea water in the previous voyage. Held, that the libellant could not recover because he had not shown that the goods were damaged while on board the steamer libeled.

In Miller *v.* Hannibal & St. Jo. R. R., 90 N. Y. Rep. 430; s. c. 43 Am. Rep. 179 (1882); rev'g. 24 Hun, 607 (1881), the bill of lading described the contents as " 30 bbls. eggs; " but the clause " contents and value unknown " was added. On arriving at their destination the barrels were found full of sawdust. Held, that the carrier was not liable unless it could be shown that the barrels contained eggs when shipped. The court say: " The sole question is whether the description of the articles in the bill of lading was a representation by the carrier

So where the language used was "contents and weight unknown," it was held that the statement in the margin of the bill of lading as to the weight of the goods was not conclusive in deciding as to the freight to be paid, but that this must be ascertained by their actual weight.[1] Nor

---

that the barrels contained eggs, because if this is the true construction of the instrument, the right of the plaintiffs to recover is unquestionable. But we are of opinion that this construction is inadmissible. Taking the whole instrument together, it imports only that the defendant had received thirty packages described as containing eggs, but the actual contents of which were unknown to defendant. The opposite view proceeds upon the theory that there is an irreconcilable repugnancy between the written and printed parts of the instrument, or that the words 'contents unknown' relate simply to the kind of eggs in the packages. It is no doubt a principle of construction that in case of repugnancy between written and printed clauses of an instrument, the written clauses will prevail over the printed. But this is a rule which is only resorted to from necessity, when the printed and written clauses cannot be reconciled. But it is the imperative duty of courts to give effect if possible to all the terms of an agreement. The construction is to be made upon a consideration of the whole instrument, and not upon one or more clauses detached from the others; and this principle applies as well to instruments partly printed and partly written as to those wholly printed or wholly written. Where two clauses, apparently repugnant, may be reconciled by any reasonable construction, as by regarding one as a qualification of the other, that construction must be given, because it cannot be assumed that the parties intended to insert inconsistent provisions. Applying these settled rules to the instrument in question, it is, we think, reasonably clear that the defendant did not make any representation as to the contents of the packages. Its agent simply certified in effect that they were described as containing eggs, accompanying this with the statement that the contents were not in fact known. The plaintiffs in making the advances were chargeable with knowledge of the contents of the bill of lading and must be deemed to have relied upon the assurance of the shipper as to the contents of the packages. The claim that the words 'contents unknown' referred simply to the kind of eggs, is manifestly untenable."

But it has been held that the words "contents and gauge unknown," in a bill of lading receipting for "barrel of molasses," must be interpreted as referring only to the quality and quantity of the molasses, not to the fact that it was molasses. Nelson v. Stephenson, 5 Duer, 538 (1856). Where a succeeding carrier has receipted for the goods in good order, and there was positive evidence of negligence, held, it was properly left to the jury whether the first carrier was liable. N. Y. Cent. & H. R. R. R. v. Eby, 12 Atl. Rep. (Penn.) 482 (1888).

[1] The "Andover," 3 Blatch. 303 (1855). In this case Nelson, J., said: "The cotton in question was part of a cargo shipped at New Orleans and consigned to the libellant at New York, he paying the freight.

in such a case is the ship or owner liable, although the amount actually delivered to the consignee is less than the amount specified in the margin as received by the carrier.[1]

This clause is generally invoked by the carrier. It is, of course, equally available to the shipper. As, for example, it has been held that under a bill of lading containing the words "contents unknown," but describing the goods shipped as domestics, the shipper could show that one of the cases when shipped contained silk goods and not domestics, and could recover their full value in case of loss, provided the carrier was not misled by the description.[2]

The bill of lading contained the clause 'contents and weight unknown.' The freight was to be paid at a certain rate per pound, and in the margin of the bill, the figures 29,782 were placed, apparently as the aggregate weight of the cotton. On the arrival of the cotton, the consignees of the ship claimed that the figures in the margin of the bill should govern in determining the weight, while the libellant insisted that as the bill of lading said 'weight unknown,' the cotton should be weighed and freight paid accordingly. . . . There is nothing in the bill of lading indicating that the weight was agreed upon by the master and the shipper, but the contrary. For, notwithstanding the memorandum in the margin as to the supposed or real weight of the cotton, the master, as is apparent, required the insertion at the foot of the bill, before he signed it, of the words 'contents and weight unknown,' thereby excluding any inference that the owner was to be bound by the memorandum. This memorandum is not even referred to in the body of the bill. . . . But, if otherwise, it could not vary the result. The bill of lading is a printed form filled up, and the words 'contents and weight unknown' are added at the bottom with a pen, clearly indicating an intent on the part of the master not to be bound by any supposed ascertainment of the weight at the time by the shipper. Any other construction would be in disregard of the clear import of the instrument, and unjust to the master and his owner."

[1] The Venner, 27 Fed. Rep. 523 (1885); The Stoga, 10 Benedict, 315 (1879); The Queen, 28 Fed. Rep. 755 (1886). In this case Brown, J., said that the burden of proving that the amount received was less than that stated in the margin remained on the carrier. But this hardly appears necessary to the decision. Shephard v. Naylor, 5 Gray (71 Mass.), 591 (1856). The same court gave a like construction to the words "more or less," added to the statement in the body of the bill of lading of the quantity of the goods received. Kelley v. Bowker, 11 Gray (77 Mass.), 428 (1858).

[2] Fassett v. Ruark, 3 La. Ann. 694 (1848).

The question in all these cases is really one of burden of proof, and this is often of great importance in the actual trial of causes where goods have been shipped at a distant port, and the obtaining of evidence in regard to the shipment is difficult or impossible.[1]

The presumption referred to is not artificial or arbitrary, and will always give way to any inference naturally to be derived from the appearance of the goods or package in which they are contained upon their arrival at the port of destination. If, for example, the package is in good condition, and it may reasonably be inferred from its appearance that the goods were properly packed and were in good order and fit for transportation when packed, it will be presumed as against the carrier that any injury to the contents took place during their transportation, notwithstanding the use in the bill of lading of the words "Weight, contents and value unknown."[2]

If the external covering of the goods is damaged when they are delivered, so as naturally to account for an injury to their contents, evidence of the condition of the goods at the time of shipment may be dispensed with.[3] If the bill of lading contain the clause "quantity guaranteed," the carrier is liable to make good any deficiency between the quantity he delivers and that specified in the bill of lading.[4]

Clauses in a bill of lading relating to the quantity or quality of the goods shipped are to be construed with reference to the other clauses in the same instrument, and effect, if possible, must be given to them all.[5]

---

[1] Wentworth v. Realm, 16 La. Ann. 18 (1861).

[2] English v. The Ocean Steam Navigation Co., 2 Blatch. 425 (1852); The "Adriatic," 16 Blatch. 424 (1879).

[3] The "Columbo," 3 Blatch. 521 (1856).

[4] Bissell v. Campbell, 54 N. Y. 353 (1873).

[5] Price v. Hartshorn, 44 N. Y. 94 (1870). In this case the clause was: "Damage or deficiency in quantity, if any, to be deducted from

SECTION III.

THE ACT OF GOD, PERILS OF THE SEAS, RIVERS, &C., AND OTHER CAUSES OF INJURY OCCURRING WITHOUT HUMAN INTERVENTION.

Strict as was the carrier's common law liability it did not extend so far as to render him liable for certain losses occurring strictly without human intervention, and which he could not by the use of reasonable care have foreseen. The expression " Act of God " was used to describe the causes of such loss or damage, and is still retained in bills of lading to express that idea. There are other terms, such as Perils of the Seas, Lakes, Rivers, and navigation, and inevitable accident, frequently found in bills of lading and used to express various causes of loss or injury, from responsibility for which the carrier is exempted, either by the operation of law or the express terms of the contract. In all such cases the rule is the same. The carrier is not liable for injuries or losses caused without human intervention, and which could not have been foreseen and guarded against by the use of reasonable skill and foresight.[1]

All of these terms are frequently used as synonymous

---

charges by consignees." It was held that this did not qualify the clauses excepting liability for loss or injury by perils of the sea, so as to make the carrier responsible for injury by such perils to the extent of the freight. The same rule of construction is stated in Miller *v.* Hannibal & St. Jo. R. R., quoted at length, *ante*, p. 292, note 1.

[1] Chicago B. & Q. R. Co. *v.* Manning, 37 N. W. Rep. (Nebraska), 462 (1888). For example, a sudden and unexpected rise of a river is the " Act of God," and if with reasonable diligence baggage cannot be removed from a station in time to prevent its being wet, the carrier is exonerated. Strauss *v.* Wabash, St. L. & P. R. R., 17 Fed. Rep. 209 (1883). The carrier is not bound to exercise extreme care and diligence to avert the consequences of such an accident as a land slide ; ordinary care and diligence are all that the law requires under such circumstances. Gleason *v.* Virginia Midland R. Co., 5 Mackey (D. C.), 356. So, also, loss by an unknown snag in the usual channel was termed an " Act of God." Smyrl *v.* Niolan, 2 Bailey (S. C.), 421 (1831). This might, perhaps, have been more properly termed a peril of navigation.

with the term "Act of God," and in some cases it has been expressly said that they were synonymous. But in others it is held that there are inevitable accidents which are not the "Act of God,"[1] and for which the carrier is responsible unless he has exempted himself by special contract in the bill of lading or otherwise.

To a certain extent this difference is probably not a mere difference of terminology, and those tribunals which have intimated that there are inevitable accidents or perils of navigation other than those arising from the "Act of God," would probably not hold the carrier exonerated from liability for losses or injury originating from them unless he had expressly contracted for such exemption. For it is well settled that "the causes which will excuse the owners and master for the non-delivery of the cargo must be events falling within the meaning of one of the expressions, 'Act of God' and public enemies; or they must arise from some event expressly provided for in the charter party."[2]

---

[1] Fisk v. Chapman, 2 Georgia, 349 (1847); Ala. Gt. So. R. R. v. Little, 71 Ala. 611 (1882). In Ewart v. Street, 2 Bailey (S. C.), 162 (1831), it was said the term "Act of God" seems to involve some notion of an accident from natural causes, such as storms, lightning, tempests, &c. In Packard v. Taylor, 35 Ark. 402 (1880), a distinction is made between "inevitable accident" and the "Act of God." In Fowler v. Davenport, 21 Tex. 626 (1858), it was held that "unavoidable accident" has substantially the same meaning as perils of the seas or the Act of God, and in Baxter v. Leland, 1 Abb. Adm. 348 (1848), "dangers of the seas," the "dangers of navigation," and the "perils of the seas," are considered to be equivalent terms.

In Walpole v. Bridges, 5 Blackf. (Ind.) 222 (1839), it was held that Acts of God were not merely those arising from natural causes, but that the term included all inevitable accidents. In Plaisted v. Boston & K. St. Nav. Co., 27 Me. 132 (1847), it was expressly held that the term "perils of the seas" was not synonymous with the term "Act of God." In Central Line of Boats v. Low, 50 Geo. 509 (1873), it was held that an unavoidable accident was not the same as an Act of God, but that the latter term implied *vis major*. See *post*, p. 303, n. 1.

[2] 3 Kent Com. 216. Crosby v. Fitch, 12 Conn. 410 (1848); Walpole v. Bridges, 5 Blackf. (Ind.) 222 (1839); Jones v. Pitcher, 7 Ala. O. S. 175 (1833). In Crosby v. Fitch, it was also said that the use of the exception "perils of the seas," in a bill of lading, did not vary the car-

But in general, it may be said that the ordinary risks commonly incident to the voyage are not excepted by the true meaning of these clauses. It is the duty of the carrier to provide means which shall be adequate to overcome ordinary perils, and it is only against liability for unusual dangers that the carrier is guarded by these exceptions to his liability,[1] and notwithstanding them the carrier is still bound by the obligations defined in Chapter IV.

But when the danger cannot with reasonable care be foreseen, and by the exercise of the ordinary and usual means cannot be guarded against, the carrier himself, if free from negligence, is not liable for the consequences.[2]

---

rier's liability, but that the carrier was not liable for injury caused by peril of the sea, whether expressly excepted or not.

[1] The Newark, 1 Blatch. 203 (1846); Tuckerman v. Stephens & Condit Trans. Co., 32 N. J. (Law), 320 (1867). A carrier is liable for injuries caused directly by a storm which would not have caused the injury if the vessel had been seaworthy. Packard v. Taylor, 35 Ark. 402; s. c. 37 Am. Rep. 37 (1880); The Howden, 5 Sawyer, C. C. 389 (1879); Dupont v. Vann, 19 How. (U. S.) 168 (1856).

[2] A sudden failing of the wind while a vessel is tacking near shore is a peril of the sea or an unavoidable accident, and for a loss so caused the carrier is not liable. Colt v. McMechen, 6 Johns. (N. Y.) 160 (1810).

In Colt v. McMechen, Kent, Ch. J., intimated that if the point had been made below that the ship ought not to have been so near the shore, he might have dissented.

Unknown shoals in the usual channel are perils of navigation. The Favorite, 2 Bissell, 502 (1871); Redpath v. Vaughn, 52 Barb. (N. Y.) 489 (1868); Boyce v. Welch, 5 La. Ann. 623 (1880); Hibernia Insurance Co. v. St. Louis Co., 120 U. S. 166 (1887); Turny v. Wilson, 7 Yerg. (Tenn.) 340 (1835); Strouss v. Wabash, St. L. & P. R. Co., 17 Fed. Rep. 209 (1883); Smyrl v. Niolan, 2 Bailey (S. C.), 421 (1831). And see The Portsmouth, 9 Wall. 682 (1869); Schloss v. Heriot, 14 C. B. (N. S.) 59 (1863); The Norway, 3 Moore P. C. N. S. 245, 262 (1865); Bazin v. Richardson, 20 Law Rep. 129 ; s. c. 5 Am. Law Reg. 459 (1851).

But if a vessel strike an obstruction which she might have discovered (as the masts of a sunken vessel which projected above the water), that is not an excepted peril, though they had been there but a short time. Merritt v. Earle, 29 N. Y. 115 (1864). In this case the ship which was run into had been sunk by a violent and sudden squall a day or two before. Held, this squall was not the proximate cause of the injury to the colliding vessel. See, also, Gordon v. Buchanan, 5 Yerg. (Tenn.) 71 (1833). A violent gale is a peril of the seas. Cochran v. The Cleopatra, 17 La. Ann. 270 (1865); Medina v. Hanson, Ib. 290 (1865). The freezing of fruit in the hold is an Act of God, no negligence being

If negligence, either of the carrier or his agents, has contributed to and is the immediate cause of the injury, the carrier is liable, although this negligence would not have caused the injury but for the Act of God, through tempest or otherwise.[1]

---

shown. The Alesia, 35 Fed. Rep. 531 (1888). Compare, however, cases in sect. 8, note 3, *post*.

Where the loss is caused by an earthquake and there is no evidence of negligence, the carrier is not liable. An earthquake is an Act of God. Slater *v.* So. Car. R. Co., 6 S. E. Rep. (S. C.) 936 (1888).

[1] Ewart *v.* Street, 2 Bailey (S. C.), 157 (1831); The Portsmouth, 9 Wall. 682 (1869); Schloss *v.* Heriot, 14 C. B. (N. S.) 59 (1863); Bazin *v.* Richardson, 20 Law Rep. 129; reported *sub nom.*; Bazin *v.* Steamship Co., 3 Wall. Jr. 229 (1851).

The Act of God which shook the dock from under the vessel was not the immediate cause of the damage. Packard *v.* Taylor, 35 Ark. 402 (1880). " Though the peril of the sea may be nearer in time to the disaster, the efficient cause without which it would not have occurred is regarded as the proximate cause of the loss." The Portsmouth, *supra ;* The Aline, 19 Fed. Rep. 875 (1883), and 25 Fed Rep. 562 (1885). See, also, Slocum *v.* Fairchild, 7 Hill (N. Y.), 292 (1843); aff'g s. c. 19 Wend. 329 (1838); The Invincible, 3 Sawyer, 176 (1874); At- wood *v.* Reliance Trans. Co., 9 Watts (Penn.), 87 (1839). Unauthorized stowage on deck is such negligence as will make the carrier liable if the goods are for that reason injured or jettisoned in a storm. The Rebecca, 1 Ware, 188 (1831); The Paragon, Ib. 322 (1836); Waring *v.* Morse, 7 Ala. 343 (1845); Barber *v.* Brace, 3 Conn. 9 (1819); Vernard *v.* Hudson, 3 Sumn. 405 (1838); The Peytona, 2 Curtis, 21 (1854); aff'g. s. c. Ware (2 Ed.), 541 (1854).

With this exception a loss by jettison is a loss by a peril of the sea, or as it is otherwise expressed, by the Act of God, or inevitable accident, if made necessary by a tempest. Gillett *v.* Ellis, 11 Ill. 579 (1850). So it is if made by the master when the ship is not in immediate danger, but when in his judgment, after due deliberation, it is required for the safety of those on board and of the ship, the goods being of such a character that they could not be safely jettisoned in a storm, and the necessity arising from injury to the ship caused by a previous storm. Lawrence *v.* Minturn, 17 How. U. S. 100 (1850); The Bergenseren, 36 Fed. Rep. 700 (1888).

In this case the goods had been stowed on deck by the shipper's consent.

And the carrier may contract for a right to jettison a deck load of cattle if necessary for the safety of the ship, without liability of the ship and cargo to general average. The Enrique, 5 Hughes, 275 (1881).

In Nill *v.* Sturgeon, 28 Mo. 328 (1859), it was held that the term " dangers of the river " was broader than the term " Act of God," but that it did not include such accidents as could be avoided by the exercise of skill, judgment or foresight. If, for example, the sheering of a

On the other hand, to render the carrier liable in such a case, it must appear that his negligence was the efficient or proximate cause of the injury, the *causa causans*. This principle is illustrated by two cases cited in the note.[1] In Astrup *v.* Lewey, the bottom of the vessel had been strained by overloading, and gave way in a storm which she would otherwise have been able to weather in safety. Here the negligence and not the storm was the real cause. Ships are expected to meet storms. It is only violent and unusual ones that are considered the "Act of God," for the consequences of which the carrier is not liable. In The Titania, a spare propeller which had been carefully and properly stowed broke loose in a storm and caused a leak. It was held that the carrier was not liable.

So where vermin are allowed to overrun a ship, damage caused by their gnawing or otherwise injuring the cargo cannot be attributed to the perils of the sea. The old rule was that the carrier was not liable for an injury by rats if he kept a cat on board the ship. Now it is held that the presence of the cat is not controlling. In Aymar *v.* Astor, it was said that the reason of this was because a better and more efficient method of ridding ships of rats had been discovered.[2] But if they gnaw a hole in a pipe

---

boat was caused by running too near a bar, or by any other imprudence, or by neglecting any proper precaution, or by the incompetence of the pilot, the carrier would be liable. See *ante*, p. 298.

[1] Astrup *v.* Lewey, 19 Fed. Rep. 536 (1884); The Titania, 19 Fed. Rep. 101 (1883); and see The Fern Holme, 24 Fed Rep. 502 (1885).

When goods were so placed as to be obviously in danger of fire, but were destroyed by fire caused in a manner that could not have been foreseen, it was held the negligence was too remote to be treated as the cause of the loss. Merch. Wharf Boat Ass'n. *v.* Wood, 2 So. Rep. 76 (1887); 3 So. Rep. 248 (1887).

[2] Aymar *v.* Astor, 6 Cow. (N. Y.) 266 (1826); The Carlotta, 9 Benedict, 1 (1877); The Isabella, 8 Benedict, 139 (1875); The Miletus, 5 Blatch. 335 (1866); Laveroni *v.* Drury, 8 Excheq 166; 22 L. J. (Ex.) 2 (1852); Kay *v.* Wheeler, L. R. 2 C. P. 302 (1867).

And even if the bill of lading in terms exempts the carrier from liability for "damage done by vermin," it will still be liable if it neglected

or in the side of the ship and water enter and injure the cargo, this damage is caused by a peril of the sea.[1]

So, although a collision caused by inevitable accident is a peril of the sea, yet if the cause of the collision should appear to be the negligence of the ship on which the injured cargo was stowed, the damage would not be attributed to a peril of the sea.[2] To guard against this risk it is now common to insert in bills of lading a clause that a carrier shall not be liable for injuries caused by collision. Such a clause is subject to the observations in the previous chapters as to the effect of negligence and the

---

to fumigate the ship before stowing the cargo. It appeared that this precaution would probably have prevented the damage from rats. Stevens v. Navigazione Gen. Italiana, 39 Fed. Rep. 562 (1889).

[1] Pandorf v. Hamilton, L. R. 12 App. Ca. 518 (1887); revg. s. c. 172 B. Div. 670 (1886); 34 Alb. L. J. 488.

The House of Lords put the decision on the ground stated by Lord Watson (p. 525): "The sea is the immediate cause of mischief." Lords Bramwell and Macnaghten quote with approval the definition of Lopes, L. J.: "Sea damage, occurring at sea, and nobody's fault." (Pp. 526, 530.)

The notes of both decisions in Gibson's Law Notes (vols. 5-7), incorrectly state that the Master of the Rolls dissented from the Court of Appeals.

The same rule was applied to the construction of a policy of insurance in Garrigues v. Coxe, 1 Binn. 592 (1809). Hazard's Adm. v. N. Eng. Mar. Ins. Co., 8 Pet. 557 (1834), was a case where worms in the Pacific Ocean had bored through the planking of a ship and so weakened it that it gave way when it struck a rock. The court say: "Underwriters insure against losses from extraordinary occurrences only, such as stress of weather, winds and waves, lightning, tempests, rocks, &c. These are understood to be the 'perils of the seas' referred to in the policy, and not those ordinary perils which every vessel must encounter."

[2] Marsh v. Blyth, 1 McCord (S. C.), 360 (1825); Sailing Ship Garston Co. v. Hickie, 56 L. J. (Q. B. D.) 39 (1886); Woolly v. Mitchell, 11 Q. B. Div. 47 (1883); Hayes v. Kennedy, 41 Penn. 378 (1861); Jones v. Pitcher, 3 Stew. & Port. (Ala.) 176 (1833); Whiteside v. Thurlkill, 20 Miss. 599 (1849); The New Jersey, Olc. Adm. 444 (1846). But while a collision without negligence is a peril of the sea, it is not an act of God, and, if there be no exceptions in the bill of lading, the carrier will be liable for damage caused by it. Plaisted v. Boston & K. Steam Nav. Co., 27 Me. 132 (1847).

Where an act of God caused delays, yet if this would not have happened if the carrier had kept his contract, he is not excused. Gulf, &c., R. Co. v. McCorquedale, 9 S. W. Rep. (Texas), 80 (1888).

burden of proving negligence, and need not here be further dwelt upon. Indeed, it has been held where the captain was misled by the shifting of a buoy in the channel, the cause of which was unknown, and injury to the cargo was caused thereby, that the loss was not within the exemptions of the bill of lading.[1]

If injury be done partly by the negligence of the carrier and partly by a peril of the sea, and the loss arising from each cause can be apportioned, the carrier will only be held liable for that portion of the loss occasioned by his negligence.[2]

Desertion by the seamen is not a peril of the sea, and the carrier will be liable for a loss occasioned thereby.[3]

The endeavor was at one time made to convince the Courts that loss by accidental fire was a peril of the sea, or inevitable accident, and that the carrier was not liable therefor. This was unsuccessful. It has long been well settled that the carrier is liable for injuries or losses from fire, unless it was produced by lightning or excepted in the bill of lading.[4]

---

[1] Reeves v. Waterman, 2 Spears (S. C.), 197 (1843). There were two dissenting opinions in this case, and the majority of the court base its opinion on the fact that this buoy was known to be unreliable, and there were other permanent land marks which should have been consulted.

[2] Tennessee v. Tardos, 7 La Ann. 28 (1852); Illinois Central R. R. v. Owens, 53 Ill. 391 (1870). In this case the contract expressly excepted all injuries caused by delay "except such as happened from collision." Delay ensued, caused partly by collision and negligence, and partly by extreme cold weather. It was held that the carrier was liable for the injury caused by the former and not for that caused by the latter.

[3] The Ethel, 5 Bened. 154 (1871).

[4] Providence and N. Y. S. S. Co. v. Hill Mfg. Co., 109 U. S. 578, 602 (1883); Garrison v. Memphis Ins. Co., 19 How. (U. S.) 312, 315 (1856); Airey v. Merrill, 2 Curtis (C. C.), 8 (1854); Slater v. Hayward Rubber Co., 26 Conn. 128 (1857); Parker v. Flagg, 26 Me. 181 (1846); Miller v. Steam Nav. Co., 10 N. Y. 43 (1852); Gilmore v. Carman, 1 Sme. and Marsh. (9 Miss.) 279 (1843); Forward v. Pittard, 1 T. R. 27 (1785); Hyde v. Trent and Mersey Nav. Co., 5 Ib. 389 (1793). Under

The term "inevitable accident" is not coëxtensive with the term "perils of the seas."   A carrier is not held liable for damage caused by an inevitable accident, although it be not especially excepted in the bill of lading.[1] But this must be understood with the same qualification that it must be such an inevitable accident as comes under the definition of an act of God.[2]

The construction to be given to these exempting clauses in a bill of lading may be modified by proof of the attendant circumstances and by a due regard to the other clauses of the contract.   For example, it was held that the sinking of a wharf boat on which goods were placed, awaiting the arrival of a boat on which they were to be transported, was not loss or damage "on the lakes or rivers" within the meaning of the bill of lading.   This

---

a Louisiana statute exempting carriers from the consequences of "accidents or uncontrollable forces," it has, however, been held that a fire without his fault was an exempted "accident."   Hunt *v.* Morris, 6 Mart. (La.) 676 (1819).

[1] Morrison *v.* Davis, 20 Penn. St. 171 (1872).   In this case the shipper was allowed to introduce advertisements and circulars issued by the carrier to show that it was the intention of the parties that the carrier should be liable even for inevitable accidents.   But see Chap. XII, sect. 3, *ante*, p. 263.

An express agreement of a carrier to become liable for such accidents would be valid.   Gaither *v.* Barnet, 2 Brev. (S. C.) 488 (1811).

But an agreement to deliver absolute in its terms is not so construed. Price *v.* Hartshorn, 44 N. Y. 94 (1870); affg. s. c. 44 Barb. 655 (1865); see, also, N. Y. Cent. R. R. *v.* Standard Oil Co., 87 N. Y. 486 (1882).

If, however, the agreement was to deliver within a certain time and extra freight was paid, the obligation would then become absolute. Harmony *v.* Bingham, 12 N. Y. 99 (1854); affg. s. c. 1 Duer, 209 (1852); and see Cowley *v.* Davidson, 13 Minn. 92 (1868).

And though a sudden and violent flood is an act of God, yet if there was opportunity to remove the goods and avoid damage, the carrier is liable.   Read *v.* Spaulding, 5 Bosw. (N. Y.) 395 (1859); Wallace *v.* Clayton, 42 Ga. 443 (1871).   And where the carrier unduly delayed in forwarding goods subsequently frozen in his station he is not discharged.   Curtis *v.* Chicago & N. W. R. R., 18 Wis. 312 (1864).

[2] *Ante,* p. 296, n. 1.   The cases cited in note 1, p. 303, are illustrations of the text to that note.

wharf boat was used as a warehouse by the railroad company, and the Court held that "on the rivers" meant in the navigation of the rivers.[1]

The cases which have already been cited in this section, as well as some others which follow, show that it is sometimes very difficult to properly apply the maxim "*causa proxima non remota spectatur*" in the determination of cases where negligence and other causes, such as storms and winds, combine to produce damage. In suits between the carrier and the underwriter, the courts have adhered strictly to the rule. It is true that the underwriter does not ordinarily insure against the gross negligence of the carrier. But still he is an insurer, and courts have often held that a disaster was caused by one of the perils insured against on the ground that this was the immediate cause (*causa proxima*) of the loss, when, if the action had been upon the bill of lading and between the shipper and carrier, it would have been held that the negligence of the carrier was the efficient cause (*causa causans*).[2]

---

[1] St. Louis & S. E. R. Co. *v.* Smuck, 49 Ind. 302 (1874); Bazin *v.* Steamship Co., 3 Wall. J. 229 (1857); Mahone *v.* Olive Branch, 18 La. Ann. 107 (1866).

[2] General Mutual Insurance Co. *v.* Sherwood, 14 How. (U. S.) 351, 366 (1852); Fireman's Insurance Co. *v.* Powell, 13 B. Munroe (Ky.), 311 (1852); Hagar *v.* New England Ins. Co., 59 Me. 460 (1871); Georgia Insurance Co. *v.* Dawson, 2 Gill (Md.), 365 (1844); Parkhurst *v.* Gloucester Insurance Co., 100 Mass. 301 (1868); Copeland *v.* New England Insurance Co., 2 Metc. (Mass.) 432 (1841); Matthews *v.* Howard Ins. Co., 11 N. Y. 9 (1854); rev'g. s. c. 13 Barb. (N. Y.) 234 (1852); Davidson *v.* Burnand, L. R. 4 C. P. 117 (1868); The Warkworth, L. R. 9 Prob. Div. 145; s. c. 51 Law T. Rep. (N. S.) 558 (1884). This was a case where the immediate cause of a collision was the way one of the ships was steered. This was due, not to the negligence of the master, but to a defect in the steering gear. It was not shown how this defect was caused, but Sir Jas. Hannen held the ship liable. Of this Brett, M. R., says (p. 147): "It was the act of a person for whose care and skill the owner was responsible, and it has been held that the negligence was the *causa causans* of the collision, though the *causa proxima* was the inability of the captain to avoid the other ship, and that inability was the consequence of the negligence of the owner's servants." This quo-

The maxim is often quoted in decisions on bills of lading, but the distinction just referred to has not always been observed.[1]   In The Portsmouth it was said that "though the peril of the sea may be nearer in time to the disaster the *efficient* cause, without which the peril would not have happened, is regarded as the proximate cause ; and there is, perhaps, greater reason for applying the rule to contracts of common carriers than policies of insurance, for, in general, negligence of the insured does not relieve the insurer."   This is perhaps the safe rule, and the court should always look at the real cause of the injury and not speculate or refine as to its ultimate cause.

For example, if the voyage is prolonged by the perils of the seas, or the vessel is obliged by such perils to put into port in distress, the carrier will not be responsible for injury to cargo, perishable in its nature, caused by delay.[2]

---

tation from the official report is condensed from the report in Law Times, p. 559. In Hamilton *v.* Pandorf, 12 App. Co. 518 (1887), the Court criticises the attempt to give to words in a bill of lading a meaning different from that of the same words in a policy of insurance.

[1] The Portsmouth, 9 Wall. 685 (1869); The Titania, 19 Fed. Rep. 104 (1883); Jones *v.* Pitcher, 7 Ala. (O. S.) 180 (1833); Packard *v.* Taylor, 35 Ark. 411 (1880); Ewart *v.* Street, 2 Bailey (S. C.), 162 (1831).

[2] The Collemberg, 1 Black (U. S.), 170 (1861); The Gentleman, Olc. Adm., 110 (1845). In such case the carrier is not liable, even if it appear that by the exercise of extraordinary care the injury might have been averted, if the master used his best judgment. The Collemberg, *ante.* But see Sherman *v.* Inman Steamship Co., 26 Hun, 107 (1882), and cases cited note 1, p. 311, *post.* If the necessity for the deviation had been caused by an unseaworthy vessel or defective supplies, and the weather had really not been unusually severe, or worse than might have been expected at the time of the year, the carrier will be liable. Marckwald *v.* Oceanic Steam Nav. Co., 11 Hun, 462 (1877). When an injury to a canal boat by sudden storm and flood might have been avoided but for the lameness of the horse drawing it, held that the carrier would not be liable unless he had expressly agreed to insure. Morrison *v.* Davis, 20 Penn. St. 171 (1852). When a loss within the exception of the contract is occasioned by previous neglect of the carrier, without which it would not have happened, he is not excused. If such a loss is unavoidably caused by the excusable delay of the carrier he will not be

So in Astrup *v.* Lewy,[1] the Court was satisfied that the storm was not of sufficient severity to have produced the injury, and that this was really caused by over-loading. It therefore held that the real or proximate cause was the over-loading. But whenever the decision of that question depends upon evidence as to the violence of the wind, and the relative probability of whether a disaster is caused by a storm of unusual violence or by bad stowage, the decision might well be different in actions between different parties between whom the presumptions and burden of proof might be different.

In General Mutual Ins. Co. *v.* Sherwood,[2] the carrier sought to recover from the underwriter damages he had to pay another vessel, for injuries to her caused by collision with his own ship. It was held that the fact that he had to pay these damages was conclusive evidence that his negligence was the proximate cause of the collision. In fact, he was obliged to aver this in his pleading.[3]

So when bad weather induces the stranding of a vessel it is ordinarily a peril of the sea, but not if it was to be foreseen and might have been avoided.[4]

These cases, when taken in connection with what has heretofore been said, seem to supply an explanation of

---

liable. But if although the delay be the proximate cause of the loss, the real and efficient cause be the negligence of the carrier, he is not excused. Bills *v.* N. Y. Central R. R., 84 N. Y. 5 (1881). It will readily be seen how much might, in such a case, depend upon which side is the burden of proof.

[1] 19 Fed Rep. 536 (1884).

[2] 14 How. (U. S.) 351 (1852).

[3] Matthews *v.* Howard Ins. Co., 11 N. Y. 9 (1854), is a similar case.

[4] The Costa Rica, 3 Sawyer, 540 (1875). In this case perils of the sea were excepted in the bill of lading. The Portsmouth, 9 Wall. 685 (1869); The Mohler, 21 Wall. 233 (1874); The Rocket, 1 Bissell, 354 (1860); Richards *v.* Gilbert, 5 Day (Conn.), 415 (1813). In Nills *v.* Mackill, 36 Fed. Rep. 702 (1888), coal dust sifting through seams in a bulkhead was held not ordinarily to be a peril of the sea, but it was said if the seams had been opened by a storm it might be.

many others where the maxim is seemingly not applied. We have seen that the ordinary perils of navigation are not regarded as included in the term "Act of God," but only such as cannot with the exercise of ordinary foresight and skill in navigation be guarded against. A gale of wind may be moderate or it may be violent. In the former case damage resulting from it may be said to be caused by a peril of the sea, but cannot be regarded as an Act of God. Thus, it has been held that if a flaw of wind which capsizes a boat is unusual and not to be expected and the boat is not over-loaded, the loss can justly be said to be caused by an "Act of God." But the court said it would be otherwise if such flaws were of common occurrence.[1]

It is the carrier's duty, as has been shown, to take all reasonable and prudent precautions to guard against the perils incident to the transportation, either of passengers or freight. If notwithstanding the use of such precautions the injury is caused to his vessel or other vehicle of transportation by one of the excepted perils, he is bound to use reasonable diligence to extricate his passengers and cargo from the consequences of the disaster. If he fail to do so, he is not entitled to the benefit of the exemption provided for by his bill of lading.[2]

---

[1] Spencer v. Dagget, 2 Vt. 92 (1829); S. P. Jones v. Pitcher, 7 Ala. (O. S.) 135 (1833).

[2] Railroad Co. v. Varnell, 98 U. S. 479 (1878); Propeller Niagara v. Cordes, 21 How. U. S. 7 (1858); Strouss v. Wabash, St. L. & P. R. Co., 17 Fed. Rep. 209 (1883); The Nith, 36 Fed. Rep. 86 (1888); The Ocean Wave, 3 Bissell, 317 (1872); King v. Shepard, 3 Story, 349 (1844); Steamboat Co. v. Bason, Harper (S. C.), 262 (1824); Bird v. Cromwell, 1 Missouri, 81 (1821); Ewart v. Street, 2 Bailey (S. C.), 157 (1831).

The Portsmouth, 2 Bissell, 59 (1868). At p. 61, Drummond, J., says : "After the vessel is stranded the master is bound to take all possible care of the cargo." This was affirmed, 9 Wall. 682 (1869). At p. 687, the Court say : "The conduct of the master after the vessel was stranded was entirely unjustifiable. It was his duty even then to take all possible care of the cargo. He was bound to the utmost exertion to save it. Losses arising from dangers of navigation, within the meaning of the exception in the bill of lading, are such only as happen in spite

There are perils of inland navigation which never entered into the consideration of navigators by sea. Among these are floods and low water, which equally embarrass the steamboats of the west. It was held in one case that low water was not a peril of navigation.[1]

But this decision is hardly sustainable on principle. Low water is a danger incident to transportation by river just as much as stranding is to carriage by sea. It was very properly held in another case that a carrier who had agreed to transport goods by river, without stipulating for any particular boat, had no right to wait two months till the river rose high enough to float his own boat, but was bound to forward the goods by a boat of lighter draft if he could, and consequently that low water under such circumstances was not a peril of navigation.[2]

While the weight of authority is that interruption of navigation by low water will excuse delay on the part of the carrier,[3] it does not follow that it will excuse absolute

---

of the best human exertions, which cannot be prevented by human skill and prudence." In this case the steamer ran aground, no lighter was sent for and no effort made to save the cargo, but the salt in question was jettisoned. The steamer was held liable.

It was, however, held in one case that where wheat was wetted by inevitable accident, the carrier was not liable for the loss, although he might have dried it. The Lynx v. King, 12 Missouri, 272 (1848). The Court in this case state the law as in the text, but as drying the wheat would have involved a suspension of the voyage and possible injury to other cargo, it was held better judgment for the captain to proceed without drying it.

[1] Cowley v. Davidson, 13 Minn. 92 (1868). In Chicago, B. & Q. R. Co. v. Manning, 37 N. W. Rep. (Nebraska), 462 (1888), it was held that high water was not an excuse for delay unless it appeared that it could not have been anticipated and avoided. Usually the burden would be on the plaintiff to show that the injury could have been avoided, although its cause was a peril excepted by the bill of lading. See Chap. XII, p. 257, notes 2, 3, ante.

[2] Collier v. Swinney, 16 Missouri, 484 (1852).

In Eveleigh v. Sylvester, 2 Brev. (S. C.) 178 (1807), a steamer struck an unknown snag, and it was held an unavoidable peril and the carrier not liable.

[3] Parsons v. Hardy, 14 Wend. 215 (1835); Bonner v. Merch. Steamboat Co., 1 Jones (Law) (N. C.), 211 (1853). But low water does not

failure to deliver the goods. When, therefore, the carrier stored the goods in a warehouse pending such delay and they were burned in the warehouse, he was held liable. The immediate cause of the injury was the fire, not the low water, and this fire occurred while his liability as carrier continued.[1]

The general rule on this subject is that a temporary obstruction to navigation, even if it compels the carrier to unload the goods, will not excuse him from carrying the goods to their destination as soon as navigation is resumed.[2]

The carrier is not liable for injury caused by a sudden and violent flood.[3]

Interruption to navigation by frost or ice is an Act of God.[4]

---

excuse delay where the carrier has made an express contract to deliver in a specified time. Cowley v. Davidson, 13 Minn. 92 (1868). See Harmony v. Bingham, 12 N. Y. 99 (1854). Even if the carrier in such contract excepts unavoidable delay, he will not be excused if he knew of the particular cause of delay at the time of his making the contract. Place v. Union Exp. Co., 2 Hilt. (N. Y.) 19 (1858).

[1] Cox v. Peterson, 30 Ala. 608 (1857).

[2] The Nathaniel Hooper, 3 Sumner, 543 (1839); Lowe v. Moss, 12 Ill. 477 (1851). See *ante*, p. 308, n. 3.

But if the obstacle to navigation be permanent it discharges the carrier from obligation to transport the goods to their destination. He must in such case deliver them to the owner. Bork v. Norton, 2 McLean, 422 (1841).

[3] Davis v. Wabash & St. Louis R. R., 89 Mo. 340 (1886). The violence of a cross current, due to the great height of water prevailing at the time, is a danger of river navigation. The Farragut, 10 Wall. 334, 339 (1870).

[4] West v. The Berlin, 3 Iowa, 532 (1856); Bork v. Norton, 2 McLean, 422 (1841).

In West v. The Berlin, it was said that in case the voyage was stopped for the season the master might store the goods for the winter. But there was evidence of a parol agreement that he should do so. In Bork v. Norton it is intimated that it might be his duty to forward by land. All these cases hold that if the consignee takes the goods at the point of stoppage, the carrier can recover pro rata freight. In the Berlin case, also, it was held the carrier was bound to provide a suitable boat, though the shipper knew the character of the one on which the goods were to be shipped. While in Bell v. Read, 4 Binn. (Penn.) 127

There are certain causes of injury, such as leakage, dampness, and the like, which are often especially excepted in bills of lading. But it is immaterial whether or not these are specifically excepted, if the efficient cause of damage be the "Act of God." In such case the carrier is not liable.[1] In one case it was held that such exemptions do not enlarge the shipper's liability for freight, and that, therefore, the carrier could not recover freight for goods rightfully jettisoned.[2] In the Nathaniel Hooper,[3] however, the Court said of cargo jettisoned, that it was "a case of general average to be borne by the ship, freight and cargo ultimately saved, and, . . . of course, the entire freight of the cargo jettisoned is to be added to the loss and allowed to the ship owner."

The explosion of a boiler on a steamboat is not a peril of navigation.[4]

In the cases that have been considered in this chapter, the weight to be given to the judgment of the master of a ship in time of peril or emergency has been frequently discussed. It is plain that he is not bound to decide upon and adopt a course which subsequent events will show to have been the best that could have been adopted. The courts will not subject the carrier or the master employed by it to any such rigorous rule. It frequently happens that the course which the master's judgment, under the circumstances as they appear at the time, indicates to be

---

(1810), it was said that to be seaworthy a vessel need only be fit for the service she undertakes.

[1] 1,200 Pipes, 5 Bened. 402 (1871).

[2] The Cuba, 3 Ware, 360 (1860).

In this case, also, certain casks were stove in during a storm and their contents partially wasted. The carrier claimed full freight but the court only allowed freight on the portion delivered.

[3] 3 Sumner, 543 (1839).

[4] Bulkley v. Naumkeag Steam Cotton Co., 24 How. (U. S.) 386 (1860); aff'g The Edwin, 1 Sprague, 477 (1859); The Mohawk, 8 Wall. 162 (1868); McCall v. Brock, 5 Strob. (S. C.) 119 (1850).

the most prudent and expedient is shown by subsequent occurrences to have been unwise. But if the facts as they appear at the time are such as to lead an experienced and intelligent navigator to conclude that a particular course is the wisest one to adopt, the carrier will not be liable, although it should subsequently appear that a different one would have been the course of safety.[1]

It is the duty of the master in cases of emergency to consider first the safety of life, and after that the preservation of property.[2]

SECTION IV.

PUBLIC ENEMY, AND CASES OF VIS MAJOR, INCLUDING IN THE LATTER THE PUBLIC AUTHORITIES, STRIKES, MOBS PIRATES, ROBBERS AND THIEVES.

The common law liabilities of carriers did not extend to losses caused by the acts of the public enemy. But the construction to be given to these words has in recent years been much considered, under circumstances to which the rule as originally laid down had never been applied. The course of decisions on this subject is an apt illustration of the flexibility of the common law.

Some of these cases arose at the outbreak of the war on the part of the Southern States. In one case, goods which had been received in New York April 10, 1861, to be trans-

---

[1] Propeller Niagara v. Cordes, 21 How. (U. S.) 7 (1858); The Portsmouth, 2 Bissell, 56 (1868); Lawrence v. Minturn, 17 How. (U. S.) 100 (1854). But in an action for subtraction of freight, where the vessel was originally delayed by negligence and charged high rates of freight in consideration of meeting boisterous fall weather, an error in judgment of the master in laying up for the winter when unnecessary, was held to prevent the recovery of more than the spring rates. There is, however, an obvious difference between actions to recover freight which had not been earned and actions for loss and injuries. Holland v. 725 tons of Coal, 36 Fed. Rep. 784 (1888). See *post*, p. 314, n. 1.

[2] Sherman v. The Inman S. S. Co., 26 Hun, 107 (1881); Turner v. Protection Ins. Co., 25 Maine, 515 (1846).

ported to Rome, in Georgia, did not reach Savannah until the last of April, where they were seized by an officer of the Confederate Government, placed in a bonded warehouse, and subsequently, after notice to the consignee, sold for failure to pay duties imposed upon them by that Government. It was held that under such circumstances the carrier was not liable, but that it had been deprived of them by an act of the public enemy.[1]

A band of marauding Indians are "public enemies," and the carrier is not liable for goods forcibly taken by them.[2]

In analogy to this rule it has been held that the carrier is not liable for not delivering goods at the pier, when such

---

[1] Hubbard *v.* Harnden Ex. Co., 10 R. I. 244 (1872). This case was decided on the authority of The Protector, 12 Wall. 700 (1871), in which it was held that the insurgents in the Southern States were public enemies at least from the time of the proclamation declaring a blockade. To the same effect are Lewis *v.* Ludwick, 6 Coldw. (Tenn.) 368 (1869); Bland *v.* Adams Ex. Co., 1 Duval (Ky.), 232 (1864).

The converse was held in Southern Ex. Co. *v.* Womack, 1 Heisk. (Tenn.) 256 (1870). In this case the goods were taken by United States troops from a Confederate carrier, and the carrier was exonerated on the ground that they were taken by the public enemy. McCranie *v.* Wood, 24 La. Ann. 406 (1872).

In Caldwell *v.* Southern Ex. Co., 1 Flipp, 85 (1866), a carrier operating within the Confederate lines claimed that he was not liable for a seizure by United States troops. The point was not decided.

In Gage *v.* Tirrell, 91 Mass. 299 (1864), the question was raised whether Confederate cruisers were public enemies. The Court say: "If they can be regarded as agents of a de facto government engaged in an actually existing war with the U. S., then the loss happened in consequence of a seizure by a public enemy." "If not they are pirates, and pirates are perils of the seas *within the exception of the bill of lading*. *Ib.* 308, 309. In Dole *v.* N. E. Ins. Co., 88 Mass. 373 (1863), which was an action on a policy of insurance against piracy which excepted "capture," it was held that Confederates were not pirates, but public enemies."

Where goods were seized or destroyed by Confederate troops, within the Confederate lines, it was held that the carrier was not liable, although the Court declined to hold that it was the act of the public enemy. It was said to be analogous to the case of goods taken from the carrier by attachment. Nashville & C. R. R. *v.* Estes, 10 Lea (Tenn.), 749 (1882).

[2] Holladay *v.* Kennard, 12 Wall. 254 (1870).

delivery was prevented by quarantine regulations at the port of delivery.[1] But on the other hand it has been held that if there be an express covenant to take on board cargo at a foreign port, the quarantine regulations of that port, even though they render the shipment unlawful, constitute no defense to the carrier in an action upon the covenant.[2] And the unlawful act of an officer of the carrier's own government constitutes no defense to the carrier, for a failure to deliver the goods, or for delay in their delivery.[3]

We have seen in the previous section that although a carrier is not ordinarily liable for losses occurring by the Act of God, he may by special contract make himself so. He may in like manner make himself liable by express contract for acts of the public enemy. Such a contract should, however, be explicit, and is not to be inferred from an agreement to deliver goods within a specified time. A contract of this latter description does not of itself imply liability for losses from the public enemy.[4]

---

[1] Bradstreet v. Heron, 1 Abb. Adm. 209 (1848). But in this case the cargo was placed on board the consignee's lighters. In Spence v. Chadwick, 10 Qu. B. 517 (1847); a different rule was applied to the case of a seizure of goods, pursuant to the Spanish law. See cases cited in the following note.

[2] Barker v. Hodgson, 3 Maule & Sel. 267 (1815). It was admitted in this case that if the performance of the covenant had become unlawful by the law of England, the carrier would have been discharged from liability. The Court does not advert to the rule that the law of the place of performance should govern. See this whole subject treated in Chap. VIII. In Hill v. Idle, 4 Campb. 328 (1815), the rule stated in the text was applied to the case of a consignee, and it was held that he was bound to remove the goods within a reasonable time and was liable in damages if he did not do so, although the delay was caused by a government regulation. See, also, Rowland v. Miln, 2 Hilt. 150 (1858). Hedley v. Clark, 8 Term. Rep. 259 (1799).

[3] Evans v. Hutton, 4 Mann. & G. 963 (1842) ; Gosling v. Higgins, 1 Campb. 451 (1808); Rowland v. Miln, 2 Hilt. 150 (1858); Seligman v. Armijo, 1 New Mexico, 462 (1870). See Porcher v. Northeastern R. R. 14 Rich. Law (S. C.), 101 (1867). See *post*, p. 316.

[4] Strohn v. Detroit &. M. R. R., 23 Wis. 131 (1868); *Ante*, p. 303, n. 1. A case arose in Illinois of a shipment over a railroad of which the

The rule as to loss or damage resulting partly from the carrier's negligence and partly from a cause which is classed as an "Act of God" was discussed in the last section. The same considerations apply to the acts of public enemies. The carrier is bound to use due precaution against capture and due diligence to rescue property that has been captured. Although it is not an insurer against such losses, it is still a bailee and bound to ordinary and reasonable care. In a case where property in the carrier's hands was seized by hostile troops, the Court held that it should have used the same diligence to remove the property of the shipper that it used in regard to its own.[1]

Some of the most interesting occasions for the application of the rule under consideration in this section have arisen in the case of strikes by the workmen and employes of railroad companies, and violence and intimidation by the strikers, with a view of preventing the carrier from employing new agents or preventing those who did not strike and who were ready and willing to work from working. After considerable discussion the courts have held that a carrier under such circumstances is not liable

---

United States authorities had, under the law, assumed military possession ; the carrier continuing to operate it under the direction of the military. It was held that the carrier was not liable for a refusal to carry, but that if it received goods and issued its bills of lading for them without exception or limitation, it would be liable as a common carrier. Phelps v. Illinois Central R. R., 94 Ill. 556 (1880). On a different state of facts the Appellate court had previously decided this case differently, but the doctrine laid down was the same in both decisions. s. c. 4 Brad. 247 (1879).

[1] Caldwell v. So. Ex. Co. (W. Dist. Tenn.) 1 Flipp. 85 (1866). So where a vessel was captured by a Confederate cruiser, but the captain was allowed to remove the personal effects of the passengers. In some unexplained way he lost the baggage of one of them. Held that the carrier was liable. Spaids v. N. Y. Mail S. S. Co., 3 Daly, 143 (1869). So it is held to be the duty of the captain of a captured vessel to do what he can in the prize court to save neutral property from condemnation. But if the captain innocently make a mistake in the course of the proceeding the carrier will not be held liable. Cheviot v. Brooks, 1 Johns. 369 (1806). See ante, p. 311, n. 1.

for delays caused by the violent acts of persons not in its
employ, although just previously they had been.[1]

At first sight these cases seem to be an exception to
the rule that mere mobs, riots or insurrections are not acts
of public enemies, but it is believed that they stand on a
different footing. The carrier's obligation is merely to
deliver within a reasonable time, and this does not mean
what, under usual circumstances, would be reasonable
time. The actual circumstances must all be considered.
It follows that delay beyond schedule time (even when
owing to the perishable character of the goods they are
injured thereby) is excused more readily than an absolute loss of or injury to goods in which delay is not a
factor.[2]

---

[1] International & G. N. R. Co. v. Tisdale, 11 S. W. Rep. (Texas),
900 (1889); Haas v. Kansas City, Ft. S. & G. R. Co., 7 S. E. Rep. (Ga.)
629 (1888); Little v. Fargo, 43 Hun (N. Y.), 233 (1887); Geismer v.
Lake Shore & Mich. Southern R. Co., 102 N. Y. 563 (1886); rv'g s. c.
34 Hun, 50 (1884). It was contended in this case that as the strike was
organized while the strikers were in the employ of the carrier, the latter
was liable for any consequences flowing therefrom, but the Court held
that this was a matter outside of their employment, and did not render
the carrier liable, and the real cause of the delay was the unlawful conduct and violence of the strikers after they left the carrier's employ.

In Lake Shore & M. S. R. Co. v. Bennett, 89 Ind. 457 (1883), the
shipper claimed that the real cause of the delay was the act of the carrier in reducing the wages of its employes, and insisting upon maintaining such reduction. This contention was overruled by the Court, and
the carrier was held not to be liable for delay in delivering according
to the agreement, which was caused by the strike.

In Indianapolis & St. L. R. R. v. Jungten, 10 Ill. App. 295
(1881), the Court said that the carrier would be liable for the delay
caused by the refusal of its employes to do their duty, but not for delay caused by the violence of those who were no longer in its employ,
provided it was diligent to secure the safety of property in the course of
transportation.

It was, however, held in White v. Missouri Pacific R. Co., 19 Mo.
App. 400 (1885), that a strike of railway employes did not excuse a
carrier for its total failure to transport goods according to its agreement.
The Court put the decision on the ground that the agreement was absolute, and that strikes were not excepted. See ante, p. 303, n. 1.

[2] When there was a special contract that the carrier should not be
liable for losses by delay, death of live stock during a delay caused
by a riot is not a loss for which the carrier is liable. The Court add,

But mere refusal of the carrier's men to work, without opposition to running of trains, will not excuse a carrier even in delay, and though he use diligence in trying to get other men.[1]

The better opinion is that a carrier who is obliged to and does deliver goods to the lawful authorities of the country where the goods are, either in transit, or awaiting delivery, or who fails to carry them, owing to the lawful order of the Court having jurisdiction of the subject matter, is not liable to the shipper.[2]

" Indeed the strict liability of common carriers, where they are without fault or negligence, does not seem to extend to losses from delay in transporting live stock and perishable property, though such delays are not caused by the act of God or the public enemies." Bartlett *v.* Pittsburgh, C. & St. L. R. Co., 94 Ind. 281; s. c. 18 Am. & Eng. R. R. Cas. 549 (1883). See *ante*, p. 105.

The same principle under similar circumstances was held in Pittsburgh, C. & St. L. R. Co. *v.* Hollowell, 65 Ind. 193 (1879), where it was expressly said, " Rioters are not public enemies." The Court say : " To make a public enemy, the government of a foreign country must be at war with the United States."

[1] Pittsburgh, Ft. W. & C. R. R. *v.* Hazen, 84 Ill. 36 (1876); Blackstock *v.* Erie R. R., 20 N. Y. 48 (1859). This case is cited approvingly in Geismer *v.* L. S. & M. S. R. Co., 102 N. Y. 563 (1886); *ante*, p. 315, n. 1. Compare Haas *v.* Kansas City R. Co., 7 S. E. Rep. (Ga.) 629 (1888).

[2] Stiles *v.* Davis, 1 Black. 101 (1861); Wells *v.* Maine S. S. Co., 1 Cliff, 232 (1874). This latter case was an action to recover for liquor taken out of the carrier's custody by the authorities of Maine, acting under the Maine liquor law. Bliven *v.* Hudson R. R. R., 36 N. Y. 405 (1867). The latter case and Stiles *v.* Davis were cases of goods taken from the carrier by the Sheriff upon a writ of attachment. In Post *v.* Koch, 30 Fed. Rep. 208 (1886), the carrier was prevented from transporting the goods, by an injunction, and this was held to relieve him from liability. Unless the carrier has issued an assignable bill of lading, the shipper has a right of stoppage in transitu, and if the carrier deliver to him it is immaterial that he exercise this power wrongfully. The Vidette, 34 Fed. Rep. 397 (1888). See *ante*, p. 313.

In Cook *v.* Holt, 48 N. Y. 275 (1872), the rule stated in the text was applied to the case of an ordinary bailment. It would have been otherwise had the sheriff merely levied an attachment, but not taken possession of the goods. Rogers *v.* Webb, 34 N. Y. 463 (1865). The true remedy of the carrier in all these cases of conflicting claims is by interpleader. 2 Story Eq. §§ 814. 817, a, b; City Bank of N. Y. *v.* Skelton, 2 Blatch. 14 (1846); German Ex. Bk. *v.* Commrs. Excise, 6

But in Massachusetts it has been held otherwise.[1]

The Court distinguishes the case from some of those just cited by drawing attention to the form of the action. In Stiles *v.* Davis, the action was in trover; whereas the Edwards case was an action upon contract. The Massachusetts Court admitted that the seizure of the goods by the sheriff was not a conversion by the carrier, but held that it was liable upon its contract for its failure to deliver them. The injustice and danger of making the carrier liable for his obedience to legal process are so obvious that it seems probable that most courts would follow the decisions cited under note 2 (p. 316), and that the form of action would be held, in this particular, to be immaterial.

It is usual in bills of lading to except loss " by pirates." Such losses now are rare, but there was a time when they were common, and when this exception was important. It seems clear that at common law a loss by pirates was not considered to be a loss by the "public enemy." Lord Holt says: " Though the force be never so great, as if an irresistible multitude should rob him, yet he is chargeable."[2] It has been in some cases maintained that a loss by

---

Abb. N. C. (N. Y.) 394 (1879); Atkinson *v.* Marks, 1 Cowen, 691 (1823); Lowe *v.* Richardson, 3 Madd. Ch. 277 (1818).

[1] Edwards *v.* White Line Co., 104 Mass. 163 (1873). In French *v.* Star Union Co., 134 Mass. 288 (1883), the goods were not attached until after the transit had terminated, and they had been placed in the carrier's warehouse, at which time, according to the Massachusetts rule, his liability as carrier had terminated.

[2] Coggs *v.* Bernard, 2 Ld. Raym. 911 (1702). In the note to this case in 1 Smith L. C. (9 Am. Ed.) 367, the editor says: " By public enemies we mean those with whom the government is at open war, . . but the violence of mobs, rioters, insurgents, constitutes no exception. Pirates come within the exception." But the authority cited does not sustain this proposition; nor does the authority cited to the same effect in Story on Bailments, sect. 526. Barclay *v.* Gana, 3 Doug. 389 (1784), holds that a carrier is liable for a loss by pirates, if it be not specially excepted in the bill of lading. In The Belfast *v.* Boon, 41 Ala. 65 (1867), the same was held of a robbery of freight on an inland river, by a body of armed men, a crime which had been made piracy by Act of Congress. The Court assume, without citing authority, that the carrier would not be liable for a loss by piracy on the high seas.

pirates might justly be said to be a loss from " perils of the seas." [1]

In any event, if there be reason to apprehend danger from violence the carrier is bound to take reasonable precautions to guard against it, and if he fail to do so, he is liable to the shipper, whether or not the violence be that of the public enemy.[2]

The words in a bill of lading—"loss by robbers,"—imply loss by violence, as distinguished from secret theft.[3]

In a later English case it was held that the words "loss by thieves" also meant loss by violence, the *latrocinium* of the civil law, as distinguished from *furtum*.[4] But it is clearly pointed out by the New York Court of Appeals in The Spinetti case [5] that the construction of like words in policies of insurance, such as the ones stated in this English decision, and which words were adopted from some of the text writers, was based on "a want of attention to the ground upon which, in earlier times, a loss by theft was not deemed covered by insurance, while a loss by piracy or robbery was." This construction was never adopted in New York.[6] In that State the words thieves, or theft, are interpreted by the Court according to their ordinary meaning. But in Tennessee it is held otherwise and the English rule is adopted.[7]

The exception of "loss by robbers" does not apply to

---

[1] Byles, J., in Russell *v.* Niemann, 17 Comm. B. (N. S.) 175 (1864); 3 Kent. Comm. 216; McArthur *v.* Sears, 21 Wend. 190 (1839).

[2] Holladay *v.* Kennard, 12 Wall. 254 (1870).

[3] Rothschild *v.* Royal Mail S. S. Co., 7 Excheq. 734 (1852).

[4] Taylor *v.* Liverpool S. S. Co., L. R. 9 Q. B. 546 (1874). The Court said the word was ambiguous and must be interpreted in favor of the shipper.

[5] Spinetti *v.* Atlas S. S. Co., 80 N. Y. 71 (1880).

[6] Am. Ins. Co. *v.* Bryan, 26 Wend. 563 (1841); aff'g s. c. 1 Hill. 25 (1841); Atlantic Ins. Co. *v.* Storrow, 5 Paige, 285 (1835).

[7] Marshall *v.* Ins. Co., 1 Humph. (Tenn.) 99 (1839).

the case of a loss which would not have happened but for the negligence of the master.[1]

The general question of the validity of contracts between the carrier and the shipper, purporting to exempt the former from liability for the negligence of his servants, has been fully considered in Chapter IV. It has there been shown that in the Federal Courts and in many of the State Courts, such contracts are held to be invalid. It was for a time contended that the decisions there cited were applicable only to contracts for transportation by land, or at most upon inland waters, and not to contracts for transportation upon the high seas. But in the Federal Courts it is now settled that no such distinction exists, and that clauses in marine bills of lading, purporting to exempt the carrier from liability for negligence of its servants, are as much against public policy and void as like clauses contained in contracts for transportation by land.[2]

The Montana was argued not only by counsel for the immediate parties to the record, but by counsel representing other parties interested in the question, and it hardly seems appropriate to repeat here the various arguments used and authorities cited on one side or the other of the case. But it will be observed that this case, like the other Federal decisions cited in Chapter IV, section 2, relate only to clauses limiting liability for negligence, and not

---

[1] The Saratoga, 20 Fed. Rep. 869 (1884); Tarbell *v.* Royal Exchange Shipping Co., 110 N. Y. 170 (1888).

[2] The Montana; Phenix Ins. Co. *v.* Liverpool & G. W. S. S. Co., 129 U. S. (1889); aff'g 22 Blatch. 393 (1884); s. c. 22 Fed. Rep. 715 (1884); aff'g s. c. 17 *Ibid*, 377 (1883); The Saratoga, 20 Fed. Rep. 869 (1884); The Brantford City, 29 Fed. Rep. 373 (1887); The Powhattan, 5 Fed. Rep. 375 (1880); rev'd on another point, 12 Fed. Rep. 880 (1882).

to those limiting the carrier's liability for wilful torts. The technical expression for such torts, when committed at sea or on shipboard, is "barratry of master or mariners." It has been held in the State of New York that a clause in a bill of lading that the carrier shall not be liable for barratry of master or mariners is valid.[1]

This clause, so far as we have been able to discover, has never come up for adjudication in the Federal Courts.[2] It is a very old one in bills of lading, and it would certainly be surprising if those courts in a proper case should refuse to sustain its validity. It does not necessarily follow that the rule laid down by those courts as to the validity of the clause, exonerating the carrier from liability for the negligence of its servants, would be applied to a case where the liability sought to be established was one for their wilful tort. The principal is not liable in an action of tort for the unfaithful, malicious, or wilful act of the agent, not committed in the course of his employment.[3]

---

[1] Spinetti *v.* Atlas S. S. Co., 80 N. Y. 71 (1880); rev'g s. c. 14 Hun, 100 (1878).

[2] Under a charter party having a covenant to keep the ship well manned, desertion of the crew is not a " peril of the sea," but barratry, and the ship is liable. But (p. 160) it is said "this risk it is competent for the owner to provide against in his contract." The Ethel, 5 Benedict, 161 (1871). When the vessel is chartered for a lump sum, the owners are not responsible for the barratry of the master appointed by them. Hart *v.* Leach, 21 Fed. Rep. 77 (1884). See The Alknomac, Bee, 124 (1798).

Where the captain being sick, shipped a man as nurse or attendant, with a promise to land him at a port where he did not intend to go, held, that if the original taking had been tortious, the ship would not be liable. "There is no proof that the captain was authorized to obtain negroes by hiring, force or strategy, and bring them to this country." If the man were a seaman or a passenger, the owners would be liable on their contract. Sunday *v.* Gordon, Blatch. & H. 569 (1837).

[3] Isaacs *v.* Third Ave. R. R., 47 N. Y. 122 (1871); Vanderbilt *v.* Richmond Turnpike Co., 2 N. Y. 479 (1849). In the Vanderbilt case the ship-owner was held not liable for damages caused by his captain wilfully and maliciously running into another ship. In Ralston *v.* The State-Rights, Crabbe, 22 (1836), it was held that under such circum-

To examine critically the numerous authorities upon this subject is not within the scope of this present trea-

---

stances the ship was liable. And in The Anna Maria, 2 Wheat. 334 (1817), the ship was held liable for the unlawful conduct of the captain as a privateer, whereby he "converted the whole transaction into a wanton marine trespass." But in these and many similar ones in admiralty, the ship is treated as itself the wrong-doer. The Tabor, 2 Bened. 331 (1868). They do not necessarily determine that the owner is also liable *in personam*. In Diaz *v.* The Revenge, 3 Wash. C. C. 262 (1814), it was held that the owners were not personally liable for the wrongful act of their captain, amounting to piracy. In Fraser *v.* Freeman, 43 N. Y. 566 (1871), defendant with two servants was endeavoring to enter upon the premises of another under a claim of right, and one of the defendant's servants killed the plaintiff's intestate who was resisting them. There was no evidence that the shot was fired by the express direction or assent of the defendant, and it was held that he was not liable. At page 569, the court quote with approval the language of Judge Cowen in Wright *v.* Wilcox, 19 Wend. 343 (1838). It is true that these cases have been very much limited by more recent decisions in the same court. Jackson *v.* Second Ave. R. R., 47 N. Y. 275 (1872); 7 Am. Rep. 448; Schultz *v.* Third Ave. R. R., 89 N. Y. 242 (1882); Day *v.* Brooklyn City R. R, 12 Hun, 435 (1877); aff'd 76 N. Y. 593 (1879); Hoffman *v.* N. Y. C. & H. R. R., 87 N. Y. 25 (1881).

But the principle stated in the text is not impaired by the latter decisions. In Stewart *v.* Brooklyn & Cross Town R. R., 90 N. Y. 588 (1882), the distinction is well stated. At page 594, the court say (referring to the Isaacs case): " That case was discussed by counsel and determined by this Court upon the assumption that the rule of the master's liability for the assault of a servant committed upon a person to whom the master owed no duty, was applicable to that case. The mind of the Court was not directed to the fact that the rule applicable to such a case does not apply to the case of an assault, committed upon a passenger by a servant intrusted with the execution of a contract of a common carrier."

In Rounds *v.* Del., Lack. & W. R. R., 64 N. Y. 129, 136 (1876), the rule as to the liability of a principal for the torts of his agents is thus stated by the Court :

" It seems to be clear enough from the cases in this State that the act of the servant, causing actionable injury to a third person, does not subject the master to civil responsibility in all cases, where it appears that the servant was at the time in the use of his master's property, or because the act, in some general sense, was done while he was doing his master's business, irrespective of the real nature and motive of the transaction. On the other hand, the master is not exempt from responsibility in all cases on showing that the servant, without express authority, designed to do the act or the injury complained of. If he is authorized to use force against another when necessary in executing his master's orders, the master commits it to him to decide what degree of force he shall use ; and if, through misjudgment or violence of temper,

21

tise. So long, however, as there are cases of wilful tort on the part of the agent for which the principal is not liable to third parties, and which, if committed by a mariner would certainly amount to barratry, so long will it be open to consideration whether the carrier may not by contract exempt himself from liability as carrier for acts, for which as principal, he is not liable at common law.

In this connection it is material to consider :

First. What is barratry ?

Second. Who can be considered as mariners ?

First. Chancellor Kent says (3 Comm. 305): " Barratry is a fraudulent breach of duty on the part of the master in his character of master, or of the mariners, to the injury of the owner of the ship or cargo, and without his consent, and it includes every breach of trust committed with dishonest views." [1]

---

he goes beyond the necessity of the occasion, and gives a right of action to another, he cannot, as to third persons, be said to have been acting without the line of his duty or to have departed from his master's business. If, however, the servant, under guise and cover of executing his master's orders, and exercising the authority conferred upon him, wilfully and designedly, for the purpose of accomplishing his own independent. malicious or wicked purposes, does an injury to another, then the master is not liable.

"The relation of master and servant, as to that transaction, does not exist between them. It is a wilful and wanton wrong and trespass, for which the master cannot be held responsible. And when it is said that the master is not responsible for the wilful wrong of the servant, the language is to be understood as referring to an act of positive and designed injury, not done with a view to the master's service or for the purpose of executing his orders."

The English cases on this subject are very fully collected in Smith's Master and Servant, 322–360. The American cases are collected in 2 Kent. Com. 259, 260, and notes; 1 Parson's Marit. Law, 391, 394, and in Story on Agency, sections 318, 456, 461. One of the most recent is Hershey *v.* O'Neill, 36 Fed. Rep. 168 (1888). The general rule is clear that the master is liable for a tort committed by a servant, only when the act committed is within the scope of the servant's employment. The difficulty has been to determine in what cases the act can be said to be within the scope of the employment. There is a distinction between cases in which the action is against the owner upon his contract, and those in which he is sued in tort. Pendleton *v.* Kinsley, 3 Cliff, 416 (1871); McGuire *v.* The Golden Gate, 1 McAlister, 104 (1856).

[1] Boehm *v.* Combe, 2 Maule & Sel. 172 (1813), was an action on a

Second. All persons who form a part of the ship's company are mariners, whether sailors or not.[1]

---

policy of insurance on specie, to be transported by land to Harwich and thence by sea to Gottenburg. The specie was stolen by the wagoner's servants. It was held that "the word barratry was large enough to include every species of fraud or *malus dolus* committed by the wagoner or servants, taking them to stand in place of the master or mariners." In Spinetti *v.* Atlas S. S. Co., 80 N. Y. 71 (1880), it was held that theft by the purser was barratry.

"No act of the master of a vessel can be deemed barratry unless it proceed from a criminal or fraudulent motive." Atkinson *v.* Great Western Ins. Co., 65 N. Y. 531 (1875); rev'g 4 Daly. 1 (1871); Lawton *v.* Sun Mutual Ins. Co., 2 Cush. (Mass.) 500 (1848); Patapsco Ins. Co. *v.* Coulters, 3 Pet, 222 (1830); Wilson *v.* Rankin, L. R. 1 Qu. B. 162 (1865).

[1] Woolverton *v.* Lacey, 8 Monthly Law Rep. 672 (1856). Conkling (Admiralty Practice, Vol. 1, p. 108, note b) says : "In the District Court of the Northern District of New York, ' porters,' whose chief business it is on board of lake steamers, employed in the conveyance of passengers, to receive, and bring on board and discharge the luggage of the passengers, have been allowed to sue as mariners, their services being essential to the proper and successful navigation of the vessel as a passenger vessel, and for the same reason this privilege has been allowed to the clerks."

In The Jane and Matilda, 1 Hagg. Adm. 187 (1823), Ld. Stowell held that a woman who acted as cook and steward, and afterwards as ship-keeper, was a mariner and could libel the ship for her wages. "The other capacity in which she served is that of ship keeper for a long space of time, in which the vessel remained in dock or harbor, during all which time she had the business of keeping the ship clean by frequent washing, and of looking to the safe custody of the stores left on board," p. 190.

In Smith *v.* The Sloop Pekin, Gilpin, 203 (1834), Judge Hopkinson held that the steward of a sloop was a mariner. In Wilson *v.* The Ohio, Gilpin 505, (1834), Judge Hopkinson refers to this case of The Pekin, and says the steward had in strictness nothing to do with navigating the ship.

So Bouvier, in his Law Dict., Vol. 2, p. 103 (15 Ed.), *sub voce* Mariner : "Surgeons, engineers, clerks, stewards, cooks, porters and chambermaids on passenger steamers, when necessary for the service of the ship or crew, are also deemed mariners, and permitted as such to sue in the admiralty for their wages." Abb. Law Dict., Vol. 2, p. 83, S. P.

In Spinetti *v.* Atlas S. S. Co., 80 N. Y. 71 (1880); rev'g s. c. 14 Hun, 100 (1878), it was held that the purser was a mariner.

Under the Statute of Nuncupative Wills, a purser is held to be " a mariner." Hubbard *v.* Hubbard, 8 N. Y. 196 (1853); The goods of Hayes, 2 Curteis, 338 (1839); *Ex parte* Thompson, 4 Bradf. 154, 159 (1856). See, also, U. S. Rev. Stat. secs. 4,573, 4,574, 4,575, 4,612. The duties of this officer in earlier days were discharged by the captain.

The words " Any act, negligence or default of the pilot, master, mariners, engineers, servants or agents of the company," are broad enough to cover the theft of a bag of gold by the purser, to whom all specie is entrusted by the carrier.[1]

If the clause purport to exempt the carrier from liability for any fault of the officers or crew "in the management of the ship," it will be interpreted to mean "in the management of the ship while the goods are on board." It will not cover the case of neglect so to prepare the ship that it should be in suitable condition for the transportation of the freight in question.[2]

SECTION VI.

DANGER OF FIRE.

Loss by fire was one of the first risks which carriers sought to exempt by a special clause in the bill of lading. It was settled long ago that in the absence of such a clause the carrier was liable for loss by fire, unless that fire was caused by lightning, although no negligence on his part concurred, and the fire was communicated to his vessel from burning buildings or other extrinsic sources.[3]

The clause by which it is agreed that the carrier shall not be liable for loss by fire is valid if the loss is not occasioned by his negligence.[4]

McLachlan on Shipping, 146, 148. The Gratitudine, 3 C. Rob. 240, 257 (1801).

[1] Spinetti v. Atlas S. S. Co., 80 N. Y. 71 (1880).

[2] Stevens v. Navigazione Gen. It., 39 Fed. Rep. 562 (1889).

[3] Providence & N. Y. S. S. Co. v. Hill Mfg. Co., 109 U. S. 578, 602 (1883); Lakeman v. Grinnell, 5 Bosw. (N. Y.) 625 (1859); Patton v. Magrath, Dudley (S. C.), 150 (1839); Hibler v. McCartney, 31 Ala. 501 (1858). See, also, cases cited in Chap. XIV, sect. 3, ante, p. 302.

[4] York Co. v. Central R. R., 3 Wall. 107 (1865); The Egypt, 25 Fed. Rep. 320 (1885). In this case the goods were discharged from the ship at night under a permit from the Collector, upon the delivery to

In some cases where the bill of lading contained an agreement to transport the goods partly by water and partly by rail, it has been held that the clause exempting the carrier from liability for damage by fire related to the water transportation only.[1] But these cases can only be upheld in view of the special language of the particular bill of lading. The exemption from liability for loss by fire is generally construed to apply throughout the entire transit, from the time of delivery to the carrier to that of delivery to the consignee.[2]

The words "dangers of fire and navigation only excepted," and "unavoidable accidents of navigation and fire excepted," mean substantially the same thing, and apply to and include loss by any fire, whether originating on the boat or not.[3]

In a case where the carrier, the owner of a steamboat

---

him of a bond to pay for goods "stolen, burned, or otherwise lost" on the wharf. The goods were destroyed by fire, and it was held that this bond did not extend the liability of the carrier, and that consequently the carrier was not liable, as the bill of lading exempted it from liability for loss "by fire before unloading, in the ship, or after unloading." In Hall v. Penn. R. R., 14 Phila. 414 (1880), the contract provided that the carrier should not be liable "for loss or damage by fire or other casualty while in transit, or while in depots or places of transportation." The goods were delayed at Pittsburgh, while in transit, owing to a strike, and were there burned in a fire, which was begun by a mob. It was held that the carrier was not liable.

[1] Barter v. Wheeler, 49 N. H. 9 (1869). The language of the bill of lading was, "the dangers of navigation, fire and collision on the lakes and rivers." Little Rock, Miss. R. & T. R. R. v. Talbot, 39 Ark. 523 (1882), is a similar case, decided on the ground that the words which followed the exemption limited it to water risks. These words were "as the R. & D. and connecting railroads assume no marine risks whatever." It was also held that a fire occurring on a wharf boat moored at her dock, which was used as the receiving depot for freight, was not a marine risk. See ante, Chap. X, sect. 3, p. 238.

[2] Scott v. Baltimore S. S. Co., 19 Fed. Rep. 56 (1884); The Egypt, 25 Fed. Rep. 320 (1885); Little Miami R. R. v. Wetmore, 19 Ohio, 110 (1869); Crocker v. The New London, Willimantic and Palmer R. R., 24 Conn. 249 (1855); Button v. The London & South Western Railway Company, L. R. 2 Q. B. 535 (1867).

[3] Swindler v. Hilliard, 2 Rich. (S. C.) 286 (1846).

on a Southern river, sought to relieve himself from liability for the destruction by fire of cotton on his boat, by
proving the custom of the business, it was held that to
have this effect the usage must be well known, established
and recognized.   It was also said by the Court that the
carrier might exempt himself from liability for loss by
fire, by showing that he had given notice that he would
not be liable for injury to cotton by fire, unless a higher
rate of freight were paid, provided this notice was given to
the shipper under such circumstances that it might fairly
be held to enter into and form part of his contract.[1]

Exemption from liability for loss by fire does not
change the right of the parties as to the payment of
freight. The carrier cannot recover freight for goods
destroyed by fire before they are delivered to the consignee, although under the terms of the bill of lading he
is not liable for their loss.[2]

SECTION VII.

LEAKAGE, BREAKAGE, SWEATING, RUST, SHRINKAGE, AND SIMI-LAR EXCEPTIONS IN THE BILL OF LADING.

Aside from the general exceptions in bills of lading
already considered, there are others, such as those specified at the head of this section, which are commonly inserted, especially in marine bills of lading. In general
they are founded on some peculiar characteristic of the

---

[1] Singleton v. Hilliard, 1 Strobh. (S. C.) 203 (1847).   This case is
referred to here because the Court seem to place the decision on the
character of the particular risk from which exemption is sought.   But
it is opposed to the current of decisions cited under Chap. X, and can
hardly be considered as authority outside the limits of the jurisdiction
in which it was decided.   Patton v. McGrath, Dudley (S. C.), 162
(1838), and Swindler v. Hilliard, 2 Rich. Law (S. C.), 286 (1846), refer
to the same custom.

[2] N. Y. & H. R. R. v. Standard Oil Co., 87 N. Y. 486 (1882); aff'g
s. c. 20 Hun, 39 (1880).

various articles mentioned in the bill of lading, which render probable the occurrence of the specified dangers. These are valid exceptions to the carrier's liability, unless the injury is brought about by the carrier's negligence, or that of his servants.[1]

If, however, the negligence of the carrier or his servants or agents contribute to produce the injury, the exception will not protect the carrier.[2]

The effect of such exemptions is to change the burden of proof as to negligence, so that when the carrier has proved that the loss was within the excepted peril he need offer no further evidence, but the shipper must prove negligence.[3]

---

[1] The Keystone, 31 Fed. Rep. 412 (1886); Wolff v. The Vaderland, 18 Fed. Rep. 739 (1883); The Pereire, 8 Bened. 302 (1853); The Delhi, 4 Bened. 345 (1870); The Jefferson, 31 Fed. Rep. 489 (1887); Mendelsohn v. The Louisiana, 3 Woods Ct. Ct. 46 (1877).

[2] The Keystone, 31 Fed. Rep. 412 (1886); Wolff v. The Vaderland, 18 Fed. Rep. 739 (1883); The David and Caroline, 5 Blatchf. 266 (1865); Dedekam v. Vose, 3 Blatch. 44 (1853); The Giglio v. The Britannia, 31 Fed. Rep. 432 (1887); The Colon, 9 Bened. 355 (1878); The Invincible, 3 Sawy. 176 (1874); Reno v. Hogan, 12 B. Monroe (Ky.), 63 (1851); Koenigsheim v. Hamburg Am. P. Co., 12 Daly (N. Y.), 123 (1883). A stipulation that machinery might be carried in open cars, the owner assuming risks of weather and rust, will not protect the carrier from damages for his negligence in omitting to cover the goods during an unnecessary delay of two days. Western & A. R. Co. v. Exposition Cotton Mills, 7 S. E. Rep. 917 (1888).

The same rule has been applied in cases where leakage or sweating were not specifically excepted, but did occur during bad weather, and were claimed to constitute a peril of the sea for which the carrier was not liable. Thus, in The Star of Hope, 17 Wall. 651 (1873), the Court say: "The defense is to the effect that sweating is one of the dangers of the seas. But if the sweating be produced in consequence of negligent stowage, the claimant is precluded from setting up the defense."

So, in The Antoinetta, 5 Bened. 564 (1872), Blatchford, J., said: "I cannot regard it as a peril of the seas to stow casks of bleaching powder in such relations to bales of grain bags that the casks, being against the skin of the ship, may become wet and destroy the wood of the casks so that by rolling of the vessel the casks will be stove and discharge their contents, so as to reach and injure the bags. The loss is not shown to be one which ordinary skill and prudence could not avoid." See The Nith, 36 Fed. Rep. 86 (1888).

[3] Where the exception in the bill of lading was of "average leakage

Where, however, the bill of lading contains a clause
that the exceptions shall not apply " unless the goods are
properly stowed," the burden is on the carrier to show
good stowage. When, as is usually the case, it is the
duty of the carrier to stow properly, his failure to do so is,
of course, negligence, which, without such a clause, it
would be the duty of the shipper to prove.[1]

Where a leakage had been caused by the working out
of a defective plug from the cask, the Court held that this
was a latent defect, and the carrier was not liable, although
the bill of lading receipted for the cask in good order.
But if the working out of the plug had been caused by
excessive motion of the cask, the shipper could show that
this was due to bad stowage.[2]

In examining the cases cited in the note to the previous paragraphs, it must be remembered that clauses exempting carriers from liability for negligence are held by
many Courts to be void, as shown in Chap. IV, sect. 2.
These Courts, in construing bills of lading, practically

and breakage," and the carrier showed that the casks were of inferior
quality, it was held that the burden was on the shipper to show negligence. Six Hundred and Thirty Casks of Sherry Wine, 14 Blatch.
518 (1878).

It was, however, said in Alabama that in order to bring the case
within the exception (breakage) it must be proved that it was breakage
without negligence. The Court says that it does not adopt the rule
that the burden is on the carrier to show no negligence. But it is diffi
cult to see the distinction.   Steele v. Burgess, 1 Ala. Sel. Cases, 207
(1861); s. c. 37 Ala. R. 247.

In Brauer v. The Almoner, 18 La Ann. 266 (1866), it seems also to
be held that the carrier must prove some unusual weather to account
for certain breakage. Where the bill of lading exempts leakage, this
does not cover leakage caused by bad stowage. But the burden is on
the libellant to show that the stowage was defective. The Britannia,
34 Fed. 906 (1888). See notes 1 and 2, ante, p. 327, and Chap. XI,
sect. 2, ante, p. 245, n. 4.

[1] Edwards v. The Cahawba, 14 La. Ann. 224 (1859). The question
of the burden of proof is well illustrated in Nelson v. The Nat. Steamship Co., 7 Bened. 340 (1874), where adjudication was made upon
losses under seven different shipments on different proofs as to each.

[2] The Olbers, 3 Bened. 148 (1869).

strike out such clauses and construe the contract as if no such clause had been inserted.[1]

A loss from stowage is not necessarily a loss from negligence. The placing of particular goods in a certain place may be necessary in order to load the ship suitably for her intended voyage. In other words, where "loss from stowage" is excepted, the carrier ceases to be an insurer against loss arising from that cause. But if due care be not used in and about the stowage of the cargo, the carrier is liable for the consequences.[2]

What will or will not constitute negligent stowage is generally a question of fact. Evidence of the customary mode of stowage is admissible as bearing directly upon the determination of this question.[3]

But the custom must be general and not confined to the particular carrier. Although if the latter has a custom as to stowage known to the shipper, and in view of which the contract is made, this will suffice. But if the experience of the trade has shown that the old method of stowage is dangerous, the carrier cannot justify himself

---

[1] The Colon, 9 Bened. 355 (1878), is an illustration.

[2] Nelson v. National S. S. Co., 7 Bened. 340 (1874). In this case the Court adverted to the fact that it was noted in the margin of some of the bills of lading that the casks were loose when shipped. The Court held that it was to be presumed that the loss of plumbago contained in these was due to the defective condition of the casks.

[3] Paturzo v. Compagnie Francaise, 31 Fed. Rep. 611 (1887); The Chasca, 23 Fed. Rep. 156 (1885); The Invincible, 1 Lowell, 225 (1868); Baxter v. Leland, 1 Abb. Adm. 348 (1848). This was a case of injury to the cargo by "sweating," as was also The Portuense, 35 Fed. Rep. 670 (1888). Baxter v. Leland and The Portuense should be compared with Mendelsohn v. The Louisiana, 3 Woods C. C. 46 (1877). Lamb v. Parkman, 1 Sprague, 343 (1857), supports the text. It is there held that under the circumstances (a hot climate) sweating is included in the express exception of "perils of the seas," because incident to the particular voyage.

In Rich v. Lambert, 12 How. 347–357 (1851), the Court said that "the conveyance of salt between decks, in a mixed cargo, was according to the established usage and custom of the trade between Liverpool and this country," and it was held that there was "no fault chargeable to the master as to the place of stowage." *Ante*, p. 245, n. 4.

for following it and is liable for a loss from sweating produced by the stowage, although loss from sweating is excepted in the bill of lading.[1]

Leakage ordinarily means leakage from the cask or other enclosure of the liquid shipped, and not leakage from the sea into the ship;[2] and where this word is used unqualified by any adjective, it extends to the loss of the entire contents of the cask.[3] When the words used are "ordinary leakage," they can be explained by parol evidence, so as to show what proportion of the contents must remain in order to constitute "ordinary leakage."[4]

"Breakage or drainage" means breaking or draining from the package injured—not from others.[5]

SECTION VIII.

DELIVERY.

Clauses are frequently inserted in bills of lading, for the purpose of limiting the common law liability of the carrier in reference to the delivery of the goods. The common law rule was that the liability of the carrier should continue, not only until the goods were delivered

---

[1] Paturzo v. The Compagnie Francaise, 31 Fed. Rep. 611 (1887).

[2] Hill v. Sturgeon, 28 Mo. 329 (1859). In this case the words used were "leaking and sinking." It was held that they did not cover a loss from sinking of the ship, produced by a leak, caused by external violence. So when the words used are "leakage, breakage and rust," it is held that they do not cover an injury caused by leakage from other goods. Thrift v. Youle, 2 C. P. Div. 434 (1877).

[3] The Helene, L. R. 1 P. C. 231 (1866). But in Brauer v. The Almoner, 18 La. Ann. 266 (1866), it was held otherwise. The Court there say that such an exception applies only to "ordinary leakage." The English case is believed to be better law.

[4] The Helene, L. R. 1 P. C. 231 (1866). In this case it was shown that a loss of one per cent. or less of the contents of the cask was considered in the trade as "ordinary leakage."

[5] The Bitterne, 35 Fed. Rep. 927 (1888).

at the pier or depot of the carrier, but until notice of their arrival had been given to the consignee and a reasonable opportunity afforded him to take them away.[1]

---

[1] This is the rule as established in the English Courts, in the Federal Courts, and in the courts of most of the States. 3 Kent. Com. 215; 2 Kent. 605. The Eddy, 5 Wall. 494 (1866); Richardson v. Goddard, 23 How. (U. S.) 28 (1859); The Peytona, 2 Curtis, C. C. 21 (1854); The Tangier, 1 Clifford, 396 (1860); Bourne v. Gatliffe, 3 Mann. & Gr. 643 (1841); aff'd 7 Ib. 868 (1844); 11 Clarke & Fin. 45 (1844); Bourne v. Gatliffe, 4 Bing. New Cases, 314 (1838); Price v. Powell, 3 N. Y. 322 (1850); McAndrew v. Whitlock, 52 N. Y. 40 (1873); Zinn v. N. J. Steamboat Co., 49 N. Y. 442 (1872); Sherman v. Hudson R. R. R., 64 Id. 254 (1876); Faulkner v. Hart, 82 N. Y. 413 (1880); The Steamboat "Sultana" v. Chapman, 5 Wis. 454 (1856); Sleade v. Payne, 14 La. Ann. 453 (1859); Chicago & Rock Island R. R. v. Warren, 16 Ill. 502 (1855). In this case the court say : " There must be an actual or constructive delivery to the owner or consignee, or to a warehouseman for storage." See the Illinois cases cited at the end of this note. Moses v. Boston & Me. R. R., 32 N. H. 523 (1856); Redfield on Carriers, sects. 110, 111; Story on Bailments, sect. 545; contra sect. 446; Graves v. Hartford & N. Y. S. Co., 38 Conn. 143 (1871). The carrier is not justified in abandoning the goods, even if the consignee refuse to receive them. Redmond v Liverpool. N. Y. & P. S. Co., 46 N. Y. 583 (1871).

The Massachusetts rule is, however, different. According to this the liability of the carrier as such terminated immediately upon the deposit of the goods on the pier or in the depot. After that the liability was simply that of a warehouseman. Rice v. Hart, 118 Mass. 201 (1875); Norway Plains Co. v. Boston & Me. R. R., 1 Gray (67 Mass.), 263 (1854); Sessions v. Western R. R., 16 Gray (82 Mass.), 132 (1860); Rice v. Boston & W. R. R., 98 Mass. 212 (1867); Miller v. Mansfield, 112 Id. 260 (1873); Stowe v. N. Y., Boston & Prov. R. R. 113 Id. 521 (1873).

The following cases hold that the consignee of goods shipped by rail must be on hand to receive them on their arrival, and is not entitled to notice :

Illinois.—Porter v. Chicago & R. I. R. R., 20 Ill. 407 (1858); Chicago & A. R. R. v. Scott, 42 Ill. 132 (1866); Merch. Despatch Co. v. Moore, 88 Ill. 136 (1878).

Indiana.—Bansemer v. Toledo & W. R. Co., 25 Ind. 435 (1865).

Iowa.—Francis v. Dubuque & Sioux City R. R., 25 Iowa, 65 (1868).

Missouri.—Buddy v. Wabash, St. L. & P. R. Co., 20 Mo. App. 206; 2 West Rep. 535 (1886).

In Jackson v. Sacramento V. R. R., 23 Cal. 269 (1863), the consignee had notice of the arrival of the goods, but the Court say that safely warehousing them completes the duty of the carrier. The Supreme Court of Pennsylvania, deciding on the law of New York, held that the carrier's usage and the course of trade would control, and that the railroad company had fully performed its duty as carrier when it

The usual form of the stipulation in maritime contracts
on this subject is in substance, that the goods should be

---

had deposited in its own warehouse the goods which the plaintiffs were
not ready to receive.   McCarty *v.* N. Y. & Erie R. R., 30 Penn. St.
253 (1858).

In New Jersey the Court said that the liability of carriers by railroad is different from that of carriers by water, and that it continues
until the consignee has had a reasonable time to remove the goods, but
that the carrier need not give notice.   Morris & E. R. R. *ads.* Ayres,
29 N. J. (Law), 394 (1862).   This language is cited by Sharswood, J.,
in Shunk *v.* Phil. Steam Propeller Co., 60 Penn. St. 114 (1869).

The Massachusetts cases cited are all railroad cases.   The courts of
that State make a distinction, based on usage, between railways and
other carriers.   Norway Plains Co. *v.* Boston & Me. R. R., 1 Gray, 263
(1854); and it is quite probable that there is a difference in the usage of
railway companies in different countries, States and towns, and also a
difference in the usage of water carriers.

In a railroad case an English court held, under the peculiar language of the contract for the shipment of a horse, that the shipper
ought to have notified the consignee, and that the carrier was not liable,
although he left the horse uncared for, without notice to the consignee,
for twenty-four hours.   Wise *v.* Great Western R. Co., 1 Hurlst. & N.
64 (1856).

Chicago & Rock Id. R. R. *v.* Warren, 16 Ill. 502 (1855), was a case
of gross negligence where the carrier would have been liable even as
warehouseman.   The goods (rags) were taken by carrier done up in
bags, and were found "lying loosely outside of defendant's depot and
out of the bags," two-thirds stolen or lost.   The syllabus says, " Carriers
must deliver to owner or consignee, and cannot rid themselves of liability until the goods are delivered to owner or consignee, *or to a warehouseman.*"   The opinion says, "Responsibility must last until that of
some other begins," and the goods were stolen "before the defendant
could reach the depot to receive them, after notice."   The right to notice not discussed.   Despatch Co. *v.* Moore, 88 Ill. 136, was a case of
connecting lines.   Goods were carried to terminus of first carrier, arrived late in evening, were warehoused, "and on the following morning" destroyed by the Chicago fire.   Defendant was held not liable.
Whether there was notice or even opportunity to tranship does not appear, and was not considered; but there could hardly have been.   This
fire broke out at night, which must have been the night of arrival.   The
contract to carry only to Chicago was proved.

Chicago R. R. *v.* Scott, 42 Ill. 139 (1866), says expressly: "*But the
rule is settled* that no notice is necessary, and if the *consignee is not* present" to receive the goods, carrier can warehouse the goods, and "his
liability as carrier ceases and warehouseman begins;" citing the Massachusetts cases.   But these cases go much farther than this and hold
the carrier discharged from his liability as carrier from the moment that
the transit ceases, and the goods are placed on the platform of the depot.

at the risk of the consignee as soon as they are delivered from the tackles of the steamer at her port of destination. Such clauses are not unreasonable and will be enforced by the courts.[1]

It is, however, clear that no obligation of the carrier is limited by such a clause, except what is expressed in the terms of the clause itself, or fairly to be implied therefrom. Such clauses do not exonerate the carrier from his liability to notify the consignee of the arrival of the goods.[2]

But transferring a car to a private line of the consignee, over which the carrier has no control, is a good delivery though the goods are not taken from the car. East St. Louis R. Co. v. Wabash, St. L. & P. R. Co., 15 N. E. Rep. (Ill.) 45 (1888); reversing 24 Ill. App. 279 (1887). Delivery to a public warehouseman, subject to the carrier's lien for freight, is a good delivery and terminates the carrier's liability. Arthur v. St. Paul & D. R. Co., 35 N. W. Rep. (Minn.) 719 (1887). After the refusal of a consignee to receive the goods the duty of the carrier is to safely warehouse. The Captain John, 33 Fed. Rep. 927 (1888).

[1] The Santee, 2 Bened. 519 (1868); s. c. on Appeal, 7 Blatch. 186 (1870); The Kate, 12 Fed. Rep. 881 (1882). In this case the words used were "the goods to be taken from the ship immediately the vessel is ready to discharge." In Woodruff v. Havemeyer, 106 N. Y. 131 (1887), the clause mentioned in the text was considered with reference to its bearing upon the charges payable by the consignee. A clause that the carrier shall only be liable as warehouseman "after the arrival at the depot," does not require the consignee to be present at their arrival. He must have notice and a reasonable opportunity to remove the goods. Louisville & Nashville R. R. v. Oden, 80 Ala. 43 (1885). Under very similar circumstances the New York Court held that the carrier was liable as an insurer, until such notice and opportunity were given. McKinney v. Jewett, 90 N. Y. 267 (1882).

[2] The Santee, 7 Blatch. 186 (1870), and see The Thames, *Ibid.* 226 (1870).

The question as to what is a reasonable opportunity to the consignee to take away the goods, is always one to be determined in view of all the circumstances of the case. For example, in The Kathleen Mary, 8 Bened. 165 (1875), it was held that notice to the consignee given on Thursday, that he could probably have some of his goods on Friday, afforded him a reasonable opportunity to go and get them.

On the other hand, in Thompson v. Liverpool & G. W. S. S. Co., 44 N. Y. Super. Ct. 407 (1879), it was held that a notice given in the morning that the goods were on the pier and must be removed during the day, was insufficient. Both these cases arose upon the construction of a bill of lading requiring the consignee to take the goods "immediately the vessel is ready to discharge."

Such a clause would not exonerate the carrier from liability for delivering the goods to some person other than the consignee.[1]

Nor would it relieve the carrier from liability for negligence in the discharge of the goods. In other words, his liability continues until the goods are safely landed.[2]

It has sometimes been attempted by the carrier to obviate the necessity of giving notice to the consignee by requiring him to be ready to take the goods from alongside (immediately the vessel is ready to discharge), and inserting a clause in the bill of lading that if not so taken by the consignee, they may be deposited on the pier or otherwise disposed of, and remain at the risk of the consignee. But even in such cases it is held that the liability of the

---

In the Alene, 19 Fed. Rep. 875 (1883); aff'd **25** *Ibid.* 562; s. c. 23 Blatch, 335 (1885), it was held (construing a similar clause) that a vessel could not be said to be ready to discharge, when the temperature was such that the goods (which in that case were oranges) could not be discharged without destroying them.

To the same effect are The Surrey, 26 Fed. Rep. 791 (1886); The Boskenna Bay, 22 Fed. Rep. 665 (1884). But in a subsequent case involving the same casualty, the bill of lading bound the consignee to receive the fruit from the ship's side, and he had notice that the discharge would be made on a certain day. He made no attempt to receive or care for the fruit, and claimed that the weather was unsuitable. Held that the carrier was not liable for injury to the fruit from frost and exposure. Bonanno *v.* The Boskenna Bay, 36 Fed. Rep. 697 (1888); and see The Alesia, 35 Fed. Rep. 531 (1888); Jacobs *v.* Tutt, 33 Fed. Rep. 397 (1888).

[1] The Santee, 7 Blatch. 186 (1870); aff'g 2 Bened. 519 (1868).

[2] Zing *v.* Howland, 5 Daly (N. Y.), 136 (1874). In like manner where a bill of lading for hams stipulated that carrier should not be liable for injury to them while at a station awaiting delivery, and that they should be delivered during business hours. They arrived Thursday. Consignee inquired for them that day and Friday, and was told they had not arrived. Held that the clause did not extend to such a case, and that carrier was liable for injury from heat during the delay. McKinney *v.* Jewett, 90 N. Y. 267 (1882). See, also, The Alene and The Surrey, *ante*, p. 333, n. 2. Special clauses of exemption are only while the goods are in transit, and cease to be applicable after the transit has ceased and the goods are warehoused, unless it is otherwise expressed. Union Pacific R. Co. *v.* Moyer, 19 Pac. R. 639 (Kansas), (1888); Tarbell *v.* Royal Exch. Shipping Co., 110 N. Y. 170 (1888).

carrier does not terminate altogether, but that he remains liable for any damage done to the goods while on the pier or in the warehouse from the negligence of his servants.[1]

Bills of lading sometimes contain clauses giving the carrier an option as to the place of delivery. In such case clauses relating to the one branch of the option cannot be considered as applicable to the other.[2]

The question has been sometimes mooted whether the delivery by the carrier of goods subject to customs duties to the officers of the customs, charged with their custody until the duty shall be paid, might not be considered as terminating his liability as carrier, and it was so held by the Supreme Court of the State of New York.[3]

---

[1] Gleadell *v.* Thomson, 56 N. Y. 194 (1874); aff'g 35 N. Y. Super. Ct. 232 (1873). The Superior Court in this case held that the carrier's liability remained in full force until notice was given to the consignee of the arrival of the goods. This construction of the particular bill of lading was not sustained in the Court of Appeals, but the judgment was affirmed for the reason stated in the text. In the same case there was a clause in the bill of lading that the carrier should not be liable for any negligence of the pilot, master or mariners. The court construed this clause from its connection with the context, to mean negligence occurring on the voyage, and held that it did not apply to the negligence of the mariners in handling the goods or dealing with them while they were on the pier, after the vessel had been moored.

To the same effect is Central R. R. *v.* Smuck, 49 Ind. 302 (1874). Even with such clauses the consignee's obligation to receive begins only when he has reasonable opportunity so to do. Tarbell *v.* Royal Exchange Shipping Co., 110 N. Y. 170 (1888).

[2] Woodruff *v.* Havemeyer, 106 N. Y. 129 (1887). In this case the first clause of the bill of lading provided that the articles "shall be at the risk of the shipper, owner or consignee thereof, as soon as delivered from the tackles of the steamer." The option was then given to the carrier to discharge the cargo at New York or Brooklyn, the consignee of cargo to pay charges thereon as expressed in the margin. These charges were for landing and wharfinger charges, and fixed the amount payable in detail. The carrier availed himself of the option to discharge on the wharf in Brooklyn, and the Court held that the defendants were liable for these charges and could not insist that the goods ought to have been delivered directly into the lighters from the ship's tackles, as they requested.

[3] Redmond *v.* Liverpool, N. Y. & P. Steamship Co., 56 Barb. 320 (1870).

But this decision was reversed by the Court of Appeals, and it was held that the custody of the officers of the customs did not, *per se*, terminate the carrier's liability, although their delivery to and storage in a bonded warehouse, pursuant to law and after due notice to the consignee, would terminate it.[1]

In all cases the requirements of the bill of lading as to the place of delivery should be complied with, and the liability of the carrier as such continues until such compliance.[2]

---

[1] s. c. on Appeal, 46 N. Y. 578 (1871). In this case the Court say (p. 587): " It may well be that if the owner fails to comply with the laws, and cannot lawfully land or remove the goods, and they are seized and taken by the officers of the government, or if, upon the omission of the owner after a reasonable opportunity is given him for that purpose, to obtain the necessary authority to remove or receive the goods, they are in pursuance of law delivered and received by the proper officers, in other words, placed in the custody of the law, the carrier would be discharged from further responsibility to the merchant. It would be equivalent to a storing of the goods under circumstances authorizing the master of the vessel to store them for the owner." In other words, it was held that the possession of the officers of the government was only a qualified possession.

To the same effect is McAndrew *v.* Whitlock, 52 N. Y. 40 (1873). This latter contains an examination of the authorities relating to the carrier's common law duty in reference to the discharge of perishable articles, but as this did not arise under any special clause in the bill of lading, it is not further referred to here.

If, however, the bill of lading exempts the carrier from liability for any specific reason, as, for example, fire, while the goods are in the custody of the customs officers, this clause will be valid. The Egypt, 25 Fed. Rep. 320 (1885). In Rowland *v.* Miln, 2 Hilt. (N. Y.) 156 (1858), it was held that if the goods were wrongfully taken and warehoused by the collector, the carrier was not thereby excused for not delivering them to the consignee, but must seek his remedy in an action against the collector.

[2] For example, in Moore *v.* Michigan Cent. R. R. 3 Mich. 23 (1853), it was held that a clause in the bill of lading binding the carrier to deliver flour "on board" at Detroit, rendered the carrier liable for loss by fire while the goods were in his warehouse at Detroit waiting the actual delivery on board the vessel.

So the reservation in the bill of lading of the privilege of re-shipping does not limit the liability of the carrier to transfer or cause the goods to be transported to the specified place of destination. The only effect of such a clause is to allow the carrier to transport the goods in a

SECTION IX.

INSURANCE.

Of late years clauses have been inserted in bills of lading, in reference to policies of insurance. They have been in two forms:

1. That if loss or injury to the goods should occur and be paid for by the carrier, he should have the benefit of any insurance effected by the shipper.

2. That the carrier should not be liable for any loss against which the shipper might protect himself by insurance.

---

vessel other than that specified in the bill of lading. Little *v.* Semple, 8 Mo. 99 (1843); McGregor *v.* Kilgore, 6 Ohio, 361 (1834); Whitesides *v.* Russell, 8 Wats. & Sargent (Penn.), 44 (1844).

So in Cain *v.* Garfield, 1 Lowell, 483 (1870), it was held that a recital in the bill of lading that the vessel was bound to a certain wharf in Charleston, followed by an agreement to deliver the goods safely " at the aforesaid port of Charleston," obliged the carrier to deliver the goods at that particular wharf, and that the liability of the carrier continued until the goods were there delivered.

A clause in the bill of lading which provided that the goods were shipped for " Valparaiso and a market," was held in Gaither *v.* Myrick, 9 Maryland, 118 (1856), to authorize the shipper to carry the goods to any place he might think desirable for a market, beyond the port of Valparaiso. An inland bill of lading which described the goods, which in that case were a package of money, as addressed to the cashier of the Artisans' Bank, was held not necessarily to involve personal delivery to the cashier, but the liability of the carrier was held to he terminated by the delivery of the money to the clerk or receiving teller of the bank while he stood behind its counter in the discharge of his duties as teller. Hotchkiss *v.* Artisans' Bank, 2 Abb. Ct. App. Dec. (N. Y.) 403 (1866).

Where there is no express privilege of re-shipment, the ship is bound to go to the place named if she can go safely. She cannot go to a neighboring port and send the goods on by lighter. The burden is on the carrier to show that the ship cannot safely go to the place named Shaw *v.* Gordon, 78 Mass. 488 (1858).

But a ship which has put into port in distress and is likely to be long delayed, is liable if she refuse to deliver goods to the owner on demand at that port. The Martha, 35 Fed. Rep. 313 (1888); and see Jacobs *v.* Tutt, 33 Fed. Rep. 589 (1888). Where the carrier has issued an assignable bill of lading his duty is to deliver only to the holder of the bill. Penn. R. Co. *v.* Stern, 119 Penn. 24 (1888); North *v.* Merch. & M. Trans. Co., 146 Mass. (1888); Weyand *v.* Atchinson, T. & S. F. R. Co., 39 N. W. Rep. (Iowa), 899 (1888); North Penn. R. Co. *v.* Commercial Nat. Bk. of Chicago, 123 U. S. 727 (1887).

22

It is very probable that in equity in the absence of the clause firstly mentioned, an Insurance Company which should, in case of loss, pay to the shipper the amount insured upon his goods, would be subrogated to his claim against the carrier.[1]

In like manner it has been held that an insurance company, upon paying the value of a house set on fire by sparks from an engine, is entitled to be subrogated to the claim of the owner against the railroad company for the injury to the house.[2] This right of subrogation, independently of contract, is not, however, an absolute one. The parties effecting the insurance may occupy such a relation to those for whose benefit it is effected, that the insurers of the cargo will not be entitled to be subrogated to a right of action against the carrier. If it appear that the insurance upon the cargo is effected for the benefit of the carrier, and the premium is paid by him, the insurer of the cargo who pays a loss upon it, will have no right of subrogation against the carrier.[3]

But wherever the right of subrogation in favor of the

---

[1] Comegys v. Vassar, 1 Peters, 193 (1828); Hall v. The Railroad Co., 13 Wall. 371 (1871); Mobile & M. R. Co. v. Jurey, 111 U. S. 584 (1883); Gales v. Hailman, 11 Penn. St. 515 (1849); Clark v. Wilson, 103 Mass. 219 (1869); Rockingham Mutual Ins. Co. v. Bosher, 39 Maine, 253 (1855); Peoria Ins. Co. v. Frost, 37 Ill. 333 (1865); Cole v. Malcolm, 66 N. Y. 366 (1876); Mason v. Gainsbury, 3 Doug. 61 (1782); Law Ass. Co. v. Oakley, 84 Law Times (Q. B. Div.), 280 (1888). From these cases and those cited in them it will be seen that the principle stated in the text is a very general one, and applies not only to carriers but to all cases where an insurer pays a loss. He thereby becomes entitled to whatever indemnity the assured had. Upon the argument that a carrier, being also an insurer, has an equal right with the underwriters, the Court, in Hall v. The Railroad Co., said that a carrier was not an insurer. This dictum does not quite agree with those of other authorities, but it is certain that a carrier has not all the rights of an insurer. Whether or not a carrier is an insurer to his freighters he has not, in the absence of contract to that effect, the right of subrogation as regards other insurers.

[2] Conn. Fire Ins. Co. v. Erie R. Co., 73 N. Y. Rep. 399 (1878).

[3] The Sidney, 23 Fed. Rep. 88 (1885).

insurer and against the carrier exists, the shipper cannot defeat it, by assigning the policy of insurance to the carrier, upon payment of the loss by the latter. In such case the insurer is entitled to have the amount paid by the carrier deducted from the claim against himself.[1]

It was to relieve the carrier from the consequences of the liability to the insurance company imposed upon him by the decisions already cited, that the clause under consideration was inserted in bills of lading. It is reasonable and valid, and prevents a rocovery by the insurer against the carrier, even though the loss be caused by the negligence of the carrier's servants.[2] Such a clause is not rendered invalid by a statute prohibiting the carrier from limiting his liability.[3]

The effect of this stipulation obviously is to deprive the insurer of his right of subrogation by a contract to which he is not a party. But to this there is no valid objection. The doctrine of subrogation always assumes that the party entitled thereto succeeds to the rights of another, and to no greater rights. The insurer is subrogated to the rights of the shipper, neither more nor less. But the insurer may himself guard against this loss by giving notice to persons dealing with him that if the bills of lading which they accept deprive the insurer of subrogation to the claim against the carrier, a higher rate of pre-

---

[1] Atlantic Ins. Co. *v.* Storrow, 5 Paige (N. Y.), 285 (1835).

[2] Rintoul *v.* N. Y. Central & H. R. R. R., 21 Blatch. 439; s. c. 17 Fed. Rep. 905 (1883). In this case the language of the bill of lading was that the carrier should " have the full benefit of any insurance that may have been effected upon or on account of said goods." Phenix Ins. Co. *v.* Erie Trans. Co., 117 U. S. 325 (1885); aff'g s. c. 10 Biss. 18 (1879); Mercantile Mut. Ins. Co. *v.* Calebs, 20 N. Y. 177 (1859); Platt *v.* Richmond, Y. R. & C. R. R., 108 N. Y. 358 (1888). Compare, also, Van Natta *v.* Mutual Security Ins. Co., 2 Sand. (N. Y. Superior Ct.) 496 (1849). In this case the carrier himself was the insured, and was allowed to recover.

[3] British & For. M. Ins. Co. *v.* Gulf, C. & S. F. R. Co., 63 Texas, 475 (1885).

mium will be charged. In such case it becomes the duty of the insured to disclose to the insurer the nature of the bill of lading which is delivered and accepted. If the shipper fail, under such circumstances, to disclose this to the insurer, he cannot recover.[1] But in the absence of fraud or concealment, or any special facts making it the duty of the shipper to disclose the terms of his bill of lading, he is not bound to make such disclosure.[2]

The clause under consideration does not, however, compel the shipper to exhaust his remedy against the insurance company. He has a choice of remedies, and may sue either the carrier or the insurer. If the carrier pay the loss, he becomes subrogated to the rights of the insured under the policy. But the failure of the insured to sue the insurer is not a defense available to the carrier.[3] From this and the cases previously cited in this section, it is manifest that the remedy of the shipper against the insurer is not the primary remedy. This is illustrated by a case in which the shipper, either inadvertently or for the purpose of securing better rates, contracted with the carrier, and also with the insurer, that each should have the benefit of his claim against the other. A loss happened and the shipper sued the insurer. It was held that the shipper had, by his contract with the carrier, disabled himself from giving to the insurer the stipulated benefit of his right of action against the carrier, and that therefore the insurer was not liable.[4]

---

[1] Tate v. Hyslop, 15 Q. B. Div. 368 (1885).

[2] Jackson Co v. Boylston Ins. Co., 139 Mass. 508 (1885). In this and the case last cited the policies were open policies, and the notice of shipment and request that the risk should be entered on the policy were given after the contract of affreightment was made. But some of the special facts out of which the duty of disclosure was held in the English case to arise, did not exist in the Massachusetts case.

[3] Inman v. South Carolina R. Co., 129 U. S. 128 (1889). If the shipper has insurance available to the carrier, the benefit of which he wrongfully refuse to allow to the latter, the carrier may set this refusal up as a counter claim in an action by the shipper. s. c.

[4] Carstairs v. Mechanics' & Traders' Ins. Co., 18 Fed. Rep. 473

The second stipulation before mentioned, in reference to insurance, is also reasonable and valid. But like all other clauses this stipulation should be construed according to the ordinary meaning of its terms, and applies, not to such unusual insurance as might be obtained by special agreement, but to the ordinary marine policy.[1] And it is not clearly settled whether, in those Courts which refuse to admit the validity of an agreement to exempt the carrier from liability for the negligence of his servants, this clause would be enforced in the case of loss caused by such negligence. It has been held that it would not be enforced, in a case where the loss was caused by defective construction.[2]

The clause in question does not apply to the case of a loss of property by theft.[3]

(1883). The Court in this case advert to the fact that the policy was effected before the goods were shipped.

[1] The Titania, 19 Fed. Rep. 101 (1883). In this case a bill of lading made in England, for transportation in an English ship to New York, provided, "The shipowner is not to be liable for any damage to any goods which is capable of being covered by insurance." Held that this was valid, but must be construed to refer to insurance "which might be obtained in the usual course of business from the ordinary insurance companies, either in the usual form, or in the customary course of business upon special application." It was held that injury from breaking loose of a spare propeller was not within this exemption, if it arose from negligence in securing the propeller, as this made the vessel unseaworthy.

[2] The Hadji, 20 Fed. Rep. 875 (1884); aff'g s. c. 16 Fed. Rep. 861 (1882). The Circuit Court cite the case stated *ante*, p. 339, in which it was held that the stipulation was valid, which gives to the carrier the benefit of the insurance effected by the shipper. But the Court add : "It is quite another thing to permit a carrier to compel the shipper, as a condition for the transportation of his goods, to enter into an independent contract with a third party for the carrier's benefit, in order that the latter may escape loss arising from his own conduct. . . The only effect that can be given to the stipulation here is by construing it as exempting the claimants from liability for any damage that the shipper could insure against, not arising from the carrier's own negligence." There is a dictum to the same effect in Rintoul *v.* New York Central R. R., 21 Blatch. 439; s. c. 17 Fed. Rep. 905 (1883).

[3] Taylor *v.* Liverpool & G. W. S. S. Co., L. R. 9 Qu. B. 546 (1874).

There is occasionally inserted in bills of lading a clause that the carrier shall insure the goods for the benefit of the shipper during some period of the carrier's possession. In such case the carrier, if it has failed to insure, is liable for a loss by fire, although the bill of lading contained another clause, exempting the carrier from liability for loss by "fire at sea or in port." [1]

SECTION X.

RESHIPMENT.

The clause often inserted in bills of lading, giving to the carrier the privilege of reshipment, is not to be extended beyond the fair meaning of its terms. It does not entail the duty of reshipment, and the carrier is not liable if he fail to reship the goods, in case of delay not attributable to his fault, as, for example, low water in a river.[2] On the other hand if he avail himself of the privilege reserved, and does reship the goods, his original liability is in no wise affected, and continues until he has safely delivered them at the port of destination.[3]

And if the clause gives him the privilege of reshipping at a particular place, he can reship only there, and will be liable if he should reship anywhere else, although the goods were lost in a storm for which the carrier would not otherwise have been responsible.[4]

---

[1] The Louisiana, 37 Fed. Rep. 264 (1889).

[2] Sturgess v. The Columbus, 23 Mo. 230 (1856); Broadwell v. Butler, 1 Newb. Adm. 171 (1854); aff'd 6 McLean, 296 (1854). But see Hatchet v. The Compromise, 12 La. Ann. 783 (1857), holding the contrary.

[3] Carr v. The Michigan, 27 Mo. 196 (1858). This case holds also that it is merely a privilege of reshipment, not of stowing on another boat. Dunseth v. Wade, 3 Ill. 285 (1840). In the latter case the clause read: "With privilege of reshipping on any good boat." It was held that the carrier, if he reshipped, must show that he placed the goods on a "good boat." Little v. Semple, 8 Mo. 99 (1843); McGregor v. Kilgore, 6 Ohio, 361 (1834); Whiteside v. Russell, 8 Watts. & S. (Penn.) 44 (1844).

[4] Cassilay v. Young, 4 Ben. Monr. (Ky.) 265 (1844). This case also

SECTION XI.

PRODUCE EXCHANGE BILL OF LADING.

Judges and statesmen, lawyers and men of business have alike lamented the evil of the lack of uniformity in the decision of questions, relating to commerce between states and nations, to which attention has been so often drawn in the pages of this book. The Legislature of our leading commercial State has made an attempt to remedy them. It has created a corporation now known as the New York Produce Exchange, the purposes of which are, *inter alia*, " to inculcate just and equitable principles in trade ; to establish and maintain uniformity in commercial usages, to adjust controversies and misunderstandings between persons engaged in business.[1]

The New York Produce Exchange has made an important attempt to perform the duties thus devolved upon it. It felt that this diversity in the decisions as to the rights of parties engaged in trade, was neither just nor equitable, and that the controversies and misunderstandings which had arisen in consequence between the carrier and the shipper, ought to be adjusted. On the one side it recognized that the carrier ought not to be exempted from responsibility for the equipment and stowage of its vessel, and that it should not be allowed to devolve this responsibility upon any ship's husband or manager. It recognized, on the other hand, that when the carrier has done all in its power to provide a proper and seaworthy vessel, manned by competent officers and crew, and has stowed her cargo on board with a due regard to the risks of the voyage, it ought not to be liable for the consequences of the care-

---

holds that this clause will not justify waiting indefinitely for another boat.

[1] Laws of the State of New York, 1862, Chap. 359, sec. 3; Laws 1868, Chap. 30, sec. 1; Laws of 1882, Chap. 36, sec. 2.

lessness of the persons entrusted with the navigation of the vessel, over whom during the voyage, in the nature of things, no supervision can be exercised. In 1886 the Produce Exchange appointed a committee, representing the carriers, the shippers, and the Average adjusters (who are really umpires between the two), and this committee, after full consideration of the subject, entered into correspondence with the Liverpool Ship-owners' Association. The representatives of both bodies adopted as a basis of their negotiations a form of bill of lading which had been recommended by the International Association for the reform and codification of the law of Nations, and discussed it article by article, until a form satisfactory to all parties had been agreed upon. The carriers agreed to strike out of the bill of lading which theretofore had been issued by them, the clauses which exempted them from responsibility for the sea-worthiness of the ship and for her proper stowage. These clauses were claimed to be valid in the English Courts and the Courts of the State of New York, and in giving them up the carrier gave up rights which were certainly important and valuable. On the other hand the shippers, fully represented as they were on the committee appointed by the Exchange, acknowledged the justice of the claim by the carrier, that it should not be responsible for the negligence of the master and mariners, to which it was in no way privy, and voluntarily agreed to accept a bill of lading containing a clause of exemption from liability for such negligence. The form of bill of lading thus agreed upon has been adopted by Commercial Exchanges in various parts of America.

In the conduct of this long negotiation the Produce Exchange was discharging the duties devolved upon it by law. It was to all intents and purposes a local legislature, and while its action certainly is not binding upon parties making contracts outside the limits of the State, yet it seems equally clear that it is binding upon those making contracts within the State of New York, until Congress shall intervene and take action in the premises.

The right of a Legislature to devolve upon a commission or officer of the Government powers of a quasi-legislative character, is now too well settled to admit of dispute. Congress, for example, has conferred upon the Secretary of the Treasury the right to make rules and regulations in reference to the whole subject of the importation of foreign goods, and the payment of duties thereon, and has authorized other officers to prescribe rules respecting matters within their jurisdiction, and these regulations have been frequently enforced by the Courts, and held to have the force of statutes.[1]

The great number of general statutes for the creation of corporations, that have been passed in all the States, is perhaps the most notable instance of the rule thus stated. The granting of charters was, in this country at least, within the power of the legislature alone. But legislatures everywhere have found it expedient to delegate this power, either to commissions, under whose authority cor-

---

[1] " This Court has too repeatedly said that they have the force of law to make it proper to discuss that point anew." Gratiot *v.* United States, 4 How. 80 (1846); *Ex-parte* Reed, 100 U. S. 13 (1879); United States *v.* Barrows, 1 Abb. U. S. 351 (1869).

The rules of Court " are made under special statutory authority, and when made have the force and effect of statutes." Matter of Moore, 108 N. Y. 280 (1888).

The Commissioners of Pilots, who were officers appointed by the Chamber of Commerce, adopted rules, pursuant to an authority conferred by statute, and these were held to be valid and binding. Sturges *v.* Spofford, 45 N. Y. 446 (1871); Cisco *v.* Roberts, 36 N. Y. 292 (1867).

The whole body of Civil Service legislation rests upon the right of the legislature to authorize an executive officer to prescribe rules, determining the manner in which persons shall be admitted into the service of the State. The validity of this legislation was expressly adjudged by the Supreme Court of Massachusetts, 138 Mass. 601 (1885), and has been frequently recognized in other cases. People *v.* Civil Service Boards, 103 N. Y. 657 (1886); aff'g s. c. 41 Hun, 287 (1886); People *v.* Common Council, 16 Abb. N. C. 96 (1884).

porations come into being, as in the case of the rapid transit legislation of the State of New York ; or directly to individuals who, under certain regulations declared by the statute, create a corporation by filing certain papers in the prescribed office.

It would seem to follow that the action of the Produce Exchage, in adopting the form of bill of lading in question, had the force and effect of a Statute of the State of New York, and that all contracts made in that form within the State of New York are valid.

The Federal Courts have never held that a contract is against public policy which is made under the circumstances just stated. They have held that a unilateral agreement, imposed by the carrier, with no freedom of choice on the part of the shipper, is against public policy. But no case has yet decided that such an agreement, entered into intelligently, after full discussion and for an adequate consideration, is against public policy or invalid.[1]

The Courts have not failed to recognize that freedom of contract is at the basis of the commercial prosperity of both England and America. They constantly declare that they do not make contracts for parties, but their

---

[1] The reason which the Supreme Court gives for refusing to enforce the clause in question is thus stated in Railroad Company v. Lockwood, 17 Wall. 357 (1873). At p. 379 the Court say : " The carrier and his customer do not stand on a footing of equality. The latter is only one individual in a million. He cannot afford to higgle or stand out and seek redress in the Courts. His business will not admit of such a course. He prefers rather to accept any bill of lading, or sign any paper the carrier presents, often indeed without knowing what the one or the other contains."

This language is repeated in The Montana, 129 U. S. 441 (1889). In the case stated in the text we see an entirely different state of affairs. The carrier's customers have themselves become a corporation. They are clothed by the legislature with power to stand out, and in the language of the Court " to higgle." They object to certain clauses which the carrier concedes. They agree to other clauses which they admit to be fair and just. The whole reasoning of the Supreme Court is inapplicable to this condition of things.

function is to enforce those which the parties themselves have made.

It would therefore seem that the rule " *Cessante ratione, cessat et ipsa lex,*" [1] should apply to the questions which may hereafter arise as to the validity of this agreement, which has come to be known as the Produce Exchange Bill of Lading.

In the history of this negotiation between the carriers and the shippers, we seem to be reading a chapter in Maine's Ancient Law. It was on the lines stated by him that the whole commercial law grew, and was gradually framed for the convenience of the mercantile community. When this law was thus forming it was common to receive evidence, either of witnesses or from the admissions of counsel, as to the usages of merchants and the course of trade, and judgment was given accordingly.[2]

The power to receive such aid is still vested in the Courts. It is the chief merit of the common law that it is flexible, and adapts itself to varying conditions of society.[3]

This distinguishing characteristic is expressed in the maxim already quoted. Of its applications there are many illustrations.[4]

---

[1] Broom, Legal Maxims, 159.

[2] Miller *v.* Race, 1 Burr. 452 (1758); Sedgwick on Construction of Statutes, pp. 3, 4.

[3] 1 Kent Comm. 472.

[4] It was well expressed by Lord Tenterden in Stone *v.* Marsh, 6 Barn. & Cress. 551 (1827): "The rule is founded on a principle of public policy, and where the public policy ceases to operate, the rule shall cease also."

The same maxim was applied to the rule that purchase *pendente lite* shall not change the rights of the parties, in Parks *v.* Jackson, 11 Wend. 442 (1833); and to the rule excluding evidence of the opinions of witnesses, in DeWitt *v.* Barley, 9 N. Y. 371 (1853); and to the rule of equitable conversion, in McCarthy *v.* Terry, 7 Lansing, 236 (1872).

A remarkable instance of the recognition by the Supreme Court of the change in the policy of the law which may be effected by local statutes is to be found in Nichols *v.* Eaton, 91 U. S. 716, 726 (1875).

The questions considered in this section have arisen in one case only, and in that the Court declined to pass upon them.[1]   The commercial community have generally acquiesced in the justice of the compromise embodied in the Produce Exchange Bill of Lading.   But if litigation should arise respecting instruments in that form, the Court before which it comes will naturally consider what is meant by the expression in the opinion of the Supreme Court in " The Montana:" " against the policy of the law."   The Court certainly did not mean the statute law. It meant unwritten law, as expounded by the Courts. This unwritten law is always subject to change by the Legislature, and has in many instances been changed. The old English statute of uses changed what had been up to that time the unwritten law relating to the effect of particular words in a conveyance.   Recent statutes in various States have changed the unwritten law as declared by the Courts, which rejected the testimony of interested witnesses, and have finally admitted the testimony even of parties to the record.   No one can dispute that Congress could lawfully pass an act, declaring that all the clauses in the bill of lading in question should be valid.   But Congress has taken no action in the premises.   In the absence of any action by Congress, it would seem clear that the Legislature of the State of New York has the power to enact that such a bill of lading should be valid if made within that State.[2]

In that case it was held that the policy of the English law as to the right to set apart property for the use of another, free from the claims of his creditors, had been changed by the general tenor of the statutes of various States of the Union, limiting the common law rights of creditors, and would no longer be enforced by American Courts of Equity.

[1] The Britannic, 39 Fed. Rep. 395 (1889).   This case was compromised, after the decision in the District Court.

[2] In Shelby v. Guy, 11 Wheat. 361 (1826), the Supreme Court say: " That the statute law of the States must furnish the rule of de-

It is true the Supreme Court has refused to recognize as authority the decisions of the Courts of the State of New York on this subject, but that is on the ground that these Courts did not correctly declare the unwritten mercantile law.   The U. S. Supreme Court has always admitted the authority of State statutes relating to transactions between merchants.   For example, State statutes relating to the negotiability of commercial paper, and to the days of grace, and other like statutes relating to commercial contracts, have frequently been recognized and enforced in the Federal Courts.[1]

It is of course impossible to predict whether the adoption of this clause under the circumstances stated, will be treated by American Courts either, (1) As an agreement for a valuable consideration to waive any defense that the clause in question is against the policy of the United States of America; or (2) Such a reference to the English law as will induce the Court to decide the questions arising under it by the law of England, and not by the law of America.   It is, however, a fact worthy of notice that the validity of the clause has been generally acquiesced in by shippers.   A curious illustration of this is to be found in the report of the Committee of the Liverpool Sailing Ship Owners' Mutual Indemnity Association for the year ending February 20th, 1888.   This states as follows:

---

cision to this Court. as far as they comport with the Constitution of the United States, in' all cases arising within the respective States, is a position that no one doubts."

[1] Shaw v. Railroad Co., 101 U. S. 557 (1879), (Bill of Lading). Scudder v. Union Nat'l Bank, 91 U. S. 406, (Bill of Exchange).   Wills v. Claflin, 92 U. S. 135 (1875), (Promissory Note).   In Peik v. Chicago & N. W. R. Co., 94 U. S. 164 (1876), the Supreme Court sustained the validity of, and enforced a statute of Wisconsin, relating to charges for railway transportation from places within that State to places without it.   In Cooley v. Port Wardens of Philadelphia, 12 How. U. S. 299 (1851), a statute of Pennsylvania imposing half pilotage fees upon vessels sailing to or from Philadelphia, was held to be constitutional, subject to the power of Congress to supersede it.

" The Committee are happy to be able to report that there are not any claims pending for loss of or damage to cargo, caused by improper navigation. This circumstance is no doubt due to the almost universal insertion of the negligence clause in contracts of affreightment."

The Ship Owners have certainly carried out in good faith the agreement on their part not to claim exemption for losses occasioned by their own neglect or fault. They have formed in England several associations for the mutual insurance of vessels by their owners, against certain claims not covered by ordinary policies of insurance. But the insurance of these associations does not extend to loss occasioned by the actual fault or privity of the member suffering the loss.

It will probably be found that the various commercial Exchanges which have adopted the form of bill of lading already referred to and which will be found in the note at the end of this chapter [1] have statutory powers similar to

---

[1] *New York Produce Exchange Steamship Bill of Lading.* Received in apparent good order and condition, by · from , to be transported by the good steamshhip now lying at the port of and bound for , with liberty to call at being marked and numbered as per margin (weight, quality, contents and value unknown), and to be delivered in like good order and condition at the port of unto , or to his or their assigns, he or they paying freight on the said goods on delivery at the rate of and charges as per margin. General average payable according to York-Antwerp rules.

It is mutually agreed that the ship shall have liberty to sail without pilots; to tow and assist vessels in distress ; to deviate for the purpose of saving life or property ; to convey goods in lighters to and from the ship at the risk of the owners of the goods but at ship's expense ; and in case the ship shall put into a port of refuge for repairs, to transmit the goods to their destination by any other steamship.

It is also mutually agreed that the carrier shall not be liable for loss or damage occasioned by the perils of the sea, or other waters, by fire from any cause on land or on water, by barratry of the master or crew, by enemies, pirates or robbers, by arrest and restraint of princes, rulers or people, by explosion, bursting of boilers, breakage of shafts, or any latent defect in hull or machinery, by collisions, stranding, or other accidents of navigation (even when occasioned by the negligence, default, or error in judgment of the pilot, master, mariners or other servants of

those which have been conferred upon the New York Produce Exchange and that the considerations as to the action of

the ship owner, not resulting, however, in any case, from want of due diligence by the owners of the ship or any of them, or by the ship's husband or manager) ; nor for decay, putrefaction, rust, sweat, change of character, drainage, leakage, breakage, or any loss or damage arising from the nature of the goods or the insufficiency of packages ; nor for land damages; nor for the obliteration or absence of marks or numbers; nor for any loss or damage caused by the prolongation of the voyage.

1. It is also mutually agreed that the carrier shall not be liable for gold, silver, bullion, specie, documents, jewelry, pictures, embroideries, works of art, silks, furs, china, porcelain, watches, clocks, or for goods of any description which are above the value of $500 per package, unless bills of lading are signed therefor, with the value therein expressed and a special agreement is made.

2. Also, that shippers shall be liable for any loss or damage to ship or cargo caused by inflammable, explosive or dangerous goods, shipped without full disclosure of their nature, whether such shipper be principal or agent; and such goods may be thrown overboard or destroyed at any time without compensation.

3. Also, that the carrier shall have a lien on the goods for all fines or damages which the ship or cargo may incur or suffer by reason of the incorrect or insufficient marking of packages or description of their contents.

4. Also, that in case the ship shall be prevented from reaching her destination by quarantine, the carrier may discharge the goods into any depot or lazaretto, and such discharge shall be deemed a final delivery under this contract, and all the expenses thereby incurred on the goods shall be a lien thereon.

5. Also, that if the goods be not taken by the consignee within such time as is provided by the regulations of the port of discharge, they may be stored by the carrier at the expense and risk of their owners.

6. Also, that full freight is payable on damaged goods ; but no freight is due on any increase in bulk or weight caused by the absorption of water during the voyage.

7. Also, that if on the sale of the goods at destination for freight and charges, the proceeds fail to cover said freight and charges, the carrier shall be entitled to recover the difference from the shipper.

8. Also, that in the event of claims for short delivery when the ship reaches her destination, the price shall be the market price at the port of destination on the day of the ship's entry at the custom house, less all charges saved.

And finally, in accepting this bill of lading, the shipper, owner and consignee of the goods agree to be bound by all of its stipulations, exceptions and conditions, whether written or printed, as fully as if they were all signed by such shipper, owner or consignee.

In witness whereof, the master or agent of the said ship has affirmed

that body already stated apply to them also. In any case it is believed that the Courts will be reluctant to decide that an agreement which all representative commercial bodies unite in, is against commercial policy.

---

to three bills of lading, all of this tenor and date, drawn as "first," "second" and "third," one of which being accomplished, the others to stand void.

Dated in   , this   day of   188   .

INDEX.

ABANDONED VOYAGE.
     effect on contract of exemption, 93.
     duty of carrier, 309.
ABANDONMENT OF INTEREST in ship and freight, 56, 70.
     not barred by abandonment to underwriters, 72.
ABROGATION OF LIABILITY.
     assent of shipper necessary to, 115.
     assent of shipper to bill of lading may be presumed, 222, 227,
         et seq.
     contract necessary for, 114.
     distinction between and limitation of amount, 119.
     notice of not sufficient, 221.
         See BILL OF LADING; LEASED LINE; LIMITATION BY
            CONTRACT; LIMITATION BY STATUTE OF SHIP-
            OWNER'S LIABILITY; NEGLIGENCE CONNECTING
            CARRIER; NOTICE; RULES AND REGULATIONS.
ACCEPTING GOODS.
     makes carrier liable for them, 93, 105, 111.
     for leased line, 111.
     reasons for not, waived by acceptance, 237.
ACT OF 1851, limiting liability of mariner.
         See STATUTE.
ACT OF CARRIER.
     error in giving wrong ticket, 165, *et seq.*
     omission to afford facilities for compliance with its rules, 220.
     cannot abrogate its liability, 221.
     when negligence of carrier contributes to loss from excepted
         risk, 235, 299, *et seq.*
ACT OF GOD.
     definition, 296, 298.
     when synonomous with perils of seas, &c., 297, 303.
     loss by deviation necessitated by defective equipment is not,
         305.
     unusual natural phenomena a question of degree, 307.
     unusual weather, 300.

DEFECTIVE EQUIPMENT—*continued*.
>   position Produce Exchange respecting, 343.
>>   See LIMITATION BY STATUTE OF SHIP OWNER'S LIA-
>>   BILITY.

DEFECTS.   See INTRINSIC DEFECTS; RECEIVED IN GOOD ORDER.

DELAYS.
>   in carrying live stock, 102, 103.
>   must not be unreasonable, 215.
>   combining with excepted peril, 237 *n.* 2, 238 *n.* 2.
>   in transporting after delivery to carrier, 238.
>   usage as to, in forwarding, 245.
>   when excusable exonerates carrier, 305.
>   caused by low water, 308 *n.* 3.
>   loss during, 309.
>   not ground for abandoning voyage, 309.
>   caused by strikes, mobs, etc., 314, 315.

DELIVERY.
>   negligence of consignee, 217.
>   manner of, should be according to usage of place of delivery, 241, 244.
>   usage of carrier, 244.
>   not complete while waiting turn to discharge, 244.
>   rule at common law, 330.
>   rule in Massachusetts, 331 *n.* 1.
>   from tackles of steamer, 333.
>   carrier's liability after notice of arrival of goods and readiness to deliver, 334.
>   when ready to discharge, 334.
>   notice of arrival, 333, 334.
>   receiving from ship's side, 333.
>   reasonable opportunity to remove, 332 *n.* 2., 334.
>   to wrong person, 334.
>   in business hours, 334 *n.* 5.
>   contracts against giving notice of arrival of goods, 334.
>   place of, 335.
>   to customs officer, 335.
>   must be according to bill of lading, 336.
>   at port, 337 *n.*
>   to bank, 337 *n.*
>   at intermediate port, 337 *n.*
>   to assignee bill of lading, 337 *n.*
>>   See CONNECTING CARRIER AND USAGE.

DESERTION.

    not a peril of sea, 302.

DETAINING passenger to collect fare, 176.

DEVIATION OF CARRIER.

    how it affects contract of limitation, 92, *et seq.*, 236, 342.

    "all rail" construed, 236.

DILIGENCE.

    proof of, 257.

    carrier bound to take precaution against perils of the sea, 298, 306, 307.

        against violence, 314, 318.

    to extricate passengers or cargo from disaster, 307.

        See BURDEN OF PROOF.

DIRECTION.

    owner assuming, 215, *et seq.*

    owner assuming, has right to expect diligence by carrier, 215.

DISCLOSURE.

    of character of goods, 206, *et seq.*

    of baggage as merchandise, 210.

DISCLOSURE OF VALUE.

    See VALUE, DISCLOSURE OF.

DISORDERLY PERSONS.

    duty of carrier as to, 154.

DOMESTIC BILLS OF LADING.

    See EXPRESS RECEIPT.

DRAINAGE.

    loss from, 330.

DRAWING room cars, 151, 164.

DROVER.

    authority to bind the owner, 276.

DROVER'S PASS, 88, 107, 265, 266.

DUTY OF CARRIER.

    carrying live stock, 98, *et seq.*

    fragile goods, 105.

    to receive and carry goods within its ordinary business, 105, 106.

    as to colored persons, 151, 152.

    as to disorderly and intoxicated persons, 154, 155.

    to furnish suitable accommodation to passenger on train, 155, 161.

    not required to carry persons injuring its own business, 157.

    to carry in reasonable time, 215.

––––––

WHOLE NO. PAGES, 442

www.ingramcontent.com/pod-product-compliance
Lightning Source LLC
Chambersburg PA
CBHW030940110726
47900CB00004B/1065